C000157652

The Production of English Renaissance Culture

The Production of English Renaissance Culture

EDITED BY

David Lee Miller
Sharon O'Dair
Harold Weber

CORNELL UNIVERSITY PRESS
Ithaca and London

Publication of this volume was supported by the Hudson Strode
Program in Renaissance Studies at the University of Alabama.

Copyright © 1994 by Cornell University

All rights reserved. Except for brief quotations in a review,
this book, or parts thereof, must not be reproduced in any
form without permission in writing from the publisher. For
information, address Cornell University Press, Sage House,
512 East State Street, Ithaca, New York 14850.

First published 1994 by Cornell University Press

Library of Congress Cataloging-in-Publication Data
The Production of English renaissance culture / edited by David
Lee Miller, Sharon O'Dair, and Harold Weber.
    p.   cm.
   "With one exception the essays gathered here were first
presented in October 1990 at the Seventeenth Alabama
Symposium in English and American Liberature"—P. vii.
   Contents: Agons of the manor / Christopher Kendrick —
State, Church, and the disestablishment of magic / Richard
Lachmann — Legal proofs and corrected readings / Joseph F.
Loewenstein — Bestial buggery in A midsummer night's
dream / Bruce Thomas Boehrer — News from the New
World / Margaret Ferguson — Dead man's treasure, the cult
of Thomas More / Clark Hulse — Treasures of culture, Titus
Andronicus and death by hanging / Francis Barker — The
picture of nobody, white cannibalism in The tempest / Richard
Halpern — Allegory, materialism, violence / Gordon Teskey.
   Includes bibliographical references and index.
   ISBN 0-8014-2961-7 (cloth : alk. paper). — ISBN
0-8014-8201-1 (paper : alk. paper)
   1. England—Civilization—16th century—Congresses.
2. Shakespeare, William, 1564–1616—Criticism and interpretation—Congresses. 3. England—Civilization—17th
century—Congresses. 4. Renaissance—England—Congresses. I. Miller, David Lee, 1951– . II. O'Dair, Sharon.
III. Weber, Harold. IV. Alabama Symposium on English
and American Literature (17th : 1990)
DA320.P76 1994
942.05—dc20   94-1036

Printed in the United States of America

⊚ The paper in this book meets the minimum requirements
of the American National Standard for Information Sciences—
Permanence of Paper for Printed Library Materials,
ANSI Z39-48-1984.

Contents

Preface

The Production of English Renaissance Culture responds to the challenge of resituating literary studies within cultural criticism. It is concerned with how the cultural treasures and values of Renaissance England are entangled with the economic and political dynamics of accumulation, production, and exchange. Focusing on the complex relations between symbolic and material economies, its nine essays locate cultural artifacts within a diverse set of social, political, and economic practices, including, among others, the development of the print trade, the reception of relics and portraits, the agrarian economics of the Diggers, the history of French and English witchcraft trials, and legal articulations of the crime of buggery. In using cultural history and criticism as contexts for literary study, the essays attend to the literary implications of social struggle and to the political and ideological dimensions of a culture that works in specific institutional settings to shape knowledge for peoples' consumption. Our contributors seek to assess the social and political functions of literary texts without reducing them to these functions.

With one exception the essays gathered here were first presented in October 1990 at the Seventeenth Alabama Symposium in English and American Literature. This program bore the title *wisemens threasure,* a reference to the last two words of the 1596 *Faerie Queene.* Echoes of this phrase in several of the essays have been allowed to stand, reminders that the metaphor of "cultural treasures" is central to our topic and that, despite the variety of their approaches and specific interests, these essays developed out of a conversation among the organizers-editors and participants-contributors, a conversation conducted over several years through an increasingly complex communications technology. *The Production of English Renaissance Culture* is truly a collaborative endeavor.

———————————

THIS VOLUME AND THE SYMPOSIUM from which it derives were made possible by generous support from several divisions of the University of Alabama, including the College of Arts and Sciences, the Office of the Provost, the College of Continuing Studies, and the Hudson Strode Program in Renaissance Studies. Research assistance was provided by Lisa Broome, Deborah D. Davis, Murrie J. G. Dixon, and Jerry Spotswood. Angela Bramlett worked patiently, cheerfully, and with unfailing accuracy through many, many versions of the manuscript.

We received valuable suggestions from Stephen Orgel, from Michael Lieb and the anonymous second reader for Cornell University Press, and at a crucial stage of the review process, from Bernhard Kendler. Our deepest debts are to the contributors (and to Catherine Belsey, whose essay from the symposium will appear elsewhere, but whose advice and encouragement have left their mark on the volume). We are grateful to these colleagues for their intellectual generosity, their promptness in meeting deadlines, and their willingness to read and respond to one another's work. Christopher Kendrick, Richard Lachmann, Gordon Teskey, Richard Halpern, and Francis Barker deserve additional thanks for the help they gave on successive drafts of the introduction.

DAVID LEE MILLER
SHARON O'DAIR
HAROLD WEBER

Tuscaloosa, Alabama

The Production of English Renaissance Culture

Introduction:
Criticism and Cultural Production

DAVID LEE MILLER, SHARON O'DAIR,
and HAROLD WEBER

The essays in this volume describe various modes and institutions of cultural production in early modern England. They attend in considerable detail to particular artifacts, including literary texts, pamphlets, portraits, saints' relics, and prison records, but whether the cultural "treasure" under discussion is Beckett's shrine or Marvell's "Upon Appleton House," the consistent effort is to assess how institutions of cultural production, together with the systems of exchange they foster, mediate its engagement with the political, social, and economic conflicts of sixteenth- and seventeenth-century England. In the words of Jonathan Dollimore and Alan Sinfield, such an approach insists "that the effectiveness of textual readings be related to the conditions in which [the texts] were and may be read; that the contests to which they have contributed and may contribute be attended to through and beyond any particular text."[1]

This characterization of cultural studies raises serious methodological questions about how exactly one proceeds to read social struggle "through and beyond" the text. As David Harris Sacks observes, "To study literature according to this insight, the literary scholar must become an historian thoroughly familiar with the events,

---

1. Jonathan Dollimore and Alan Sinfield, "Culture and Textuality: Debating Cultural Materialism," *Textual Practice* 4 (1990): 98.

ideas, and institutions of the age that he or she investigates. This means acquiring a full command of the relevant historical sources and the debates on their interpretation, and not merely dipping here and there into the modern historical literature for arguments to support one's claims."[2] The insistence on "full command" is faintly authoritarian, a symptom of the scholarly anxiety aroused by imperatives to study what Carolyn Porter, in a shrewd critique of Stephen Greenblatt's "cultural poetics," has called "the horizonless field of the social text."[3] A field without horizons is difficult to imagine, let alone "command."

The first question confronting cultural theory, then, is the question of totality: How can we conceive of or represent society as a whole? Other questions follow from this one: How much of the social order, and which parts of it, should we bring to bear on any particular cultural artifact? What kinds of mediations are necessary in order to describe adequately the impact of particular social formations (sodomy laws, agrarian reform, the slave trade) on plays, poems, and novels? What in particular is the role of ideology? Should cultural criticism proceed as a form of ideological critique? If so, what ideological functions will we attribute to culture? To what extent can we argue that literary texts are privileged sites for the critique of ideology, or that they are somehow uniquely transgressive or disruptive of social orthodoxy? How do we respond to theories that see ideology as secondary to institutional or economic forces? What criteria should be used to assess explanatory models within cultural criticism? Is agency to be understood as psychological, discursive, or institutional? Does the project of cultural studies entail a theory and history of subjectivity? If so, do we conceive the subject as collective or individual? Do we seek a sociological or a psychoanalytic model of subjectivity? And what about our own agency and subjectivity: if "there is no document of civilization that is not at the same time a document of barbarism" (in Benjamin's celebrated phrase), how can modern criticism achieve the detachment needed to assess the implication of past cultural texts in political repression? In short, what value or cogency do we claim for cultural criticism, and on what basis?

Questions such as these cannot be conclusively answered either by

2. David Harris Sacks, "Searching for 'Culture' in the English Renaissance," *Shakespeare Quarterly* 39 (1988): 474.

3. Carolyn Porter, "Are We Being Historical Yet?" *South Atlantic Quarterly* 87 (1988): 782.

theoretical formulations or by the results of practical research; rather they will be answered differently in different contexts. Yet they are not pointless. Such questions serve to guide the specific work of cultural criticism, which shuttles between theory and practice as it reiterates and refines the problems it cannot lay to rest. The essays herein suggest varying, sometimes speculative answers to these questions, at the same time as they advance our specific understanding of various cultural artifacts and add to our empirical knowledge of early modern England.

The empirical tendencies of "old historicism" direct its research toward the local and the particular, away from problems of how to describe the social totality. Cultural studies rejects this pragmatism in its effort to conceptualize the systems and institutions that condition particular situations, yet there is little consensus as to just how the particular and the systemic are related. Marxism and postmodernism tend to influence this discussion in opposing ways, Marxism traditionally emphasizing precisely the kinds of deep structural determinism and "master narrative" that Lyotard, for example, calls into question. The "new historicism" in Renaissance literary study often finds itself suspended uneasily between these alternatives, resorting to the strategic use of anecdote to finesse theoretical problems raised by its analyses. The danger in this reticence, as various critics have shown, is that at crucial moments it can yield to prematurely totalizing conclusions, in a way that tends to reify partial explanations.[4]

The problem of conceptualizing totality has been central to Marxist social theory from the beginning, so it is not surprising that strains of revisionist Marxism play an important role in modern cultural theory. Christopher Kendrick, in "Agons of the Manor," links the notion of "relative autonomy"—the idea that different institutions and social processes develop independently of one another, each according to its own dynamic—with that of "uneven development." He assumes, in

4. This is Porter's argument. Francis Barker offers a forceful critique of Greenblatt and Geertz in the longer version of his essay, which appears under the the title "'A Wilderness of tigers': *Titus Andronicus*, Anthropology, and the Occlusion of Violence" in the author's *Culture of Violence: Essays on Tragedy and History* (Manchester: Manchester University Press; Chicago: University of Chicago Press, 1993). The editors are grateful to Professor Barker for consenting to the publication in this volume of an excerpted version, a decision for which we assume the responsibility.

other words, that because the political, economic, and cultural realms each have their own logic and temporality, developments in any one sphere will tend to be out of step with the others. But Kendrick's model of the historical process also stipulates that the principle of totality will intervene to limit the autonomy of the separate dynamics: sooner or later they will catch up with one another, clashing or interfering so as to trigger abrupt adjustments.

Kendrick's consideration of Marvell's "Upon Appleton House" and of Cressy Dymock's project for agricultural improvement makes sophisticated use of the notion of relative autonomy, allowing him at once to define the English "revolution" as principally a cultural event and yet to retain the notion of economic determination: the revolution represents a "moment of truth" in which the irreversible transformation of the agricultural base is poetically "registered." This argument attributes a clarifying function to Marvell's poem, whose form and style respond to the entrenchment of agrarian capitalism. At the same time, Marvell's aesthetic practice has mixed consequences: by "explaining away" contradictions inherent in the new productive relations that have emerged on the manorial estate, it tends at once to "inure the subject" to such contradictions and to create a position from which they may be regulated.

The economic determinism of Marxist historicism has often been challenged, notably by Max Weber, whose social theory emphasizes the proliferation of bureaucracy in its drive to "rationalize" all aspects of public life in technically advanced Western societies.[5] The debate in social theory between Marxists and Weberians is of considerable interest to cultural studies; it enters our volume in Richard Lachmann's "State, Church, and the Disestablishment of Magic," which argues that structural and ideological change in early modern Europe is driven less by class conflict than by competition among elite factions. These factions are defined by institutional interests and affiliations, which emerge as an indispensable level in the analysis of social conflict. Lachmann demonstrates that we can account for specific variations in the timing and location of witch trials only by attending to competition among institutionally differentiated elite factions (the

---

5. A useful point of entry into the sociological debate over Marx and Weber is the introduction to *Classes, Power, and Conflict: Classical and Contemporary Debates*, ed. Anthony Giddens and David Held (Berkeley: University of California Press, 1982), pp. 3–11.

crown, the gentry, the church hierarchy, the magnates) for both material and symbolic capital.

Lachmann's essay is immediately concerned not with literary studies, but with the cultural conflict surrounding witchcraft and magical practices—a topic of considerable interest to literary scholars—and with the relative success of different explanatory models in accounting for the *timing* of witchcraft trials. In refocusing our attention on institutional competition within the power structure of the early modern state, Lachmann offers a structural explanation of how, when, and why a relatively settled situation of negotiation, which tended to remove institutions and social practices from active political conflict, could be critically reconfigured to criminalize previously tolerated practices and so recruit the judicial apparatus as an instrument of political domination.

This insight has important implications for the tendency among literary scholars influenced by Foucault to focus on the operations of state power. Joseph Loewenstein addresses this issue in "Legal Proofs and Corrected Readings," arguing contra Foucault that penal strategies are secondary to economic forces in the crown's effort to enforce censorship during the Restoration. Loewenstein examines the role of the Stationers' Company, which sought to protect its trade monopoly by enforcing crown policy. His essay, by formulating a conception of authorship in which ideological control provides an "idiom" for market competition, shifts our focus from ideology to economics, from product to production, and from the absolutist claims of the Stuart monarchy to the state-sponsored monopoly exercised by the Stationers' Company.

In Loewenstein's model of cultural production the author does not disappear but is dispersed throughout the system of manufacture; the monarchy struggles to produce an "author's text" in the face of an opposition London print trade determined to resist the fixing of authorship in a single act or figure of composition. The construction of the author emerges, then, as a reactionary move in the power struggle that resulted when print culture began more and more powerfully to fashion the public sphere within which monarchical and parliamentary authorities vied for supremacy. Loewenstein's focus on the mutuality of interest between two specific institutions, the crown and the Stationers' Company, matches Lachmann's insistence on institutional relations as the central dynamic of social conflict, even as his emphasis on the priority of trade protectionism suggests that, at least in the instance of Restoration censorship, the engine driving such conflict is finally the economic as mediated by institutions. In both essays, it is the conjunction of economic and institutional dynamics that explains the operations of state power.

Among the concepts that cultural criticism relies on to theorize the social and political functions of culture, and hence to conceptualize the sphere of culture in relation to economic and institutional forces, is that of hegemony. Not a static totality but a totalizing process, hegemony is a dominant discursive formation that saturates lived experience by means of its success in articulating diverse social elements and subject positions; it also encounters resistance from competing articulations and must therefore be continually renewed and, in the process, transformed.[6]

Bruce Boehrer, in "Bestial Buggery in *A Midsummer Night's Dream*," analyzes a particular hegemonic system by tracing the links of symbolic equivalence through which potentially disruptive conflicts involving gender and sexuality are recontained by the social order. Boehrer locates the metaphoric complexity of Shakespeare's comedy in a series of sexual transformations that violate but also sustain gender and class distinctions, paradoxically reaffirming marital and social harmony through bestial metamorphosis. Titania's humiliating passion for an ass, orchestrated by Oberon to assert his domestic sovereignty, epitomizes the play's production of bestiality as a species of moral entertainment. Bestial transformation in Shakespeare's play offers itself strangely as a pattern of moral instruction, as the play establishes sexual limits which it then transgresses, its social arrangements and discursive practices *producing* bestiality as a pretext for political self-justification. For Boehrer, "a moral economy of monsters" sustains the Renaissance discourse of sexual and domestic propriety.

Although he refers to social and political formations such as the family and the courts, Boehrer focuses principally on the analysis of discursive practices, citing judicial records to establish that Eliz-

---

6. For recent contributions to the theorizing of hegemony, see Ernesto Laclau and Chantal Mouffe, *Hegemony and Socialist Strategy: Towards a Radical Democratic Politics*, trans. Winston Moore and Paul Cammack (London: Verso, 1985), and Robert Bocock, *Hegemony* (London: Tavistock, 1986).

abethan buggery is first of all "a crime against ideas," and only secondarily an occasion for judicial displays. In "News from the New World," Margaret Ferguson emphasizes instead the intersection between ideological and material orders, and the contradictions that mark it. In Aphra Behn's *The Widow Ranter* and *Oroonoko*, Ferguson discerns a strategy of sympathetically representing and legitimating forbidden modes of behavior by punishing the most transgressive characters with deaths presented as inevitable; these texts engage both the emerging cultural imperative against miscegenation and the eagerness of Restoration London to enjoy sensationalized reworkings of Shakespeare's *Othello*. Ferguson explains this system of sacrifice and legitimization by placing Behn's literary life and works in a range of contexts including debates over the nature of woman, conventions regarding the semantics and aesthetics of blackness, and economic institutions as different as the international slave trade and the literary marketplace. Because women, like noble slaves, are at once victims and beneficiaries of an emerging international marketplace in which books and bodies become commodities, Behn oscillates between criticizing and endorsing the colonial project and the hierarchies, sexual, social, and racial, which it served. As commodities, too, both play and novella profit in a morally ambiguous way from the slave trade, marketing images of slaves at once as worthy objects of moral and political sympathy and as exotica that will promote the sale of books and theatre tickets.

The contradictions that concern Clark Hulse in "Dead Men's Treasure" also involve the complex relationship between the material and symbolic realms. He begins with the architecture of Beckett's shrine at Canterbury, where a middle layer of gold acts as a "transitive term"— both true and metaphoric gold—to mediate the contradictory convergence in the relics themselves of both putrefaction and glorification. Hulse scrutinizes the exchange of material and symbolic capital at the shrine, seeking the tropes that enable exchanges between incommensurable forms. In this analysis Hulse's argument intersects with Lachmann's—both are concerned with the production and circulation of institutional magic—but where Lachmann seeks to account for specific breaks in the cultural economy of magic, Hulse analyzes in detail how one version of that economy worked. Moreover, in contrasting the symbolic-financial transactions of the shrine with the political upheavals in which More's relics were caught up, Hulse seeks to grasp the historical transition between very different cultural economies—one distinctly medieval, the other already discernibly "modern." John Colet's visit to the shrine gives a fascinating glimpse of how an emergent, counter-hegemonic articulation seeks to redeploy the terms of the existing system, but it also suggests the limitations of the discursive: when Henry VIII and his ministers used the repressive apparatus of the state to effect a violent transformation of the medieval church, they transferred the material wealth of the shrine not to the poor but to the royal coffers. Hulse analyzes the transactions between material and symbolic capital that sustain Lachmann's elite institutions and suggests how the nature of such transactions was transformed in England by that decisive restructuring of institutional relations we call the Reformation.

Besides conceptualizing the place of culture within a larger social order, cultural studies needs also to characterize the work of its artifacts: what ideological functions do they perform, what social agency do they possess? As a group, the essays in this volume offer varied and complex accounts of the functions performed by different cultural texts and suggest that a structural theory of cultural agency is best able to explain the often contradictory ideological effects we attribute to a given text.

In examining the way violence functions in *Titus Andronicus*, Francis Barker's "Treasures of Culture" shows how the play blocks recognition of judicial violence in Elizabethan England. Barker takes issue with the new historicist emphasis on sovereign power as constituted through public spectacle; he argues that we must resist the temptation to aestheticize politics, for both the Shakespearean text we study and the Renaissance culture we produce conspire to obscure the institutionalized barbarity through which the social order maintained itself. Though the extreme brutality of *Titus Andronicus* has led many to question its place in the Shakespeare canon, Barker uncovers the play's mystification of its cruelty, an effect it achieves through structures of opposition that encode violence as the product of savagery. The play enacts an anthropology wherein violence is staged as a "spectacle of the exotic," located not in the civilized state, our state, but in the wilderness beyond its borders. Barker shows how a "descriptive ethnography" of the Roman ceremonies and rituals represented in the play reveals both a structural anthropology and a "civil" sphere that ground themselves on a pre-cultural realm of the barbarous. Through this anthropology, the boundary between civilization and its horrific other is constituted by—and as—culture.

In "'The picture of Nobody,'" Richard Halpern also attends to the strategies of cultural ethnocentrism, examining a discursive practice of occlusion and erasure that he labels "white cannibalism." Using Gonzalo's ideal commonwealth in *The Tempest*, Halpern charts the way in which European colonialism extracted cultural as well as material treasures from its New World colonies. This commonwealth is derived (via Florio) from Montaigne's description of the Tupi Indians of Brazil, but Gonzalo Europeanizes this alluring vision of masterless freedom, communal ownership, and paradisal ease in order to "digest" and assimilate an alien culture. This erasure of the material origins of symbolic capital reveals one of the crucial ideological functions of colonial discourse, which reinforces cultural hegemony by detaching radical political ideas from their New World matrix in order to rearticulate them within a less threatening classical tradition. "What America adds," then, is not a distinct class of texts or themes but a new signifying dimension: elements that in the European tradition have been *merely* utopian acquire an unprecedented deictic value. As the "author" of a colonialist utopia, Gonzalo offers a singular demonstration of the way utopian discourse tended to make this deixis unreadable by rewriting "New World" as "Nowhere."

This account of textual agency contrasts sharply with that presented by Gordon Teskey, who sees literature as exceeding the ideological system in which it nevertheless participates. The pleasure of allegory, or more broadly of "transforming life into meaning," contains for Teskey an element of unavowed delight in the spectacle of subjection. In "Allegory, Materialism, Violence," he explores the complicity of allegory in concealing the rift between form and matter that characterizes the metaphysics of idealism. When this rift is figured as a gendered conflict between feminine *materia* and masculine form, an ideology of rape emerges within the discourse of philosophical idealism. In this ideology, the conceptual hierarchy's need to seize and elevate matter as the medium through which it can inform a realm of particular beings is served by what Teskey calls a "poetics of capture." This poetics typically obscures the violence of capture and rape behind female personifications who embody their imprinted meanings gladly. But the greatest practitioners of literary allegory, Teskey argues, disclose the violence latent in this pleasure. Thus his reading of the *Inferno*, canto five, seeks to recover the brutal candor of Dante's text from beneath layers of evasion spun by a critical tradition intent on rationalizing, rather than acknowledging, "the thrilling violence of the transcendentalizing project" at the heart of the *Commedia*.

Taken together, the essays in this volume depict cultural agency as a site of contradiction, marked by the convergence of institutional, economic, and technological dynamics. Hegemony develops out of the complex interplay among these diverse political and social forces. Such an understanding of hegemony envisions the work of culture generally and of intellectuals in particular as central to the process by which relations of dominance and submission are socially reproduced. Hegemony in this sense functions as a symbolic system, promulgated through the kinds of institutions Louis Althusser called "ideological state apparatuses," by means of which ideology secures its effects, promoting the interests of socially dominant groups and forestalling effective dissent.

What function can we then claim for cultural criticism? Cultural studies may see itself as contesting a given hegemony by seeking to foreground and then to disarticulate hegemonic systems of symbolic equivalence in order to forge others in their place. Since the concept of hegemony subsumes discursive practices within the larger social field, this aim may be extended to broader analyses of cultural production. At the same time, the possibility remains that in busily dismantling the hegemonic structures of early modern England we are unwittingly forging links in a contemporary hegemony.

This problem does not admit of a definitive answer, but our first step should probably be to reframe it in terms of the institutional dynamic of the modern university. In assessing the debate over canonicity, John Guillory has argued that the figuration of literary works as treasures, which ostensibly celebrates their power to preserve and convey "values," actually marks their function in the system of educational institutions. "The real social process," he maintains, "is the reproduction not of values but of social relations." The form of canonicity signified by the trope of value is "not a property of the work itself but of its transmission"; the trope works, however, to objectify the process of reproduction, thereby fostering an illusion in which the canonical text "appears to reproduce itself" and so to be "inexhaustible."[7]

Conventional literary study reproduces social relations in highly mediated ways. But it collaborates with the mystification of value first of all in the interest of self-perpetuation. "The institution," says Guillory, "elicits out of its very structure a demand for the subordination of the specificity of works to the canonical form, and this subordination is recognizable in pedagogic practice as a homogenizing of dogmatic content, the universal truths discovered and rediscovered by the 'truly great'" (496). If such a demand does arise from the structure of the institution, then to resist the demand is, however indirectly, to work against or upon that structure. And if "subordination of the specificity of works to the canonical form" is indeed the content of the institutional demand, then one way to resist it is to undo the subordination, using the specificity of texts to challenge the homogenizing force of canonical form.[8] So long as educational institutions continue to circulate cultural treasures as the coin of universal truth or enduring value, there will be reason to intervene at the level of practice with research and teaching that apply the historical "specificity of works" like a solvent to the corrosions of dogmatic content, or that try, in Walter Benjamin's phrase, to "brush history against the grain."

We are implicated in the process of reproduction because we have access to that process, because we participate in the ways that educa-

---

7. John Guillory, "Canonical and Non-canonical: A Critique of the Current Debate," *English Literary History* 54 (1987): 494–95.

8. Guillory's essay represents a major contribution not only to the debate on the canon but to the understanding of the social role of literary pedagogy, on which see also Margaret Ferguson, "Afterword," in *Shakespeare Reproduced: The Text in History and Ideology*, ed. Jean Howard and Marion F. O'Connor (London: Methuen, 1987), pp. 273–83. Guillory argues that ideologically the literary canon participates in attempts to secure the prestige and the *use* of educational apparatuses of credentialization for the purpose of legitimating or delegitimating particular disciplines and discourses. It does this in his account as a highly mediated way of reproducing social relations. The tendency of Guillory's argument as we read it is curiously at odds with its academic style. The most radical implication of this argument, though unstated, is that universities should seek either to disengage their pedagogical practices from procedures of credentialization or to transform those procedures drastically in order to legitimate excluded fields and languages. Such a program would risk its own authority insofar as that authority derives from the apparatuses of credentialization to be disavowed or transformed. It could thereby risk the basis of our own reproduction as literary scholars within the university.

tional institutions take advantage of their "relative autonomy" to re-
negotiate the terms of their cultural mission. Such a prospect of institutional negotiation is limited; it assumes our inescapable professional implication in the barbarism of contemporary civilization, regardless of the degree of horror with which we contemplate the massive human and ecological violence of the postindustrial state. We
cannot, on this view, rise to anything quite so decisive as Francis Barker's closing gesture of repudiation: "I, for one, will not be party to that
violence, nor to its occlusion. Nor to its 'anthropology.'" Despite the
appeal of this political imaginary, we turn finally to Gordon Teskey's
model of divided agency, which illuminates Dante's courage in exposing the violence of the moral systems sustained by his poem. Dante
the writing subject cannot finally reconcile his critique of divine provi-
dence with his complicity, cannot coordinate them within the same
subjectivity. It is not by consolidating a subject-position of political
detachment, we suspect, but by choosing carefully how and when to
move among the subject-positions available to us that literary intellectuals can best use our teaching and writing to dismantle orthodoxies
within and beyond the modern university.

1

Agons of the Manor

"Upon Appleton House" and Agrarian Capitalism

CHRISTOPHER KENDRICK

The three works considered in this essay respond in direct and obvious ways to the political shock of the Interregnum's onset, and to the opening it presented; my argument will have them negotiating the shock and exploring the opportunity by way of sustained symbolic encounter with the secular and ongoing crisis that characterized agrarian property relations in early modern England. My main focus will be Andrew Marvell's "Upon Appleton House," and the questions asked of its strategy will organize the entire argument. But I will also give close attention to two other works, both of them utopian proposals—one more economically minded in its offered "solution," the other expressly political—which have been less studied than Marvell's poem but can more readily be seen as responses to the agrarian crisis specifically. The first is a proposal for a new way of draining and developing the fens, authored by one Cressy Dymock and published in 1653 by Samuel Hartlib, in whose circle of scientific correspondents Dymock was enrolled as an expert on agrarian improvement. The second, more familiar work is not a text but a project: the enterprise, undertaken in 1649 by a few groups known as Diggers and

I thank the editors for reading the manuscript of this essay so carefully and for offering such helpful criticism. I am also grateful to James Holstun, Joseph Loewenstein, and Richard Halpern for criticizing draft versions.

apparently led as well as sponsored by Gerrard Winstanley, of collectively cultivating waste and common lands.[1]

My principal reason for treating these works together is to sketch the outlines of a discursive configuration that responds so lucidly to the contradictory entrenchment of agrarian capitalism that it ought properly to be called revolutionary. By this I mean that the emergence of the "triadic" system of landholding and labor organization (consisting of commercial landlord, capitalist farmer, and copyholding or propertyless hired hands) is so surely registered by these works that there can be no question of returning to, or of salvaging the comparative humanity of, some previous settlement; in these texts, I will maintain, all refeudalizing strategies are discredited in advance as solutions to the crisis, or rather take on a new status as secondary qualifications or overdeterminations of more fundamental strategies or structures. This will not, of course, be to hold that these texts' reference to capitalism is utterly lucid or unmistakable. Instead they register capitalist productive relations in a somewhat partial or distorted way—most strikingly by insistent reference to one of the chief dialectical *effects* of these relations' emergence, that constant pressure for enclosure and engrossment which dates at least from the time of *Utopia* to that of *The Deserted Village*. It seems safe to assert that, well before Marvell wrote, this pressure had come to enjoy a virtually technical status as a distinct dynamic. By the mid-seventeenth century, enclosure and engrossment might indeed be thought of not just as the phenomenal forms of agrarian capitalism but as its active principles.[2] I assume in what

1. I would stress in advance that I will not be discussing Winstanley's texts so much as the form of the project they advocate.

2. The best case for the primary importance of the relations of production in determining the course taken by the British economy has been made by Robert Brenner. See especially his concluding essay, "The Agrarian Roots of European Capitalism," in *The Brenner Debate: Agrarian Class Structure and Economic Development in Pre-Industrial Europe*, ed. T. H. Aston and C. H. E. Philpin (Cambridge: Cambridge University Press, 1985), pp. 213–327. An informative discussion of enclosure and engrossment may be found in J. A. Yelling, *Common Field and Enclosure in England, 1450–1850* (Hamden, Conn.: Archon Books, 1977). The tenor of Yelling's careful study is to reinforce, while qualifying and further specifying, the argument of R. H. Tawney's great *Agrarian Problem in the Sixteenth Century* (1912; New York: Burt Franklin, 1967). Unless the context indicates otherwise, I use *enclosure* in its general sense (which refers to the putting up of fences around plots of land). I ordinarily do not use the word to mean the appropriation of common or waste lands, which was only one among many specific forms taken by enclosure. (It is not necessary, for my purposes here, to rehearse the various kinds of enclosure—unitary, piecemeal, by agreement, and so on; the interested reader can consult Yelling for these.) My "practical" historical assumption in this essay is that for the greater part of the sixteenth and seventeenth centuries enclosure

follows that it is above all through their insistent allusion to this dynamic in its seeming autonomy that the works under consideration not only recognize, but also formally respond to or "negotiate" with, the new principles of capitalist economy on the land. Thus even while conjuring the past, these texts raise basic questions as to the shape those principles will and should take in the future.

CAPITALISM AND BOURGEOIS REVOLUTION

Since suggesting that these texts are revolutionary implies that the social and political events of the 1640s and early 1650s constituted a revolution in some sense, my main argument will perhaps seem dated, at least to many of those who have followed the historiographical disputes over the Civil War for the last twenty years or so. "Revisionist" historians claim to have invalidated the "Whig-Marxist" notion that what happened at mid-century was a revolution. Instead, they tend to argue, the Civil War was a rebellion, admittedly a great rebellion, gone awry. This usually means that the war was in its inception really an intra-class phenomenon, the result of aristocratic faction or disaffection; that "social issues," other than those of a narrow constitutional or procedural nature, were never seriously debated (or at least not until the rebellion went out of control, at which point the issues raised were by definition expedient and marginal); and that the events at mid-century had no lasting effect on the nature of political (read: aristocratic and monarchical) power.[3]

---

was primarily important for indirectly re-enforcing capitalist productive relations, which it did by weakening customary forms of tenure rather than by directly expropriating large sections of the peasantry. Put another way, I assume that enclosure was chiefly instrumental in undermining what Marxism calls "feudal possession" rather than in forcibly dispossessing the peasantry—though I would of course agree that in the long run this is a distinction without a difference. I use the term *engrossment*, likewise, in its strict (less narrowly pejorative) sense, as the conjoining or amassing of plots, or more generally as the process by which the normative size of the farm was increased.

3. For an informative description of the debate, see R. C. Richardson, *The Debate on the English Revolution* (London: Routledge, 1989). The essential revisionist references and arguments can be found, usefully summarized and mustered by a right-wing revisionist, in J. C. D. Clark, *Revolution and Rebellion: State and Society in England in the Seventeenth and Eighteenth Centuries* (Cambridge: Cambridge University Press, 1986). Conrad Russell's works, *The Causes of the English Civil War* (Oxford: Oxford University Press, 1990) and *The Fall of the British Monarchies, 1637–52* (Oxford: Oxford University Press, 1991), now offer the most positive and comprehensive revisionist account avail-

An assessment of the motives and merits of revisionist arguments lies beyond the scope of this essay. I will only observe here what their characteristic rhetoric sufficiently indicates (such-and-such an idea is a "non-starter," so-and-so were not real "players" in the game, and so on): that these arguments are chiefly phrased in the *negative*. I would suggest, accordingly, that it is with the revisionist case as with empiricist positions in general: that it can seem effective only if formulated as a series of falsifications of the chief propositions supporting those "Whig-liberal" or Marxist explanations which have been worked out in detail. Nonetheless, though weak "in themselves," revisionist arguments have been strong enough as rebuttals, it seems, to have called the whole paradigm of bourgeois revolution into question, estranging or defamiliarizing it in such a way that it now becomes necessary to rethink its defining differences and specific utility. The consensus among Marxist as well as liberal historians of all stripes seems to be that the case for the bourgeois revolution could use rearguing in light of the revisionist attack, which has not been confined to seventeenth-century England but has known its French version as well.[4]

---

able of the midcentury crisis. For more recent (and critical) responses to revisionist contributions, see the essays in *Conflict in Early Stuart England: Studies in Religion and Politics, 1603–1642*, ed. Richard Cust and Ann Hughes (New York: Longman, 1989); Perry Anderson, "A Culture in Contraflow—II," *New Left Review* 182 (July-August 1990): 121–30; Ellen Meiksins Wood, *The Pristine Culture of Capitalism* (London: Verso, 1991), chaps. 7 and 8—surely the most polemically devastating critique of revisionist commonplaces available; and Robert Brenner's remarkable "Postscript" to his *Merchants and Revolution* (Princeton: Princeton University Press, 1993), whose early pages respond especially to Conrad Russell's recent work.

4. The point about empiricism is Fredric Jameson's. The Cust and Hughes collection cited above offers evidence that the revisionist attack has instigated, at least in the case of the English Revolution, a more cautious and categorically aware reassessment of the institutional history, and of the histories of the various levels, of the English social formation—a reassessment that seems to be leading to the qualified redemption, often enough, of older (liberal and Marxist) positions. One example of such reassessment is the essay by J. P. Sommerville demonstrating, pace Conrad Russell, that there really were basic differences of opinion about the proper relation of king and parliament. See also Sommerville's *Politics and Ideology in England, 1603–1640* (London: Longman, 1986). An equally important sort of reassessment concerns the significance of Civil War county histories, of which a great many were produced during the 1970s and early 1980s; these studies, while modest in their individual aims—that of telling how it was and how the politics worked in the particular county in question—were less so in their collective aim, which was generally understood to be the demonstration that nothing so general or unified as a revolution could have taken place in seventeenth-century England. There seems to be an increasingly broad realization that to demonstrate this last, the local studies would need explicitly to engage an axiom laid down some time ago by Lawrence Stone, namely that particularism and absolutism went hand in hand

As evidence of this estrangement of the revolutionary paradigm, we might usefully review two Marxist works on France and Britain respectively, George Comninel's *Rethinking the French Revolution* and Robert Brenner's "Bourgeois Revolution and the Transition to Capitalism." Both writers acknowledge the power of certain revisionist criticisms of traditional Marxist versions of these events. Comninel explicitly questions the wisdom of *retaining* the term "bourgeois revolution," and Brenner clearly shares some of his reservations. The reasons for their skepticism are comparable, yet suggestively opposed. Comninel holds that since generalized commodity production cannot be said to have existed in France until the 1870s or so, and since the battle between ruling-class factions was over resources commanded by the state rather than over the form of productive relations, there can have been little enough that was capitalist about it. Brenner argues that since manorial capitalism already predominated in England by the 1640s, and since the aristocracy had more or less successfully adjusted to the new property relations by then, there was nothing really revolutionary left to accomplish—though he is at pains to stress that the unrevolutionary issues at stake were quite important ones all the same.[5]

Now this is rethinking bourgeois revolutions with a vengeance. To avoid false impressions, I should stress that neither Comninel nor Brenner accepts the problems usually posed by revisionist historiogra-

---

from the early sixteenth century (see Stone, *The Causes of the English Revolution, 1529–1642* [London: Routledge, 1972]); in other words, these studies ignored the national-political conditions of county "autonomy." Ann Hughes's essay, in the above collection, is good on this matter; likewise Brenner's "Postscript" (see esp. pp. 645–50). From most Marxist standpoints, the defining revisionist arguments usually appear as local or provisional objections to Marxist explanatory narratives. Few revisionists pay what a Marxist would recognize as systematic attention to the economic organization of society, and none that I know show signs of having cultivated even an unsympathetic appreciation of the complexity of the Marxist concept of determinacy.

    5. George C. Comninel, *Rethinking the French Revolution: Marxism and the Revisionist Challenge* (London: Verso, 1987); Robert Brenner, "Bourgeois Revolution and the Transition to Capitalism," in *The First Modern Society: Essays in English History in Honour of Lawrence Stone*, ed. A. L. Beier et al. (Cambridge: Cambridge University Press, 1989), pp. 271–304. This last sentence needs to be qualified in light of Brenner's recent book, which I cannot adequately treat here. Brenner argues that the Long Parliament's attack on Laud, Strafford, and kingly prerogative in 1640–41 amounted to a *legislative* revolution; he sees the reforms of these years as of major structural consequence, persisting in their effect even after their literal reversal in the Restoration. The second Civil War and Commonwealth, on the other hand, are somewhat marginalized in his narrative; they are explained conjuncturally and are treated as having less determinate long-term effects.

phy. Both their arguments are offered as resolutely Marxist ones; in criticizing the traditional concept of bourgeois revolution, they both indeed claim to free Marxism of uncritical (i.e., bourgeois) elements—Comninel by exposing the revolution as a liberal myth, Brenner by demonstrating its participation in a Smithian problematic. Before considering some of their assumptions, I want to acknowledge and stress that whether one finds their rejection of the conventional notion of the bourgeois revolution convincing or not, Comninel and Brenner are surely right to assume that it *can* be jettisoned. The revolution is an issue that can and will be debated in (and of course outside) Marxist circles; how the debate comes out will obviously have a direct impact on the way the actual history of the capitalist mode of production is mapped.[6] But it is by no means a core proposition in Marxism that the transition from feudalism to capitalism must "in the ordinary course of things" be effected or sealed by a bourgeois revolution. As a historical concept, the bourgeois revolution is not like, say, the tendency of the rate of profit to fall. This tendency is a basic structural law under capitalism—so basic that its disproof would seriously vitiate Marxism's scientific status. The same cannot be said of the theory of bourgeois revolution. It is best to be clear about this distinction.

That said, I want to express doubt as to whether Comninel's and Brenner's positions on the revolution "problem" are theoretically adequate. It seems difficult to deny their arguments against the applicability to France or England of the undiluted model of revolution, the strong form of the theory, according to which you have a bour-

---

6. It seems that those who argue for or emphasize some version of a "persistence of the old regime" thesis are likelier to line up against the revolution or to emphasize the respects in which it failed—though bourgeois revolution and the persistence of the old regime are not incompatible notions. For an influential example of a Marxist work that emphasizes the persistence of the old regime, see Tom Nairn, *The Enchanted Glass: Britain and Its Monarchy* (London: Radius, 1988); for an equally important Marxist interpretation of the political history of late nineteenth- and early twentieth-century Europe from the vantage of this "thesis," see Arno J. Mayer, *The Persistence of the Old Regime: Europe to the Great War* (New York: Pantheon, 1981). Colin Mooers, in *The Making of Bourgeois Europe: Absolutism, Revolution, and the Rise of Capitalism in England, France and Germany* (London: Verso, 1991), ably defends and updates a more traditional concept of revolution and of bourgeois history against arguments often associated with the persistence of the old regime "thesis." Perry Anderson's brief essay on the notion of the bourgeois revolution, in his *English Questions* (London: Zone Press, 1992), offers what is easily the most theoretically advanced and illuminating sketch of the problems involved in defining the notion and describing the thing.

geois revolution when a bourgeois class or faction seizes and reworks the power apparatus (primarily the state), thus putting itself in a position to effect a transformation in property relations (whether this means overthrowing older forms of property or consolidating and extending capitalist relations). But disproving the case, only rarely made, for the English bourgeois revolution in this strong sense requires no great historiographical effort. What is more difficult to show is that the transition was not *sealed* in the Interregnum, in either political or cultural senses or both. Thus, let it be granted that the transition to capitalism had established itself at the economic level, it can still be argued, and often has been, that the Cromwellian moment put an end to absolutist reaction and thus helped secure capitalist relations, even if it did not secure *itself* institutionally.[7] Again, let it be argued that the absolutist reaction was doomed to fail anyway, and that the struggles in the forties clearly did more than was necessary (in fact did *too much*) to dissuade would-be absolutisms of the future, it might still be maintained that Cromwell's revolution knew what amounted to a collective "moment of truth," during which the ruling classes' conditions of existence were indeed clarified and the sociocultural landscape redefined in such a way that it was impossible to return to things as they were before save through a massive effort of ignorance, impossible to live with the lessons learned except by the practice of some sort of collective bad faith.[8]

The following discussion of Marvell's poem, and of the projects of Dymock and Winstanley, is intended to offer a limited corroboration of this last, "culturalist" hypothesis. But before turning to these works, we can begin to situate them, however generally, if we pause to reflect briefly on the reasons for both the difficulty and the desirability of making a case for the revolution. We need above all to locate the structural determinants that explain why the concept of revolu-

7. This is the position on the revolution now more or less shared by Christopher Hill and Lawrence Stone. See, e.g., Lawrence Stone, "The Results of the English Revolutions of the Seventeenth Century," in *Three British Revolutions: 1641, 1688, 1776*, ed. J. G. A. Pocock (Princeton: Princeton University Press, 1980); and in the same volume, Christopher Hill, "A Bourgeois Revolution?"

8. C. B. Macpherson's *Political Theory of Possessive Individualism: Hobbes to Locke* (Oxford: Clarendon Press, 1962) can be read as making a strong (if mostly implicit) case for taking the revolution this way. I think especially here also of Olivier Lutaud's argument that Winstanley was influential in the later seventeenth century even though, or only as, his memory was repressed; see his *Winstanley: Socialisme et Christianisme sous Cromwell* (Paris: Didier, 1976), pp. 457–65.

tion seems to be afflicted by a kind of uncertainty principle, so that
locating the bourgeois revolution in any particular moment makes
one aware immediately of the social dynamics that escape it, and more
particularly of the discrepancy between socioeconomic and political
dynamics. But given the ineradicable character of this problem, we
first need to explain why one continues to want to locate a revolution
somewhere, why one doesn't want to consent too readily to a "non-
revolutionary" account of the transition to capitalism as a series of
class struggles, each of them locally and temporally bounded, each
with winners and losers, each with utterly unintended systematic consequences.

One's resistance to such a pragmatic view of the transition will
rouse familiar suspicions of a catastrophist or triumphalist bias on
Marxism's part; Marxists want the bourgeois revolution because they
need it as a type or shadow of things still to come. Note, though, that
to grant that these suspicions have weight (and I imagine they do) is
not necessarily to have consigned the theory of revolution to the conceptual wastebin; for to say that an idea serves a symbolic need is not
necessarily to say that it is inaccurate or unrealistic. In any case, the
principal theoretical reason for resisting a pragmatic or ceaselessly
transitional view of the transition lies elsewhere, in one of the specific
differences of the capitalist mode of production, namely the separation that it institutes between the economic and the political levels.
From Marx's analysis one learns that the capitalist economy exhibits
an autonomous and contradictory dynamic—a dynamic formally opposed to political coercion and regulation—and determines the national territory as the arena of its newly intensive logic.[9] Since the
capitalist mode of production is in its very nature totalizing and separating, and since it is inherently contradictory, it stands to reason
that in its installation (however gradual its seizure of the productive
forces might turn out to be) totalizing backlashes and adjustments
would be required at the political level. It also stands to reason that
these adjustments, along with the contradictions of the new system,
would be registered at the cultural level as well as the political. If one
accepts Marx's analysis of the capitalist system in its essential features,
then it would seem that a non-revolutionary transition, a transition

9. See Karl Marx, *Capital: A Critique of Political Economy, Volume One*, trans. Ben
Fowkes (New York: Vintage Books, 1977), chap. 25 ("The General Law of Capitalist
Accumulation"), and *Capital, Volume Three*, trans. David Fernbach (New York: Vintage
Books, 1981), pt. 3 ("The Law of the Tendential Fall in the Rate of Profit").

without radical breaks and renewals, is what would really need explaining.

Meanwhile, the difficulty of locating the revolution at any particular moment is likewise given by the formally constitutive separation of the economic and the political under capitalism, but is determined by another aspect of this separation: not the totalizing movement, the unity of the capitalist economy per se, but rather its extreme abstractness or generality, its peculiarly conceptual or (more provocatively) unconscious character, which is what is at issue in all those puzzling passages of *Capital* where Marx stresses that what he analyzes doesn't exist anywhere exactly, and indeed can't exist anywhere in the "pure" form in which he is describing it. Under capitalism there exists a constitutive disequivalence between the economic and the other levels, such that the other levels always in a certain sense qualify or transgress the logic of capital. Forms of legality and of the state may be more or less compatible with the capitalist mode of production, but there exists by definition no capitalist state or legality, and compatibility is in its nature a situational category (so that the institution of parliamentary democracy might in a certain context actually hinder the development of capitalist relations).[10] Since the capitalist mode of production is by its nature radically overdetermined, to put it in Althusserian terms, or since capitalist development is by its nature combined and uneven, to put it in Trotskyist, it will often prove difficult to *locate* the revolution except provisionally and "tactfully."

The revolution is to be sought, then, because of capitalism's totalizing character, and it is elusive because of its overdetermined character. I can now state the wager I am making in this essay, the operating assumption that my argument attempts to "prove": that the bourgeois revolution, *understood as a cultural moment of truth*, should provide fairly direct access to the structural contradiction and discontinuity, the totalizing dynamism and the overdetermination, of the capitalist fact (i.e., of the basic structure of social reality under capitalism). Though there is no question that the examination of three texts can prove beyond doubt that a revolution took place, I believe that these texts can cogently be understood as revolutionary documents—as unconsciously grasping and giving figuration to a new social ontology, and thus as turning a cultural corner.

10. I take this to be one of Bob Jessop's main points in his *Capitalist State: Marxist Theories and Methods* (New York: New York University Press, 1982) and the best justification for his argument against "a general theory of the state."

MARVELL REWRITES JONSON:
PERAMBULATING/CAPITALIZING THE MANOR

I will begin and end with Andrew Marvell's "Upon Appleton House," a work probably composed between 1651 and 1653.[11] Though I will not have a great deal new to offer in the way of close readings of the poem, I would not wish to deny that the poem's chief distinction lies in the rich verbal texture of its individual stanzas; indeed my interpretation will assume some prior appreciation of Marvell's manner with the stanza, which, to call on a conventional and inevitable analogy, makes one think of a landscape painter experimenting with different kinds of perspective effects, and testing them against one another, in discrete sections of a painting.[12]

But I am chiefly interested here in the narrative format within which this stanzaic production takes place. It is well known that the country-house poem undergoes an enlargement in "Upon Appleton House." The principal justification for the distension surely lies in the superior importance of the house's owner, who merits big praise: the great Lord Fairfax, recently retired to the country an unhappy man, having subdued the kingdom.[13] But the distension's aesthetic or "strictly literary" justification lies of course in its actual modus operandi, or rather in the effects procured through the definitive introduction into the country-house poem of what remains something of a foreign body—the "perambulatory" genre that Marvell most likely picked up from Saint-Amant, one of Fairfax's favorite poets.[14] These

11. Fairfax resigned as general of the parliamentary army in late June of 1650, and Marvell evidently composed the poem after that event. Marvell seems to have left Fairfax's service in late 1652 or early 1653. See Pierre Legouis, *Andrew Marvell: Poet, Puritan, Patriot* (Oxford: Clarendon Press, 1965), pp. 18, 91. In an as yet unpublished essay, Derek Hirst and Steven Zwicker make an interesting case that the poem addresses Fairfax's political situation in the summer of 1651 and was written then. (I am grateful to Steven Zwicker for allowing me to read this essay in draft.)

12. Marvell's "perspectivism" is virtually a critical commonplace by now. But Rosalie Colie's reading of "Upon Appleton House" is more sensitive to Marvell's perspectival and painterly effects than any other I have encountered; see her *"My Ecchoing Song": Andrew Marvell's Poetry of Criticism* (Princeton: Princeton University Press, 1970), esp. pp. 201–18.

13. See R. I. V. Hodge's summary of Fairfax's career in his *Foreshortened Time: Andrew Marvell and Seventeenth-Century Revolutions* (Totowa, N.J.: Rowman and Littlefield, 1978), pp. 132–40.

14. For Saint-Amant's influence, see Colie, *"My Ecchoing Song,"* pp. 221, 288, and William McClung, *The Country House in English Renaissance Poetry* (Berkeley: University of California Press, 1977), pp. 148–53. Fairfax's translation of Saint-Amant's "La Solitude" is printed in M. A. Gibb, *The Lord General: A Life of Thomas Fairfax* (London:

effects may be most readily characterized in terms of fragmentation: virtually all of the poem's critics testify to the tendency of Marvell's poem to dissolve, and of Appleton House simultaneously to decompose, into their constituent parts and marks. But "fragmentation" and "decomposition" are of course extremely general terms; to specify their character in the poem we need to focus more narrowly on its narrative format, and to describe the immediate generic "cause" of decomposition. Generically speaking, then, what happens in Marvell's poem is that the basic perambulatory fiction of the *interrupted stroll* punctuates in a new way the metaphorical survey of the estate ordinarily walked by the country-house poet, turning what were before the various oriented *stages* of a *circuit* into what have become more or less independent *segments of* or *sketches along* an *itinerary*. The understood movement between the segments of "Appleton House," the silence between its stanzas, brackets each place or item off from the larger circuit, setting the marks of the estate free to develop their own "qualities" or mini-narratives, and indeed positively encouraging their further "enlargement." Meanwhile, as this happens, the poet's personality—meaning here his impressionistic powers, his scenic or figurative capacity—moves into the middle of the manor's things, even while his character—his judicial powers, his capacity as socially representative moralizer—disappears into the silence between segments and stanzas, taking shelter in those blank spaces where (so one is made to feel at any rate) all the controlling choices are made.

Thus much by way of an initial, more or less bare, description of the new genre, the "perambulatory country-house poem"; we can now begin to ask after the *meaning* of Marvell's revision of the lyric kind associated with the names of Penshurst and Ben Jonson. In one of the better readings of the poem, William McClung has gone far toward capturing what should be grasped, I think, as an ideological consequence of the new generic mix: "Marvell," he says, "departs from the societal assumptions of the country house genre. Like his

---

Drummond, 1938), pp. 283–87. One might, of course, describe the generic composition differently; in view of the similarities between "Appleton House" and Marvell's other lyrics, an especially strong case can be made for simply reading the poem as pastoral. For one such reading, an incisive argument that the poem exposes the representational limits of Marvell's preferred general idiom, see Jonathan Crewe, "The Garden State: Marvell's Poetics of Enclosure," in *Enclosure Acts: Sexuality, Property, and Culture in Early Modern England*, ed. Richard Burt and John Michael Archer (Ithaca: Cornell University Press, 1994); I am grateful to Jonathan Crewe for letting me read his essay in draft.

predecessors, he defines a virtuous house in terms of its appropriateness and utility, but the ends to which the house and its master's life
are directed are religious rather than ethical and concern man's spiritual rather than social obligations."[15] One might debate the centrality
or the genuineness of the poem's concern with Fairfax's spiritual obligations. But McClung is surely right to see the poem as marking an
important stage in the rapid demise of the country-house ethic, and to
emphasize the absence of any represented community, of any rou-
tinely festive meal shared in ancient hall, as in Jonson's pleasant Penshurst fiction. The farmers and farmers' daughters who accompany
Jonson on his return from touring the Sidney estate, bearing gifts of
food that will be reciprocated—these customary residents of the man-
or are replaced, in "Appleton House," by the crew of tawny mowers in
the "meadow" section of the poem. Marvell evidently did not even
contemplate the mendacity of bringing his mowers into the great
lord's hall, and to give him credit one feels it would have been an
indignity practiced on both parties. The mowers celebrate their harvest, if it is theirs, in the meadow; and they will evidently return to
their village, which apparently lies beyond the manor's vanishing
point.[16]

   But the change is a matter not just of the reapers' depicted "inde-

15. McClung, *Country House*, pp. 160–61. Cf. also Raymond Williams's remarks on
the increasing separation of the house from the estate in the chapter on the country-
house poem in *The Country and the City* (London: Chatto and Windus, 1973), pp. 55–60.
Though this chapter has been influential, Williams's essential point, that this separation
is determined by the entrenchment of wage labor, or in other words by capitalist
relations of production, is more often than not glossed over. I am indebted to the early
chapters of Williams's work, and particularly to his brief analysis of "Upon Appleton
House."

16. "Villagers" chase their cattle into the mown meadow in stanza 57, ll. 451–52, so
there is a village around somewhere. References are to the poem as printed in *Andrew
Marvell: The Complete Poems*, ed. Elizabeth Story Donno (Baltimore: Penguin, 1972).
Subsequent citations will appear in the text. For a stimulating article on the significance
of Marvell's mowers, see Rosemary Kegl, "'Joyning my Labour to my Pain': The Politics
of Labor in Marvell's Mower Poems," in *Soliciting Interpretation: Literary Theory and
Seventeenth-Century English Poetry*, ed. Elizabeth D. Harvey and Katharine Eisaman Maus
(Chicago: University of Chicago Press, 1991), pp. 89–118. Kegl provides evidence that
mowing was highly waged, if seasonal, work, and suggests that Marvell, in the mower
poems, makes his pastoral swain a mower both in order to bring pastoral up to date
(mowers having replaced shepherds as the best representatives of the rural laboring
kind) and to return it to the seriousness of pre-Elizabethan or early humanist pastoral.
It is perhaps worth noting that Marvell's reference, in the meadow section of "Appleton
House," is evidently to a mowing crew, and that so far as one can tell mowers and
villagers are assumed to constitute two separate groups.

pendence," telling as that is, but also of the manner of the depiction. To grasp the decline of the country-house ethic in its determinacy, one needs especially to attend to its formal mediation. Just as a distance has appeared between tenants and manor house, so does an un-bridgeable rift exist between signification and reference in their rep-resentation. What is especially striking about Marvell's reapers is that they are not so comfortably symbolic as Jonson's farmers and clowns. They are both more and less conventional, more and less realistic, than Jonson's creatures: they work and sweat, but sweat too much, so that one feels they may originate as the products of the playful phrase "sweet sweat."[17]

McClung states that country-house ideals (the values of communal appropriateness and utility) are still espoused in "Appleton House," though redirected, and in one sense he is obviously right to say so: Marvell does reiterate the basic country-house values. Yet those values don't really bear repeating in the idiomatic confines of Marvell's poem; as McClung elsewhere recognizes, they are not simply redi-rected but deformed in their very reassertion. That the manor of Appleton House has been decisively removed from the village, that the communal ethos of Jonson's house has been subverted and re-placed by what is in effect an individual ethic, is never so apparent as when the "essence" of that ethos is "actually"—that is, all too "real-istically" and yet conventionally—represented within the estate's so-ber frame. For Marvell does find room for hospitality, alongside Fair-fax's more commodiously quartered humility, in the architectural description of the opening stanzas. The most telling lines come in stanza 9:

> A stately frontispiece of poor
> Adorns without the open door:
> Nor less the rooms within commends
> Daily new furniture of friends.

Do frontispiece and furniture represent turgid people or lively orna-ment? If more space were devoted to the description of friends and poor, if they were freed from their figurative encasement, the ques-tion would not pose itself. But as things stand, reflection reveals an allusion, more or less explicit, to the familiar process by which what was once architecturally functional is retained, eventually, as mere

17. See stanza 54, ll. 425–32.

decoration, becoming more narrowly functional or sheerly architectural in the process. So the wit must flash here partly at the expense of the cheap artifice of Fairfax's Protestant *habitus*, which for a reflective instant is made to seem willing to tolerate a few images, idols of charity, in place of the real thing, as long as they save some pounds and don't clash with the spartan tone of the accommodations.

The historical significance of this "functionally" motivated reduction of the hospitable ethos to decoration appears more plainly to view when we set it more definitely in relation to Jonson's *ur*-poem, and see it as continuing and redefining a crucial Jonsonian strategy. It will be remembered that Jonson's circuit in "Penshurst" also roughly describes a hierarchy; it begins with the estate's natural marks and then moves to and up its social gradient. But either Penshurst was atypical or not all its residents are included. Just where nature turns to culture in his poem, and where a line or two might have been devoted to the laborious rung of society (small copyholders, say, or hired hands), Jonson places instead a series of images that, though prettied up and classicized, are yet not so decorated as to have lost all recognizable traces of their original production in the land of Cokayne.[18] The copyholders are not effaced, exactly; but they are only recognized in the "immemorial" but now dated signs of their desire, plundered and painted over so as to render them of service in the new aristocratic order of things. The profound effrontery of Jonson's vision of country-house generosity, often remarked in a general way, may perhaps be most precisely appreciated here, in this substitution and distortion. Penshurst does not actually acknowledge the laboring class. It does not make "subject-citizens" of them by imaging them. It rather evokes their memory, at need, in the very act of wrenching their fantasy to a new use. It thus in effect destroys, in "taming," the collective imagery of peasant desire, and by implication also disorients the older feudal ethos that originally accommodated that desire, and whose reincarnation its ancient pile is supposed to announce in its very form.

What Jonson's images of officious fish, then, did to Cokayne and the older feudal ethos, so Marvell's lively furniture now, under cover of increased brazenness, does to the generous neo-feudal ethos that Jonson "first" celebrated. But the analogy doesn't end here. For Jon-

18. See Don E. Wayne, *Penshurst: The Semiotics of Place and the Poetics of History* (Madison: University of Wisconsin Press, 1984), pp. 38–44.

son's redaction of Cokayne is not just motivated by effrontery, nor is Marvell's overly figurative hospitality simply a mockery. It has often been noticed that the courtly depiction of Penshurst's underwater supply (*officious* fish and *emulous* eels) tends to recall and disturb the distinction—a founding one within the poem—between Penshurst and opposed architectural versions (evidently courtly and extravagant) of neo-feudalism. The decorated remains of Cokayne thus raise questions about the social basis of the Penshurst ideal that bring their own answers with them: in other words, the message written into its fishes' overmannerly sacrifice is that Penshurst's architectural nostalgia is animated by much the same will to distinction, and records much the same contempt for labor, as the false splendor of the houses "built for show"—predicated as both monuments are on the common conquest and displacement of the smallholding class. So in Marvell do the remnants of *neo-feudal* generosity (for example, the frontispiece of poor) efface the distinction between (foreign) architecture and sober frame, and thus raise questions as to the true (social) basis of Fairfax's protestant ethic.

This last point can be put in generic terms, and generalized, if we note that the frontispiece and furniture of the stanza just discussed are the somewhat extreme, but by no means atypically curious, products of the poem's governing pictorial bent, or of the action of perambulatory figurative practice on country-house materials. Let Jonson's classicized Cokayne serve, as it well might, as the best figure for the hospitable circuit, the generous movement, of Penshurst. Then Marvell displaces Cokayne further, fragmenting it and diffusing it over the surface of his estate/poem. In this way he *fully* internalizes the linked, founding oppositions that had remained relatively external and objective in the ur-poem: the oppositions between the house built for show and the "ancient pile"; between artificial (or built) and natural architecture; and between the permanent, objective virtue of the estate and the perpetuating, participatory virtue of the patron and poet (a *figured* opposition, but one distinctly implicit in the fiction by which Penshurst is addressed as a person). My point here is that in the process of internalizing and collapsing these defining country-house distinctions, Marvell refigures the very ontology of the manor.

Thus—to illustrate the movement of the last distinction—in Jonson's poem the house is *addressed*, and this personification doesn't just afford a face-saving way of praising the patron Sidney and of lending historical solidity to the Sidney family's primitively recent accumulation of honor. By situating the house as auditor, the personification also objectifies social virtue, and thus not only marks out the function of the patronized poet but indeed justifies his seat at the table—since, to make the house's virtue speak, he must communicate with its good things.

Marvell is of course altogether less oral; not *to* Appleton House, note, but *upon*. He does not *address* the house, he pens a series of short reflections of and upon it—he mirrors the house that mirrors Fairfax's virtue—and thus from the poem's opening lines both house and representation lose their distinctness and solidity. Consider the following well-known stanza, in which the house's architectural athletics are described. Marvell may be seen here "realizing" or "literalizing" Penshurst's personification, along with a Vitruvian ideal of man as measure:

> Yet thus the laden house does sweat,
> And scarce endures the Master great:
> But where he comes the swelling hall
> Stirs, and the square grows spherical,
> More by his magnitude distressed,
> Then he is by its straitness pressed:
> And too officiously it slights
> That in itself which him delights.
>
> (ll. 49–56)

You might say we get the idea even if we don't the picture: Fairfax's presence is as masculine and fertilizing as it is modest. But I think the house's strenuous efforts slight the message they are ostensibly intended to convey; the turbulence of the picture impresses more than the weight of the moral theme. Marvell's house is so witty within its sober frame that it cannot even be located, much less addressed.

Accordingly, we can plausibly find a literalizing play in Marvell's chosen preposition: "upon" both glances at a sexual sense (just recall how Marvell cavorts in the woods, and how women sum this manor up) and at a proto-romantic one (Appleton may just be your very nice English farm, but the poem for all its disorder contains a fairly continuous "prospective" dimension; so at times being upon Appleton House is as good as being upon a peak in Darien). But surely the main play on "upon" is generic and locative: the eclipsing of the distinction between poem and house/manor, between frame and witty decoration, leaves the reader suspended awkwardly above the house, hunting a manor whose distinguishing marks have been buried, but which has become all the more haunting and real for that. The poem no longer takes the form of a dialogue with the estate; it has become its epigraph, or epitaph, even as it reads the estate itself as such. To resort to linguistic language once more: by mingling with the signifying chain, the estate breaks free of the signified and becomes the (absent) referent at which the poem can now only make forays. Or again, we might say that in becoming so emulous, in taking on so much character, the estate wins itself an unconscious too.

The other significant oppositions in the narrative structure of "To Penshurst" are also collapsed, and I will turn to these in due course. But we are already in a position to ask after the context in which this narrative transformation should be read. At the instigation of what agency does Marvell find it necessary to collapse the old distinctions and "de-objectify" his (Fairfax's) manor? From my introductory comments, it should be apparent that I assume there must be more than one agency at work; nonetheless I would contend that the poem's formal shift "ultimately" discovers the peculiarly abstract and discontinuous ontology associated with capitalism, whose particularity always transgresses against the truth of its total form, whose actual existence is always non-identical with its determining structure or concept. The narrative format of "Appleton House" is designed above all, I'd argue, to register (or reflect) this normative disequivalence—to consolidate its recognition—and then to negotiate with or react against it, to model it, in various ways. It's no accident, surely—it testifies to where capitalism existed most purely in English social reality—that this disequivalence is allegorically located on the manor, whose abstract and questionable shape is the indirect but insistent "theme" of the poem. Capitalism, we might say, is unconsciously figured as the manor in "Appleton House," and the manor is nowhere known except in the collapsing gap between representations, the silent stroll between stanzas, the perspectival principle that both frames and skews the stanza's impressionistic contents, whether these be pictorial or narrative or moral-thematic in kind. The capitalist manor constitutes the questionable ground on which the traditional poetic and thematic materials of the poem must now assert their meanings; or put the other way around, manorial capitalism imputes new meaning to such materials, relativizing their old values to unknown ends.

A contemporary analogy might help to clarify this reading. I would

suggest that Marvell discovers, in his metaphorical survey, an answer
and a problem that correspond to those that William Petty unveiled
and came up against in his great Irish survey.[19] Petty, when confronted with the question how to value land, or construct farms of
equal value, solved this problem by discovering the labor theory of
value, that is, that land was the more or less indifferent locus of an
abstract value other than itself; yet also, and unsurprisingly, he proved
unequal to this discovery, and continued to consider land as the
source or qualitative harbor of value. This same contradiction is figuratively instituted and kept up by the narrative format of Marvell's
poem; and my reading of the poem will be complete, logically speaking, even if only sketched in the barest way, when we note that in
keeping up the contradiction, in its insistent contextualizing or deval-
uing of its thematic materials, the poem tends, allegorically at any
rate, to its solution: it imposes the truth of the discovery of abstract
value and exposes the relativity of the manor itself as a merely customary form, arbitrarily related to the conduct of its various segments
or sketches, which have come variously to house and respond to the
curiously abstract, still foreign, power of capital itself.

MANOR AS GARDEN, GARDEN AS MANOR: THE
REPOSSESSION OF THE DEMESNE

One can anticipate two rather different kinds of objection to this
reading. First, that the poem is not about a manor, at least in its
economic aspect, at all: the poem concerns just the house, or rather
what could actually be seen from it (meadow and park)—the decorative image of the manor then, and not the thing itself. It might be
added to this that the poem focuses only on the decorative image of
the manor because it is really all about Fairfax, or intends mainly to
provide his retiring conscience with an hour's relief.

The second anticipated objection would have it that this reading is
radically unhistorical, that capitalism is on my brain rather than in
Marvell's poem, that however accurate a description of the poem may
have been provided, it needs to be re-thematized or -contextualized,
because capitalism doesn't emerge as an integrated system, or exert
any such systematic effects as I am claiming anyway, until much later

19. See David McNally, *Political Economy and the Rise of Capitalism: A Reinterpretation*
(Berkeley: University of California Press, 1988), pp. 47–53.

(the late eighteenth or possibly the nineteenth century). I think there is much to be said for the former, more formalistically positivist, objection; the latter, historicist-positivist (or revisionist) objection seems both more difficult to answer and more misguided, even though I would agree that capitalism probably shouldn't be spoken of as an integrated or total system until at least the nineteenth century. I will go some way toward addressing the first objection, especially, by showing how Marvell, in collapsing the other two country-house oppositions I've mentioned, symptomatically negotiates with the new arbitrariness and discontinuity of the manor. I can perhaps allay some historicist doubt by locating these same, or related, responses to the manor at work in other contemporary developments.

Though Marvell immerses himself in the marks of his chosen estate at a length unrivaled by any other country-house poet, we nonetheless, it's true, see less of it than we do of others. The reapers harvest hay and cattle are commoned in the meadow; still, the space of Marvell's manor is more recreational, and thus seems more restricted, than any of his precursors'.[20] I believe we can grasp the contradictory principle at work here if we recognize that Marvell treats the grounds as if they were an extension of Fairfax's garden. The very presence of Fairfax's formal garden in Marvell's poem has symptomatic significance: as Don Wayne points out, Jonson omits Penshurst's garden from his circuit, and we may speculate that this was partly because to describe the garden would call in question the constitutive opposition between the house's lack of architectural finish and the abundance of natural architecture boasted of on the grounds.[21] Fairfax's military garden demonstrates that this particular opposition has been ambushed: not only has Marvell realized the lack of architecture in the

20. An exception might be made of Thomas Carew's *To Saxham*, in which the poet visits the manor at a time when the house is snowbound, and so cannot tour the grounds; yet, though the space of Saxham is certainly cut off or restricted, it's also centripetal and dense—Carew's strategy, a sacralizing one, involves making a great mystery of the fact that, and the means by which, all the products of the estate migrate to its hearth—so the final "spatial impression" left by the poem is of an enclosed plenitude.

21. See Wayne, *Penshurst*, pp. 107–8, 117–18. Wayne suggests that, though the garden was crucial to the symbolic program imbedded in the grounds and house of Penshurst Place, its symmetry was unappealing to Jonson's rougher, archaizing aesthetic; accordingly, Jonson "seems to have shifted the metaphor [of garden-paradise] from the garden to the estate as a whole . . . the image of paradise [becomes] that of a magically ordered disorder. . . ." Marvell might be read as revealing this projection of the garden onto the estate—of uncovering the principle at work as such—even as he extends its sphere of activity and elaborates its effects.

manor house by making it embody Vitruvius' "natural" principles and
thus de-objectifying it; he has also literalized the notion of a natural
architecture, and follows Fairfax's lead by diffusing the architectural
principle across the house's vista in a series of twisting frozen frames.
Those inclined to doubt that the meandering poet should be perceived as a kind of natural gardener might recall the poet's final
description of Appleton as "heaven's centre, Nature's lap, / And paradise's only map" (lines 767–68).

I propose that we should read Marvell's extension of Fairfax's formal garden into the wilder anthology of the body of the poem much
as we should read the comparable phenomenon in the history of
manorial gardens. From Roy Strong's history of English gardens, one
learns that in the earlier part of the seventeenth century, fashion came
to require a more intensive remodeling of the garden plot, a remodeling that resembled in its chief features and its technical apparatus, if it
wasn't indeed partly derived from, the improvement of farmland
through the practice (especially) of up-and-down husbandry and the
floating of meadows. And we learn of the tendency toward larger
gardens, which extended over more and more of the estate: Strong
instances John Evelyn's design for a 100-acre garden, in the mid-
1650s, as the culmination of this movement toward the huge (nor-
matively Baroque) garden. Strong's nostalgia for an aristocratic utopia is too powerful to let him orchestrate his garden history with the
history of capitalist farming (in the way Anne Bermingham, whose
lead I am following here, does in her book on later landscape painting).[22] But he makes it possible to venture that the intensification and
extension of gardens must have been aimed not only at separating the
aristocratic element, and the house, from the classes who actually ran
and serviced the manor, but also at symbolically repossessing the demesne, or rather what have become the swelling—increasingly enclosed and engrossed—leasehold lands. It must have amounted to a
kind of "symbolic enclosure," which apparently grew bolder and
more impenitently luxurious in pace with the loosening of rents and
the consolidation of the triadic system.

If you take Marvell's anthology this way, as a "symbolic repossession" of the demesne, then the objection that the poem is only about
the manor's vista is met. For it is precisely in transforming the vista

22. See Roy Strong, *The Renaissance Garden in England* (London: Thames and Hudson, 1979) and Ann Bermingham, *Landscape and Ideology: The English Rustic Tradition,
1740–1860* (Berkeley: University of California Press, 1986).

into a garden, in divorcing the house from the manor, that the poem manages to be "about," and attempts to locate, the manor.

But I would want to press a little further than this, and suggest that the revolutionary character of this text lies less in this literary enactment of the actual practice of symbolic enclosure than in the poem's jumbled rehearsal and anticipation of garden possibilities, of the history of garden types. The allusion to the late medieval enclosed garden in the compressed character of Maria suggests a quasi-systematic intention; but what is most impressive is Marvell's anticipation, in the meadow and forest sections respectively, of picturesque and romantic moments of later garden history. Marvell can anticipate in this way, I think, because within the enclosure of his manor he rehearses, in figurative and outlandish form, the very principles of enclosure and engrossment that are no longer, now, felt to threaten, but rather to constitute the manor's social existence.

MARVELL, DYMOCK, AND THE ANTICIPATORY STREAMLINING OF CAPITALIST LANDSCAPE

That Marvell figuratively registers the principles of agricultural "improvement" will seem more plausible if alongside his poem we consider an especially striking proposal drawn from the sphere of agricultural (or "improving") discourse itself. Cressy Dymock's short pamphlet, "A Discoverie for Division or Setting out of Land," re-fashions and -systematizes enclosing and engrossing principles much more directly and single-mindedly, and to more patently anticipatory ends, than does Marvell's poem. The pamphlet provides a better, less fallible "proof" than the poem for the existence and nature of the dynamic of improvement; accordingly Dymock offers comparatively privileged access to the state of agrarian productive relations, whose relatively advanced or capitalist character, so goes the necessary inference, conditioned and encouraged the very appearance of an improving dynamic, and which thus constitutes the symbolic raw material to which the poem, as well as the pamphlet, may be seen finally, if rather transparently, to respond.[23]

23. Both the transparency and the "ultimate" character of these works' responses to agrarian capitalism are important for my larger argument, and I present the following interpretation of Dymock both to anchor Marvell's text more concretely, to bring it more clearly into contact with the historical Real, and also to forward the argument for

The project set out in "A Discoverie" originated, Dymock tells us,
as a scheme for the drainage and restoring of fenlands. When the
scheme found no takers among fen developers, Dymock published
his plan, in 1653, in the form of two letters to Samuel Hartlib, that
utopian reformer of all trades.[24] On publication, the scheme effectively becomes more strictly utopian, in the sense that it is no longer
directed just at the fens (though Dymock hasn't given up all hope on
that front), but has designs on British land-division in general; the
scheme would suffer from lack of water, but its principles could be
imitated in any mixed farming region. Though its publication by
Hartlib means that it would have reached that part of the British
audience most interested in technical reform and improvement, I
know of no evidence that Dymock's text was especially popular (it was
not republished), or that it was actually used by contemporaries as a
model. Since his plan obviously required that individuals or small
groups of projectors be granted rather sweeping powers of revision
with respect to agrarian labor processes and landscape, and since by
1653 the time of political compromise had already in effect been
entered upon, it can hardly be surprising that the plan made no
immediate impact on land-division in general. Still—even if he was

---

cultural revolution, to insist on the comparative transparency of capitalist class struggle
in the Cromwellian moment. For the first purpose, Dymock's text is serviceable by
virtue of its difference from Marvell's poem and its similarity with other agrarian tracts
(its participation in the same problematic). For the second purpose, Dymock's work
serves by virtue of its similarity with Marvell's text and its difference from other economic texts (its extremely advanced or "unpragmatic" character).

24. Dymock, *A Discoverie* (London, 1653), pp. 1–2. The title sheet of the pamphlet
reads as follows: A Discoverie / For Division or Setting out of Land, / as to the best
Form. / Published by *Samuel Hartlib* Esquire, for / Direction and more Advantage and
the Profit of the Ad- / venturers and Planters in the FENS and other / Waste and
undisposed Places in England / and IRELAND. *Whereunto are added some other Choice /
Secrets or Experiments of / Husbandry. / With a Philosophical Quere concerning / the Cause of
Fruitfulness. /* AND / An Essay to shew How all Lands may be / improved in a New Way to
become the ground / of the increase of Trading and Revenue / to this Common-wealth.
Only Hartlib's name appears on the title page, and an introductory letter by Hartlib
opens the pamphlet. Dymock is known to be the author of the land-division scheme
because he signs the letters describing it. It's also worth noting that Dymock offers the
second letter to clarify the first; a second letter about a new invention or recommenda-
tion is not an uncommon occurrence in Hartlib's publications, but evidently Hartlib or
someone in his group wanted further explanation, especially as to how all the ditch
digging required by the plan could be economically feasible. For such biographical
information about Dymock as is known, see Henry Dircks, *A Biographical Memoir of
Samuel Hartlib, Milton's familiar friend* (London: John Russell Smith, n.d.), pp. 90–95.
(Dircks's preface is dated 1865.)

forbidden his role as the Luther of land-division, and even though he was not retrospectively recognized as its Newton—Dymock's scheme presents an exceptionally clear case of a concrete anticipation. For as Yelling has pointed out, once it became routine practice, in the early eighteenth century, for Parliament to grant the right to enclose manors and farms to individuals in a position to seek it, the kind of rationalized remodeling actually carried into effect bore a remarkable resemblance to the innovation for which Dymock had argued.[25]

The reader of Dymock's proposal will not be inclined to feel that this "prophecy" is an accidental or particularly uncanny matter. For Dymock is a modest, pragmatic, departmentalized utopian: with publication, his scheme doesn't become utopian "on its own"; it finds its place as part of a larger collective project, Hartlib's Macaria, where it is as subject to the proof of experience, and to revision, as any other of Macaria's departments.[26]

25. Yelling notes that parliamentary enclosures grew more boldly rational with time; it was especially the second wave of these enclosures, beginning around midcentury, that might have been modeled on Dymock's diagrams; so Dymock was about a century ahead of his time. Yelling is particularly good at situating Dymock's text within the history of its proper discursive field, and deserves quoting at some length: "The gradual application of systematic thought to agriculture, which is so pronounced a feature of the writings of our period, inevitably came to involve the problem of how best to organize farm territory. It is worth considering briefly the conclusions that were reached; not because these theoretical considerations necessarily formed the basis of practical schemes, but because they illustrate the principles towards which any rationalisation had to aim. The first and most general problem was to arrange the land around the farmhouse in such a way as to maximise the economy of labour on the farm itself. To this there is a definite answer, provided many times during the parliamentary enclosure period: 'The first great benefit resulting from an enclosure is contiguity, and the more square the allotments are made, and the more central the buildings are placed, the more advantages are derived to the proprietors in every respect.' The solution is one that is not difficult to perceive once the problem has been formulated. It was possibly the lack of opportunities for effecting such model plans in practice that causes writers such as Fitzherbert to advocate a less revolutionary approach" (*Common Field*, pp. 120–21). Yelling's quotation is from T. Stone, *A General View of the Agriculture of the County of Lincoln* (London, 1794). For parliamentary enclosure, see Yelling, *Common Field*, pp. 134–44.

26. For Macaria, see Gabriel Plattes, *A Description of the Famous Kingdome of Macaria* (London, 1641). Plattes was one of the original members of the Baconian circle for which Hartlib served as clearing house, press agent, and lobbyist. His pamphlet, published by Hartlib, describes in its projected kingdom the beneficial consequences of Baconian experimental principles as institutionalized in, and applied to society by, a streamlined paternalist state. In his correspondence, Hartlib came to use "Macaria" as the name both for his own circle and for his manifold operations, aimed as these were at some such society as Plattes had described. For an extensive treatment of the Hartlib circle and of Macaria's various departments, see Charles Webster, *The Great Instauration: Science Medicine and Reform, 1626–1660* (New York: Holmes and Meier, 1976).

Still, what is most striking about Dymock's proposal is just how radical it is within its own chosen department of improvement, a department that Dymock indeed more or less creates, as a specialized field, in this fragmentary pamphlet. His radicalism can be seen, quite literally seen, in the diagrams attached to the pamphlet—one of two model manors (Figure 1.1), and the other of an individual farm or manor farm (Figure 1.2). Dymock attributes considerable authority to these "Charts" (or this "Contrivance," as he prefers to call them), and when you consult them it is easy to understand why. With Marvell in mind, we might imagine that one of the perspectival aids used by Renaissance painters to help install geometrical space on their canvases has fallen into the world of the farm. For one basic property of the diagram is that if it were put into practice it would be legible in the land itself, which would be reinscribed according to simple geometrical rules, much in the way that urban utopias and new cities of the continental Renaissance tended to be.[27]

27. The reader is apparently forced to register the formal effects of Dymock's radical stance in a particularly graphic way when, a short way into his pamphlet, Dymock casually refers to these diagrams as "the Plats here intended to every mans view," as if it were already known what these were. We then realize, in the absence of any description forthcoming, that we can go no further into the pamphlet until we have located and consulted these plots, which are attached, folded up, between Dymock's first and second letters. One need not subscribe to Louis Marin's notion of utopian form to see that the maps are the text, the true pamphlet, in this pamphlet utopia, and the text itself only commentary. This commentary should not be thought to add to the real text in any positive way, but only hedges round its reason, "lest any mistake should be," says Dymock, explaining why he writes his letters at all, "in the not rightly understanding my meaning, or the nature of the thing" (p. 2). It might be argued that perspectival culture knows its explicit and integral advent into the English utopian tradition in this little-known agrarian work; perhaps it is no accident, if that is so, that perspective "takes hold" of utopia in the form of a proposal for land-division, rather than as an architectural or city-building proposition. I would note here two significant "themes" determined by the symbolic emergence of perspective in the land, which I have not the space to discuss in the body of the text. Both of these can be specified by observing a discrepancy between scheme and commentary. First, though one comes away from the commentary feeling that the individual farm should really be circular, and the manor, so as to accommodate it, square—in other words, though the commentary suggests that Dymock's is essentially a yeoman's utopia, the schemes are quite impartial as between farmers and landlords: they make it plain that both manor and farm may be arranged either in the round or the square—i.e., that in the new layout they are essentially *interchangeable* units, distinguished only by size. Second, little in the commentary, read on its own, would lead one to predict the schemes' seemingly unmistakable hieroglyphic or esoteric aspect. One thinks here of Walter Benjamin's reflections on the fantastic element in nineteenth-century arcades and visions of the future: "In the dream in which every epoch sees in images the epoch that follows, the latter appears wedded to elements of ur-history, that is, of a classless society." See Susan Buck-

The more urgent point to make in this context, however, is that the utopian character of Dymock's proposal—in the sense of its aesthetic integrity, its apodictic distance from the real—raises the question of the proposer's intention in a sharp way. Even though his proposal is lucid, indeed just because of that, Dymock must explain a great deal to make the application of his contrivance clear; again, just because his proposal is so removed from reality it "goes without saying," though it is easy to forget, that the explanation of the diagram's application will be an explaining away. It is obvious what the diagram explains away: fen society and culture, if you take the water literally,[28] or, quite simply, the village, if you think of the proposal as one for land-division in general, and take the water as streamlined hedge (i.e., to represent fences). This point, that Dymock's is first of all if in effect an agrarian clearance proposal, ought not to be forgotten, for it is basic to what follows even if my purposes here require a focus on the logic of Dymock's scheme in its constructive aspect, its positive form.

That the application of geometrical space to the manor can even be conceived, of course, attests the relatively advanced, technical character of agrarian problems in reality. Dymock's contrivance asks to be read, indeed, as a kind of technical-reflexive response to a question posed by a century and a half of improving practices: "What is the ideal shape of the improved farm?" Dymock imagines his plan will have the quasi-magical, fertilizing effects he predicts because it will solve at a stroke the two thorniest problems still besetting British farming, the chief stumbling-blocks remaining in the way of achieved improvement. First, it nullifies common and especially waste lands simply by casting its imaginary net over these (imaginarily) uncultivated spots.[29] Second, and even more crucially for him, it serves as an instrument to distinguish interests: the main obstacle to increased production, Dymock claims—what keeps good men from taking part in the historic mission of improvement—is the "unremediable intanglements or intermixture of interest"[30] of English farmers, or in other

Morss, *The Dialectics of Seeing: Walter Benjamin and the Arcades Project* (Cambridge: MIT Press, 1989), p. 113 and chap. 5.

28. For a good history of local responses to fen development schemes during the civil war—responses that testify dramatically to the existence of a distinctive fenland culture or cultures—see Keith Lindley, *Fenland Riots and the English Revolution* (London: Heinemann Educational Books, 1982).

29. See Dymock, *A Discoverie*, p. 3.

30. Ibid., pp. 3–4.

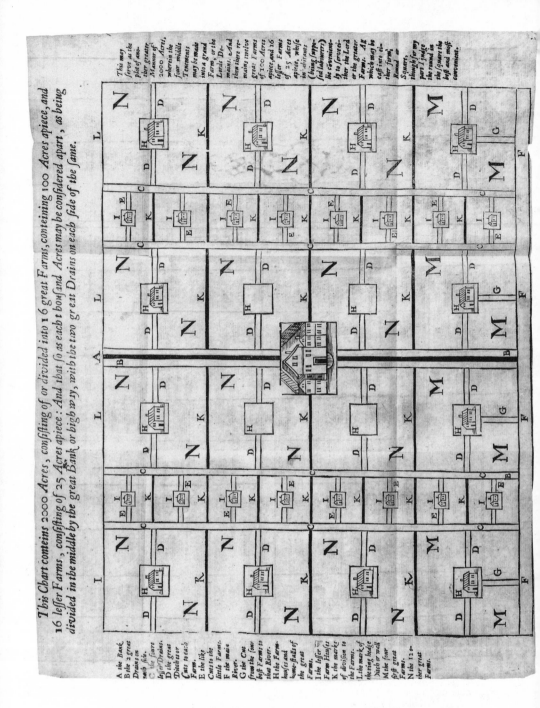

Figure 1.1. Dymock's first chart: The manor. Courtesy The Newberry Library

words, the continuing dispersal of the plots of individual farms across the territory of the village—what is increasingly felt as the *fragmentation* of English farms. Perspectival space, as Dymock uses it, puts an end to such fragmentation; it sets the tenant farmer squarely in the middle of a space that is his to do with as he will, without interference from unruly neighbors.

Once the tenant-farmer occupies the center, more specific answers can be provided to the question of what makes the ideal farm; the farmer's imaginary, unitary control of his space allows a problematic of relative utility to emerge in a well defined and seemingly natural shape. The most obvious advantages of the grid plan concern the disposition of animals and the fixed plant of the farm, the two main topics upon which Dymock's commentary dwells. The terrible entangling of interests is most noxious, it transpires, for rendering the appropriate handling of animals impossible. So Dymock dedicates a good deal of his pamphlet, unexpectedly but winningly, to an analysis of the creatures in light of the specific utility for which their natures qualify them. The pigeon, for example, is an inefficient and noisome bird, annually consuming six times its weight in stolen grain;[31] pigeons won't make it onto Dymock's ark, if he has his way, and shouldn't onto any serious farmer's. Amusing as such an implicit fiat may be, it raises interesting questions. One might ask, for example, whether any recourse would be allowed the fellow with aristocratic tastes, who'd like to bag the occasional pigeon. I sense that Dymock would be willing to accommodate this retrogade desire—he doesn't say he wants to do away with pigeons—but only in a highly regulated way.

The general problem raised here takes on a more integral form, and receives a more programmatic, if still implicit, solution, in Dymock's discussion of the shape of his individual farm. A great advantage of his grid scheme, again, is that the individual farmer can arrange things as he wants within his own square, and Dymock's text vividly communicates the appeal of this freedom. But he himself has rather definite, not to say rigid, ideas on the matter, and he can't help defending their rationality so passionately as to connect them rather forcefully into the general scheme. It's clearly partly a matter of taste; but taste is here, one wants to say, in its very singularity and contingency, even less than is usually the case a simply personal and contingent affair. In the second letter, one reads an apology for the pres-

31. Ibid., pp. 4–5.

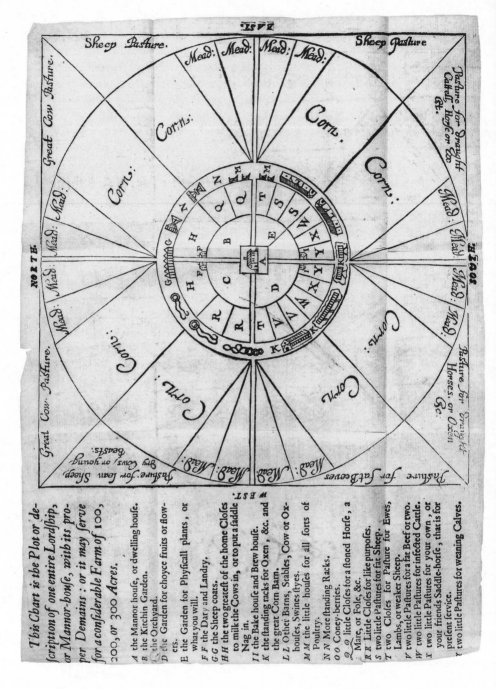

This Chart is the Plot or description of one entire Lordship, or Mannor-house, with its proper Demains : or it may serve for a considerable Farm of 100, 200, or 300 Acres.

A the Mannor house, or dwelling house.
B the Kitchin Garden.
C the Orchyard.
D the Garden for choyce fruits or flowers.
E the Garden for Physicall plants, or what you will.
F F the Dary and Landry.
G G the Sheep coats.
H H the two gratest of the home Closes to milk the Cows in, or to put a saddle Nag in.
I I the Bake house and Brew house.
K the standing racks for Oxen, &c. and the great Corn Barn.
L L Other Barns, Stables, Cow or Oxhouses, Swines styes.
M M the little houses for all sorts of Poultry.
N N More standing Racks.
O O Coney-berries.
P P little Closes for a stoned Horse, a Mare, or Fole, &c.
R R Little Closes for like purposes.
S two little Pastures for fat Sheep.
T two Closes for Pasture for Ewes, Lambs, or weaker Sheep.
V two little Pastures for a far Beef or two.
V two little Pastures for infected Cattle.
W two little Pastures for your own, or your friends Saddle-horse, that is for present service.
X two little Pastures for weaning Calves.

Figure 1.2. Dymock's second chart: The individual farm. Courtesy The Newberry Library

ence, within the scheme of the individual farm, of an aesthetic of
rounded, layered enclosure;[32] and as one gathers the details of this
plan, one comes to realize that Dymock's aesthetic bridges the gap
between the general and the particular—that it mediates the antinomy between what we might call pure economic reason, on the one
hand, and the farmer's independence, on the other, by socializing the
latter while supplementing the former. Dymock advocates the construction of a series of belts around the center of the farm: the first
ring consists of house and delicate gardens; the second of orchards
and kitchen gardens; the third of closes for various domestic purposes (brewing, for example); the fourth, which should be undivided,
will contain the foldstead (sheds for animals); and the fifth, far and
away the largest, will contain the great closes of fields, meadows, and
pastures.

Now one ought not to underestimate the rationality of this plan.
Dymock explicitly wants to reduce the total distance traveled on the
farm, to and from the various "departments"; he wants to increase the
farmer's surveillance capacity; and he wants to separate noisome from
domestic, "healthy" places (that is why the foldhouse is an undivided
ring on the outskirts of the domestic center). There is a passionate
implicit interest, beyond this, in the very fact of separating the various
laboring functions from one another, or in what we might call the
analytical clarification of the labor process (though it must be allowed
that Dymock does not get very far in the actual analysis of the various
functions). I doubt whether this clarification could have been managed so well by a non-circular arrangement (the corner pastures, of
course, are quite distinct as things stand, and an undivided ring di-
vides arable from domestic more clearly than an undivided square
belt would have). Dymock's farm might well be called a manufactory
utopia, or, to use a more technical term, a utopia of the formal sub-
sumption, for it shares with manufactory capitalism the same essential
role of elucidating the means of production by extracting it from its
traditional social matrix, and thus of reducing labor-time, increasing
productivity, by making an agrarian equivalent to simple cooperation
possible. It would require considerable ingenuity to invent a more
purely reasonable plan than this one.

Nonetheless, the scheme contains an incompletely acknowledged
aesthetic dimension, and contradiction; or rather, we become aware

32. Ibid., esp. pp. 19–22.

of contradiction (at least one) when we realize that there are competing spatial logics or configuring impulses, which have taken on an
irrational or compulsive (read: aesthetic) character. The round
scheme betrays a compulsive character, for example, when Dymock
says he would have the farmhouse built in a circular shape, too—not
the first plan for a circular manor,[33] but a remarkable architectural
departure all the same, which is perhaps why it isn't recorded on the
scheme. Or again, consider the following long sentence, the discursive
climax of the first letter, in which Dymock epitomizes his preferred
arrangement:

> Finally, here your house stands in the middle of all your little world
> (which you may build as your purse and fancy directs, though I could
> say something as to that in particular, which I take to be as effectuall if
> need were) enclosed with the Gardens and Orchards, refreshed with
> the beauty and odour of the blossomes, fruits and flowers, and the
> sweet melody of the chirping birds, that again encompast with little
> Closes, that all young, weak, or sick Cattle may be fostered under your
> own eye without losse or inconvenience, and all bound together as with
> a girdle, (and surely never had the old proverb, ungirt, unblest, a fitter
> or fuller sense or application) and all that covered again, as with a fair
> large cloak of Meadow and Tillage, to which you may commit the cor-
> ner pasturage, the Cape if you please, or the Sleeves to the Coat (for a
> Coat as well as a Cloak will serve to cover either knavery or foolery) of
> old customes or negligence.[34]

Layers of round enclosure for your farming comfort—this much is
clear anyway. If parts of the passage are elusive, that is largely, I'd
suggest, because Dymock's enthusiasm swamps the idea he wants to
communicate; to put it another way, it's that the idea in question
clearly retains something of a fetish character—that Dymock is trying
to sell his contrivance by linking it to a rather replete fantasy of
(among other things) safety and sanity. In context, this emphasis on
rounded enclosure works primarily to indicate the limits of the compatibility between reason and independence, thus attributing to the
distinction between the two maps, the opposition between the circular
farm and the rectangular manor, the force of a contradiction. This

33. Ibid., p. 19. See Mark Girouard, *Robert Smythson and the Elizabethan Country
House* (New Haven: Yale University Press, 1983), p. 26, for a design for a circular house
by John Thorpe.
34. Dymock, *A Discoverie*, pp. 10–11.

discordance between circular and perpendicular evidently derives from, and corresponds in a general way to, a contradiction at the heart of the dynamic of improvement between what we might characterize in terms of the economic rage for accessibility, on the one hand, and the proprietary desire for unitary control, on the other. The aesthetic dimension of Dymock's manor-farm should in the first place be grasped *organically*—that is, as a quasi-technical response to the question posed by the improving dynamic—even though the circular aesthetic strikes one as secondary, and indeed plays a compensatory role, premised as it is on the rectangular logic of the larger manor.

Yet however organic, the aesthetic does indeed seem to possess a life of its own. I would argue that it wins its independence, or becomes architectural, with the recognition that the odd spaces in the scheme enact a kind of "secondary" secondary compensation, constituting a series of "compromise" topoi and introducing a third, differential or modalizing, aesthetic level or logic, what we might call a subdued aesthetic of uneven development. You can begin to see how this is if you attend to Dymock's pasture-corners, which appear in his picture of the farm as imperfect triangles, and are glossed in his commentary (in the passage quoted above), with some syntactic ambiguity, as the cape of old custom. The ambiguity suggests some ambivalence on Dymock's part, an ambivalence stirred, one assumes, because pasture is the least laborious, least apparently productive category of farm land. But the pasture is a picturesque, if apologetic, feature. In it, Dymock's system confesses its link to the traditional—wasteful, negligent, aristocratic—farm, while recoding it as a purely aesthetic touch, which ought to give satisfaction to those customary desires understood still to be at work within the rationalizing farmer's soul. Even while implicitly confessing to the pasture/waste's economic backwardness, the commentary makes it symbolically or emotionally functional, and so effects a kind of compromise between the system's two other configuring impulses.[35]

35. I am not suggesting that pasture was in fact relatively unproductive, but only that it is coded thus in the passage in question. In Hartlib's popular *Samuel Hartlib His Legacie or An Enlargement of the Discourse of Husbandry used in Brabant and Flanders* (London, 1651), Sir Richard Weston argues that the high incidence of pasture and meadowland in England is what makes it richer than other countries (p. 49). Although I have not had the space to address the gender implications of Dymock's arrangement, it is important to note that agrarian improvement seems to have been somewhat contradictorily coded, both as the feminization of the farm and the containment of femininity. Witness this interesting passage, again from Weston: "In the times of *Papistry*, all in this

But the contradiction between manor and farm is then more clearly resolved in the scheme itself, in the place where the corners of
waste/pasture move inside the ring of arable, and assume the perfectly triangular shape, now, of the meads. Once we see that these triangles, which bring the waste in domesticated form into the farm, allude
to traditional village farming, and enact the symbolically subdued
return of the *strip*, we gather that there is a full-blown compensatory
system at work in the scheme. The village is not just explained away; it
returns, in diminished form, and it will abide. History, by undergoing
synchronization, is allowed to stake a distorted, limited claim within
the shifting terrain of the enclosed and engrossed farm.

To return now to "Appleton House": it will be remembered that I
introduced Dymock's tract mainly as a way of lending conviction to
the suggestion that Marvell, in symbolically repossessing or enclosing
the demesne, could also be rehearsing garden history, understood as a
series of responses to definite phases of enclosure and engrossment,
in advance. If Dymock can grasp the principles of improvement securely enough to forecast a future phase of enclosure in its essential
form, then there is no good reason not to understand Marvell as
forecasting the response. I believe that meadow and forest sections of
"Appleton House" might indeed be read as offering a kind of utopian
dialectical counter-image to Dymock's utopian manor. If space permitted, I could support this suggestion by exploring a series of possible analogies. Isn't Marvell's manor in a sense an earnest yeoman
poet's utopia?—the utopia of a poet who's learned his technique from
the best, most advanced foreign models? Doesn't the application of
technique go along with a femininization of the manor? Could Marvell, in the wood, be analyzing his birds within an implicit problematic

---

Island were either *Souldiers* or *Scholars*; *Scholars*, by reason of the great honours, privi-
ledges, and profits (the third part of the *Kingdome* belonging to them) and *Souldiers*,
because of the many and great warres with *France, Scotland, Ireland, Wales*. And in those
times *Gentlemen* thought it an honour to be carelesse, and to have *houses, furniture, diet,
exercises, apparel*, & yea all things at home and abroad, *Souldier*-like: *Musick, Pictures,
Perfumes, Sauces* (unlesse good Stomocks) were counted perhaps unjustly, too effemi-
nate. In *Qu. Elizabeth's* dayes *Ingenuities, Curiosities*, and Good *Husbandry* began to take
place; and then *Salt Marshes* began to be fenced from the Seas; and yet many were
neglected, even to our dayes" (p. 52). If the pastures, in Dymock's scheme, are to be
associated with old masculine negligence, then the neatly triangular meads, which I will
cast below both as resolving the antinomy between round and square, comfort and
reason, and introducing a new spatial logic of development into the scheme, would
seem also to bridge the distance between masculine and feminine farm-spaces.

of relative moral utility? Is it an accident that both "Appleton House" and Dymock's manor consistently allude to the same two religious subtexts, the contrasting typological narratives of Eden and Ark?

But I must limit myself to considering two further, closely related strategies implicit in Marvell's narrative format and more or less explicit in Dymock's scheme, to which it thus helps to direct attention. Marvell not only symbolically repossesses the demesne in the wood and meadow sections; he also, and perhaps more primarily, takes symbolic possession of the waste. And I believe that this possession proceeds by way of an aesthetic of uneven development comparable to that which we've just witnessed emerging in Dymock, though much more complexly and fully instituted.

MARVELL, WINSTANLEY, AND THE ANTINOMIES OF ABSOLUTE PROPERTY

To exposit these strategies will require another detour, or rather the brief discussion of a distinctly different project of "rural development"—the collective (and collectivist) occupation of wastelands carried out in 1649–50 by a few groups who came to be known as the Diggers, and recorded and sponsored in a series of remarkable pamphlets by Gerrard Winstanley. The relevance to "Appleton House" of this "digression" can be seen if we turn to the lines that lie at the symptomatic core of the strategies of possession and synchronization to which I've just referred. In the meadow section, after the reapers have danced their dance and piled and removed the haycocks, Marvell describes the appearance of "A new and empty face of things, / A levelled space, as smooth and plain / As cloths for Lely stretched to stain" (ll. 442–44). Then, after two more analogies, the narrative is taken up again:

> For to this naked equal flat,
> Which Levellers take pattern at,
> The villagers in common chase
> Their cattle, which it closer rase;
> And what below the scythe increased
> Is pinched yet nearer by the beast.

(ll. 449–56)

The reference here is most transparently to the Diggers, or True Levellers,[36] and its most obvious aim, a thoroughly conventional one, is to trivialize radical heretics by implying that their grievance is against ineradicable natural differences (Spenser's leveling giant makes the same point in Book V). But to leave it at that, as a bad and tired joke, is to ignore the technical possibilities, the perspectival compression, of these lines. It is well to recall Marvell's painterliness here, and, more narrowly, what Colie called his perspectivism. If Marvell is the most painterly poet in the language, he is so less because of the iconographic and visual genre references scattered through his verse (though these are of course important in themselves, and provide directive context), than in regard of his manifest technical interest in the relations between linguistic and visual media, and in the possibility of producing "reality effects" in verse equivalent to those of a Vermeer or a Rembrandt. This interest is especially obtrusive in Marvell's habitual "floating" of relative clauses and pronouns—a common enough poetic practice, to be sure, but so common in Marvell that the shifting reference of clauses takes on an unusual figurative force, estranging and unveiling the spatial-gestural signified of ordinary syntax much in the way the more customary practice of poetic tropes estranges everyday diction. Since, in this poem's stanzas, so many relative clauses underscore their relativity by shifting their affiliations, one comes to regard all "shifters" with a canny eye; one waits for a new reference, better than the one first or "automatically" made, to discover itself and to present a new line of sight, a new image. The analogy would seem to be with the kind of attention one brings to anamorphic pictures—that species, for example, in which, upon the viewer obtaining or stumbling upon the right angle, a picture of the royal couple emerges from what had been a landscape, or a pornographic scene protrudes from the pope's wrinkled physiognomy.

The reader runs across one such example of "syntactic anamorphosis," I'd propose, in the first *which* clause in the above stanza. Syntactic custom makes it harder for a *which* clause to refer forward than backward (though of course a forward reference was much eas-

36. More precisely, the reference lumps Levellers together with Diggers, as if there were no difference between them; an obvious aim is to discredit the more politically dangerous group (the Levellers) by associating it with one completely beyond the pale. (That this was a common propagandistic move is testified to by the Levellers' frequent outright repudiations of the communistic sin and by their acceptance of the sobriquet "Leveller" in the mode of ritual disavowal [see their repeated references to their own party as "those they call Levellers" or "the levellers (so called)"].)

ier in Marvell's time than it would be today, when such arrangements are generally felt to be stilted and "undemocratic"). But it makes better *sense* for the analogy to be drawn with the villagers, or with their collective action, than with the flat or its nearly razed blades of grass: Levellers, being people, can more easily imitate villagers (especially when they act "in common") than flats, however equal. Once you see this angle, the odd allegorical resonance of "naked equal flat" is modified somewhat; if the Levellers are imitating villagers chasing cattle, then they are involved in an allusion to village riots, another name for which was enclosure riots, and the naked equal flat starts to look like a poetic version of Dymock's first plat: it is what the land becomes, what is left over, after enclosure. Thus a view opens of what I would maintain is a convincing interpretation of the Diggers' historical meaning. What Marvell is "really" saying is that the Diggers model themselves on the practice of collective commoning in the new context determined by enclosure. If this is the repressed sense of the passage, if what the lines limn in true perspective is a picture of the Diggers' structural strength, then Marvell's strategies of possession and uneven development become more comprehensible.

Whether or not the Diggers constituted a serious threat to the social status quo, their remarkable tenacity cries out for explanation, and suggests some structural source. It could not just have been hunger and desperation, any more than it was just religion, that made them weather nearly a year of constant legal and physical intimidation, first on George's Hill, and then at Cobham.[37] To explain their persistence we need first to ask after their strategic resources, to discover the symbolic logic of their project. How and why did Winstanley's experimental and materialist religion lead him, after his communist revelation, to George's Hill?[38] Why did his communism limit itself to the common lands, leaving enclosed lands to the elder brothers—not just in practice (the explanation for that, of course, is not far to seek), but also, to a large extent, in theory?

37. For the Diggers' story, and for stimulating discussion of Winstanley's pamphlets, see George H. Sabine's introduction to *The Works of Gerrard Winstanley: With an Appendix of Documents Relating to the Digger Movement* (1941; Ithaca: Cornell University Press, 1965); Robert W. Kenney's introduction to his edition of *The Law of Freedom in a Platform* (1941; New York: Schocken Books, 1973); Christopher Hill, *The World Turned Upside Down* (New York, 1976); and Lutaud, *Winstanley* (note 8, above).

38. For the communist revelation, see *Works of Gerrard Winstanley*, ed. Sabine, pp. 190–98 and p. 315. For Winstanley's initial George-Hill pamphlet, see "The True Levellers Standard Advanced," pp. 245–50.

The Diggers had many resources, of course, but two seem particularly decisive. The first has often been noted. Keith Thomas some time ago observed that the Diggers should probably be understood as continuing the tradition of squatting on common and (especially) forest land by groups of vagrants and cottagers, a practice which, though fugitive, was approximately as perennial as the rural depopulation that accompanied primitive agrarian accumulation.[39]

But the Diggers were distinguished squatters, for they preached what they practiced. They tried to *legitimate* squatting. Winstanley has several arguments as to why the Diggers should have the commons—arguments from political and social emergency, from equity, from his version of Norman Yoke theory—but no one of them makes his case so profoundly as his occasional, apparently naïve, punning insistence that the common people should have the common land because both are, after all, common[40]—as if the language itself recognizes some deep affinity between these people and those places.

How might Winstanley have come to assume such an affinity? Perhaps this can best be understood as the end result of enclosure debates. J. A. Yelling has suggested that enclosure came to symbolize the whole complex process of rural modernization partly because the debates over enclosure in manorial and village courts provided the only forum in which the issues raised by modernization could be publicly mooted. Questions concerning rights to commons occupied much of the discussion.[41] It seems that in the course of this long-term debate the communal character of property relations in the village was displaced from village lands and focused anew on the commons. And, since continued access to the commons was of overwhelming importance to those whose tenure was inferior or insecure, you can see how the commons would have come to be associated with the poor, to represent especially their prerogative. If this was the effect of the debates, then Winstanley's appropriation of wastes and commons for the poor and common people, and his assumption that the commons should be communally cultivated, seem much less radical, less apocalyptic than they might strike one at first.

Nonetheless, it should be stressed that Winstanley's "take" on the

39. See Keith Thomas, "Another Digger Broadside," *Past and Present* (1969): 57–68.
40. Cf., e.g., *Works of Gerrard Winstanley*, ed. Sabine, p. 196: "For as the inclosures are called such a mans Land, and such a mans Land; so the Commons and Heath, are called the common-peoples."
41. Yelling, *Common Field*, chap. 1.

debates is a millennial one; and that Winstanley's material God, the God of so much popular religion, makes it possible for him to extrapolate from them in the way that he does, and to experience the enclosure movement as caught up in a dynamic with utopian ends. One sees it happening in the pamphlets of early 1649: Winstanley's impersonal, spreading God, the Christ rising in us all, stakes a special claim to the common lands: when the Diggers occupied George Hill they were the spreading God returning to paradise.

To describe the project in a structural way, now: the Digger intervention is predicated upon a millennialist misrecognition of the ends of the enclosure movement and, by extension, of the capitalization of the manorial economy. It assumes that enclosure is rendering not just private property but also common land "absolute," and attempts to put an end to the process by extraditing the new pockets of communal space from the exclusive, enclosing space of private property, or of what Winstanley calls kingly power. This extradition will activate a battle, already latent in the soil, between opposing tenancy spaces— which is what the vagrant squatters have—unknowingly—been about all along.

The specific virtue of the Diggers' misrecognition of utopia in the common lands would seem to be that it affords a way, a place, of thinking the unity of the rural laboring class, in preparation for their practical, political structuring. It has generally been insufficiently stressed (and is crucial to my larger argument here) that Winstanley's millennialism paved the way for strategic, political thinking; it conditioned the appearance of the problem of how to organize the rural poor and dispossessed, even while setting limits, finally, to the problem's lucid elaboration.

The Diggers did have a plan. Their strategy involved exploiting the crisis and indecision in the ranks of the ruling class to establish a network of Digging communities. In the course of its being set in place, the network would take on the character of an agrarian strike. This is especially plain in the first two Digger pamphlets, where Winstanley warns his readers, in decidedly ominous tones, that no one should any longer work for a master. But the aim throughout was to create a solidary ethos of masterlessness, and to use the lure—and threat—of freedom to draw off the landholding class's wage-labor force. They would then be in a position to deliver what we might call the Digger petition (for the sake of a contrast with the Leveller petition). The Digger petition would only be addressed after some (provisional) organization had been achieved, and would be sent, not to Parliament or the Army Grandees, but to the landholding class where they lived. The Digger petition would turn the tables on the lords of manors, and make them understand from within the "cry of necessity" that Winstanley came to describe, in *The Law of Freedom*, as constituting the origins, when and as long as it is heard, of good government.[42]

Now if Marvell anamorphically recognizes the Digger strategy in the passage above, the special urgency of the meadow and forest sections of the poem, the intensity with which he applies hard-won poetic technique to what, under the Diggers' aspect, are symbolic commons and waste, is comprehensible. It is an effort to stifle the cry of necessity before it gets to the diaphragm, to possess the commons, absolutely, for his lord.

This is the context, I believe, in which one can best appreciate the extent to which *Upon Appleton House*, however much it may honor Fairfax's line, amounts to a surreptitious celebration of absolute property, premised as its praise is on his manor's independence of customary ties and obligations, whether to monarch or village. If Fairfax's hall, unlike Penshurst's, accommodates no villagers' repast, neither do his rooms play mystic host to a monarch. And even Fairfax's line, though honored at length, is selfish on scrutiny. Jonson addressed Penshurst as a way of endowing Robert Sidney with a spuriously deep line. Marvell is handicapped, of course, by the historical accident that Fairfax was without a male heir; but it is no accident that he praises Fairfax by depicting his virtue as absolute, or irreducible to his line— virtually (or metaphorically) at one, that is, with his estate, his property. This is the message implicit in the passage usually read as the thematic climax of the poem, though its oddity has generally gone unnoticed by critics:

> Hence she [Maria] with graces more divine
> Supplies beyond her sex the line;
> And like a sprig of mistletoe
> On the Fairfacian oak does grow;
> Whence, for some universal good,
> The priest shall cut the sacred bud,
> While her glad parents most rejoice,
> And make their destiny their choice.

(ll. 737–44)

42. See *The Law of Freedom in a Platform*, ed. Kenney, pp. 83–87, esp. p. 85.

In other words, it is a good thing that Fairfax and Vere didn't have a son, since it lets them prove that he really owns his line: he will prove it by giving it all away. But this proof will come only after they have improved the line, in what would traditionally have been one of its wasted members (that is, in Maria, who in the poem's last section is metaphorically equated with the manorial paradise—the logic is clear), yet more thoroughly, and much more economically, than Marvell has cultivated the decorative waste of Fairfax's estate.

Marvell prepares this thematic climax, grounds it structurally, by making his house metaphorical from the first stanza on. Penshurst was opposed to Elizabethan and Jacobean great houses (those, evidently, that had learned some superficial classical language); and the opposition remains pretty securely literal. Penshurst, we might say, is metonymic in relation to Sidney—the setting of and for his virtue— and synechdochic in relation to Britain—a piece of what is good about it. But the sober frame of Appleton House is not opposed to other places in this way. It is filled with its own tension between the foreign and domestic, the cultivated and natural; the "original" opposition is internalized, and the house has a strained, strictly metaphorical status—it simply *is* Fairfax, or the poem, or England, or all these things at once. Or if it isn't these things exactly, it's what they should be, the model of or for them. This revision is tailored, clearly enough, to Fairfax's greatness, which remains without rival; those who say that this country-house poem is really all about the owner have some reason for saying so. But it is tailored to more than that; Marvell's generic revision is by no means simply panegyric. I would contend, indeed, that the theme of absolute property "originates" with this metaphorical attempt at reducing an older, metonymic opposition. What happens in the poem's course, then, as the metaphor stamps property and its attendant vexation upon the grounds of the estate, is that the original problem this poem, if it's all about Fairfax, must after all address, is repositioned while being ignored, and "explained away" into the fabric of the manor.

That problem is Fairfax's regret for what he turned out to have accomplished, his ambivalent desire for a return to the old regime,[43] and it is clearly alluded to and indirectly engaged at least twice in "Upon Appleton House": first in the legendary department of the poem, which narrates the story of the first Fairfax's legally violent

43. See M. A. Gibb, *The Lord General: A Life of Thomas Fairfax* (London: Drummond, 1938), pp. 208–26.

appropriation of the manor; and second, in the meadow section, where Marvell unwittingly instigates a massacre of harmless and improvident rails. A major function of the nunnery section is evidently to provide a fable of origins, a historical code in terms of which the house's oppositions, the poem's metaphorical strain (but also Fairfax's own dilemma) can be understood—a task accomplished in the notion of Protestantism's necessary original sin. So Fairfax's problem is not his fault, it is his progenitor's, or Protestantism's; one can't be expected not to repeat an original sin. A major function of the meadow and forest sections then is to suggest that Fairfax's sin is not simply his ancestor's, or Protestantism's, fault either. Catholicism and Protestantism return in these sections, but they are not the same; they return as a complex logic of manorial impulses and impressions, and only the metaphorical structure, only the manor itself in its increasingly absolute form, is the same. Thus when Marvell repeats Fairfax's sin, in the meadow section, by telling the reapers they are on the way to the promised land (situating them typologically), it would seem that Thestylis' bloody response, in its literalism, its primitive superstition, can be read as a return of Catholicism. But she is also something new—a very different heretic from the subtle nun who speaks for the convent community in the fable of origins. Likewise with Marvell's vegetable epiphany in the forest, at the climax of which he likens himself to some great Prelate of the Grove: another return of Catholicism, but in a metaphysical and *libertin* guise now. In such playful repetitions of the original sin, in such figurative violence, Fairfax's historical problem, along with the original historical explanation, are not being forgotten, exactly, but redisposed, explained away into the structure of the manor.

CONTRADICTION AND OVERDETERMINATION: THE NECESSITY OF THE POLITICAL AS A DISCRETE INSTANCE

We might now briefly review the moments or symbolic impulses of Marvell's new genre, the perambulatory country-house poem. The first and most basic of these moments, the one that keeps returning in the poem and in my exposition, is that of structural discovery. In this moment, as we might conceive it, the poem comes up against the jarring abstraction of capitalist productive relations and refuses to let

go of the shock; instead it chooses ceaselessly to reproduce the disequivalence these relations bring with them, in order both to disclose
and to exploit the manor's new relativity, its difference from itself. To
exploit: for this is not a passive recognition, nor is it only recognition
that is on the poem's agenda. Even while discovering the manor's
newly abstract form, Marvell undertakes—at what we might for convenience' sake call a second, more concrete and purely strategic
level—symbolically to remodel it. He does this by putting in play what
I've called strategies of repossession, strategies that although "physically" coterminous are by no means logically congruent, responding
as they do to distinct anxieties. In the second moment, the land Marvell walks through in the body of the poem—which is evidently the
land within view of the house—stands for the land of (what was once)
the demesne, and Marvell, by making a garden of the "visual demesne," is reclaiming the real thing for the aristocracy and asserting
their continuing difference from the "new" landholding class of capitalist farmers (the sort of interest expressed with idiosyncratic purity
in Dymock's "contrivance"). In the third moment, the land of Marvell's poetic survey stands for waste and common land, and Marvell,
by occupying and systematizing its unruliness, "reclaims" (but perhaps a more accurate word here would be "steals") from the peasantry
and common people a site affording crucial symbolic support for
their political agency (an agency whose ambiguous place, both within
and without the new system, and whose potential structural strength,
are expressed with premature clarity by Winstanley).

Both these strategies proceed partly by way of what I've called an
aesthetic of uneven development; the latter strategy, especially, cannot
be separated from the effects of dynamic incongruity consequent
upon the de- and re-contextualization of materials previously (but
now as it were permanently) disparate, or rather from the aesthet-
ically self-conscious practice of such effects. These effects appear in
many spheres, of course—I certainly have not discussed them all—
but I take it that the manorial situation is decisive here, conferring on
all these appearances the character of unconscious allusions to the
principles of enclosure and engrossment. Dynamic incongruity is thus
above all registered as a spatial "event": like Dymock's, if less schemat-
ically, Marvell's manor seems to contain discrete spatial logics, which
govern discordant "plays of space." If this incongruity were not so
paradigmatically spatial, that is, if Marvell were not so clearly tapping
the force of uneven development before instituting, or in order to

institute, its aesthetic practice, one might speak of Marvell's aestheticization of incongruity as an impulse in its own right, as a fourth
moment in the poem's generic structure. But since, in tapping uneven
development, Marvell in effect discloses the peculiarly overdetermined dynamic native to capitalism, his aestheticization of incongruity partakes of the moment of discovery. The aesthetic of uneven
development, in other words, is only partly strategic. We might say
that its aim, first of all, is a simple recognition of the capitalist dynamic, but that in accomplishing this it also succeeds in explaining away
the damage attendant on capitalism's agrarian emergence. In promoting (thus in a sense accomplishing) a structural recognition, it incidentally enacts a strategic justification.

But it is the poem's moment of "discovery," I have assumed
throughout, which especially marks it as revolutionary. For this discovery presupposes, as I hope has become clear, the dramatic expansion of the cultural sphere, the sudden access of social consciousness,
which the events of the 1640s had produced, and indeed, if in a
somewhat perverse way, is premised on the promise of liberation they
at times held forth. Accordingly we might conclude by briefly spec-
ulating as to what good the revolution is in "Appleton House," insofar
as it is present to, and informs, the poem's narrative makeup. Or, to
put the same question another way: insofar as Marvell's "unruly practice" of an essentially utopian aesthetic of uneven development or
ceaseless overdetermination has it as its principal effect to preserve
the "moment of discovery," and to draw out the poem's encounter
with capitalist abstraction, what role or function does it ultimately
play? The answer to this question is difficult to pin down and perhaps
should not be assayed so directly. But I would suggest that the aesthetic works, as discovery, in two basic ways.[44] Its first, most literal aim
must simply be to inure the subject to the paradox of absolute property, or in other words, to the newly overdetermined character of capitalist contradiction, the systematically unevenly developed nature of
capitalist development. The attempt to possess the common land is
doomed to miss its mark, sociologically speaking, and Marvell's poem
makes us aware of this even as it symbolically occupies the common.

But there would seem to be a second aim, implicit in this first. The
aim is not to solve the problem of property but to work through it so

44. The conclusions that follow have been much influenced by Manfredo Tafuri,
Architecture and Utopia: Design and Capitalist Development, trans. Barbara Luigia La Penta
(Cambridge, 1987).

as to situate it, to put the subject in a position to regulate contradictions now perceived as inevitable, or perhaps to institutionalize their regulation. Critics have often noted that by the end of Marvell's poem, his advice to retreat inside has a very hollow ring; and some have suggested that Marvell, in praising Fairfax so extensively, was working his way away from him, and toward his future political career as a public servant dedicated to those concrete gains that the Revolution did achieve.[45] I would agree with them, and note that this was one matter, at least, on which Winstanley's path converged with Marvell's: in *The Law of Freedom in a Platform*, his utopia of 1653, Winstanley may be seen to be implicitly criticizing himself for what we could call his former religious economism.

According to these works, then, the manorial economy may be what counts—it may lie at the heart of the midcentury crisis and revolution. But while the manor poses the basic, moving problems, its survey provides no final answers. The works' firm recognition of these capitalist facts, I am suggesting, marks a decisive shift within the cultural landscape of what is now a capitalist nation beyond backsliding, its many reservations figured into account as *functional* nostalgia.

45. See Hodge, *Foreshortened Time*, pp. 157–58.

2

State, Church, and the Disestablishment of Magic

Orthodoxy and Dissent in Post-Reformation England and France

RICHARD LACHMANN

Beginning in the sixteenth century, an increasing number of people in England and France came to doubt that Catholic priests were the only, or even the preferred, practitioners of magic. Smaller but rapidly growing numbers of English and French went further and denied the reality of magical power, whether claimed by priests or by their rivals. Officials within the Catholic and Protestant churches of England and France, and from the lay governments of the two nations, embarked upon a number of campaigns (which sometimes worked at cross-purposes from one another) to eliminate unofficial practitioners of magic and to make popular religious beliefs conform to official standards of orthodoxy.

At times, efforts to enforce religious orthodoxy were directed against specific targets whom clerical or secular officials defined as witches and then sought to exterminate. Although the long-term decline of magic and short-lived and localized campaigns against witches were intertwined in contemporary minds (and often conflated in modern scholarship on that era in English and French history), it is critical that we differentiate those two phenomena for two reasons.

I acknowledge financial support from the National Endowment for the Humanities and the Society for the Scientific Study of Religion. I have benefited from the advice of Mary Fulbrook, Dominique Julia, Allen Liska, Theda Skocpol, and the editors of this volume.

First, on purely logical grounds, we cannot assume that causal factors used to explain a generalized decline of magic over several centuries in England and France can also account for witch trials that were confined to specific times and places in the two countries. Second, there is ample evidence that disbelief in magic led to tolerance as well as repression of witches. My task in this essay is to identify the particular causal factors that account for differences in the timing and quality of skepticism toward magic and for the repression of witches in the two countries, and thereby find a surer basis for understanding the interactions between those two phenomena.

It is important to begin by defining magic and witches. Medieval theologians contrasted prayer with magic. As Keith Thomas says, "A prayer had no certainty of success and would not be granted if God chose not to concede it. . . . Magic postulated occult forces of nature which the magician learned to control." Thus, magic by definition was anti-Christian, an effort to harness devilish or occult forces to alter God's plan. The Christian concept of prayer depended upon the willingness of a conscious God to respond to supplication. Most medieval Europeans, including Catholic clerics, however, blurred the clear theological distinction between prayer and magic. In their claims and practices, medieval clerics encouraged the laity to believe that "the medieval Church [was] a vast reservoir of magical power, capable of being deployed for . . . any human aspiration." As a result, almost all Catholics believed that "the Church was a magical agency, no less than a devotional one." We can therefore, without being anachronistic, use the term *magic* to refer to both the "white" magic of the Church and the "black" magic of wizards and witches. Most medieval Europeans believed that white and black magic were equally efficacious and differed only in that the former was derived from God and the Catholic Church, while the latter was achieved through pacts with the Devil or by drawing upon occult powers not sanctioned by the Church. Witches were defined, by medieval Europeans, as practitioners of black magic.[1]

In the first section of this essay, I highlight the great variations in the timing and intensity of witch trials across early modern Europe and note that such trials were concentrated in specific times and places. It is important to note the rarity and variability of witch pros-

1. Keith Thomas, *Religion and the Decline of Magic* (New York: Scribner's, 1971), pp. 41, 45, 47.

ecutions because most of the historical and theoretical literature on witch trials and the decline of magic addresses one or the other without explaining the causal connections between skepticism toward magic and the persecution of witches.

THE PROBLEM OF WITCH TRIALS: PERIODIZATION AND GEOGRAPHY

Despite the almost universal belief in the devilish sources of black magic, English and French clerics did not attempt to root out popular expressions of magic prior to the Reformation. Such passivity was not characteristic of all European clergies in those centuries. Witchcraft trials in the northern regions of Italy and Spain reached a peak in the fifteenth and early sixteenth centuries ("official zeal for exterminating witches had largely evaporated in Spain and Italy before it had even begun to appear in certain other lands"), whereas witch trials in Hungary, Poland, and Sweden intensified only after 1650.[2] In France there were few witchcraft trials before 1500 or after 1670. For example, Robert Muchembled's[3] survey of the number of sorcery trials in what is now the Departement du Nord and a small portion of Belgium indicates a dramatic rise following the Reformation, peaking in the early seventeenth centuries:

YEARS	1351– 1400	1401– 1450	1451– 1500	1501– 1550	1551– 1600	1601– 1650	1651– 1700	1701– 1790
Number of sorcery accusations	2	7	11	23	68	110	67	6

In England, witchcraft was a crime only in the years 1542–47 and 1563–1735. There is no evidence of prosecutions in the first period. In the later period there may have been as many as one thousand executions, although three hundred seems a more probable estimate.[4] Most of those executions fell into the years 1580–1600 and

2. Geoffrey Scarre, *Witchcraft and Magic in Sixteenth and Seventeenth-Century Europe* (Houndsmills: Macmillan, 1987), pp. 20–22.

3. Robert Muchembled, *La sorcière au village* (Paris: Gallimard, 1979), p. 131.

4. Alan Macfarlane, *Witchcraft in Tudor and Stuart England: A Regional and Comparative Study* (New York: Harper, 1970), p. 62; Christina Larner, *Witchcraft and Religion: The Politics of Popular Belief* (Oxford: Blackwell, 1984), pp. 71–72.

1645–47.[5] In any case, the numbers of trials and executions in England and France were slight compared with the far greater bloodbaths in the witch panics and inquisitions in Switzerland, Austria, and Germany from 1561 to 1670. At the height of witch accusations and executions, only 15 percent of English defendants in witchcraft trials were executed, compared with 49 percent in Muchembled's data for the Departement du Nord, and more than 90 percent in German-speaking regions of Europe.[6]

Witch prosecutions in England and France, and elsewhere in Europe, were concentrated in time and place. Trials were held at those rare moments when lay or clerical prosecutors realized a need to find and punish witches. In most years and most localities witches were neither found nor punished by authorities.[7] Almost all English witch trials occurred in the 1580s and 1590s and in the years 1645–47; most of those trials were concentrated in Essex, Kent, Norfolk, and Suffolk.[8]

THE DECLINE OF MAGIC: THREE PERSPECTIVES ON WITCH TRIALS

With the exception of Keith Thomas's *Religion and the Decline of Magic*, studies on the decline of belief in magic and the persecution of witches in England and France suffer from a lack of attention to the causal interrelationships between rising skepticism toward magic and the concentration of witch trials during the sixteenth and seventeenth centuries in England and France. Scholars of witch trials assume either a continuing general belief in magic and hence in the efficacy and danger of witches, or an elite disbelief in the claims of popular

5. Thomas, *Decline of Magic*, pp. 449–51.

6. Scarre, *Witchcraft and Magic*, p. 30; Eastern European execution rates were comparable to that in France, while Geneva's rate was similar to England's. Of course, these data do not reflect those people who were accused of witchcraft but never formally tried and hence never came to be acquitted, or not executed despite convictions. From the limited documentation available it appears that such pre-indictment dismissals were more common in England than on the Continent and quite rare in German-speaking areas, suggesting that the real execution rate is even lower than 15 percent for England, and perhaps even higher than the formal data indicate for German-speaking Europe. France, again, falls somewhere in the middle.

7. Robert Muchembled, *Les derniers bûchers: Un village de Flandre et ses sorcières sous Louis XIV* (Paris: Ramsay, 1981), pp. 94–205.

8. Thomas, *Decline of Magic*, pp. 449–52; Macfarlane, *Witchcraft*, pp. 28, 61–63.

magicians as the motivations for prosecuting witches. Thomas's contribution is to trace how beliefs in magic and views of witchcraft
changed in early modern England. The factors he highlights, however, are inadequate to explain the timing and geographic concentration of witch trials in England, let alone account for differences in the
manifestation of those phenomena in France.

Thomas's compelling study of magic in England draws upon the
broadest set of sources. He demonstrates that until the seventeenth
century, religion—both Protestant and Catholic—was intellectually
compatible with magic, even as clerics competed with lay wizards,
cunning men, and witches for the custom and allegiance of the populace. "The [Catholic] Church did not deny that supernatural action
was possible, but it stressed that it could emanate from only two possible sources: God or the Devil."[9]

Thomas shows how the constant Catholic use of prayer and holy
objects to secure everyday ends provided the intellectual base for lay
magicians to claim that magical forces were present outside the
church and could be mobilized by cunning men for ends desired by
their customers rather than for those rarer ends sanctioned by the
Church.[10] Although the Church of England often, and the Puritans
almost always, denied the reality and efficacy of magic whether practiced by priests or the laity, Protestantism, by intensifying belief in the
immanence of the Devil, reinforced the idea that magical powers were
at large in the world. Indeed, by denying the value of ritual exorcism
and instead arguing that faith and works were the only ways to ward
off evil, Anglican and Puritan ministers drove fearful lay people to
the remaining Catholic priests, and to white witches and those ministers of radical sects who remained eager to practice exorcisms of one
variety or another.[11]

If in the first century after the Reformation the Catholic Church's
loss of its virtual monopoly over the practice of magic opened opportunities for rival magicians, in the long run Protestant espousal of
rationalism and championship of the efficacy of man's works created
an intellectual climate which undermined belief in magic. First the
Protestant elite of the seventeenth century, and later a growing sector
of common people, rejected the possibility of magical power.[12]

9. Thomas, *Decline of Magic*, p. 255.
10. Ibid., pp. 25–50, 253–63.
11. Ibid., pp. 469–97.
12. Ibid., pp. 641–68.

Thomas's emphasis on the primacy of intellectual over institutional factors in explaining the decline of magic derives from his finding that in England most people abandoned faith in magic *before* the development of more effective scientific and medical techniques for controlling nature and alleviating suffering. "The change which occurred in the seventeenth century was thus not so much technological as mental. In many different spheres of life [efforts to control poverty, improve agriculture, reform the state, and above all in scientific explanation] the period saw the emergence of a new faith in the potentialities of human initiative."[13]

By taking magic seriously as an intellectual enterprise, Thomas is able to expose the "tautological character [of] Malinowski's argument that magic occupies the vacuum left by science."[14] Each system won adherents primarily from the premises it proposed for the relationship between humankind, God, and the physical world, and only secondarily from its operative accomplishments. Magic declined, in Thomas's view, because first an elite and then the majority became less and less accepting of its intellectual premises.

Science appealed to some groups sooner than to others, however, and rejection of magic did not lead all skeptics to advocate state sanctions against its remaining practitioners. Thomas often describes, but does not identify the causes of, variations within England in attitudes toward magic and its practitioners. Specifically, he does not explain divergences between the intellectual rejection of magic and a willingness to prosecute magicians. Puritans were the first in England to deny the possibility of manipulating magical forces in this world, yet they were reluctant allies, and at times hostile opponents, of the repeated efforts by officials of the Church of England to prosecute popular magicians, even as Anglicans remained unwilling to abandon totally the practice of magic themselves. Meanwhile, equally well educated ministers and lay members of radical sects embraced magic even as they tried to differentiate their practices from those of Catholics or private wizards. Nor does Thomas account for the concentration of attacks on witches in a few English counties and during the 1580s and 90s and the brief 1645–47 period.[15]

Thomas's work stands alone in its analysis of the shifting intellectual bases of belief in magic. All other scholars have studied early

13. Ibid., p. 661.
14. Ibid., p. 667.
15. Ibid., pp. 256–61, 449–51.

modern beliefs about magic only to the extent necessary to explain
the existence of fears of witches and the eruption of witch trials.
Thus, all other sociologists, historians, and literary critics have in fact
analyzed witch trials as a species of "crime control." In so doing, they
all have made explicit or implicit use of one of what Allen Liska, in a
review, describes as the three social-science approaches to crime control: "structural functionalism," "conflict," and the "economic."[16]

Structural functionalists see crime control in general, and witch
trials in particular, as proxies for deep social conflicts. Members of a
society are most active in finding and prosecuting witches and other
sorts of "criminals" in times of "social anxiety." Nachman Ben-Yehuda
argues that the main persecutors of witches were Catholic inquisitors
who were reacting to the weakening of clerical authority and saw the
campaign against witches as a way to advance their specific institutional interests and bolster the power of the Church. The inquisitors
were supported by a populace that was anxious over the breakdown of
a communal medieval order. Peasants angered at violations of traditional customs turned on single women, whose sexual freedom and
employment as wage laborers made them symbols of the challenge to
a family-based village order and easy targets for denunciation as
witches.[17] Similarly, Alan Macfarlane, in his history of English witch
trials, sees witches as violators of traditional standards of charity, hospitality, and social dignity within peasant communities.[18]

Cultural and literary historians of England are virtually unanimous
in sharing an implicit and perhaps unconscious attraction to the structural functionalist perspective elaborated by sociologists and anthro-
pologists. Peter Stallybrass sees the "function" of witchcraft beliefs as
"one way of asserting distinctions . . . including definitions of political and familial roles." Analyzing the "function" of witchcraft in *Macbeth*, Stallybrass finds that Shakespeare and his audience associated
witchcraft "with female rule and the overthrowing of patriarchal
authority which . . . leads to the reversals in the cosmic order [and]-
. . . in the patriarchal order. . . . The conclusion of the play rees-
tablishes both the offended . . . father . . . and the offended
son/king," with the witches' evil supplanted by a restored order. The

16. Allen Liska, "A Critical Examination of Macro Perspectives on Crime Control,"
Annual Review of Sociology (1987): 67–88.
17. Nachman Ben-Yehuda, "The European Witch Craze of the 14th to 17th Centuries: A Sociologist's Perspective," *American Journal of Sociology* 86 (1980): 1–31.
18. Macfarlane, *Witchcraft*.

opposition of witchcraft to order in *Macbeth* parallels the actual function of witch trials in Stuart England, which, according to Stallybrass,
was "a particular working upon, and legitimation of, the hegemony of
patriarchy" by destroying poor women who were made to embody less
easily identifiable challenges to social order.[19]

Several cultural historians provide support for the notion that
witch trials were prompted by actual changes in social relations and
the resulting challenges to social order. The concern for upholding
patriarchy was reflected in and mediated through changes in family
structure which were felt most strongly among the elite. Lawrence
Stone describes the late sixteenth and seventeenth centuries as the era
of the "Restricted Patriarchal Nuclear Family," which "saw the decline
of loyalties to lineage, kin, patron and local community. . . . [T]he
nuclear family . . . became more closed off from external influences,
either of the kin or of the community. But at the same time, both state
and Church, for their own reasons, actively reinforced the pre-
existent patriarchy within the family."[20] Stone describes the imposition of legal control in conjunction with increased paternal force as
compensation for a decline in community restraints upon women and
children.[21] Stuart Clark contends that the Renaissance notion of correspondence among divine, princely, and patriarchal powers "endowed acts of social disorder with a significance far beyond their
immediate character, attributing to them repercussions in every other
plane of 'government.'"[22] Witch trials, especially of women who were
seen as the main attackers of patriarchal rule, thus became the prime
means of restoring proper social relations at all levels of governance.
Clark believes such "a contextual reading of Renaissance demonology . . . surely confirms the view that [the genesis and decline of
European witch trials] were related to the fortunes of an entire world-
view."[23] As David Underdown states it, witch trials, and milder sanctions against "scolding" women, were concentrated in a period of
declining neighborliness and rising disorder, exemplified by the increasing number of independent women and masterless men. The

19. Peter Stallybrass, "*Macbeth* and Witchcraft," in *Focus on Macbeth*, ed. John Russell
Brown (New York: Routledge, 1982), pp. 190, 201, 190.

20. Lawrence Stone, *The Family, Sex and Marriage in England, 1500–1800* (New York:
Harper, 1977), p. 7.

21. Stone, *The Family, Sex and Marriage*, pp. 151–218 and passim.

22. Stuart Clark, "Inversion, Misrule and the Meaning of Witchcraft," *Past and
Present* 87 (1980): 111.

23. Clark, "Inversion, Misrule and the Meaning of Witchcraft," pp. 126–27.

concern with order and the persecution of witches were responses to "a real threat to order in both social and familial relations in the century after 1560."[24] Underdown finds the greatest efforts to discipline the poor and to punish unruly women in those areas where traditional order had been disrupted by migration, enclosure, and the rise of industrial by-employment and agrarian wage labor.[25]

Continental scholars of witchcraft are the main adherents of a conflict approach, viewing the control of such "crimes" as instruments and indicators of class conflict. Continental studies of magic focus their attention on social differences between wizards and their supporters on the one hand, and inquisitors and skeptics on the other. Emblematic of this approach is Carlo Ginzburg's essay "High and Low." Ginzburg argues that in the Catholic Church throughout the medieval and Renaissance periods St. Paul's admonition against moral pride, *noli altum sapere*, "had been interpreted as directed against the intellectual curiosity of heretics about matters of religion . . . as the standard authority against any attempt to overcome the boundaries of human intellect . . . that is 'do not seek to know high things.'"[26]

Ginzburg contends that the religious and secular elites of Europe condemned religious heresy, political subversion, and freethinking science as equally serious challenges to the mutually supporting authority of church and state, both of which were sustained by "the time-honoured image of the cosmos." Witchcraft and science were attacked by elites because of the "possibility of drawing subversive analogies from the 'new science' [and from popular systems of magic] to religious and political matters." Ginzburg suggests that individual atheists and leaders of radical political movements also were aware of the subversive potential of science and magic.[27]

Ginzburg's suggestive essay finds support in the work of many French scholars. Muchembled studies witch trials in France and the Low Countries. He argues that both lay seigneurs and clerics associated sorcery with popular challenges to the absolutist state and Catho-

24. David Underdown, "The Taming of the Scold: The Enforcement of Patriarchal Authority in Early Modern England," in *Order and Disorder in Early Modern England,* ed. Anthony Fletcher and John Stevenson (Cambridge: Cambridge University Press, 1985), p. 135.

25. David Underdown, *Revel, Riot and Rebellion: Popular Politics and Culture in England, 1603–1660* (Oxford: Clarendon, 1985), pp. 20–40.

26. Carlo Ginzburg, "High and Low: The Theme of Forbidden Knowledge in the Sixteenth and Seventeenth Century," *Past and Present* (1976): 30.

27. Ibid., pp. 33, 35.

lic Church. Witches were identified at moments when peasants mobilized to resist royal taxes and conscription demands for war. Such popular mobilization, and therefore witch prosecutions, were most common in areas where seigneurs exploited peasants most intensely (and peasants therefore had no surplus margin to pay the added taxes) and where clerics were poor and with low prestige (and thus most likely to call in outside inquisitors to bolster their positions). Witch trials were furthered as well by divided peasant communities (divisions which were the result of increasing state tax and seigneurial rent demands). The tiny minority of well-off peasants feared the black magic of the mass of poorer peasants and aided the inquisitors by offering the names of uppity poor peasants as witches.[28]

Scholars who utilize the structural functionalist and conflict approaches offer plausible explanations for the motives of the men who prosecuted witches in early modern England and France. Their arguments, however, are inadequate as causal explanations. They fail to explain why the fears and interests they describe did not result in continual and massive campaigns to find and exterminate witches. Both approaches are unable to account for the rarity and the nonoccurrence of witch trials. Further, neither theory accounts for the differences in the targets and achievements of witch trials and broader anti-magic campaigns in the two countries.

Specifically, a convincing analysis must explain both why the English state and Anglican Church concentrated their efforts and enjoyed their main successes in suppressing political practitioners of magic, while the French state and Catholic Church tried to suppress all practitioners of magic, whether or not they had overt political interests, and why in France clerics took the lead in asserting that most witches were frauds, while in England Anglican ministers were the last elite to doubt the power of magic in everyday affairs. Further, a full theory must highlight the causal connections between differences in witch trials and the variations in beliefs about magic in En-

28. See Muchembled, *Culture populaire et culture des élites dans France moderne* (Paris: Flammarion, 1978); Muchembled, *La sorcière*; and Muchembled, *Les derniers bûchers*. Other studies which link magic with popular radicalism and find a class interest in the repression of sorcery include John Delumeau, *Catholicism between Luther and Voltaire* (1971; London: Burns, 1977), pp. 161–74; Philippe Joutard, *Les camisards* (Paris: Gallimard, 1976), pp. 59–90; Dominique Julia, "La religion—histoire religieuse" *Faire d'histoire, nouvelles approches* (Paris: Gallimard, 1974), pp. 137–67; and Robert Mandrou, *Magistrats et sorciers en France au XVIIe siècle: Une analyse de psychologie historique* (Paris: Plon, 1968).

gland and France. A theory must answer why pre-Reformation French kings and aristocrats were so much more active in the practice of magic than their English counterparts, why the secular use of magic to solve everyday problems was practiced mainly by commercial wizards in post-Reformation England, but still by priests in post-Tridentine France, and why the actual declines of magic in the two countries followed different courses: in England, politically oriented magic largely disappeared by the end of the seventeenth century, even though quotidian uses of magic by wizards continued into the nineteenth century, while in France both political and practical uses of magic continued through the Revolutionary era.

A theory of the interrelationships between witch trials and the decline of magic must address the *capacities* as well as the *interests* of witch prosecutors and anti-magic campaigners. Absent the means, motives cannot produce change. Only the third social-science approach to crime control, the economic, even begins to address the issue of capacities for combating the crime of witchcraft and for transforming beliefs about magic. Scholars working from this perspective would note that variations in the rate of witch trials mirror differences in the resources inquisitors were able to draw from their communities.

Elliott Currie argues that witch prosecutors in early modern Europe all had an interest in exaggerating the danger of witchcraft in order to draw more resources from their communities to finance their witch-hunting enterprises. Currie pictures witchcraft control in Continental Europe as "a large-scale industry" in which the identification of witches fueled popular hysteria, leading governments and churches to allocate ever more resources to witch hunters to find more witches, and thereby making the danger of witchcraft appear ever more ubiquitous and dire.[29] Only in England, where strong common law protections saved defendants from torture and self-incriminating confessions to imaginary deeds, was the sense of witchcraft's extent and the resultant demand for more witch hunts limited.

Currie's economic model of the mutually reinforcing generation of demand and supply also oversimplifies history. The "communities" of Europe responded in various ways to witchcraft and witch trials. A theory must explain from whom and why witch hunters sometimes received support for their efforts, but more often did not. Further, a

29. Elliott P. Currie, "Crimes without Criminals: Witchcraft and Its Control in Renaissance Europe," *Law and Society Review* (1968): 21.

theory must explain how witch hunters and religious reformers developed the capacities to act on their and their supporters' interests, and how limited capacities yielded limited results. I attempt to answer those questions in the remainder of this essay.

ELITES

The shortcomings of the scholarship described in the previous section stem in large part from the authors' lack of specificity in identifying the instigators of witch trials and reform campaigns. The "societies" and "communities" discussed by scholars from the structural functionalist and economic perspectives are reified categories that obfuscate, not clarify, historical analysis. The descriptions of a unified "elite" or dominant "class" by adherents to the conflict perspective ignore the serious intra-class conflicts that accompanied the class struggles of this era. Not all of Renaissance English or French society, nor even all of a unified ruling class or elite, agreed on the dangers of witchcraft and the appropriate means for combating black magic and ensuring religious orthodoxy. We must remember that the peak period of witch trials in England and France were also the centuries of Reformation and Counter-Reformation when societies and ruling groups were marked by divergent interests, and when their individual and collective capacities for action were sapped by intramural struggles.

A satisfactory explanation of the phenomena under consideration can only be constructed with a theory of social structure which allows for more exact distinctions than the oppositions of society vs. threatening deviants and criminals, or of high rulers vs. low masses, offered by the three perspectives of the previous section. For this essay, I employ a model of conflicting multiple elites.[30] Elites are defined as a group of rulers having the capacity to appropriate resources from non-elites and inhabiting a distinct organizational apparatus. The power, prestige, and income of elites are derived from their organizational capacities. Thus, high-status individuals and families outside of such organizational apparatuses are not, according to this definition,

30. Richard Lachmann, *From Manor to Market: Structural Change in England, 1536–1640* (Madison: University of Wisconsin Press, 1987); and Lachmann, "Class Formation without Class Struggle: An Elite Conflict Theory of the Transition to Capitalism," *American Sociological Review* (1990): 398–414.

part of an elite and, I would predict, are not able to secure power and resources to accompany their prestige.

Each elite has two fundamental interests: to preserve its organizational capacity against challenges from rival elites and to reproduce its exploitative relation vis-à-vis the producing class. Each elite's capacity to pursue its interests derives primarily from the structure of relations among the various coexisting elites and only secondarily from the interclass relations of production.

My essential argument, and challenge to past scholarship on witch trials and the decline of magic, is that changes in perceptions of magic and witchcraft were products primarily of shifts in elites' interests in defending their organizational apparatuses against rival elites who employed magic, and only secondarily offensives against non-elite practitioners of magic. Each elite's capacities to act upon its interests by prosecuting witches or by orchestrating campaigns of religious reform were circumscribed by the capacities of rival elites. Shifts in elite capacities for action against witches and other magical practices followed elite conflicts that transformed the structure of elite relations and therefore the relative capacities of each elite.

TOLERANCE OF WITCHCRAFT IN PRE-REFORMATION ENGLAND AND FRANCE

The mediating effect of elite structure upon magico-religious beliefs and practices is evident in the virtual absence of witch trials in pre-Reformation England and France. Three possible factors, alone or in combination, could account for the paucity of witch trials in England and France at a time when such trials were passing their peak in Italy and Spain: the clergy's inability to find and punish popular magicians; a lack of demand for unofficial magic due to the populace's satisfaction with the access to supernatural aid provided by clerics, kings, and aristocrats;[31] and the clergy's tolerance for popular practices that did not threaten their prerogatives. The first factor would be economists' explanation of choice, with their emphasis upon resources available to prosecutors. The second factor is noted by Thomas, while the third is

31. Explaining the rise of witchcraft and witch trials only *after* the Reformation, Thomas observes that "the Reformation took a good deal of the magic out of religion, leaving the astrologers and cunning men to fill much of the vacuum" (*Decline of Magic*, p. 638).

suggested by my elite conflict model, which portrays an elite's actions as responses to threats to that elite's organizational capacities. Neither the structural functionalist nor the conflict models are able to generate explanations for the lack of witch trials.

The first reason appears the most doubtful. The Catholic Church established the Office of the Inquisition and the Dominican order, both charged with finding and punishing heretics, in the thirteenth century, and both were active and successful in Spain and Switzerland, though not in France and England, in the fourteenth and fifteenth centuries.[32] The organizational capacity of the French church advanced dramatically in the century following the Hundred Years War and preceding the Reformation. The number of clerics grew dramatically, and bishops exercised greater control over the priests in their dioceses.[33] Clearly, French and probably English clerics as well possessed the organizational means to prosecute witches in the fifteenth century.

Thomas provides extensive documentation to support his view that the second factor, the ample provision of magic by church officials, kings, and aristocrats, was characteristic of pre-Reformation England. Delumeau provides similar evidence for France in that era. Priests used the Christian sacraments to meet their parishioners' secular needs and thereby demonstrate their magical powers. The wine and wafer of Holy Communion were fed to sick people and animals. Baptismal water was poured on fields to improve the harvest. Animals were baptized to ensure their fertility and productivity. Parishioners turned to their priests for exorcisms of plagues, requesting, for example, that church rituals be used to banish insects and rodents.[34]

Thomas's and Delumeau's evidence of official magic in England and France does not in itself demonstrate the relative absence of unofficial magic prior to the Reformation. The paucity of historical evidence of popular magical practices, aside from that revealed at or concocted for witch trials, makes it impossible to prove or disprove Thomas's hypothesis. Thomas assumes that the decline in official toleration of clerical magic and the rise in witch trials after the Reformation are the cause and effect of an intervening rise in popular magic. However, comparative analysis raises doubts about the adequacy of

32. See Ben-Yehuda, "The European Witch Craze," pp. 8–11.
33. Delumeau, *Catholicism between Luther and Voltaire*, p. 3.
34. Thomas, *Decline of Magic*, pp. 25–50; Delumeau, *Catholicism between Luther and Voltaire*, pp. 168–70.

his explanation. Elsewhere in Europe witch trials peaked before the Reformation, at a time when Catholic clerics still were active practitioners of magic. Clearly there was plenty of unofficial magic, or at least of official fears of witchcraft, in pre-Reformation Switzerland, Spain, and Italy. Further, witch trials declined in England and France (and intensified elsewhere in Europe) during the late seventeenth and eighteenth centuries even as popular beliefs in magic and employment of wizards continued. The absence of witch trials does not indicate an absence of magicians, nor is an increase in such trials necessarily due to a real increase in popular magic.

Thomas's theory is valuable for identifying the role of the Reformation in England (a role paralleled by the reforms of the Counter-Reformation in Catholic France) in the decline of belief, on the part of lay and clerical elites, in the propriety of using magic for secular ends. Thomas, however, fails to anticipate another question raised by comparative analysis of witch trials: Why did some elites at certain times and places fear as well as scorn, and therefore prosecute, unofficial magical practices? That question can be answered only by tracing changes over time in the ways in which each elite succeeded and failed to use magic to augment its power.

My elite conflict model would predict that English and French elites perceived popular magic as a threat, and attempted to act on those perceptions by initiating witch trials and campaigns to reform popular beliefs, in those periods when their control over religious institutions came under challenge from rival elites and from subordinate classes. In the next section I offer support for that prediction by tracing the correlation between a stable division of control over clerical resources and magical authority among English and French elites on the one hand, and the absence of witch trials on the other hand, before the Reformation. The following two sections examine the causal relationship between elite conflicts and witch trials and campaigns of religious reform in the post-Reformation era.

THE INSTITUTIONALIZATION OF MAGIC IN PRE-REFORMATION ENGLAND AND FRANCE

Clerics were forced to share control over the income and authority of the English and French Catholic Churches with lay elites. The extent of encroachment by lay elites upon the institutional autonomy of the clergy was somewhat different in the two countries, yet in each case remained stable in the centuries leading up to the Reformation. With their joint control over the Church remaining relatively uncontested, neither the Catholic Church as an institution nor the claims of magical powers which each elite derived from its organizational authority offered terrain for elite or class conflict in England or France prior to the Reformation.

Catholic clerics were most likely to have their claims to a monopoly on magical power challenged when and where their institutional autonomy had been compromised as well. Clerics, in both England and France, claimed unique understanding of a body of knowledge—Catholic doctrine—and asserted that only they could perform the task of curing souls. Clerical competence and access to the supernatural powers God had vested in the Catholic Church were certified by appointment to church offices. Clerics, by virtue of holding office, were guaranteed incomes through tithes and other church claims on feudal production.

In fact, the existing corps of the Catholic Churches of England and France were forced to share control over clerical appointments and revenues with the monarchs and aristocrats of their nations. Both English and French monarchs enjoyed the right to name the archbishops who headed the Catholic archdioceses in the territories under their control. The English kings of the pre-Reformation period generally exercised that power unilaterally, while French rulers often had to cede their appointment authority to the great nobles who exercised de facto control over provinces within the French nation.[35]

At lower levels, the English church was far more autonomous than its French counterpart. Few English nobles controlled clerical offices prior to the Reformation.[36] Most English clerics were named by their ecclesiastical superiors. In contrast, the majority of French clerical offices were filled by aristocrats and urban merchants who enjoyed de facto patronage rights to those offices.[37]

Control over offices translated into income rights as well. Kings in

35. Christopher Hill, *Economic Problems of the Church: From Archbishop Whitgift to the Long Parliament* (Oxford: Oxford University Press, 1963), pp. 3–5; J. J. Scarisbrick, "Clerical Taxation in England, 1485 to 1547," *Journal of Ecclesiastical History* (1960): 45; Pierre Blet, *Le clergé de France et la monarchie: Etude sur les Assemblées Générales du Clergé de 1616 à 1666*, vol. 1 (Rome: Université Grégorienne, 1959), pp. 88–89; Michèle Bordeaux, *Aspects économiques de la vie de l'église aux XIV et XVe siècles* (Paris: Librairie Générale de Droit et de Jurisprudence, 1969), pp. 197–202.

36. Hill, *Economic Problems of the Church*, pp. 53–58.

37. Bordeaux, *Aspects Economiques*, pp. 66–68; Philip T. Hoffman, *Church and Community in the Diocese of Lyon* (New Haven: Yale University Press, 1984), pp. 7–10.

both nations, and the ruling magnates in some French provinces, used their authority to name archbishops as leverage to demand "gifts" from the clerics within their territories. French aristocrats also demanded a share of the income from their appointees' offices, while the more autonomous English priests were able to keep most of the income that accrued to their offices.[38]

The extent to which kings and aristocrats were able to appropriate clerical offices and incomes affected their capacities to claim magico-religious authority as well. English and French kings used their institutional positions as heads of their nations' Catholic Churches to endow their secular offices with magical powers, allowing them to become *rois thaumaturges*. Kings in both countries pre-empted the clergy's magical claims by healing the sick, using the ritual objects of their secular rule much as priests used the sacraments to minister to their subjects' temporal needs.[39]

Lesser English nobles, lacking control over institutional sites within the Church, were unable to make magical claims. However, many French aristocrats and corporate bodies of urban notables were able to appropriate spiritual as well as economic and political resources from the Church. French nobles attached the clerical assets and priestly services under their control to the lay religious confraternities they headed. Thus French aristocrats often were able to situate themselves as mediators between the clergy and laity, directing the Church's magical powers toward spiritual and temporal ends of their own choosing. Although few French nobles were able to make personal claims to magical powers comparable to those of the king, lay confraternities became the sites, and their aristocratic heads the objects, of popular appeals for magico-religious intervention in this life and the next.[40]

The incapacity of the English and French clergy to challenge existing claims by lay elites upon church assets and to magical powers, and

38. Scarisbrick, "Clerical Taxation," pp. 41–50; Felicity Heal, "Clerical Tax Collection under the Tudors: The Influence of the Reformation," in *Continuity and Change: Personnel and Administration of the Church of England, 1500–1642*, ed. Rosemary O'Day and Felicity Heal (Leicester: Leicester University Press, 1976), pp. 97–112; and Blet, *Le clergé de France*, vol. 1.

39. Thomas, *Decline of Magic*, pp. 194–204; Marc Bloch, *The Royal Touch: Sacred Monarchy and Scrofula in England and France*, trans. J. E. Anderson (London: Routledge, 1973).

40. John Bossy, "The Counter-Reformation and the People of Catholic Europe," *Past and Present* 47 (1970): 51–70; Bordeaux, *Aspects économiques*, pp. 66–68; Hoffman, *Church and Community*.

the offsetting inability of lay elites to extend their grasp over the clergy's temporal and spiritual powers, served to remove the Catholic Church as an institution and magic as a practice from the terrain of active political conflict. The available historical evidence does not allow us to draw a direct causal connection between the elite "settlement" concerning religion prior to the Reformation and the lack of witch trials in England and France during that era. In the following sections on the post-Reformation period, however, I provide a causal explanation for that correlation, which allows us to reach some conclusions on the relative explanatory power of each of the theories on witch trials.

ELITE CONFLICT IN THE REFORMATION

The Reformation disrupted the long-standing stalemate among elites over the control of clerical assets and authority. In both England and France, Protestants and Catholics fought each other and among themselves to impose their own beliefs upon everyone else, to fill clerical offices with their ideological allies, and to divert church income and assets to their own ends and often into their own pockets. There is no need to enter into the long-running debate over the factors that contributed to making a majority of the English, but only a minority of the French, leave the Catholic Church. What is at issue here is the extent to which particular elites were able to incorporate, within the institutions under their control, pieces of the authority and assets once controlled by relatively autonomous clergies and the strategies those elites adopted to protect their newly appropriated resources from challenge by rival elites.

The degrees to which the Catholic Churches of England and France had retained autonomy from the monarchs and lay landlords of their nations in the pre-Reformation period determined the success of crown efforts in the sixteenth century to nationalize religious institutions under the guise of the Reformation or Counter-Reformation. The strength of the English church's institutional autonomy weakened the clergy's position in English politics. Since lay landlords lacked influence over clerical appointments and were opposed by ecclesiastical courts in land tenure conflicts, they had no interest in preserving church authority and assets. In contrast, French nobles, who controlled clerical appointments and the revenues of church offices, wanted to preserve the formal autonomy of the Catholic church from royal appropriation. Of the 129 men appointed as bishops during the reign of François I (1514–47), 93 were nobles of the sword who came from families that held land and headed military companies independent of the crown. The majority of bishoprics were kept within nobles' families, and incumbent bishops enjoyed de facto right to name successors.[41] Consequently, when kings submitted their fiscal and legal demands to assemblies of bishops, clerics enjoyed sufficiently strong ties to provincial nobles to resist royal threats to their interests.[42] French clerical subordination to their aristocratic kin saved clerical property from being expropriated by the crown.

In contrast, the English church's autonomy from county landlords meant that the monarch needed to control only the few dozen clerics at the top of the hierarchy. The hierarchical character of the church, the absence of ties between lower-level clerics and lay landlords, and Henry VIII's domination of the bishops enabled the king to gain parliamentary ratification for the transfer of revenues and assets from the clergy to the crown. Through the Dissolution, the monarch assumed rights to all English manors held by the monasteries—a third of all English farmland.[43]

The Henrician Reformation sparked massive popular resistance by unreformed Catholics who sought to protect the offices and properties of their priests. That opposition culminated in the 1536 Pilgrimage of Grace and related rebellions which were joined by poorer monks and by prosperous and poorer peasants alike, and supported by some landlords who had been excluded from royal patronage.[44] Popular opposition to the Reformation forced Henry VIII to share the spoils of the Dissolution in order to maintain the support of his lay collaborators in Parliament and in the counties. The crown sold estates, benefices (the right to collect tithes in a parish), and advowsons (the right to appoint the occupant of a parish ministry) to laymen both

41. J. H. M. Salmon, *Society in Crisis: France in the Sixteenth Century* (New York: St. Martin's Press, 1975), pp. 80–83.

42. Blet, *Le clergé de France*, vol. 1.

43. Hill, *Economic Problems of the Church*, pp. 3–5.

44. T. H. Swales, "The Redistribution of the Monastic Lands in Norfolk at the Dissolution," *Norfolk Archaeology* 34 (1969); Christopher Haigh, *The Last Days of the Lancashire Monasteries and the Pilgrimage of Grace* (Manchester: The Chetham Society, 1969). The vehemence of opposition to the Reformation is powerfully conveyed elsewhere in this volume in Clark Hulse's discussion of Thomas More's death and the cult of his martyrdom.

to win their support and to raise money for the wars that consumed the last years of Henry's reign.[45]

In England, control of clerical offices passed quickly through the crown's hands in the sixteenth century, and came to be held by gentry based in the counties. Parish tithe rights became the property of lay landholders.[46] From the middle of the sixteenth century on, most English ministers were appointed and paid at the pleasure of the lay owners of benefices and advowsons. Neither crown nor clergy were able to enforce legal provisions against lay interference in clerical activities or against simony.[47] Ministers' weak legal positions allowed gentry to use their ownership of benefices and advowsons both to divert tithe revenues away from spiritual ends and to enforce ministers' conformity to the varied theological tastes of their patrons rather than to the new orthodoxy dictated by the hierarchy of the Church of England.

Lay English (and Scottish) owners of benefices, advowsons, and manors had to champion religious pluralism in order to guard their control over former monastic properties from efforts by the hierarchy of the Church of England to reassert old claims to estates, parish livings, and offices. Once Elizabeth I had secured royal control over the episcopacy at the end of the sixteenth century, she began to support the Anglican clergy's efforts to regain its former properties and powers. Her Stuart successors became increasingly bold in their attempts to weaken the gentry, and improve their own fiscal positions, by backing the claims of their clerical lackeys.[48] In response to the developing crown-clerical alliance, Puritans and less ideologically committed gentry had to choose between tolerance for radical sects and alliance with the crown to suppress dissent, in either case compromising authority over their own ministers.

French kings never were able to directly appropriate much clerical property. Instead, the crown took advantage of splits within provincial

45. Frederick C. Deitz, *English Public Finance 1558–1641*, vol. 2 (London: Cass, 1964), pp. 139–50; Joyce Youings, ed., *Devon Monastic Lands: Calendar of Particulars for Grants 1536–1558*, vol. 1 (Devon: Devon and Cornwall Record Society, 1955).

46. Hill, *Economic Problems of the Church*, pp. 50–73; Rosemary O'Day, "Ecclesiastical Patronage: Who Controlled the Church?" in *Church and Society in England: Henry VIII to James I*, ed. Felicity Heal and Rosemary O'Day (Hamden, Conn.: Archon, 1977), pp. 37–55.

47. Hill, *Economic Problems of the Church*, pp. 63–69.

48. O'Day, "Ecclesiastical Patronage"; Hill, *Economic Problems of the Church*, pp. 39–49, 307–45 and passim; Felicity Heal, "Economic Problems of the Clergy," in *Church and Society in England*, pp. 99–118.

blocs of lay elites, occasioned by the Wars of Religion, and of Papal concessions in the Concordat of 1516 (which was spurred by Papal fears of Protestant seizures of church properties in France), to make incremental gains in control over clerical offices and to increase royal taxes on church income.[49] By the end of the sixteenth century, the crown had appointed its own clients to a majority of French arch-bishoprics, replacing appointees from magnate families not suffi-ciently subservient to the crown.[50]

The key to gaining appointment to, and control over the resources of, clerical offices became loyalty to the king and his allies, rather than membership in autonomous provincial cliques. Loyalty to Catholicism counted for little in crown determinations of such appointments. In-deed the crown at times supported Protestants' claims upon benefices as a way of stripping clerical revenues from hostile provincial Catholic aristocrats.[51] Where the French crown could not gain direct control over clerical appointments, it alternately supported one faction or another in return for the lion's share of revenues seized by the crown's allies from the losing side.[52] The crown often precipitated religious conflict when it attempted to expand its income by empowering a religious or corporate body to collect taxes or control resources pre-viously under the authority of a rival. French elites appealed to co-religionists abroad, or formed alliances of convenience with their religious opponents, to bolster their positions in domestic factional disputes.[53]

French clerical benefices were controlled mainly by high church officials, who were forced to give an increasing share of tithe income to the crown through annual "gifts," clerical taxes assessed by the crown on each diocese.[54] Parish priests' incomes, except for the rare clerics who controlled their own benefices, were determined by crown

49. David Parker, *La Rochelle and the French Monarchy: Conflict and Order in Seventeenth-Century France* (London: Royal Historical Society, 1980), pp. 46–94; J. H. Shennan, *Government and Society in France, 1461–1661*, Historical Problems: Studies and Documents 7, gen. ed. G. R. Elton (New York: Barnes, 1969), pp. 16–19; Blet, *Le clergé de France*, vol. 1, pp. 88–99.

50. J. A. Bergin, "The Decline and Fall of the House of Guise as an Ecclesiastical Dynasty," *Historical Journal* (1982): 781–803.

51. Salmon, *Society in Crisis*; Louis Guéry, *Mouchamps: Histoire d'une paroisse vendéenne* (Fontenay-le-Compte: Luissaud, 1981).

52. Parker, *La Rochelle*, pp. 46–94.

53. Russell J. Major, "The Crown and the Aristocracy in Renaissance France," *American Historical Review* (1964): 631–45; Michael J. Hayden, *France and the Estates General of 1614* (Cambridge: Cambridge University Press, 1974), pp. 54–67.

54. Blet, *Le clergé de France*; Ivan Cloulas, "Les aliénations du temporel ecclésias-tique sous Charles IX et Henri III," *Revue d'histoire de l'église de France* 44 (1958): 5–56;

edicts which set the minimum salaries that clerical and lay controllers of benefices were required to pay the parish clerics from the decreasing portion of tithe revenues left after meeting the crown's demand for taxes.[55] The French crown, in the course of the sixteenth century, transferred authority to collect parish tithes from autonomous clerics and aristocrats to clerics and aristocrats under its control. That shift was accompanied by greater crown control over appointments to clerical offices and over the disposition of tithe revenues (parceled out variously to the crown itself, to the Pope, to lay clients of the crown, and to support parish priests and their spiritual activities). The crown also allowed its leading allies in each locality to select clerics who would meet their spiritual needs, even though the religious beliefs of crown clients varied from province to province and town to town.

RELIGIOUS INTERESTS AND MAGICAL POWER

Elite attitudes toward magic were bound up in the wider web of interests surrounding religious offices and properties. This is not to claim that elites determined their views of magic after calculating their political interests. Rather, people of Renaissance England and France responded to the ideological confusion of their era—the proliferation of religious sects, competition among magical practitioners, growing skepticism about humanity's capacity to mobilize supernatural forces in this world combined with optimism about the possibility of discovering and manipulating the forces of nature—by evaluating the character of magical claimants along with the content of their assertions. In other words, people of the Renaissance decided what to believe in part by settling upon whom to believe.

Offering spiritual allegiance to a priest, minister, or magician had political and economic as well as spiritual consequences. Lay people tended to trust magical practitioners whom they were able to control (or who were subordinated to the same authority as they were) and to fear magicians who were immune from their power. People who found that all claimants to magical power were beyond their influence, or were allied with their enemies, tended to become skeptical of

Jean-Pierre Gutton, *Villages du Lyonnais sous la Monarchie (XVI–XVII siècles)* (Lyon: Presses Universitaires de Lyon, 1958).

55. Timothy Tackett, *Priest and Parish in Eighteenth-Century France: A Social and Political Study of the Curés in a Diocese of Dauphine* (Princeton: Princeton University Press, 1977), pp. 120–29.

the very possibility of mobilizing supernatural forces in this world through the use of magic.

My hypothesis of affinities between institutional interests and belief in, fear of, and skepticism toward particular magicians and toward the very possibility of magic can be tested by examining the contrasts between the targets and achievements of anti-magic campaigns in England and in France. To the hierarchy of the Church of England and to its royal guardians, all other magicians were challengers to the Anglicans' self-proclaimed monopoly on access to divine power. The Anglican denunciations of rival magicians paralleled similar dictums by their sixteenth-century contemporaries in the French Catholic Church.

The stances of the official churches of the two nations toward magic varied in two significant ways. First, the French Catholic Church took the lead, in the seventeenth century, in educating the laity to its realization that most unofficial magicians were frauds rather than genuine instruments of the Devil, while in England Anglican ministers were the last elite to doubt the ubiquity of white and black magic in this world. Second, French clerics enjoyed strong support from the crown and lay elites in their anti-magic campaigns, while in England the gentry successfully attempted to undermine Anglican prosecutions of witches in almost all instances and only rarely instigated its own trials of witches in secular courts. These differences in the sources of intellectual leadership for skepticism toward magic (clerical in France, lay in England) and in lay support for clerical attacks on magic (strong in France, negative in England), affected the differences in the post-Reformation practice of magic. In France Catholic priests were the prime purveyors of magical solutions to quotidian problems, whereas in England commercial wizards filled most of the demand for such services. In England the political uses of magic were successfully suppressed by the end of the Civil War even as commercial wizards continued to be left alone by state and church, while in France state and church battled with limited success against both political and commercial uses of magic through the end of the Ancient Regime.

In England, only the bishops and ministers of the Church of England, joined at the end of the sixteenth century by their royal sponsors, sought to restore a unified hierarchy of religious authority in the nation. From their perspective, rival ministers and practitioners of magic were at best misguided, but were more probably instruments of the devil. The Anglican dream of reestablishing a monopoly of religious power required challenging the spiritual as well as the institutional legitimacy of their rivals and proving the unique correctness of their own divine authority. That dual task appeared more righteous and urgent when the enemies of Anglicanism were viewed as instruments of the devil.[56] However, the Church of England's capacity to suppress rival practitioners of magic—whether Catholic, dissenter, or commercial wizard—was severely limited by a series of post-Reformation Parliamentary Statutes and by rulings of lay judges that restricted the jurisdiction of ecclesiastical courts.[57]

The Anglican hierarchy was the only English elite with a clear and unchanging opposition to popular magic during the entire period from the Henrician Reformation through the Civil War. In contrast, the other three elites—crown, magnates, and gentry—shifted their views toward magic over time, and, in the case of the latter two, suffered from internal splits within counties. Such divisions prevented those elites from acting upon their opposition to magic through much of this period. Gentry interests in tolerating or suppressing popular religion and magic were shaped by their stance toward pluralism which responded, in turn, to crown policies toward gentry control over clerical properties. Gentry capacities to act upon their interests increased as crown and magnate capacities declined.

Crown tolerance of elite pluralism and popular religious dissent underwent a transformation toward the end of Elizabeth I's reign. After the Reformation, Henry VIII, Edward VI, and their advisers tolerated religious dissent (except for movements in support of the deceased Catholic clergy, which they crushed as a way of weakening clerical autonomy).[58] That policy was reversed during Mary's brief reign; however, her purges were directed against Protestants in gen-

56. Claire Cross, "Churchmen and the Royal Supremacy," in *Church and Society in England*.

57. Ralph Houlbrooke, "The Decline of Ecclesiastical Jurisdiction Under the Tudors," in *Continuity and Change*, pp. 239–57; Houlbrooke, *Church Courts and the People during the English Reformation, 1500–1642* (Oxford: Oxford University Press, 1979), pp. 7–20, 214–60, and passim.

58. Anthony Fletcher, *Tudor Rebellions* (London: Longman, 1968), pp. 21–47; Michael Scott Harrison, *The Pilgrimage of Grace in the Lake Counties, 1536–1537* (London: Royal Historical Society, 1981).

eral and not focused on magicians.[59] Up through the last two decades of the sixteenth century, "with the clergy only dubiously protestant, the political subordination of the church [of England] had still been a matter of concern to the government" and so the crown was still supportive of gentry claims to authority over clerical offices and properties.[60] Thus through the end of the sixteenth century, gentry could still entertain the desire of suppressing popular religious and magical movements without having to fear that they would provide an opening for a crown-Anglican alliance to enforce orthodoxy on them as well.

Crown control over the Anglican clergy was solidified by the end of Elizabeth I's reign. As a result crown policy began a shift, which accelerated under James I and intensified during Charles I's reign, toward aiding Anglican attempts to reclaim church authority. At the end of the sixteenth century the fusion of crown and clerical interests in opposition to dissent affected gentry attitudes toward popular religion and magic. Before that moment, the gentry could oppose popular magic and radical sects without having to fear crown support for an attack by the Church of England on their religious autonomy. Once Elizabeth I shifted her policy to ally with the episcopacy, the gentry's prime religious interest became the protection of their dissent, even if that meant tolerance for lower class magic and religion. As the gentry consolidated power in the counties during the reigns of James I and Charles I, Puritans for the most part became "more confident in the ability of wealth to prevail in a system of free competition, and were prepared to accept congregational Independency as the price of alliance with the sectaries."[61]

Distrust of the Anglican episcopate and of the surviving Catholic priesthood, both of which made strong though conflicting claims to magical power, predisposed dissenters to skepticism toward all magical claims. Many dissenters went further and denied Anglican and crown assertions of any form of divine power.[62] Such "rationalism"

59. Alan G. R. Smith, *The Emergence of a Nation State: The Commonwealth of England 1529–1660* (London: Longmans, 1984), pp. 80–82.

60. Hill, *Economic Problems of the Church*, p. 33.

61. Ibid., p. 345.

62. Ibid., pp. 39–45; Bossy, *The English Catholic Community, 1570–1850* (London: Dennter, 1975), pp. 52, 278–80; Mary Fulbrook, *Piety and Politics: Religion and the Rise of Absolutism in England, Wurttemberg and Prussia* (Cambridge: Cambridge University Press, 1983), pp. 102–29.

among elite dissenters was reinforced in turn by fear of the consequences that would follow from a successful Anglican assertion of a
monopoly upon the legitimate use of magic.

The dissenters' rejection of magic in toto did not lead them, for the
most part, to replace the Church of England's campaigns against popular magic with independent efforts to suppress witches and magicians. The institutional pluralism which dissenting ministers and their
sponsors demanded to secure their own positions was linked of necessity to tolerance for the dissenting beliefs of other ministers and of
common preachers and wizards. The institutional location of dissenting ministers and their lay sponsors predisposed them to oppose Anglican efforts to enforce orthodoxy against any targets.

How then can we explain the two waves of prosecutions of witches
in England, which were mounted by laymen and heard in courts
dominated by the gentry? Those prosecutions were concentrated in
two periods, the 1580s and 1590s and 1645–47.[63] While there were
trials and at least one execution in every English county, Essex stands
out as having the greatest concentration of executions in both periods. In the earlier period, Kent also had an above average number of
executions. In the latter period, Norfolk and Suffolk joined Essex as
centers of the anti-witchcraft campaign.[64] The two periods, though in
different ways, were unusual conjunctures when the gentry (at least in
the counties with the greatest numbers of witch trials) possessed both
the interest and the capacity to attack popular magic.

Table 2.1 offers a graphic summary of the interest and capacity of
the four principal English elites in each period from the Henrician
Reformation to the end of the Civil War. As noted above, the crown's
interest switched from opposition to support of the Church of England's continuing desire to suppress dissent. At no point, however,
did either of those two elites possess the capacity to carry forward
such interests, either alone or in concert. The Church of England's
independent judicial apparatus had been crippled by the joint efforts
of the crown and lay county elites in the first decades after the Reformation. The crown had always depended upon the efforts of unpaid
laymen who filled county offices to carry out royal edicts.[65] Thus the

63. Thomas, *Decline of Magic*, pp. 449–51; Macfarlane, *Witchcraft*, p. 28.

64. Macfarlane, *Witchcraft*, pp. 61–63; Thomas, *Decline of Magic*, pp. 450–52.

65. Vernon K. Dibble, "The Organization of Traditional Authority: English County
Government, 1558 to 1640," in *Handbook of Organizations*, ed. James G. March (Chicago:
Rand, 1965), pp. 879–909.

Table 2.1. Elite interest in and capacity for the suppression of magic

	1536 Henrician Reformation	1547–53 Reign of Edward I	1553–58 Reign of Mary I	1558–1603 Reign of Elizabeth I	1603–23 Reign of James I	1623–40 Reign of Charles I	1640–48 Revolution/ Civil War
Crown							
Interest	–	–	–	–..+	+	+	+
Capacity	–	–	–	–	–	–	–
Church of England							
Interest	+	+	+	+	+	+	+
Capacity	–	–	–	–	–	–	–
Magnates							
Interest	+/–	+/–	+/–	+/–	+/–	+/–	+/–
Capacity	B	B	B	–	–	–	–
Gentry							
Interest	+/–	+/–	+/–	+/–	–	–	+/–
Capacity	–	–	–	+/–	+/–	+	+
				Essex Kent			Essex Norfolk Suffolk

For Interest: + elite has interest in suppressing magic
– elite is not interested in suppressing magic
+/– elite is divided over whether or not to suppress magic
–..+ crown's interest shifts from – to + in this period
For Capacity:
+ elite has the capacity to suppress magic
– elite does not have the capacity to suppress magic
B elite's capacity to suppress magic is blocked by the crown
+/– elite has the capacity to suppress magic in certain counties but not others

enforcement of religious orthodoxy depended upon the cooperation of magnates and gentry.

During most of the period from the Henrician Reformation to 1600, the gentry, regardless of their interests, lacked the organizational capacity to mount campaigns to suppress popular religion. The machinery of county government remained in the hands of magnates —some of whom still sought to control clerical offices for their own purposes, and who did not see popular challenges to gentry authority as threats to their own interests.[66]

By showing a mix of attitudes (denoted by the $+/-$) on the part of both magnates and gentry, Table 2.1 depicts the stalemate of forces within the counties in the years between 1536 and 1558. Lay landlords were divided among Catholic, Puritan, and Anglican allegiances. In no county was there sufficient denominational unity among magnates and gentry to overcome the objections of elite members of minority sects to concerted efforts to impose orthodoxy. Where Catholic or Puritan magnates were followed by gentry in attempting to impose those faiths in a county, the crown intervened against what it regarded as threats to royal supremacy over the church.[67] In contrast to the French pattern, the English crown allowed pluralism but not local attempts to establish minority religious monopolies. While the crown and gentry of the pre-Elizabethan era lacked the capacity to enforce their faiths, they did have the institutional means to veto efforts by rivals to enforce orthodoxies of which they disapproved.

Where the crown had removed magnates from power, counties often suffered from political vacuums for decades, as the crown sought to prevent the formation of new autonomous political forces. By the time the gentry achieved political hegemony in most counties, the crown's shifting policy toward the Anglican church had ended gentry interest in turning its new local power against popular religious dissent and magical practices. Essex and Kent were the only counties in which the gentry coalesced into "tight" blocs prior to a shift in crown attitudes toward the church, and thus in gentry attitudes toward pluralism.[68] Only in those two counties did the gentry

66. Lawrence Stone, *The Crisis of the Aristocracy 1558–1641* (Oxford: Oxford University Press, 1965), pp. 257–70, 725–45.

67. Stone, *The Crisis of the Aristocracy.*

68. Elsewhere (Lachmann, *Manor to Market*, pp. 84–100, 128–34) I have offered the following criteria for gauging the "tightness" of gentry political hegemony within a

achieve the capacity to take unilateral action against popular magic
while they still possessed an interest in so doing.

The second wave of witch trials in 1645–47, occurred when elite
interests and capacities again coincided. The Civil War had fractured
the gentry political blocs in most counties. Only in those counties
where factional divisions had been resolved did the gentry regain the
capacity to pursue lower class religious enemies. The conjecture, in
1645–47, of the royalists' imminent defeat and the heightened radical
threat created a renewed gentry interest in limiting pluralism and in
attacking popular magic. After Charles I had been decisively defeated
the gentry turned on their anti-royalist allies among the lower classes,
attempting to expel radical elements through purges in the New
Model Army, attacks on radical political forces, and witch trials to
counter popular assertions of access to magico-religious power.[69]

Only in Essex, Suffolk, and Norfolk had the gentry recreated unified county governments with the capacity to mount witch trials in

---

county: (1) a jump in the portion of manors controlled by gentry versus king, clergy,
and magnates; (2) absence of a dominant magnate or magnates capable of using armed
force and/or patronage to intimidate lesser landholders and bring them within a
magnate-led political machine; and (3) an increase in the total membership of the
county Commission of the Peace, and a shift to a majority on the county Commission of
Justice of the Peace with local as opposed to national or mixed orientations. Control
over manors in most counties had shifted to the gentry by the latter half of the sixteenth
century, as pointed out by Lawrence Stone and Jeanne C. Fawtier Stone, *An Open Elite?:
England 1540–1880* (Oxford: Oxford University Press, 1984), pp. 181–210. Essex and
Kent stand out in terms of the second and third criteria. Those two counties, along with
Norfolk and Suffolk, were among the first in which Elizabeth I successfully eliminated
magnate power. In Norfolk and Suffolk, however, the gentry did not form a cohesive
bloc until the early 1600s, whereas in Essex and Kent locally based gentry, with little
connection to the royal court, came to dominate the county Commissions of the Peace
in the 1560s and 1570s. For Essex, see William Hunt, *The Puritan Moment: The Coming of
Revolution in an English County* (Cambridge: Harvard University Press, 1983); for Kent,
see Alan Everitt, *Change in the Provinces: The Seventeenth Century* (Leicester: Leicester
University Press, 1969), Peter Clark, *English Provincial Society from the Reformation to the
Revolution: Religion, Politics and Society in Kent 1500–1640* (Sussex: Harvester, 1977),
C. W. Chalkin, *Seventeenth-Century Kent: A Social and Economic History* (London: Long-
mans, 1965); and for Norfolk and Suffolk, Diarmaid MacCulloch "Power, Privilege,
and the Country Community: Politics in Elizabethan Suffolk," Ph.D. diss., Cambridge
University, 1977, offers the best analysis on the sixteenth-century disarray and
seventeenth-century cohesion of gentry in those two counties. For a survey of gentry
political organizations across English counties, see Anthony Fletcher, "National and
Local Awareness in the County Communities," in *Before the English Civil War: Essays on
Stuart Politics and Government*, ed. Howard Tomlinson (London: Macmillan, 1983),
pp. 151–74.

69. Christopher Hill, *The World Turned Upside Down: Radical Ideas during the English
Revolution* (London: Penguin, 1972).

time to meet the gentry's momentary political interest.[70] After the decisive gentry victory over both royalist and radical forces, popular magic no longer represented a political threat. Apolitical wizards were tolerated because the absence of viable radical political movements emptied magic of its millennial content, reducing it to a quotidian service for the superstitious. The gentry no longer had an interest in pursuing witches.

Catholic skepticism toward magic had first been enunciated at the Council of Trent in 1564 when impostor sorcerers were distinguished from true practitioners of black magic. In 1601, lay judges of the Paris Parlement began to punish impostor sorcerers as a category of criminal separate from real witches although equally dangerous and deserving of execution.[71] Despite those conceptual advances, neither lay nor clerical judges possessed the institutional capacities to pursue many witches or to educate the populace to the difference between rare cases of witches who actually had made pacts with the devil and the more common fraudulent witches. As noted above, Catholic clerics' institutional and spiritual powers in the early sixteenth century were still under challenge from the crown, aristocrats, and corporate bodies. No French elite was willing to allow another the authority to regulate magical power, since each elite continued to assert its control over spiritual forces and clerical offices.

As clerics were incorporated within the absolutist state, and their income and power were distributed to provincial and then national lay elites, elite conflict over clerical assets was resolved and the French Catholic Church gained institutional resources and cooperation from lay elites and judicial officers to carry out the post-Tridentine attack upon real and false witches and a reform of popular practices. The causal primacy of institutional over ideological factors in the initiation of anti-magic campaigns is demonstrated by the geographic location as well as the timing (beginning more than a century after the Council of Trent) of reform efforts by the Catholic hierarchy. Tridentine reforms were most successfully carried out in those provinces where bishops were appointed by royal governors who exercised control

70. William Hunt, *The Puritan Moment*; Diarmaid MacCullouch, "Politics in Elizabethan Suffolk."
71. Robert Mandrou, *Magistrats et sorciers*, pp. 28–85.

over lesser nobles and over lay courts, especially the Parlements, and who enjoyed the support of the crown.[72]

Once all French elites, Protestant and Catholic, were incorporated within the absolutist state, the exercise of magical power was no longer a criterion for, or a reflection of, the distribution of clerical assets. Magic ceased to be a basis for elite competition. Aristocrats and urban elites, both Catholic and Protestant, abandoned their claims to magiçal powers in the late sixteenth and seventeenth centuries and acquiesced in the suppression of such practices within confraternities and during holidays under their control. Reformist bishops and clerics took over direction of the confraternities in an effort to enforce a catechism formulated at the Council of Trent but not widely taught in France until the seventeenth century. Lay elites accepted visitations from reforming bishops and the growing presence of priests from the new evangelical missions. The number of Jesuits in France rose from one thousand in 1556 to fifteen thousand in 1600. There was a similar growth in other orders—Capucins, Ursulines, Visitandines, Daughters of Charity, Trappists, and Dominicans. By 1700, each diocese in France had at least a few monasteries, often doubling the number of priests in the diocese.[73]

In 1653 the crown's final defeat of the aristocratic Frondes ushered in more than a century of relative peace among French elites.[74] Elite

72. Jean Delumeau, *Catholicism between Luther and Voltaire*; Cynthia A. Dent, "Changes in the Episcopal Structure of the Church of France in the 17th Century as an Aspect of Bourbon State-building," *Bulletin of the Institute of Historical Research* 48 (1975): 214–29; Jean Mauzaize, *Le rôle et l'action des Capucins de la province de Paris dans la France religieuse du XVIIe siècle*. 3 vols. (Lille: Université de Lille, 1978).

73. Delumeau, *Catholicism between Luther and Voltaire*, pp. 75–83. The source for the summaries, in this and the subsequent three paragraphs, of lay elite attitudes toward reforms in the Catholic Church, and of clerical efforts to transform lay religious beliefs and practices are: Dominique Julia, "La Réforme Posttridentine en France d'après les procès-verbaux pastorales: Ordre et Resistance," *La società religiosa nell'età moderna* (Naples: Guida Editori, 1973), pp. 311–415; Delumeau, *Catholicism between Luther and Voltaire*, pp. 65–83, 256–92; Hoffman, *Church and Community*, pp. 71–97 and passim; Jean-Claude Dhotel, *Les origins de catéchisme moderne: D'après les premiers manuels imprimés en France* (Paris: Aubier, 1967); Louis Pérouas, *Le diocèse de la Rochelle de 1648 à 1724: Sociologie et pastorale* (Paris: Sevpen, 1964), pp. 222–86; Jeanne Ferté, *La vie religieuse dans les campagnes parisiennes, 1622–1695* (Paris: Vrin, 1962), pp. 201–369; André Schaer, *Le clergé paroissial catholique en Haute Alsace sous l'ancien régime, 1648–1789* (Paris: Sirey, 1966), pp. 134–80; Alain Croix, *La Bretagne aux 16e et 17e siècles: La vie—la mort—la foi*, vol. 2 (Paris: Maloine, 1981), pp. 1155–246.

74. William Beik, *Absolutism and Society in Seventeenth-Century France: State Power and Provincial Aristocracy in Languedoc* (Cambridge: Cambridge University Press, 1985), pp. 3–5 and passim; Richard Lachmann and Julia Adams, "Absolutism's Antinomies:

magic neither helped its practitioners to control clerical assets nor threatened the positions of other elites. Elites perceived magic as a danger only when it was invoked by popular magicians who inspired or directed peasant rebellions.[75] Magic, then, was reduced to a source of danger to the French ruling class without providing a source of power to any elite in that class against another. Under such conditions, provincial lay elites and parish clergy became more receptive to the long-standing position of Catholic intellectuals and Paris Parlement judges that most magicians were frauds rather than true witches in pact with the devil.

The new skepticism toward witches was reflected in the reception given to the *Traité des superstitions*, which was written by a Parisian doctor of theology, Jean-Baptiste Thiers. First published in 1679, Thiers's four-volume work elaborated in exhaustive and exhausting detail the century-old Tridentine distinction between witches employing true black magic and charlatans who preyed on superstition to convince the masses that their fraudulent claims to supernatural power were real:

> One can not deny that there are magicians or sorcerers . . . without visibly contradicting the canon and civil laws, and the experience of all centuries and without shamelessly rejecting the irrefutable and infallible authority of the Church which so often throws down the thunderbolts of excommunication against them in its sermons.
>
> That there are sorcerers is indisputable; but, if in fact [they] are actually sorcerers is often very doubtful, because often one accuses of being sorcerers those who in effect really are not.[76]

Thiers's work evoked a tremendous response from clerics and educated lay people alike. The book and numerous pamphlet-length summaries of its conclusions were printed by bishops for distribution to clerics and educated parishioners. In the last decades of the seventeenth century, Thiers's writing and its imitators served to justify an intensification of trials against practitioners of magic who were, for

---

Class Formation, State Fiscal Structures and the Origins of the French Revolution," in *Political Power and Social Theory: A Research Annual,* ed. Maurice Zeitlin, vol. 7 (Greenwich, Conn.: JAI Press, 1988), pp. 154–68.

75. Yves Castan, *Magie et sorcellerie à l'époque moderne* (Paris: Albin Michel, 1979), pp. 175–242.

76. Jean-Baptiste Thiers, *Traité des superstitions.* 4 vols. (Paris: Compagnie des Librairies, 1741), 1:132, 137; the translation is my own.

the most part, now recognized as frauds rather than as black witches.[77]

During the eighteenth century, elite skepticism became so strong that prosecution of witches largely was abandoned in favor of efforts to stamp out popular religious practices through education and clerical supervision. Prosecutions were employed only during times of peasant rebellions, and then radical witches were usually tried for crimes of sedition rather than for sorcery.[78] The crucial manual of this period was *Traité de la police*, written in 1722 by Nicolas Delamare, founder of the national police. Delamare explains the need for police to track down charivaris, feasts of fools, displays of skill by wizards, and all other "profane" activities, not to enforce religious orthodoxy, which he trivializes, but to head off political rebellion. In Delamare's view, magicians were obvious frauds and therefore their activities were matters for the police rather than for the clergy.[79] The abrupt decline in the number of sorcery trials at the end of the seventeenth century,[80] and the subsequent rapid growth of the national police force in the eighteenth century, indicate that French elites—lay and clerical—shared Delamare's perspective.[81]

I have focused here on the rise of elite skepticism toward magic and on efforts by lay and clerical elites to suppress magical practices among non-elites. By the middle of the seventeenth century in England, and the beginning of the eighteenth century in France, elites were convinced both that witches were frauds rather than instruments of the devil and that magic had disappeared as a significant threat to their command of ecclesiastical institutions and the social hierarchies that they headed. Although elites were successful for the most part in eliminating magico-religious threats to their power, there is ample evidence of continuing popular belief in everyday magic, of demand for commercial wizards in eighteenth and nineteenth—and even

77. Mandrou, *Magistrats et sorciers*.
78. Delumeau, *Catholicism between Luther and Voltaire*, pp. 293–322; Yves-Marie Bercé, *Croquants et nu-pieds: Les soulèvements paysans en France du XVIe au XIX siècle* (Paris: Gallimard, 1974); Joutard, *Les camisards*.
79. Nicholas Delamare, *Traité de la police* (Paris, 1722), Book 1 and passim.
80. Muchembled, *La sorcière*, p. 131.
81. Delumeau, *Catholicism between Luther and Voltaire*, pp. 308–22.

twentieth—century England.[82] In the face of the continued popu-
larity of magic, and the powerful revival of magical practices and
pagan rituals in the festivals of the French Revolution,[83] one might
ask then what did the anti-magic campaigns of Renaissance England
and France accomplish?

I began by noting that existing theories view the decline of magic
and witch trials as products of generalized rationalizing trends, ubiquitous class conflict, or the breakdown (real or perceived) of a medieval social order and as a result are unable to account for variations in
the timing and intensity of anti-magic campaigns. In reviewing the
historical evidence from England and France, we find that elites lost
interest in manipulating supernatural forces themselves as the possibilities of increasing their control over clerical institutions were
closed. The timing and manner in which specific elites lost the opportunity to compete for clerical assets varied in the two countries and, as
a result, the sequence in which English and French elites rejected
magic differed as well.

In England, control over the offices, lands, and legal authority once
held by the Catholic Church remained in dispute from the beginning
of the Henrician Reformation until the end of the Civil War. The
relatively long duration of elite conflict for control of clerical institutions and religious authority had two major consequences for lay
beliefs and practices. First, the long competition among Anglican,
Catholic, and lay magicians, who offered differing conceptual bases
for their varying claims, in itself induced skepticism. Second, the
Tudor crown's interest in weakening the Anglican clergy in the sixteenth century, which was followed by the gentry's interest in protect-
ing the autonomy of their ministers and clerical properties from the
seventeenth-century Stuart-episcopate alliance, provided more than a
century of almost uninterrupted elite protection for pluralism, with
first the crown and then the gentry being sufficient to block the
united efforts of the other elites to induce conformity.

Gentry skepticism and support for pluralism combined to estrange
that elite from the Anglican ministry. Through most of this period,
Anglican ministers continued to believe that supernatural forces
could be manipulated in this world through white magic by them-

82. Thomas, *Decline of Magic*, pp. 663–68; James Obelkevich, *Religion and Rural
Society: South Lindsey 1825–1875* (Oxford: Clarendon, 1976), pp. 259–312.
83. Mona Ozouf, *Festivals and the French Revolution*, trans. Alan Sheridan (Cambridge: Harvard University Press, 1988).

selves and through black magic by their enemies. Anglicans' continued allegiance to the medieval model of magic was compatible with
their interest in regaining a monopoly on magico-religious power.
However, continuing elite challenges—led first by the crown, then by
the gentry—rendered the clergy incapable of acting on their beliefs
and interests.

The gentry's hold on former clerical properties and on the allegiance of their ministers depended upon their capacity to fend off
challenges from the Church of England. To do so, the gentry first
allied with the crown and later constructed county-based political
blocs capable of resisting the Stuart-Anglican alliance. The gentry's
interest in religious pluralism dictated a tolerance for magic even
after its social, intellectual, and political distance from Anglican as
well as royal, Catholic, and popular magical practices turned most
members of that elite into skeptics. Only in the rare moments when
crown support or crown defeat opened the strategic space for gentry
authoritarianism did the gentry in those counties where they had
developed the organizational capacity translate their skepticism into
action to suppress magical practices.

Elite conflict over religious assets fostered gentry rejection of magic, yet those same conflicts severely limited gentry interests in acting
against magicians. The post–Civil War terms of gentry political hegemony in the counties set the limits within which popular beliefs and
practices developed. The non-elites of Restoration England turned
for practical aid to commercial wizards, and for solace to those dissenting denominations which were tolerated because they had abandoned any promise of summoning supernatural forces for social
transformation.[84]

In sixteenth-century France, clerical assets were quickly transferred from provincial magnate-headed blocs to a national structure
of patronage centered on the crown. The struggles of the Wars of
Religion hastened that process of centralization and forced laymen to
locate themselves politically, and often geographically, in a bloc that
could ensure access to a cleric of their choice. Before, during, and
after the Reformation and Wars of Religion, all clerics remained dependent upon lay patrons. Religious conflicts in France changed the
identity of clerics' patrons and hence the brand of religion that patrons required from their priests and ministers.

84. Hill, *World Turned Upside Down*, pp. 361–86.

Once Catholic and Protestant lay elites had achieved relatively uncontested authority over the clerics in their localities, French Catholic
priests and Protestant ministers were freed to fulfill their roles as
religious practitioners and to try to enforce the orthodoxies of their
denominations—which for French Catholics in the late sixteenth and
seventeenth centuries came to include the discovery and enforcement
of Tridentine limitations on magic—without jeopardizing their hold
over clerical offices. As French clerics' institutional subordination to
lay elites freed them to pursue their interest in policing magic, it also
made clerics dependent upon lay support for the means to educate
and punish popular magicians and their followers. Thus the anti-
magic campaigns in France, as in England, started and stopped, intensified and slackened in response to lay elites' perceptions of their
interests and as elite and class conflicts transformed each elite's capacities to act upon its interests.[85] During the sixteenth and seventeenth
centuries, when lay elites saw popular magical beliefs and practices as
a threat, the French Catholic Church was provided with the resources
for a new corps of priests for education, and lay courts prosecuted
witches found by clerics. Once political dissent was distinguished
from superstition in the eighteenth century, witch trials abruptly less-
ened, even as priests continued to teach a Catholic piety that had been
drained of its magical aspects and its emotional intensity.

Elites and to some extent others in England and France became
more skeptical toward magicians and their claims during the Renaissance. The degree to which lay and clerical skeptics attempted to
enforce conformity to their views depended, however, upon their perception of a threat to their interests from magicians and their fol-
followers. This comparison of anti-magic campaigns in England and
France suggests that elites weighed such a threat primarily in terms of
their control over clerical properties and powers. Such control, in
turn, was determined primarily by the structures of relations among

85. It is on this point that my elite conflict model in general, and my analysis here of
witch trials in particular, can be read as a refinement of the economistic approach to
crime control critiqued by Liska in "Crime Control." Interest in controlling crime is not
constant across society, as assumed by economists (and by Stallybrass and others working within a structural functionalist perspective). Each elite has a specific interest in
combating, ignoring, or aiding each variety of "crime," and that interest changes
through elite and class conflict. Further, the capacity to act upon interests cannot be
reduced to a generalized measure of economic resources. Capacity also is specific to
social structural sites, and therefore changes as elite and class conflicts transform social
relations.

lay and clerical elites. Those structures also determined who had the capacity to persecute witches and thereby selected the timing, the geographic and social locations, the targets (black witches or char-latans), and the strategies (counter-magic, witch trials, or education) employed by elites to eliminate the dangers which uncontrolled magic appeared to pose to their social worlds.

3

Legal Proofs and Corrected Readings

Press-Agency and the New Bibliography

JOSEPH F. LOEWENSTEIN

The following exposition offers a way of knowing something that we may already know. It proposes an unusual object of scrutiny, an unusual site of probabilities, but one that might be particularly apt for the purpose of knowing the past as a region of labile origins.

One of Michel Foucault's great achievements, though it is not solely his, is the critique of the historiographically premature reification of the subject. This, the largest project of *The Order of Things*, is carried out in miniature in the essay on authorship, as a critique of the premature reification of the author as the subject of discourse, the author as literary agent.[1] Although Foucault intended, by this intervention, to alleviate the pressure of the subject on cultural theory, his brilliant underlying premise, that the *personality* of discourse has a history, points squarely in the opposite direction, toward a history of authoriality.[2] I want to pursue the implications of that premise, to supplement the history of the author, by offering some notes on the *stationer* as an agent of discourse, on what might be termed the authoriality of the press.

---

1. Michel Foucault, "What Is an Author?" in *Textual Strategies: Perspectives in Post-Structuralist Criticism*, ed. Josué V. Harari (Ithaca: Cornell University Press, 1979), pp. 141–60.
2. For Foucault's own struggle with these opposing tendencies in his analysis, see ibid., pp. 157–59.

Students of early modern cultural agency can hardly conduct their inquiries without grappling with the essay on authorship.[3] Since what follows is in many ways a homage to Foucault's project, I wish to qualify my assent *to* that project. As a resistant reader of Foucault's sketch of the problematics of authorship, I find that my misgivings center on his main thesis, that the institution of the author is preeminently a cultural defense specific to the threat of *semantic* proliferation. I detect in this thesis a distortion identical to that which Bourdieu finds endemic to anthropology: "The anthropologist's particular relation to the object of his study," he writes, " . . . inclines him to a hermeneutic representation of practices, leading him to reduce all social relations to communicative relations."[4] Like Bourdieu, I mistrust the hypertrophy of the discursive within cultural theory. I believe it can be demonstrated that, at least in early modern England, the need to restrain meaning—a need nearly without agents, a pressure nearly without vessels, a desire at once for, of, and against the discursive—was secondary to the local need to restrain economic competition. Because it seems to me that cultural history needs the distinctions, however crude and inelegant, between speech and labor, and between conversation and market exchange, I give an account in which ideology—in its pre-Althusserian sense—plays second fiddle to economy.[5]

This conviction leads me to quarrel with perhaps the most influential corollary of Foucault's thesis, his assertion that discourse "has always been subsequent to what one might call penal appropriation," that the discursive act "was a gesture fraught with risks before becoming goods caught up in a circuit of ownership."[6] On the contrary, early

3. To personalize this further: I am finishing a book on the development of intellectual property from the middle of the fifteenth to the middle of the seventeenth century, on the place of the book in the early modern English economy, on the history of proprietary ideas among English writers, on invention and copyright, on genius and monopolistic competition. As this project nears completion, I find that I have been struggling with Foucault's essay at nearly every stage of my reflections. For a report from an earlier stage in this struggle, see my "*Idem*: Italics and the Genetics of Authorship," *Journal of Medieval and Renaissance Studies* 20 (Fall 1990): 205–24.

4. Pierre Bourdieu, *Outline of a Theory of Practice*, trans. Richard Nice (Cambridge: Cambridge University Press, 1977), p. 1.

5. For a rough-and-ready but nonetheless effective defense of this distinction, see Perry Anderson, *In the Tracks of Historical Materialism, The Welleck Library Lectures* (London: Verso, 1983), pp. 40–44.

6. Foucault, "What Is an Author?" p. 148. It is worth remarking that the claims on behalf of the penal, specifically the claims to analytic and (often) temporal, priority, are notably relaxed in Foucault's late work.

modern English authorship may be more a product of trade protectionism than of ideological control. It is easy enough to discern the pattern of practical subordination of penal to economic strategies in the practices constituting authorship at an advanced stage, in 1709, when the Statute of Anne was promulgated. According to the interpretations of the courts of the mid-eighteenth century, the Statute of Anne had secured authorial copyright, but at the moment of its promulgation the novelty of the statute had to do with the fact that it put the stationers' trade monopoly on a new footing. The stationers had fought hard for this legislation, having failed to secure the renewal of the Licensing Act of 1662, the original aim of their appeals to Parliament. Although this milestone in the history of intellectual property law might therefore be described as a reaction to the lapse of a censorship mechanism, it is important to see the continuity of interest unmasked by the legislative history: the trade organization that secured passage of the new property law was the same trade organization that had sought the renewal of licensing. The pursuit of such legal controls had been the Stationers' strategy since 1557, and perhaps earlier: virtually every new development of the English *licensing* system, the chief mechanism of print censorship, begins with a proposal from the stationers. Not surprisingly, the landmarks of this censorship—the Stationers Charter of 1557, the Star Chamber Decrees of 1586 and 1637, the Licensing Acts of 1643 and 1662—contain within them trade protections, more particularly, protections for the most heavily capitalized sectors of the book trade; the protections far outstrip the ostensible function of suppressing heresy and sedition.[7] It would be foolish, of course, to minimize the importance of censorship to liter-

---

7. The literature on the history of the book trade is nearly as voluminous as that on the history of censorship. For useful studies that feature the intersection of these two histories in Tudor and Stuart England, see Frederick Seaton Siebert, *Freedom of the Press in England, 1476–1776: The Rise and Decline of Government Controls* (Urbana: University Press of Illinois, 1952), Howard W. Winger, "Regulations Relating to the Book Trade in London from 1357 to 1586," *Library Quarterly* 26 (1956): 157–95, W. W. Greg, *Some Aspects and Problems of London Publishing between 1550 and 1650* (Oxford: Clarendon, 1956), Cyprian Blagden, *The Stationers' Company: A History, 1403–1959* (London: Allen, 1960), and Lyman Ray Patterson, *Copyright in Historical Perspective* (Nashville: Vanderbilt University Press, 1968). Authorship was not made part of the structure of press censorship until the Star Chamber decree of 1637, when it was required that the name of the author be printed along with that of printer and publisher, this as a condition of license. The legal force of the decree evaporated with the abolition of Star Chamber, though authorship was again given a place within censorship in the short-lived 1642 parliamentary Licensing Edict and again in the 1649 Printing Ordinance.

ary culture, foolish even to minimize its importance to the evolution of proprietary authorship, as if ideological labor were inimical to market controls. But perhaps the soundest description of the early history of English authorship is simply this: in the disseminative sphere, ideological regulation provided an idiom for the pursuit of monopolistic competition.

Having made these stipulations, I wish to reconstitute the case for ideological discipline and punishment within the cultural history of the text. To do so is to discover a very un-Foucauldian way to alleviate the pressure of the subject within bibliography, not by explaining away the subject (the tendency of Foucault's archaeology) but by dispersing it. If this persists in jostling Foucault's project it is even more disturbing to that far more problematic one, the project of the New Bibliography, which was to increase the pressure of the subject on the surface of texts.

In 1901, Ronald McKerrow, not long out of Cambridge, attacked a now-forgotten work of literary antiquarianism, and in so doing announced a research program that was to have decisive effect on literary scholarship. He insists in his review that "until some curious inquirer makes a thorough investigation into all the technical details of Elizabethan printing, and from this and a comparison of handwritings arrives at some definite statement of the relative probability of various misreadings and misprintings, emendation must remain in much the same state as medicine before dissection was practised."[8] Sixty years later, the research program that McKerrow announced had been so productive that bibliography was regarded, not as a complex of problems, but as a method, a mechanical routine; this was a misperception, albeit one which its foremost practitioners of the fifties and sixties may themselves have encouraged. Of late bibliography has come under more rigorous and perhaps more appropriate criticism. McKerrow's project, the project he shared with W. W. Greg, Alfred Pollard, and Percy Simpson, thereafter with Graham Pollard and Fredson Bowers, and after that with Charlton Hinman and with Bowers's students, was "to present the best detailed text of an author

8. Cited in F. P. Wilson, *Shakespeare and the New Bibliography*, rev. and ed. Helen Gardner (Oxford: Clarendon, 1970), p. 5, from McKerrow's review of K. Deighton, *The Old Dramatists: Conjectural Readings* in the *Modern Language Quarterly* (1901).

in a form as close to his intentions as can be managed," to "recover and guard the purity of an author's words," "to try to pierce this veil of the printing process and to restore, however imperfectly, the authority of the manuscript." The phrases are Bowers's, but not idiosyncratically his.[9] The aspiration to determinacy within the bibliographical project, the possibly anxious and certainly premature reification of authorship, the fetishization of handwritten text—all of these are vulnerable to at least mildly corrosive philosophical critique.[10] Patient *historical* critique has been slower in accumulating, but it has accumulated (thanks to Kirschbaum and, later, McKenzie, Taylor, Warren, Werstine, and Blayney).[11] This historical critique has been fruitful, sometimes dazzling. We have come to accept that multiple versions of genetically related texts could circulate simultaneously without provoking crises of reception, without any diminution of the power of books to compel attention, indeed, without any substantial disturbance of Early Modern semiosis. We are beginning to assess the complex relations between manuscript circulation and publication in print. We are more at ease with anonymous and collaborative authorship. We are no longer so quick to lament textual "corruption" as an aesthetic blemish or as an ontological lapse. Having thus enabled us to sluff off a degree of positivist anxiety, the loyal opposition to the New

9. Fredson Bowers, from "Current Theories of Copy-Text, with an Illustration from Dryden," "Textual Criticism and the Literary Critic," and "Some Relations of Bibliography to Editorial Problems," published separately but collected in *Essays in Bibliography, Text, and Editing* (Charlottesville: University Press of Virginia, 1975), pp. 279, 307, and 35.

10. The most elegant formulations are in Stephen Orgel, "What Is a Text?" *Research Opportunities in Renaissance Drama*, ed. David M. Bergeron (1981): 3–6 and Jerome J. McGann, *A Critique of Modern Textual Criticism* (Chicago: University of Chicago Press, 1983).

11. Leo Kirschbaum, *Shakespeare and the Stationers* (Columbus: Ohio State University Press, 1955); D. F. McKenzie, "Printers of the Mind: Some Notes on Bibliographical Theories and Printing-House Practices," *Studies in Bibliography* 22 (1969): 1–75 and "The London Book Trade in the Later Seventeenth Century, The Sandars Lectures," 1976 (photocopied typescript); Gary Taylor and Michael Warren, eds., *The Division of the Kingdoms: Shakespeare's Two Versions of "King Lear"* (Oxford: Clarendon Press, 1986), Gary Taylor, "The Rhetoric of Textual Criticism," *Text: Transactions of the Society for Textual Scholarship* 4 (1988): 39–57; Stanley Wells et al., *William Shakespeare: A Textual Companion* (Oxford: Clarendon Press, 1987); Paul Werstine, "McKerrow's 'Suggestion' and Twentieth-Century Shakespeare Textual Criticism," *Renaissance Drama* n.s. 19 (1988): 149–73, and "The Textual Mystery of *Hamlet*," *Shakespeare Quarterly* 39 (1988): 1–26; Peter W. M. Blayney, *The Texts of "King Lear" and Their Origins*, 2 vols., *Volume 1: Nicholas Okes and the First Quarto* (Cambridge: Cambridge University Press, 1982). Those familiar with this newest New Bibliography will recognize how very deeply the present essay is indebted to the work of McKenzie and Blayney.

Bibliography maintains the heuristic utility of the concept of textual authority, which can now be construed as a *historical* problem: we have adopted a more analytic approach to the institutions of that authority. As we shift the focus of our attention from the cultural artifact to the cultural system, from cultural product to cultural production, the text, and even the author, cools and loses incandescence, begins to relinquish its status as an intellectual fetish. Less impressive, more interesting.

Thus, despite the attacks inflicted on the core project of the New Bibliography, despite the decentering of author's text, bibliography thrives and for that shift Greg, Pollard, and McKerrow deserve much credit. They were ambitious polemicists, eager to bring their researches into public scrutiny, and they therefore did a good deal more than edit texts. Each of them made efforts to organize and publish the documentary record of early book production. Greg's calendar of the Stationers' Register, Pollard's short-title catalogue, and McKerrow's introduction to historical bibliography provide the raw materials, not just for a questionably positivist editorial tradition, but also for several chapters in that general history of English textuality which remains to be written.

Consider, for example, proposals of the psychological agency of print, those large concerns of an Ong or a McLuhan. If the slogan on a new banner reads "Texts Are Historical Agents," we are nonetheless a long way from writing a history of such interpellative functions of literacy as they posited; to write such a history would be to initiate an *Ideologiekritik* which would be anything but crude. The appropriation of oral culture, the rise of London's dialect (a key feature of post-feudal recoding), the spread of alphabetism and of disciplined orthography, the domestication and individualization of worship by means of printed service books and other devotional texts—these are all still imperfectly chronicled, yet they are essential elements of early modern, and late modern, English subjectivity. The history of each of these interpellations might be eloquently framed from within a historiography of the book trade. Certainly, those who wish for a historiography which features the mutual determinations of ideological and social formations will find the Stationers' Company a more interested and energetic agent of such interpellations than, say, the crown, which has been the usual focus of inquiry for literary and cultural historians. For a genetics of modernity we need to take our researches outside the lineage of the absolutist state.

But in order to ease the transition to a properly bibliographic historiography, we might begin an account of the discursive personality of the stationer from well within the lineage, with a volume compiled by the king's printer, Leonard Lichfield, to honor the birth of Prince Henry in 1640.[12] As is inevitable given the highly allusive verse proper to such occasions, the poems in the anthology have their ambiguities, but they are generally celebratory. Lichfield's own contribution catches a crucial nuance in the specific materiality of print:

> The Schollers now, like *Volunteers*, professe
> As Loyall Service in the learned *Presse*,
> As those that drink Your Twelve-pence: They would Fight,
> Should You command, as willingly as Write.

Although in matters of property and within the law of evidence, handwriting holds a privileged place, printing had accumulated far greater political heft and potency, a fact to which Lichfield's verses somewhat clumsily give witness. This poem on the birth of Henry as anthological occasion indicates that the heft of print could be ominous and dangerous. First the pun on "press," which indicates a new vulgarity, a massing within literary culture. The tone is light enough: a somewhat mechanical wit operates here within a confidence that writing and physical violence are easy to distinguish. Yet, as Lichfield knows or as his idiom naturally indicates, they are not worlds apart. Literary competition is certainly distinguishable from political strife, but the poem is nerved by the plain knowledge that political strife cannot be constrained by such customary distinctions, however witty:

> They throng'd to put in Verses: and made there
> Friends for a place, as when Your Courts appeare.
> May there be only such Contentions.

Historical context firms these lines, gives them an edge. Not only has competition for patronage become routinized, not only has it lost its decorous exclusivity. In 1640, all throngs were unstable, threatening imperfectly manageable contentions. Over a decade of historicist criticism makes it unnecessary to insist that historical context is not located safely *outside* such a volume as Lichfield's, but it may still be

---

12. Lichfield (1604–57) was the son of John Lichfield, the second official printer to Oxford University, whom he succeeded in 1635.

worth pointing out that the publicity of print culture had become constitutive *of* that context. That pen and sword, or rather press and army (mass medium and massed men), are especially commutable is just what keeps the biblical figure that closes Lichfield's epigram from being merely mechanical:

> May there be only such Contentions; let
> My FOUNTS to give you Joy, for ever sweat.
> But unto such as do oppose Your Throne
> May every Letter be a *killing* one.[13]

To assert the commutability of pen and sword, the force of print, as Lichfield does may seem merely an academic figure, the dream-work of an impotent intelligentsia. This has been the dismissive response offered recently to those who assert the determining power of aesthetic production. With respect to the late Renaissance, the figure might easily be described as a fantasy specific to frustrated humanism, yet it is not Kyd or Jonson or Wither, but the king's printer who here protests the verity of the figure. In the campaigns of mid-1642, Lichfield mounted his press on a wagon and followed the king's forces, publishing tenders of pardon to such local followers of Essex as would lay down their arms without a fight. In Buckinghamshire, Lichfield closed such a proclamation of pardon with an epistle to the queen:

> *Madam,*
> That Traytrous and *Unletterd* Crew
> Who fight 'gainst *Heaven*, Their *Soveraigne*, and *You*,
> Have not yet stain'd my Hallowed FOUNTS, The spring
> Must needs be Cleare that issues from the King.

The patent, that is, which grants Lichfield the status of King's Printer absolutely royalizes the productions of his press. There is evidence of partisan publishing under Elizabeth and James, but as long as markets remained uncertain and distribution networks inefficient purely industrial forces had inhibited the development of firmly discriminated book production and the stationer with an invariant partisan output had remained exceptional. Lichfield's "stainless" record of royalist production was, of course, one of the luxuries entailed by his patent, but by representing mixed production as adulteration or

13. *Horti Carolini Rosa altera* (London: Leonard Litchfield, 1640), e4^v.

taint, these lines suggest a novel development within book culture, the industrial embrace of ideological discrimination: partisan publishing was becoming a means of delineating and securing market sectors.

Then comes the old figure, invigorated by circumstance:

> *Presses* of Old, as Pens, did but incite
> Others to Valour; This *It Selfe* did fight:
> In Ranks and Files these *Letters* Marshall'd stood
> On Dismall *Edg-Hill-day*, yet 'twas not blood
> They boaded by their Black, for Peace they sought
> And Teem'd with Pardons while the Rebells fought.

The teeming press figures in a rhetorical complex that unites the king's clemency with his genetic bounty: mercy, insemination, dissemination. In the next lines comes a new invention; the compositor's case, image of order, becomes the object of rebellious violence. This is not Lichfield's invention, but the rebels': at Edgehill, Lichfield's press fell under physical attack and his type-case was overturned:

> Yet those that found it on that Boysterous day
> Tooke't for some *Dread Commission of Array*;
> And thought each Letter *Theta*, every Point
> To give a Period to a Life or *Joynt*;
> They *Plunder'd*, and so turn'd it ore and ore
> As that th'had ne're used their Neck-verse worse before;
> So Anagrammatized each *Comma* in't
> That *Babel-London* has not put in Print
> More confused Nonsense . . . [14]

Lichfield's political and rhetorical opportunism, his skill at appropriating the figurations of rebellion, make him particularly interesting. Nervously alert to advantage, he is quick to register the various means by which print culture secured itself, politically and economically. The fonts are recovered and sorted; the press, remounted, now flaunts its power.

It goes without saying that Lichfield's militant publishing is grossly inefficient, a royalist printer's conspicuous production. Proclamations need not be printed in the field; and handwriting—filling in blanks in a printed text—is a far more efficient means of localizing a general

14. *A Proclamation of His Majesties Grace, Favour, and Pardon to the Inhabitants of His County of Buckingham* (London: Leonard Litchfield, 1642).

pardon. Lichfield's campaign is calculated—if the term doesn't over-dignify his behavior—to make a *spectacle* of the royalist press, to display a press restored to the incunabular function of reproducing an authoritative handwriting. His gallant poetizing, his rush to the scene of battle, make a show, not of independent authorial subjectivity, but of the submission of the printing subject to instrumental service of the clement royal author.

The occasional motives for such a show are not far to seek. First is the abolition of the Star Chamber in 1641, which had washed away the ground of the stationers' monopoly. As King's Printer, Lichfield's own monopolies were largely independent of those industrial protections policed by the Stationers' Company and secured by the Star Chamber Decrees of 1586 and 1637, but he no doubt registered the new uncertainties within the book trade and valued his own patents the more jealously. Even the royal privileges fell vulnerable in this climate, for anti-monopolist energies had flared along with anti-royalist ones: in *Scintilla* the privileges of the Company and of such patentees as Lichfield are equally scourged. It was a nervous monopolist who wheeled his press into battle.

Lichfield must have had another motive as well. The Buckinghamshire epistle comes less than a year after the vehement parliamentary debates over the Grand Remonstrance had issued in a more particular and more vehement debate over whether to *publish* the Grand Remonstrance.[15] As soon as the Remonstrance had passed,

15. Clarendon's account of the debate on publication (*History of the Rebellion and Civil Wars in England Begun in the Year 1641*, by Edward, Earl of Clarendon, ed. W. Dunn Macray, 6 vols. [Oxford: Clarendon, 1888], 1:419–20 [iv.52]) may be exaggerated, but the violence of the confrontation is corroborated by both D'Ewes's *Journal* (*The Journal of Sir Simonds D'Ewes from the First Recess of the Long Parliament to the Withdrawal of King Charles from London*, ed. Willson Havelock Coates [New Haven: Yale University Press, 1942]) and Sir Edward Nicholas's manuscript "History of the Long Parliament" (B.L., Add. MSS, 31954, f. 1856; cited in D'Ewes's *Journal*, ed. Coates, pp. 186–87). William Strode seems to have betrayed an intention that the Grand Remonstrance be published on 11 November; within a week anxieties about publicity were so intense that the House determined to suppress all printed or manuscript reports on the proceedings in parliament. The negotiation of the decorums of publicity was wonderfully uncertain: Sir Edward Dering lost his seat in the House by publishing his speeches against the propriety of publishing the Remonstrance. Materials on the Grand Remonstrance are conveniently assembled in John Forster, *The Debates on the Grand Remonstrance: November and December, 1641* (London: John Murray, 1860); see also, Willson H. Coates, "Some Observations on 'The Grand Remonstrance,'" *Journal of Modern History* 4 (1932): 1–17.

George Peard moved its publication; Forster's assessment of the political maneuverings is telling:

> It was not then announced for the first time, but had substantially been confessed all through the debate, that the Declaration was meant as an appeal to the people. And so far from the desire to "protest" [the publication of the Grand Remonstrance] having arisen naturally and suddenly out of . . . [Peard's announcement], the protest had been concerted as a party move, and made known to the King's servants before the Declaration was voted. The intention was obvious. It was meant to divide, and by that means destroy, the authority of the House of Commons. It was a plan deliberately devised to exhibit, before the face of the country, the Minority as in open conflict against the Majority, and as possessed of rights to be exercised independently.[16]

We stand here near the beginning of that long revolution whereby the authority of parliamentary government came to be negotiated within a public sphere constituted by print culture. Fielding might argue in 1748 that "to canvas those high and nice Points, which move the finest Wheels of State, Matters merely belonging to the Royal Prerogative, . . . in Print, is in the highest Degree indecent, and a gross Abuse of the Liberty of the Press," but this indecency had become quite normal by the 1720s, when M.P.s began regularly to publish their speeches and to engage in journalism.[17] Historians of the eighteenth century, and particularly French historians like Chartier and Darnton, have recently made much of the function of print in the constitution of a specifically political public sphere. But it seems to me worth insisting that this development was substantially anticipated— as was so much in pre-Revolutionary France—by developments in pre-Revolutionary England, worth insisting that the assault on English political journalism originates, not with Fielding, but with James and Charles Stuart.[18] By the 1640s, the political stakes were easy enough to gauge. In 1641, when censorship collapsed, political journalism—newsletters reporting on developments in Parliament—

16. Forster, *Grand Remonstrance*, pp. 320–21.

17. Henry Fielding, *The Jacobites' Journal and Related Writings*, ed. W. B. Coley. The Wesleyan Edition of the Works of Henry Fielding (London: Wesleyan University Press, 1975), p. 290.

18. Joseph Frank, *The Beginnings of the English Newspaper, 1620–1660* (Cambridge: Harvard University Press, 1961), pp. 6, 14.

issued in a sudden torrent. The first weekly of printed domestic news was inaugurated in November—there were three such weeklies in operation before the year was out—and the author of the utopian *Macaria* predicted that "the art of printing will so spread knowledge that the common people, knowing their own rights and liberties, will not be governed by way of oppression."[19] Lichfield's press-caisson is a strike against such a revolutionary press.

The key determinant for English book culture, what gives it its special momentousness in comparison to continental book culture, is the monopoly of English book production granted to the London Stationers in 1557.[20] The monopoly led in opposing directions. During the sixteenth century, the London Stationers' Company took upon itself much of the responsibility for ideological policing as a means of justifying its privileged position. Thus, in order to *protect* the monopoly, the Stationers' Company had contributed to the development of national surveillance. As the trade matured, the Stationers had had to develop efficient networks of national distribution in order successfully to *exploit* their monopoly. Ideological policing could not prevent the eventual emergence of an opposition press—abiding labor unrest internal to the Stationers' Company seems to have contributed to this emergence—and the opposition press found it easy to exploit established distribution networks for the swift and often clandestine circulation of its production.[21] The political effect of the monopoly was to concentrate opposition printing in London, to impose thereby a specifically political and even more specifically anti-royalist idiom on the various forms of economic and religious opposition, and to provide for the efficient dissemination of texts generative of an opposi-

19. Charles Webster, *Utopian Planning and the Puritan Revolution* (Oxford: Research Publications of the Wellcome Unit for the History of Medicine, 1979), pp. 72–73; and Frank, *English Newspaper*, pp. 20–24.

20. The Stationers' monopoly must be qualified in one important way. In 1534 Cambridge University was authorized, by letter patent, to set up a press under its own jurisdiction. No effort was made actually to establish a Cambridge University press until the late 1570s, at which point the London Stationers' Company mounted a campaign against it. Still, the 1586 Star Chamber Decree for the regulation of the press makes allowances for university presses at both Oxford and Cambridge (this before Oxford had received a patent similar to that allowing for a Cambridge University press, which it did in 1636 thanks to the efforts of Bishop Laud). By 1649, provisions were also made for the operation of a Bible press in Finsbury and another press at York.

21. After the restoration, and once L'Estrange had established his authority, clandestine distribution became a good deal more complex; see D. F. McKenzie, *London Book Trade*, pp. 28–29 and J. Walker, "The Censorship of the Press during the Reign of Charles II," *History* 35 (October 1950): 227–28.

tion by no means united, but surprisingly political in orientation and national in the horizon of its attentions.

So these years mark a double revolution in English political culture. First, in formulating the Grand Remonstrance Parliament allowed itself to act without the unanimity traditionally necessary for English corporate action. (To gauge the rupture here, note that William Chillingworth was sent to the Tower, nonetheless, for insinuating that "wee had sides and parts in the howse.")[22] Mark Kishlansky's forthcoming history of this procedural revolution will no doubt explore the contribution of the press to the shift to mere majority rule: after all, the press had rendered the existence of faction an undeniable and abiding feature of public experience.[23] But for our purposes the second aspect of the revolution in English politics is more telling. Swords were drawn in Parliament over the motion to remonstrate, in print, with the people.[24] Thus, long before Fielding, the privacy of parliamentary deliberation is breached as Parliament appropriates the press as one of the chief organs of its now enlarged and now riven power.[25] This is a major landmark in the history of the *English* public sphere, though in a quest for concurrent origins this history might be traced to the newsbooks of the previous decade.[26] As a theory of representation became more crucial to English politics, the circularity of representation became a practical guarantor of the political: in the 1640s, the press began its emergence as necessary to the reciprocal representativity of Parliament and people.[27] For royalists—now co-

22. *The Journal of Sir Simonds D'Ewes*, p. 234.

23. For Mark A. Kishlansky's preliminary observations on the shift to majoritarianism, see *Parliamentary Selection: Social and Political Choice in Early Modern England* (Cambridge: Cambridge University Press, 1986), pp. 20, 71–72, 228.

24. *The Journal of Sir Simonds D'Ewes*, p. 186.

25. Christopher Hill gives a useful overview of the response of the English press to political developments in the early 1640s in *The Collected Essays of Christopher Hill*, 3 vols. (Amherst: University of Massachusetts Press, 1986–87), Volume 1: *Writing and Revolution in 17th Century England*, pp. 40–42, 44–50. For the terms of the debate on the publication of the Grand Remonstrance, see, in particular, the speech of Sir Edward Dering on November 22, 1641 ("I did not dream that we should remonstrate downward, tell stories to the people, and talk of the King as of a third person," cited in Forster, *Grand Remonstrance*, p. 292) and of Sir Benjamin Rudyard on the same day.

26. The resistance to the volubility of a specifically political, journalistic press is apparent in the 1632 decision of the king's council to ban all newsbooks; Folke Dahl, "Amsterdam—Cradle of English Newspapers," *Library*, 5th ser. (1949–50): 166–78, but see also Frederick Seaton Siebert, *Freedom of the Press*, pp. 155–56.

27. On representation, see Hannah Fenichel Pitkin, *The Concept of Representation* (Berkeley: University of California Press, 1967).

alescing into royalist parties, perhaps even *a* party—English politics
was being stained by public ink, and precisely this figure, however
banal, conditions Lichfield's insistence on the purity of his enterprise,
the protest that *his* fonts are hallowed: "The spring / Must needs be
Cleare that issues from the King. . . . 'Twas not blood / they boaded
by *their* Black" (my emphasis). Lichfield's press-caisson squares off
against that of Joseph Hunscutt, who printed the Remonstrance for a
rebellious Parliament.[28]

The newsletters of the 1630s had already begun to expose parliamentary debate to public scrutiny, provoking Selden to ask, "Shall the
Councells of Parliaments bee layd on stalls and shall any divulge
them?" D. F. McKenzie, surely the most daring historical bibliographer of our day, has begun a chronicle of this constitution of a political public sphere.[29] It is among other things the sphere of attributive
shenanigans—the newsletters frequently published spurious or mis-
attributed parliamentary speeches—and these early publisher's tricks
were soon taken up by M.P.s themselves, as they created a genuinely
public political forum.[30] This is the innovation over which men drew
swords in 1641 and this is why a royalist printer might wish to spec-
tacularize his press. The public sphere on the eve of the Revolution is
characterized by that riven textuality described in Jonson's *Staple of
News*, one in which an agile book trade swiftly splits signature and pen
name, dislocates the circumstance of utterance from the sphere of
circulation, furthers the mutual alienation of speech and writing, and
widens the fissure between private intention and public appropriation.[31] In a reaction to the rhetorical turbulence of newsbook publica-

28. *The Thomason Tracts* [s.1.: s.n.] 1641, I, 48 Microfilm. Ann Arbor, Mich.: University Microfilm International, 1977.

29. Cited in McKenzie, *London Book Trade*. McKenzie is not, of course, starting from
scratch: he can draw on the work of parliamentary historians and genealogists of
modern journalism. In *English Newspaper*, Frank notes (p. 20) that speeches made in
Parliament had been occasionally published since the middle of the reign of Elizabeth.

30. See *The Journal of Sir Simonds D'Ewes* for January 25 and February 9, 1641–42;
see also Forster, *Grand Remonstrance*, pp. 289–90n.

31. This taxonomy of sociolinguistic schism will be recognized by theorists of the
rift between oral and scribal practice: one of the chief cultural functions of the press is
to harden the boundary between speech and writing. Paul Ricoeur investigates how the
distinction between speech and writing operates on the consciousness of historicity in
"The Model of the Text: Meaningful Action Considered as a Text," *Social Research* 38
(Autumn 1971): 529–62. Though his argument mainly serves to defend the fundamentally hermeneutic methods of historiography, by exposing the phenomenological
homology of events and (written) texts, his analysis also suggests how a print culture—
which is to a certain degree describable as a "hyperscribal" culture—promotes the

tion and pamphleteering, with its threats to the positional stability and personality of opinion, Lichfield puts his press on wheels, makes of it an Early Modern Olivetti; he hauls it onto the battlefield in order to secure a crucial full proximity of the merciful royal author, the royal printer, the political occasion, and the printed text. "The spring / Must needs be Cleare that issues from the King." His reworking of the old scribal figure—the pen as fount—like his effort to preserve for the press the physical mobility of the scribe is technologically and historically regressive, reactionary in a rich sense. The stationer who prints a newsletter is too much an agent of discourse; Lichfield manages his self-promotion by volubly effacing his own agency.

The press in the public eye; subservient to the will of its author; improving on, but not competing with manuscript production; its fidelity on full display—literary historians will recognize this as Jonson's ideal press. To complete the description by noting that the products of this ideal press are subject to immediate if not prevenient censorious scrutiny will give us almost precisely the press of Parliament's 1642 Licensing Edict: the rebels who topple Lichfield's licensed type-case may be said to have anticipated Milton's similar attack in *Areopagitica* by two years.[32] But Lichfield's press, excellent both for the visibility of its functioning and its transparency to authorial will, is above all the press sought by the heirs of the New Bibliography. By this I mean to suggest that twentieth-century bibliography has borrowed many of the methods of Stuart censorship to force the norms and procedures of the printer's mystery into visibility; both censorship and bibliography protest all that is clandestine within dissemination. Indeed, both censorship and traditional bibliography protest discursive mediation itself and seek its exposure and elimination.

---

apprehension of events as texts, the alienation of perlocutionary effect from intention, and, thus, the inscription of political "science" within agency itself. (It might be argued that the press gives the "Machiavellian moment" in political thought an inflection towards functionalism.) I suggest that Ricoeur's analysis can serve as a phenomenology of the public sphere constituted by print.

32. It might be more accurate to identify Lichfield's press with that constituted by the 1649 "Act against Unlicensed and Scandalous Books and Pamphlets," for that act responds explicitly to "the mischiefs arising from weekly pamphlets." For a richly contextualized account of the 1642 Edict, see Abbe Blum, "The Author's Authority: *Areopagitica* and the Labour of Licensing," *Re-membering Milton*, ed. Mary Nyquist and Margaret W. Ferguson (New York: Methuen, 1987), pp. 74–96.

Because "books are not wholly dead things," because of the inde-
terminacy of originative agency within that public sphere constituted
by the press, English censorship had long been *theoretically* confounded by seditious printing: where was the treason? who was the
traitor? The Star Chamber Decree of 1586 had instituted monetary
penalties for unlicensed printing and had authorized the Wardens of
the Stationers' Company to punish offenses by causing "all such pryn-
tinge presses and other Instrumentes of ymprintinge to be Defaced,
melted, sawed in peeces, broken, or battered at the smythes forge,"
which looks for all the world like a displacement of the traitor's hanging, drawing, and quartering onto the printing press itself.[33] In a
sense, this mutilation of the press elaborates the logic of book-
burning, which incorporates the heretical book as biblio-heretic, incorporates *only* to encorpse. Although a Henrician statute on the
books had given legal articulation to the idea of treasonable writing
(26 Henry VIII, c.13) and an Edwardian statute had extended the
domain of the treasonable word to printing (1 Edw. VI, c.12), the
state showed itself reluctant to entertain the possibility of a traitor-
stationer, as opposed to a traitor-press: it is worth noting, worth
remembering, that only one stationer, the Roman Catholic William
Carter, was executed for treasonable publication before 1664.[34] By
pursuing total scrutiny of books, Tudor, Stuart, and Commonwealth
censorship avoids address to the problems of personality specific to
book culture. It thus aims to confine verbal transgression to autogra-
phy and speech.[35]

33. I cite the Star Chamber decree as transcribed in Patterson, *Copyright*, p. 241.
34. Carter's offenses were first alleged in late 1579, shortly after the uproar over the
publication of Stubbe's *Gaping Gulf*. He was accused of publishing a variety of papist
pamphlets, including one asserting Mary of Scotland's claim to the throne, but kept
silent during his examination before the Court of High Commission and escaped
death. Soon thereafter he was arrested for another publication, but even under torture
again resisted self-incrimination. On January 10, 1584 he was finally convicted of high
treason.
35. The early Tudor statutes articulate a calculus of verbal intention. 1 Edw. VI c.12
provides that to deny the king's supremacy over the church or his claim to the throne or
to compass to deprive the king or the king's heirs of their estate or titles *by spoken word*
became treasonable on the third offense; such denials or compassings were treasonable
on the first offense if committed by written word (or by deed—the discursivity of deed,
the performative status of the written, the commutability of written word and deed are
also entailed within the calculus of treason). Hudson sustains the calculus within his
comments on *De Libellis Famosis* (1600), the case on which the modern law of seditious
libel rests; William Hudson, *A Treatise on the Court of the Star Chamber, Collectanea Jurid-
ica*, ed. F. Hargrave, 2 vols. (London: Brooke, 1791–92), 2:104.

This is a paradoxical situation, since it is precisely the power of the press to produce new political solidarities, to precipitate novel ideological "classings," that had produced the emergent sense of the word as political agent. If speaking had been taken as evidence of treason as early as 1402, it is still the case that the treasonable *word* becomes an abiding problem only in the sixteenth century.[36] Within the shifting development of the Tudor law of treason (and despite parliamentary reluctance to broad constructive extension of the law of treason during the first half of the century), specifically verbal treasons were conspicuously elaborated, a development coincident with the elaboration of print censorship.[37] Print remains, as it were, the unspoken motive of early modern regulation of speech and writing. By emphasizing prevenient scrutiny, the Tudor state attempted to exclude verbal transgression from print culture; thus excluded, treason, libel, and schism could be made to conform to traditional forms of criminal agency. And so with bibliography: the total scrutiny of the printed book is instituted in order to identify anomalous acts of semantic production—variants—so that they may be eliminated, so that we may restore an author's text.[38] Again, censorship and bibliography seek the dissolution of the book.

36. Isobel D. Thornley, "Treason by Words in the Fifteenth Century," *English Historical Review* 32 (1917): 556–61.

37. See John Bellamy, *The Tudor Law of Treason: An Introduction, Studies in Social History*, ed. Harold Perkin (London: Routledge and Kegan Paul, 1979), chaps. 1 and 2.

38. This is why modern bibliography and early modern censorship are so obsessed with dramatic production. (This is *one* reason why bibliography wrestles with the drama. McKerrow, Greg, Pollard, and Simpson no doubt respond to the prestige of Shakespeare, to the immediate pressure of contemporary Shakespeare bibliography, and to the pleasure of a communal scholarship which the prestige of Shakespeare and the bibliographical tradition had made so convenient; I do not wish to scant the power of sheer cultural momentum.) Given the conditions of Elizabethan and Jacobean dramatic publishing, the bibliographic dream of restoring an author's text was always really a deeply relished editor's nightmare. Stephen Orgel ("The Authentic Shakespeare," *Representations* 21 [1988]: 1–25), Jonathan Goldberg ("Textual Properties," *Shakespeare Quarterly* 37 [1986]: 213–17), and Leah S. Marcus (*Puzzling Shakespeare: Local Reading and Its Discontents* [Berkeley: University of California Press, 1988], pp. 43–50) have elegantly elaborated what others have often remarked, that the drama cheerfully disperses, or at least threatens to disperse, the author's text. The litany, spoken trippingly, from obvious to less so: the printed text gives only the words; actors speak more, and less, than is set down for them; playwrights make playhouse revisions not recorded in the copy for printed texts; acting companies also make such revisions; copy for printed dramatic texts varies far more widely in provenance and notational convention than does that for most other early printed texts; copy for printed dramatic texts is seldom autograph, seldom even a first fair-copy of autograph; acting companies frequently attempted to thwart the circulation of printed plays; the relation between multiple

As the mechanisms of anonymous publication became more pol-
ished, legal regulation adjusted its procedures. Isobel Thornley tells
us that when the Tudor treason acts "expired or were repealed in the
early seventeenth century, treason by words disappeared with them,
and Coke could hold it to be no part of English law," but this was to be
only a momentary disappearance.[39] If the mediating press was the
repressed motive of the Tudor law of verbal treason, it could not but
return as an object of legal scrutiny within the public sphere of the

---

editions of early dramatic texts tends to far greater complexity than the relations
between multiple editions of non-dramatic texts; most playwrights had no direct economic interest in the printing of their plays; reproduction rights for dramatic texts
were appreciably less stable than those for non-dramatic texts. These things we know,
thanks to the New Bibliography. And these things have been argued, arguments which
would further interfere with positivist dramatic editing: that, with noteworthy exceptions, copy for printed dramatic texts was prepared with less care than was the copy for
non-dramatic texts; that proofreading of dramatic texts was more lax than that of non-
dramatic texts; that, owing to some special status of the drama, most playwrights simply
cared less about fidelity of transmission than did, say, poets. Solving the particular
problems of print transmission, a project Greg took to be a special case, however
complex, of scribal transmission, only introduces a spiraling problematic. Bibliography
imagines an author, whom it takes as an origin, the sole subject of intentions; it imagines an autograph manuscript, which it takes to be a preeminent material product, the
medium of intentions; it imagines a reading, the object of intentions, a paradigmatic
consumption of a printed text which is itself imagined as a mimesis of the scribal
mimesis of authorial intention. But the authorial origin of drama is multiple, it has no
preeminent material product, its consumption is obtrusively dispersed, and it disrupts
mimetic hierarchies.
     Drama thus scandalizes bibliography. It is hardly a failing of the New Bibliography
that its practitioners never admitted as much. Yet their work repeatedly—and
fruitfully—responds to the scandal. Greg's career was given over to demonstrating how
broad was the range of possible sources of dramatic copy-text, how various could be the
sources of textual anomaly and variant. And Pollard's great work, the Short-Title Catalogue set aside, is a provisional account of the interactions among stationers, acting
companies, and authors. Their particular concern with the drama forced them to
engage with complexities that compromise their editorial principles. Few bibliographers between that first generation and our own—Kirschbaum is the notable
exception—came so close to admitting the intransigence of the obstacles to a restored
author's text. Though we now once again grapple with the mediations of the stage—
even make an honored place for those mediations in our criticism—we have not yet
confronted the intransigent mediations of printing.
     39. Thornley, "Treason by Words," p. 558, citing the *Third Institutes*. In the early
seventeenth century, the law of seditious libel underwent important elaborations. In the
case *De Libellis Famosis* Coke distinguished between defamation of private persons and
defamation of magistrates (see William Searle Holdsworth, *History of English Law* [Lon-
don: Methuen, 1922–72], 8:336–37). Meanwhile the common law courts began to
discriminate degrees of publicity—again a calculus of mediation—by distinguishing
between slander and libel, thus making way for articulate distinctions between writing
and printing.

Interregnum. After a decade of parliamentary wrangling over the regulation of the press, the *publication* of printed works alleging the tyranny or illegitimacy of the government was made treasonable by an act of July 1649; at the Restoration the *printing* of works compassing the king's harm or death became treasonable.[40] Although the press lost and recovered a place within the law of treason, it maintained and strengthened a degree of recognition within the considerably more supple law of seditious libel. According to a statutory tradition running from the reign of Edward I through that of Elizabeth, the publisher of seditious libel may be imprisoned until the "inventor" be brought before the Court; the "inventor" of seditious libel is punishable at common law; the reporter or disseminator is punishable under statutory law.[41] By thus describing a relatively autonomous criminal agency for the libelous publisher, early modern law proved more resourceful than modern bibliography, which still shuns the challenge of anonymous composition, of texts to which fully individualized intention can never be conveniently restored. In yet another attempt to rouse textual scholarship from the dream of a restored author's text, I want to instance a couple of stationers' books of the Restoration, books that excited the censor and threw the bibliographer into a frenzy.

Let me begin with *The Speeches, and Prayers of some of the Late Kings Judges*, a book that presents the dying words of the recently executed regicides in the inflammatory accents of the martyrdom. The book was printed late in 1660 by Thomas Creeke and Simon Dover for Thomas Brewster, and it was discovered three years later when L'Estrange and his men raided the premises of the bookbinder Nathaniel Brooks. L'Estrange was trying to round up a group of radical stationers whom he called "the Confederates," this at a moment when he

40. It is worth noting that judges, not comfortable with the personal confusions of assimilating publication to invention, avoided trials under the act. These acts simply specify the drift of an interpretive tradition that had developed in Star Chamber before its dissolution, a tradition developed out of *De Libellis Famosis*: in the course of construing the case it was proposed that there was no distinction at law between inventing sedition and publishing it (Siebert, *Freedom of the Press*, pp. 118–19 and Holdsworth, *English Law*, 5:209 and 8:338–39). Coke held (5 Co. Rep. 125a–b) that cases of criminal defamation could be dealt with by indictment at common law as well as by proceedings in the Star Chamber, but Star Chamber proceedings were far more efficient, and the judicial prosecution of censorship was not taken up within the common law courts until the Restoration. For a useful introduction to Restoration press censorship, see Walker, "The Censorship of the Press," pp. 219–38.

41. Siebert, *Freedom of the Press*, p. 118.

had acquired the patent on the two official newsbooks and was in a far way of securing a monopoly of English print journalism.[42] It was one of the grimmest affairs of a grim time, made particularly nasty by the fact that Creeke, one of the printers, had in 1661 been hauled in on a different charge; on that occasion L'Estrange had so worn him down that he turned king's evidence. On information from Creeke, L'Estrange managed to arrest Giles Calvert, probably the most daring and highly principled radical printer of the Interregnum. During the ensuing months, as the king's security and L'Estrange's power increased, no printer who had dealt with Creeke could feel secure. And surely the round-up of 1663 was no surprise.

The trial was held four months later, and Creeke was interrogated first.[43] He admitted to having printed the first thirty-six folio pages—the court had determined that offending passages did not begin until page 45—and expressed his belief that Dover had printed the rest of the book. Brewster, the bookseller, though close to death, was the most eloquent of the accused, gallantly and perhaps ever so slyly emphasizing that Creeke's printing put him squarely outside the reach of the indictment. Brewster built his defense on two arguments: that he was not familiar with the contents of the book and that, since the speeches published in the book had originally been delivered in public, the dissemination of the work, in print, was simply the preservation of a public record and not an original libel. Dover's contribution to the defense—that the book was printed before the 1662 Licensing Act—seems to have had some influence with Chief Justice Hyde, though the judge was quick to point out that Brewster and Brooks were still *selling* the book in 1663. Hyde focused most closely on Brewster's arguments. With respect to the claim that publishing in print was categorically different from public speaking, that it possessed inherently lower degrees of agency, Hyde was derisive: "This

42. He failed in his monopolist campaign, being dependent for news on the newsletter system that was falling under the exclusive control of the Secretaries of State, who themselves managed to secure a monopoly of printed news from 1666 to 1679; Peter Fraser, *The Intelligence of the Secretaries of State and their Monopoly of Licensed News, 1660–1688* (Cambridge: Cambridge University Press, 1956), pp. 35–49, and George Kitchin, *Sir Roger L'Estrange* (London: Kegan Paul, 1913), pp. 141–54; on the round-up, see Kitchin, *L'Estrange*, pp. 112–25.

43. *An Exact Narrative of the Tryal and Condemnation of John Twyn, for Printing and Dispersing of a Treasonable Book, with the Tryals of Thomas Brewster, Bookseller, Simon Dover, Printer, Nathan Brooks, Bookbinder* (London, 1664). The not unconventional statement of license on the title page of this account—"Published by AUTHORITY"—possesses a special resonance.

they publish, and say it was spoken publickly, let it be upon his own soul that did it; for in case he did it, no man knew it but those that heard it: But to *publish* it all over *England*, (3000 of the first Impression, and a second). This is to fill all the Kings Subjects with the justification of that horrid murther [of Charles I]."[44] At the sentencing Hyde insisted that publishing this book might have been punishable as treason. He may have had in mind the new and until then untried provisions of the 1661 Act for the Safety and Preservation of His Majesties Person, which added seditious printing—though not seditious publishing—to its catalogue of treasonable behavior. But the men were indicted at common law, and Hyde conducted the case as a libel trial. The procedure in the case established a devastating precedent, for Lord Hyde ruled that the jury was only to find on the fact of publication, and that it lay with the court to find whether the publication was in fact libelous, a legal situation which prevailed until 1792.[45]

Brewster's first line of defense, that he didn't know what he was publishing, has particularly interested bibliographers. He is certainly lying, but his efforts to make it a colorable lie command attention. Creeke claims that Brewster gave him the first thirty-six pages to print; Brewster concurs. But the proofreading was not performed in-house: Creeke claims to have delivered proof-sheets to Giles Calvert's servants on some occasions, and on some occasions to Brewster's. There is probably nothing unusual in the arrangements thus described: the jury in this trial was composed primarily of stationers and the examination gives no special emphasis to these procedures. But conventions of division of labor gave a cautious stationer a degree of safety, or "deniability." Neither Creeke nor Dover ever read the book they were printing. Creeke never saw Brewster with the proofs, nor had Brewster ever been seen in possession of a complete manuscript copy of the book. Dover never saw the first half of the volume; Creeke never saw the second half. The book was completed at the binder's shop, but a binder has no call whatsoever to read what he stitches up. His alibi might have been better had he been sewing a small-format volume: an octavo must be infolded, some pages sealed and so rendered illegible until a purchaser attacks them with a paper-knife.

Brewster, Dover, and Brooks were found guilty and punished, but

---

44. *Exact Narrative*, p. 47; this aspect of Brewster's defense was specifically weakened by the fact that the book contained transcriptions, not just of public speeches, but also of private correspondence.

45. Holdsworth, *English Law*, 8:342–44.

their strategem was by no means discredited. In 1683 Thomas Brad-
dyl was arrested for printing *The Growth of Popery*, but because he had
only printed three sheets of the book, he had to be released. L'Estrange felt thwarted by the release but "did not much wonder at it, the
printer being commonly out of distance of a full discovery where the
copy is divided into several houses, besides the difficulty of proving a
printer conscious to the matter of the book."[46] As the stationers' corporate authority declined before the burgeoning jurisdiction of the
common law courts, the press contrived further to atomize the discursive subject, resorting to forms of production so fragmented that no
textual laborer could be proven "conscious to the matter of the book."

Sometimes, rarely, notoriously, L'Estrange could make his case.
Around 4:30 in the morning, about a week before his discovery of the
volume of regicide speeches at Brooks's bindery, he raided the
printshop of John Twyn, which he had kept under surveillance for
several consecutive nights. When L'Estrange came to the door, Twyn
and his apprentices were in the middle of printing off sheet D of a
seditious book entitled *A Treatise of the Execution of Justice*. They seem
to have been hurrying their work, but the testimony at Twyn's trial is
uncertain on this point; L'Estrange alleged that Twyn was trying to
finish in time to get the book into circulation in the north as part of
the agitation for the rising of mid-October.[47] What makes this less far-
fetched than many of L'Estrange's imputations was Twyn's admission
that he had recently received moneys from Elizabeth Calvert's maid-
servant. It was well known that Elizabeth, now widowed, still maintained a commitment to such radical publishing as she and her husband had fostered for the previous two decades. At any rate, although
it took L'Estrange about a quarter of an hour to break down Twyn's
door on the morning of the 7th, Twyn and his apprentices had not
succeeded in covering their tracks. The formes had been broken, but
not completely; unperfected sheets lay on the tympan, and many
sheets which had been tossed out the window and down a set of back
stairs were recovered, some still wet, so Twyn's responsibility for printing the books was undeniable. A complete manuscript copy was found
on the premises and Twyn was indicted on a charge of treason.

46. Cited in McKenzie, *London Book Trade*, p. 22.
47. As to their haste, see the evidence given by Twyn's apprentice, Joseph Walker
(*An Exact Narrative*, p. 14), L'Estrange (p. 20), and Thomas Mabb (p. 23). Concurrent
printing was almost certainly going on: both presses were in use; some of the sheets
were perfect and some imperfect.

Seventeenth-century trials for treason do not provide good models of judicial procedure. The court had wide discretion and its standards of evidence were extremely lax. It was under little pressure to build a finely calibrated case, so its distinctions were rough and ready. That its procedure and distinctions correspond so poorly to what we might expect is what makes the case so instructive.

Twyn was tried at the same session as were Dover, Brewster, and Brooks, before the same jury, of which stationers made up half, with Lord Hyde again presiding. In his defense Twyn argued, as would Brewster two days later, that he was simply a poor man trying to make a living. He claimed not to know who was the author of his manuscript copy—a claim that the court seemed to respect, since no effort was made to secure the information by torture. Thus the case of treason had to be made in the absence of an inventor, or author, of treason. Coke was skeptical about the legal foundations for verbal treasons, as has already been noted, but he had made some provision for the problem, arguing (*Third Institute*, 14) that publication of books compassing the king's death could be construed as treason, but his arguments had not yet been brought to bear in court. In the Brewster-Dover-Brooks portion of the session, the court dealt most harshly with Brewster, the bookseller, who seems to have organized the printing and publication of the regicide speeches, but since Twyn denied having received the manuscript from Calvert's maid, and since Elizabeth Calvert and her household had managed to flee London during L'Estrange's purge, there was no focal industrialist who could be identified as the origin of discourse. Therefore Twyn had to be so identified before he could be lawfully hung, disemboweled, decapitated, and quartered, the first English stationer ever convicted of treason.

The case against Twyn was made to hang on whether or not he knew what he was doing. According to the published account of the trial, L'Estrange had asked Twyn at his arrest what he had thought of the book, to which Twyn replied, "Methought it was mettlesome stuffe, the man was a hot firey man that wrote it."[48] L'Estrange wanted to focus the case on this remark, for he seems to have instructed all his witnesses to feature these phrases in their testimony before the court. But Lord Hyde and Judge Keeling, who assisted Hyde in the examination of the witnesses, show themselves far more

48. This is by no means an exaggeration: the author insists that "if ever there was a season which required the Lord's people to sell their garments and buy swords it is now" (*An Exact Narrative*, p. 20).

interested in bibliography than in literary criticism. The court builds its case on the specific procedures of book production in Twyn's shop. Hyde and Keeling seem more intent on establishing that Twyn himself assisted in the printing, more intent again in establishing that Twyn had participated in setting type for the book, but most intent of all in proving that Twyn had read proof. Thrice in the course of examining Twyn's apprentice, who was the main witness in the case, Hyde returns to the subject of proofreading, seeking to establish to whom proof sheets were taken, whether copy was present where proofs were taken, whether Twyn had been seen reading proof, how much time had passed before proofs were returned and whether corrections had been made in Twyn's own hand, and the loyal apprentice does everything he can to prevent the assembly of a unified scene of proofreading, with Twyn seated in his kitchen, comparing the proofsheets before him against the copy beside him on a dresser, and writing the corrections.

Indeed, it is clear that, from the moment of his arrest, proofreading was to be the focus of *Rex v. Twyn*. L'Estrange reports that "I did ask him in the house of the Constable: Who corrected this? the Corrector must certainly know what it was. Said he, *I have no skill in correcting*. But when I speake of *correcting*, I mean who *revised* it, *overlooked* it for the press; *I read it over*, sayes he." We can see Twyn fumbling towards a defense during this first interrogation. At his sentencing, having seen on what his fate was hanging, he is clearer: "I never read a word of it." But at the outset, he attempts to discriminate between correcting and reading, between two types of editorial intervention, one semantic—modifications on behalf of political orthodoxy, or political radicalism, or logic, or rhetoric—and one—how to put this?—non-semantic, orthographic, aesthetic, typographical. Perhaps "bibliographical": Twyn was adjusting the printed to the handwritten word. The distinction will not bear much scrutiny, and L'Estrange denies it. To read proof is "to know what it was," "to be conscious to the matter of the book." To read proof is to become subject to penal interpellation as the origin of discourse. In the absence of an author, to read proof is to write.

> He to his study goes, and there amiddes
>   His Magick bookes and arts of sundry kindes,
> He seekes out mighty charmes, to trouble sleepy mindes.
> Then choosing out few wordes most horrible,

(Let none them read) thereof did verses frame,
With which and other spelles like terrible,
He bad awake black Plutoes griesly Dame,
And curses heaven, and spake reprochfull shame
Of highest God, the Lord of life and light.[49]

Of course, Archimago is not a printer, and his crimes would have fallen under the jurisdiction of the court of High Commission, at least up until its dissolution in 1641, after which the Court of King's Bench would have had jurisdiction in the case. Archimago is not a printer, but, since he is an imitative poet of the least inventive sort, assembling his verses from the commonplace books of the black arts, his criminality resembles Twyn's. By dint of the dubious originality of their production neither may be simply subjected to a specifically criminal interpellation. Spenser's warning about Archimago's text, "let none them read," alerts us, however, to the same dangerous threshold across which Twyn transgressed. *Lasciate ogni speranza*, for ye who enter here cross over into criminal agency.

A distinction should be made, for Twyn puts his signature to criminal agency, demonstrates his reading by correcting proofs in his own hand. (In the trial, composing—setting type—is *not* enough to prove reading and therefore insufficient evidence that the industrial threshold of writing has been crossed. Dover had set type for the book of regicide speeches, but because he had not read proof, he was deemed less culpable than the bookseller Brewster, and was treated more or less as an accessory.) Twyn's reading is nodal, corresponding to malice in a libel trial, but his crime is dispersed across the entire process of text production, and it is therefore more diffuse than that inveigling reading from which Spenser warns us. But Anne Ferry has recently argued, as part of her effort to engage Foucault's historiography of the discursive field, that Spenser's exceptionally elastic use of the verb "to read" finds its semantic center in the laborious construction of meanings difficult of access, a bringing to light of senses largely hidden by signs visual and verbal. Spenser's reading is a nodal cognitive labor instanced in different interpretive practices, unlike Twyn's nodal practice among practices. Ferry further observes that in the few cases in Spenser in which "to read" means to comprehend a written

49. Edmund Spenser, *The Faerie Queene*, ed. A. C. Hamilton, Longman Annotated Poets (London: Longman, 1977), I.i.36.7–37.6.

text—the incidence of the term to describe the comprehension of spoken words is rather higher—the activity implies a wider responsiveness and deeper connoisseurship, a fuller effort and graver susceptibility than is implied in the modern use of the verb—or, at least, as it is used by those who don't teach literature for a living.[50] Twyn was part of an industry that was steadily specifying the act of reading, reconstituting its social base, and transforming its affect. But the efflorescence of censorship in the seventeenth century—censorship's great moment—surely has to do with a fear of democratizing the experience of the undiminished affectivities still residual in post-Spenserian reading. Those affectivities were what necessitated the licensing of books in the first place, and as their power has subsided so that necessity has been felt to have lapsed. Now it is the image or the rhythmic spoken word which must be subject to surveillance and, if need be, banished from discourse.

One phase of my argument ends here, with the description of a criminalized reader-response. But it may be useful to remark that the trial of John Twyn has proven more important to bibliographers than to legal historians. Since literary criticism has not yet recovered its once-central interest in paleography and bibliography, this trial is not as familiar to literary scholars as it should be. Two facts to be gleaned from these trials unsettle received bibliographic wisdom, by which I mean the bibliographic orthodoxy of Greg, Pollard, and McKerrow, and especially as it has been transmitted by Hinman; these facts can be made to speak to us of authorship. The first has to do with shared printing. The testimony in Dover's case makes it clear not only that shared printing of single books was not unheard of, but that there were norms for such production routines. That pamphlet went through two impressions and the work was split between Dover and Creeke in precisely the same way for each edition: as Creeke testified, "to the best of my Remembrance I Printed the same that I did before. . . . That's usuall, he that Prints the First, doth Print the same of the Second" (p. 43). Despite this evidence, Bowers has asserted—strenuously and vehemently—that this is an unusual practice, that it tends to show up in large productions, and that "it was fairly common in Restoration play quartos produced in a hurry to take advantage of the author's night. But," he goes on, "such shared printing was not

50. Anne Ferry, *The Art of Naming* (Chicago: University of Chicago Press, 1988), pp. 9–27.

common about 1600 except for massive books."[51] Bowers may be right here; certainly we have reason to suppose that the practice of shared printing might have spread during an age of increasing censorship as a means of sustaining the confounded personal agency of stationer's labor. But Bowers gives no evidence for his assertion, and I am interested by his truculence. A serious historical bibliographer might wish to assemble the typographic evidence for shared printing, to trace as precisely as possible the history of this diffusion of agency. Bowers angrily dismisses the matter.

More interesting is the evidence provided by these trials for the practice of proofreading. McKenzie and Blayney have both cited the trials as sources of technical information.[52] To summarize their conclusions: even in cases of extreme haste, Restoration printers made sure proof was read against copy. They either sent proofsheets out of the shop for correction elsewhere, or they employed an in-house corrector, or, when budgets were extremely tight or extreme secrecy was required, they themselves read proof. That this was an almost invariant practice has huge implications for textual scholarship. It would be redundant for me to recount the elegant arguments of Blayney and McKenzie from which these implications emerge. Suffice it to say that the normal procedure of reading proof against copy means that printing on a given book could not proceed without interruption except in extraordinary cases. Twyn took between an hour and an hour and a half over each quarto forme, roughly twenty minutes per page. If it is true that this interruption is a norm, the fact destroys a good deal of bibliographical argument about type shortage and compositorial practice, which in its own turn could discredit large traces of Hinman's heroic account of the setting of Shakespeare's First Folio, that is, *if* standards for proofreading an impressive folio in 1623 were as high as they were for proofreading some seditious pamphlets in 1663. When McKenzie first began teasing out these implications in 1969, Hinman admitted, to his credit, that "some of us have been much less demanding about what we accept as probative evidence . . . than we should have been."[53] Alas, Bowers responded to

51. I take the citation from Bowers's review of Gaskell's *New Introduction to Bibliography*, "McKerrow Revisited," *Papers of the Bibliographical Society of America* 67 (1973): 109–24.

52. McKenzie, *London Book Trade*, pp. 22–23, 30–31, and Blayney, *The Texts of King Lear*, 1:41, 197–99.

53. Charlton Hinman, "Shakespearian Textual Studies: Seven More Years," *Shake-

Philip Gaskell's formulation of the McKenzie position (and Blayney has scourged him for it) that such an "account of proofreading and correction . . . is pure moonshine for the average commercial book produced in the Elizabethan period."[54] Blayney notes that Bowers is here discussing that great Elizabethan book, Shakespeare's First Folio.

I have no intention of holding Bowers up to ridicule. His position may have begun to erode—though not because we have managed to come up with a detailed history of shared printing or proof correction. Still, that position still possesses a sanctified orthodoxy, so it is worth asking why the Greg-Bowers-Hinman model of textual mediation has proved so sturdy in the face of damaging evidence. This question can be framed and reframed in ways that will, I think, imply some answers. The questions with respect to shared printing: why does bibliography resist the conception of a text dispersed and reassembled between authorial propagation and commodity consumption? Why do we resist the intrusion of complex models of industrial mediation into a simple semiotic model of textuality? And if the answers here are self-evident, having to do with that disposition to protest mediation that characterizes both censorship and bibliography, then why, on the other hand, does bibliography prefer the model of negligent production, poor workmanship? Why cling, for example, to Hinman's pessimistic assessment that Jaggard "was largely indifferent to the accuracy of his text"?[55] If the printshops of Twyn, Dover, and Creeke are normal, then we should expect the Folio to have been prepared slightly more carefully than was Twyn's *Execution of Justice*. And if Twyn's hurry means that his procedures represent a minimal

---

speare 1971: Proceedings of the World Shakespeare Congress, Vancouver, August 1971, ed. Clifford Leach and J. M. R. Margeson (Toronto: University of Toronto Press, 1972), p. 42, cited in Blayney, *The Texts of King Lear*, 1:204.

54. Bowers, "McKerrow Revisited," p. 117, and cited, sharply, in Blayney *The Texts of King Lear*, 1:203; see also Bowers's earlier reaction to the McKenzie-Gaskell position, and to Hinman's respectful response to McKenzie, in "Seven More Years," pp. 50–51. Bowers's own account of the place of proofing in the process of book production, the account that he is implicitly defending, is "Elizabethan Proofing," *Joseph Quincy Adams Memorial Studies*, ed. James G. McManaway, Giles E. Dawson, and Edwin E. Willoughby (Washington: Folger Shakespeare Library, 1948), pp. 571–86; see also Bowers's "Established Texts and Definitive Editions," *Philological Quarterly* 41 (1962): 1–17; reprinted in *Essays in Bibliography, Text, and Editing* (Charlottesville: University of Virginia Press, 1975), pp. 364–66. For Gaskell on proofreading, see his *New Introduction to Bibliography* (Oxford: Clarendon Press, 1972), pp. 110–17.

55. Charlton Hinman, *The Printing and Proofreading of the First Folio of Shakespeare*, 2 vols. (Oxford: Clarendon, 1963), 1:227.

standard of care in text preparation, then a cheap quarto play-text—
to choose precisely the paradigmatic object of New Bibliographic
scrutiny—should be no worse. That means that we should expect any
printed book to be read at least once against copy. In fact, Simpson,
McKenzie, and Blayney provide plenty of circumstantial evidence to
imply that, for large productions designed to impress, a book would
go through two or three stages of proofreading, all this *before* the stop-
press corrections that give us the textual variants that send bibliographers into their ecstasies. Implication: a printed book was adjusted to
its copy before printing got fully under way.[56] Therefore, stop-press
corrections are not likely to represent the principal adjustment to
copy (indeed, why check copy against proof *during* a print run?); stop-
press corrections may just as well represent an adjustment of the page
to common sense. A page in print *might* be read against copy, but,
likely as not, stop-press corrections would involve the correction of
obvious typographical errors—for which copy is unnecessary. During
the process other adjustments might be made that reflect . . . what?:
authorial intervention at the printshop; an emendation to clarify a
passage that has fallen under someone's, anyone's, casual glance; a
change. Most often we *cannot know* how manuscripts influence textual
variability. The change at press is an act of writing.

"A printer," said Lord Hyde to his jury, "A printer, he is a publick
Agent." Thus Hyde; thus Eisenstein.[57] Autograph is effaced by printing; authorship is set adrift on stationery tides. If the New Bibliography resists the evidence of Twyn's proofreading, it is because that
evidence confounds the dream of a systematic, scientific regress to
manuscript. According to Justice Hyde and Surveyor L'Estrange—
and they should know—to read proof is to write, or at least to share in
the work of writing.[58] We need not frame this primarily as a problem

56. Blayney, *The Texts of King Lear*, 1:200–202.

57. Although Eisenstein is synecdochic here, she is also in many ways the very
progenitrix of the new cultural historiography of print. The present essay can be little
more than a supplement to her great speculation, *The Printing Press as an Agent of
Change: Communications and Cultural Transformations in Early-Modern Europe*, 2 vols.
(Cambridge: Cambridge University Press, 1979).

58. Those among my readers who are familiar with the modern tradition of bibliographical theory will note that this argument may be situated within what may be called
the Tanselle-McGann debate (itself a theoretical reenactment of the Bowers-Gaskell
confrontation) and situated, roughly, on the McGann side of the argument. For an
introduction to the basic terms of this confrontation, see G. Thomas Tanselle, "The
Editorial Problem of Final Authorial Intention," *Studies in Bibliography* 29 (1976): 167–
211, and Jerome J. McGann, *Modern Textual Criticism*. It may be observed that the

extrapolated from manuscript: to read proof is part of printing; to write is to begin to go into print. As Bowers and L'Estrange survey the seventeenth-century English public sphere they shudder at the spectacle of ramified mediation.

"A printer, he is a publick Agent." The printer is, indeed, so much an agent of discourse that royalists like Lichfield had to figure out a way to restrain that originative agency, and that political potency, without ceasing to print; the printer is so much an agent of discourse that radicals like Calvert and Twyn had to destroy the unity of the productive process in order to defend themselves from being treated like traitors, the inventors or authors of treason. To defer once more to Justice Hyde—he is instructing the jury—"It is high time to take notice of this dispersing of pamphlets." What we should notice in the evidence of that dispersal is that the seventeenth-century press was becoming authorial: the constitution of authorial property as we know it, the legal constitution of authorship as such, is in some measure a reaction to the proliferation and dispersal of authorial functions across the field of dissemination, a crisis of ramified mediation. The proofreading episode is simply a node in that crisis, an attempt to stabilize and locate originality in the discursive field, without the traditional apparatus of authorial origination—"writing." Surely the historical bibliographer need not shudder over "this dispersing of pamphlets"; surely we are not so resistant to collaborative labor in the cultural sphere nor so hostile to the constitution of a public sphere that the history of the discursive field is to remain forever a history of privacies. We no longer need as a theory of the modern text the unfounded model of epistolary communication, discourse as a passing of notes. Twyn's head and quarters were dispersed to the several gates of the city; can we not now recognize that he died as a cause?

---

constraints of editorial practice have produced polarizations in textual theory that constitute some slight obstacle to constructing a nuanced history of textuality. It is therefore worth recalling Greg's shrewd dictum—Greg in the idiom of the late Foucault: "authority is never absolute, but only relative" ("The Rationale of the Copy-Text" [1950–51], reprinted in W. W. Greg's *Collected Papers*, ed. J. C. Maxwell [Oxford: Clarendon, 1966], p. 374).

4

Bestial Buggery in
A Midsummer Night's Dream

BRUCE THOMAS BOEHRER

Although no one has paid much sustained attention to the fact, *A Midsummer Night's Dream* is patently about bestiality.[1] On the most immediate level, Titania's animal passion for the asinine Bottom climaxes the play's fairy subplot. In the process, this passion tests the bounds of Elizabethan theatrical decorum; Titania leads Bottom to a

I am grateful to David Lee Miller, Harold Weber, Arthur Kinney, Margreta de Grazia, Sharon O'Dair, Stephen Orgel, Jeanne Addison Roberts, and Bruce Smith for helping me with early versions of this essay. Likewise, I am indebted to my co-participants in the 1990 SAMLA session, at which I originally presented a shorter version of the work, and to my colleagues in the 1990 Folger Library/NEH Institute "Shakespeare and the History of Taste," at which I completed much of the necessary research.

1. Jan Kott's early discussion of the play in *Shakespeare Our Contemporary*, trans. Boleslaw Taborski (New York: Doubleday, 1964), emphasizes the element of bestiality more than most; yet even for Kott, Titania's bestiality is simply one element of the play's larger focus upon a Brueghelesque "sexual demonology" (p. 220). And while his more recent work in *The Bottom Translation: Marlowe and Shakespeare and the Carnival Tradition*, trans. Daniela Miedzyrzecka and Lillian Vallee (Evanston: Northwestern University Press, 1987) includes a thorough and suggestive discussion of the relations between bestiality in Apuleius' *Golden Ass* and *A Midsummer Night's Dream* (pp. 35–40), it does not attempt to extend that discussion to other elements of the play's structure. Deborah Wyrick's remarks about the bestiality parallelism in Shakespeare and Apuleius are perhaps typical of the overall trend in scholarship ("The Ass Motif in *The Comedy of Errors* and *A Midsummer Night's Dream*," *Shakespeare Quarterly* 33 [1982]: 432–48): "Subliminal erotic perversity notwithstanding, the audience's predominant response to the dalliance between the ass and the Fairy Queen is one of amusement" (p. 444). And Joseph R. Summers dismisses the issue with an air of finality (*Dreams of Love and Power:*

bed of flowers, embraces and kisses him, and woos him with some of
the play's most extravagantly sensuous verse:

> Come sit thee down upon this flow'ry bed,
> While I thy amiable cheeks do coy,
> And stick musk-roses in thy sleek smooth head,
> And kiss thy fair large ears, my gentle joy.[2]

Oddly enough, this moist rhetoric emerges from an exercise in household discipline: Oberon's plot to drug his wife with an aphrodisiac and
thereby reassert his own domestic sovereignty—what Paul Olson has
called "an orderly subordination of the female . . . to the more reasonable male."[3] Apparently, that is, one enforces traditional marital
order and decency by indulging certain kinds of *in*decency, both within the moral economy of Shakespeare's play and within the political
economy of Oberon's marriage. This contradiction reappears elsewhere in the play as a symbolic coupling of human erotic desire to
animal objects.

    Oberon, for his part, expresses at least two different—and not fully
compatible—attitudes toward his queen's humiliation. On the one
hand, he warns Titania that it will be a kind of just recompense for
her insubordinate refusal to surrender her changeling page: "Well;
go thy way. Thou shalt not from this grove / Till I torment thee for
this injury" (II.i.146–47). The torment, these lines imply, is entirely
merited, and later Oberon almost suggests that it is technically
necessary—as if there were no way to win his quarrel with Titania
other than to force her to make love to a jackass (or at least a "lion,
bear, or wolf, or bull" [II.i.180]): "Ere I take this charm from off her
sight / (As I can take it with another herb), / I'll make her render up
her page to me" (II.i.183–85). From this standpoint, Titania would
seem in fact to be punishing herself, and thus Oberon can emerge as
her benefactor at play's end, taking "pity" on her (IV.i.47) and

---

On Shakespeare's Plays [Oxford: Clarendon Press, 1984]): "As almost every audience
recognizes, the scenes between Bottom and Titania do not descend to nightmarish
bestiality" (p. 11).

    2. *A Midsummer Night's Dream*, IV.i.1–4, in *The Riverside Shakespeare*, ed.
G. Blakemore Evans et al. (Boston: Houghton Mifflin, 1974). Further citations of
Shakespeare's works are from this edition and appear parenthetically in the text.

    3. Paul A. Olson, "*A Midsummer Night's Dream* and the Meaning of Court Mar-
riage," *English Literary History* 24 (1957): 95–119.

moving—out of his own native goodness and decency—to "undo /
This hateful imperfection of her eyes" (IV.i.62–63).

Yet alongside this view of matters, Oberon also expresses a distinct
sense of pleasure—indeed, almost a salacious delight—in his wife's
degradation. Thus when Puck first reports to him that "Titania
wak'd, and straightway lov'd an ass" (III.ii.34), his response is one of
unqualified satisfaction: "This falls out better than I could devise"
(III.ii.35). He later refers to the spectacle of Titania's sleeping in
Bottom's arms as a "sweet sight" (IV.i.46). And his treatment of his
enfeebled queen involves a good measure of open ridicule:

> Meeting her of late behind the wood,
> Seeking sweet favours for this hateful fool,
> I did upbraid her, and fall out with her.
>
> . . .
>
> When I had at my pleasure taunted her,
> And she in mild terms begg'd my patience,
> I then did ask of her her changeling child;
> Which straight she gave me.
>
> (IV.i.48–60)

In short, Oberon may claim to regret Titania's disobedience and to
desire nothing more than to be "new in amity" (IV.i.87) with his
queen, but he also revels in the chance to make sexual sport of her.

For Oberon, then, Titania's plight is both hateful and delightful,
and his language enables him to disavow any moral responsibility for
degrading her while it simultaneously promotes her as an article of
good theatrical fun. In the most obvious sense, such rhetoric legitimates fantasies of male authority: Titania is reduced to her husband's
power, exposed to an audience, and placed in sexual bondage to a
donkey, and all these events are represented as the inevitable consequence of her own misconduct. She has, as it were, brought them on
herself—to both Oberon's and the audience's broad amusement. The
play thus exacts a sort of "encoded revenge" upon womankind in
general and the principle of female sovereignty in particular;[4] yet in
the process it places both Oberon and the audience in a potentially

4. Annabel Patterson, "Bottom's Up: Festive Theory in *A Midsummer Night's
Dream*," *Renaissance Papers* (1988): 34. Patterson's revision of this essay in *Shakespeare and
the Popular Voice* (Oxford: Basil Blackwell, 1989) drops the specific phrase quoted here
while retaining the general sense of the passage.

uncomfortable position, for it identifies the return to traditional domestic order with—of all things—bestiality. As Jonathan Dollimore
has recently observed of perversion in general, "the clear implication
is that civilization actually depends upon that which is usually thought
to be incompatible with it."[5] The fairy king solves his marital problems by openly transforming his wife into the erotic bondslave of an
ass; what, then, does that make him?

The present essay takes this question as central to *A Midsummer
Night's Dream*'s exploration of marital arrangements and household
order. From this standpoint, the unproblematical distinction between
human and bestial nature—a distinction to which Shakespeare's comedy might at first seem fully committed—ultimately emerges from
the play as neither unproblematical nor particularly distinct. The
play's various discursive mechanisms force human nature to amal-
gamate with animal nature and vice versa; Titania's unnatural wifely
disobedience produces winds, fogs, floods, and diseases of cattle, as
well as her amorous encounter with Bottom (II.i.81–117); Bottom is
clearly both man and animal, although various metonymic references
to him as an ass (III.ii.34; IV.i.76; etc.) invite us to consider him
wholly beast. As author of Titania's and Bottom's relationship—as
well as the various other relationships which comprise the play—
Oberon himself participates in the dalliance of people with animals,
and this dalliance subtends the humanity of the very institutions (marriage, patriarchy, monarchy) he seeks to underwrite. In short, *A Midsummer Night's Dream* is about bestiality because the social arrangements it promotes take bestiality as their raison d'être; they assume
that human nature is in constant danger of corruption from the bestial and/or female other, and that it must therefore be continuously
and rigorously policed. They promote themselves as the proper vehicles for such policing. And thus they manufacture the bestial
prodigy—the Bottom and Titania—as a means of political self-
justification.

A MAN NEEDS A MARE

This argument assumes that the urge to bestiality finds its ultimate
source in the institutions that ostensibly oppose it—that, to use

5. Jonathan Dollimore, "The Cultural Politics of Perversion: Augustine, Shakespeare, Freud, Foucault," *Textual Practice* 4 (1990): 179.

Foucault's words, it consistently provokes "a kind of generalized discursive erethism" within western culture.[6] In effect, that is, conditions in *A Midsummer Night's Dream* should be at their most bestial and disnatured exactly when the play promises that all is (or is rapidly being) restored to order. Puck makes this promise very plainly to the sleeping Lysander, and the terms in which he does so deserve to be studied:

> The country proverb known,
> That every man should take his own,
> In your waking shall be shown.
> Jack shall have Jill;
> Nought shall go ill:
> The man shall have his mare again, and all shall be well.

(III.ii.458–63)

According to Puck, the play's action will obey the dictates of proverb; "all shall be well" when a proprietary relation is reasserted between men and women, allowing "every man [to] take his own," and this proprietarism gains concrete illustration in the parallel promises that "Jack shall have Jill" and "The man shall have his mare again." Jack is to Jill as man is to mare—that is, as owner is to owned. The desire of characters and audience alike finds what Terry Eagleton has called "its own natural, stable form" as male dominion within marriage,[7] and this is apparently what it means for all to be well within the context of *A Midsummer Night's Dream*.

But of course these lines raise other possibilities as well. In particular, they do not really specify what it means to say that Jack is to Jill as man is to mare; the terms of the correspondence remain disturbingly imprecise. For if woman qualifies as man's fit sexual companion by assuming the status of commodity (i.e., by being like a mare), then a mare, too, may be a man's fit mate; the text's parallelisms acknowledge no qualitative difference whatever between a man's relationship with his woman and that same man's relationship with his horse. In fact, quite the contrary: Puck's language plays off a long-standing emblematic identification of sexually active women with mares. Described in

6. Michel Foucault, *The History of Sexuality—Volume 1: An Introduction*, trans. Robert Hurley (New York: Vintage Books, 1980), p. 32.

7. Terry Eagleton, *William Shakespeare* (Oxford: Basil Blackwell, 1986), p. 20.

medieval bestiaries as "the most lustful of female animals,"[8] the mare appears in such early texts as the *Ancrene Riwle* as a metaphorical placeholder for the wanton woman; thus the *Riwle* counsels unchaste women to unburden themselves to their confessors by bluntly exclaiming, "'Sir, God's mercy! I am a foul stud mare, a stinking whore.'"[9] Similar language pervades late medieval play-texts like *Mankind*, where New-Gyse, interrupting Mercy's windy advice on how a man should govern his horse ("Yf a man haue an hors, and kepe hym not to hye, / He may then reull hym at hys own dysyere"),[10] exclaims, "Ande my wyf were yowur horse sche wolde yow all to-samne";[11] apparently, that is, New-Gyse's wife is like a horse in that she can both resist male governance and at the same time "to-samne" (i.e., disgrace or shame) her male governors. Furthermore, this traditional identification of woman with mare has a disturbing tendency to appear at unexpected places within the Shakespeare canon—as when Antigonus in *The Winter's Tale* protests of Hermione, "If it prove / She [is unchaste], I'll keep my stables where / I lodge my wife" (II.i.133–35). Indeed, to carry the point further, Renaissance court records reveal the mare to be far and away the most commonly abused animal in cases of bestial buggery (see Appendix); it is almost as if, once woman had been made a mare by the processes of metaphor, mares then began to assume the qualities and status of women as well.

Of course, Bottom's asinine metamorphosis reverses the gender-troping of such identifications. Where Antigonus, Puck, the *Ancrene Riwle*, and generations of rustic Englishmen all seem determined to turn women into animals, Shakespeare's Oberon makes the *man* a beast and leaves his wife in her original form. Yet in either case the troping preserves a symmetry more important than any question of who gets to be the donkey this time, for all such transformations take as their immediate object the disparagement of the woman's identity. Hence Bottom's own personality remains outstandingly unimpaired throughout his interlude with Titania; indeed, a large part of his comic incongruity derives from the fact that his desires as beast—for headscratching, belly-cheer, and deferential service—remain so perfectly faithful to his human character. It is Titania, on the other hand,

8. Anne Clark, *Beasts and Bawdy* (London: J. M. Dent, 1975), p. 81.

9. Quoted in ibid., p. 81.

10. *Mankind*, pp. 234–35, in *Chief Pre-Shakespearean Dramas*, ed. Joseph Quincy Adams (Boston: Houghton Mifflin, 1924).

11. Ibid., p. 242.

whose humanity is more fundamentally impeached by the entire exchange, for she—not Bottom—clearly cannot distinguish a bestial love-object from a human one. In this sense, at least, Bottom's transformation happens more to Titania than to Bottom himself. The result is an ideological identity of interest between locally dissimilar animal transformations, all of which offer roughly the same moral: turning a woman into an animal degrades the woman, and turning a man into an animal also degrades the woman.

The insistency of this message betrays its overdetermination. Emerging again and again out of contradictory circumstances, it repeatedly figures sexual difference in ways that privilege the man. Yet by the same token, such figurations place male privilege itself in a position of dependence upon the humiliated, bestialized female other—without whom the concept of male sovereignty would not be thinkable and to whom it must therefore constantly refer for the invidious comparisons that lend it identity. Various theoretical models—among them the Marxist, feminist, psychoanalytic, and post-Saussurean—may arguably be invoked to account for this dependence, but it is not my intention to dwell upon any such model. Instead, I maintain that Renaissance bestiality texts typically concern themselves with exploring the boundaries of human character and that in the process these texts repeatedly encounter social distinctions—between man and woman, peer and commoner, virgin and pervert, and so forth—that interfere with the equally fundamental distinction between human and animal nature. The unilinear moralizing of Renaissance bestiality texts can never finally foreclose this interference; underlying the obsessive formulation of social difference is an unavoidable sense of human mixedness—an ontological catachresis—that simply will not go away. Yet, from the standpoint of the moralizing texts themselves, that is all the more reason for the moralizing to continue.

Thus, to use Harold Brooks's phrase, *A Midsummer Night's Dream* seems determined to construct men and women as "alien species,"[12] and as a result all of the play's romantic couplings are in an important sense zoophilic. Hermia refers to the ardent Demetrius as a "serpent" (III.ii.73), and in a much-discussed nightmare she envisions Lysander as "smiling" at her while another serpent eats away her heart

12. Harold F. Brooks, ed., *A Midsummer Night's Dream* (New York: Methuen, 1979), p. cxii.

(II.ii.144–50).[13] More suggestively still, Helena can thus represent
herself—in relation to her beloved Demetrius—as a dog:

> I am your spaniel; and, Demetrius,
> The more you beat me, I will fawn on you.
> Use me but as your spaniel; spurn me, strike me,
> Neglect me, lose me; . . . .
> What worser place can I beg in your love
> (And yet a place of high respect with me)
> Than to be used as you use your dog?

(II.i.203–10)

Helena's orgy of self-abasement finds its definitive expression as a
sinister kind of puppy love. Hence the erotic charge of her remarks,
which formulate her passion precisely as the state of being owned.
Demetrius' eventual marriage to Helena comments further upon
what it means to use a person "as you use your dog," for it is this very
marriage that consummates Helena's erotic wishes and rewards her
abject fidelity.

If, then, the moral of *A Midsummer Night's Dream* is that men should
sow their oats among the most alien of mares, this mixed metaphor
gains its ideal embodiment in the union of Theseus and Hippolyta.
Herself the mother-to-be of a mythic figure famous for preferring
horses to women,[14] Hippolyta is also preeminently an object to be
possessed; thus, as scholars regularly observe,[15] Theseus woos her

13. Norman N. Holland ("Hermia's Dream," in *Representing Shakespeare: New Psychoanalytic Essays*, ed. Murray M. Schwartz and Coppélia Kahn [Baltimore: Johns Hopkins
University Press, 1980], pp. 1–20) has commented upon the obviously phallic and
sexual quality of this dream, describing the serpent-image in Erik Erikson's terms as
"*intrusive* or *penetrating*" (p. 7) and hence as a figure of "violation" (p. 11). Marjorie B.
Garber (*Dream in Shakespeare: From Metaphor to Metamorphosis* [New Haven: Yale University Press, 1974]) has similarly associated the serpent with "violation and betrayal" as
well as "male sexuality" and has argued that Hermia "separates Lysander, the beloved,
from the serpent with whom she instinctively identifies him"—thus seeking to compen-
sate for her own sexual anxieties (pp. 72–73).

14. Harold Brooks has thoroughly catalogued the various sources and analogues of
A Midsummer Night's Dream (pp. lviii–lxxxviii), and has in the process pointed out that in
North's Plutarch—apparently the principal source for the story of Theseus and
Hippolyta—the Amazon queen is named Antiope. The name Hippolyta derives instead from Chaucer's *Knight's Tale*. Yet Brooks adds that Seneca's *Hippolytus* stands as a
major "neglected source" for Shakespeare's comedy (p. lxii) and thus could easily have
added a classical coloring to Shakespeare's choice of names.

15. Louis Adrian Montrose, "*A Midsummer Night's Dream* and the Shaping Fantasies
of Elizabethan Culture: Gender, Power, Form," in *Rewriting the Renaissance: The Dis-*

"with [his] sword" and wins her love by defeating her on the battlefield (I.i.16–17). As bride, Hippolyta becomes part of the spoils of
war, only problematically distinct from such booty as weapons, gold,
and horses; moreover, she relates to Theseus conspicuously through
the medium of hunting-animals. Thus she can kindle what at least
one reader regards as a spark of sexual jealousy in Theseus by talking
about a pack of hounds:[16]

> I was with Hercules and Cadmus once,
> When in a wood of Crete they bay'd the bear
> With hounds of Sparta. Never did I hear
> Such gallant chiding.
>
> (IV.i.112–15)

Theseus responds with a peevish and aggressively phallic description
of his own animals:

> My hounds are bred out of the Spartan kind;
> So flew'd, so sanded; and their heads are hung
> With ears that sweep away the morning dew;
> Crook-kneed, and dewlapp'd like Thessalian bulls;
> Slow in pursuit; but match'd in mouth like bells,
> Each under each. A cry more tuneable
> Was never hollow'd to, nor cheer'd with horn,
> In Crete, in Sparta, nor in Thessaly.
>
> (IV.i.119–26)

Theseus vies with Hippolyta's former male companions—Hercules
and Cadmus—through the medium of their hunting-dogs, and the
dogs themselves, their heads encompassed by great folds of skin and
their bodies dewlapped and bullish, serve implicitly as surrogates for
the male member. Mine are the same as Hercules' and Cadmus',
Theseus argues—only better.

Thus *A Midsummer Night's Dream* seems determined to construct its
various marital unions as analogues to (or extensions of, or coincident
with) the sexual conjunction of people and animals. Given the play's
peculiar discursive framework, zooerastia emerges as "integral to just

---

courses of Sexual Difference in Early Modern Europe, ed. Margaret Ferguson et al. (Chicago:
University of Chicago Press, 1986), pp. 70–71.

16. Brooks, *Dream*, p. civ.

those things it threatens,"[17] figured and refigured repeatedly within
the space of human domestic relations. Moreover, bestiality arguably
encompasses a large part of the play's overt eroticism; the spectacle of
Titania and Bottom embracing and sleeping together comes as close
to enacted sexual intercourse as any scene in Shakespearean comedy.
In short, *A Midsummer Night's Dream* takes pains to establish sexual
limits that it then transgresses, through metaphor and innuendo and
overt representation, as often as possible, and this act of transgression
constitutes a good measure of the play's appeal to its audience. In
overall effect, *A Midsummer Night's Dream* is a bit like a Protestant
marriage-manual constructed out of animal pornography.

SOME MONSTERS

Documented cases of bestiality are rare in early English records (Lawrence Stone's lengthy *Family, Sex and Marriage in England, 1500–1800*
does not mention a single one), but nonetheless they do occur. I have
assembled a quick survey of relevant court records in the Appendix to
this essay, and these records confirm the disciplinary rigor with which
animal sodomites were occasionally handled; however, the recorded
prosecutions acquire a literary/discursive character over and above
the administration of physical punishment. This is not to deny that
real people were tried, punished, and even executed for bestial buggery; they most certainly were. Yet the minuscule number of such
trials; the extreme inconsistencies of sentencing, which could range
from a virtual handslap from the church courts to hanging under the
common law; the massive contrast between the heated language of
Renaissance moralists and legal theorists and the trickle of prosecutions for buggery of any kind; and the occasional way in which bestiality charges were tacked on to other, more serious accusations as a kind
of judicially unnecessary lily-gilding—all these suggest that the rhetoric of bestiality was in some basic ways more important than the crime
itself. This investment in rhetoric becomes clearer when one thinks of
bestiality as being, in effect, a victimless crime; after all, in the absence
of a vengeful or abused human plaintiff, what can bestiality prosecutions possibly redress? The offended party would seem to be not an

17. Dollimore, "Perversion," p. 189.

individual human being but rather a kind of abstract linguistic principle of what human beings ought to be. To this extent, bestial buggery is a crime against ideas, not people.

As such, it elicits inevitable judicial displays, some of which culminate in the execution of the offending party. But the execution becomes largely subservient to the discourse that demands it, and indeed, as long as the discourse itself is satisfied through some ritual of exorcism or purgation, capital punishment may even be deemed unnecessary. The really important thing is not that a particular poor bugger be hanged, but that the judiciary apparatus be seen to work. To this extent, Renaissance buggery laws may parallel Jean-Christophe Agnew's sense of the function of the medieval marketplace; they comprise "a ritually defined threshold" of the human community,[18] a threshold that is progressively blurred by the "new liquidity" of Renaissance social/theatrical relations.[19] Court buggery records themselves are therefore overwhelmingly concerned with maintaining or reestablishing the threatened boundaries. In 1519, for instance, the ecclesiastical court presiding over Tetchwick, Buckinghamshire, reports that one Richard Mayne, a watercarrier, "joined himself carnally with a mare, and a certain Elizabeth Parsons noticed this and reported it."[20] The court records, which take care to describe the process of human intervention whereby the suspect was brought to justice, do not mention a penalty; but later in 1525, a certain William Franklin appeared "in the parish church of Brisley" in Norfolk, to answer the charge of "having had sexual intercourse with an animal."[21] In this case the defendant was found guilty, although he produced four testifiers in his defense; for punishment, he was ordered "to go in procession publicly, as a penance, and to offer a penny candle before the high image."[22]

Franklin's token penalty may or may not have been standard for such offenses; however, it is certainly out of keeping with the dire precept of Leviticus:

---

18. Jean-Christophe Agnew, *Worlds Apart: The Market and the Theater in Anglo-American Thought, 1550–1750* (Cambridge: Cambridge University Press, 1986), p. 32.

19. Ibid., p. 59.

20. Cited in *Before the Bawdy Court: Selections from Church Court and Other Records Relating to the Correction of Moral Offenses in England, Scotland, and New England, 1300–1800*, ed. Paul Hair (London: Elek, 1972), p. 147.

21. Ibid., p. 152.

22. Ibid.

If a man lies with a beast, he shall be put to death; and you shall kill the
beast.
If a woman approaches any beast and lies with it, you shall kill the
woman and the beast; they shall be put to death, their blood is upon
them.[23]

Thus the Catholic court's ruling also runs counter to the severe rhetoric of Puritans like Thomas Beard, whose *Theatre of Gods Judgements*
(1597) is roughly contemporary to *A Midsummer Night's Dream*:

It is not for nothing that the law of God forbiddeth to lie with a beast,
and denounceth death against them that commit this foule sinne: for
there have been such monsters in the world at sometimes, as we read in
Caelius and *Volterranus*, of one *Crathes* a sheepheard, that accompanied
carnally with a shee goat, but the Buck finding him sleeping, offended
and provoked with this strange action, ran at him so furiously with his
hornes, that hee left him dead vpon the ground.[24]

Beard's peasant, unlike William Franklin, suffers to the full extent of
the Mosaic law and, ironically, the vehicle for his punishment is a kind
of miraculous *deus ex capre*. Justice and piety emerge from the traditional animal symbol of lust, and Beard solemnly warns his readers
against fornicating with beasts, noting that "there have been such
monsters in the world at sometimes."

To this extent, of course, Beard is himself in the business of making
(or at least repackaging) monsters, and of retailing them to the highest bidder; thus the *Theatre of Gods Judgements* regales its readers with a
mind-numbing sequence of adulteries, murders, fornications, incests,
and rapes—as well as tyranny, sodomy, dancing, and playacting (this
last in a book that likens itself to a theater). Beard himself, despite the
lurid and muckraking quality of his work, seems more or less oblivi-
ous to the irony of his own position, and yet it is not nearly as distant
from that of William Franklin's judge as Beard himself might insist.
For Beard's own authority, as writer and as moralist, demands a steady
supply of William Franklins: of aberrations to be disciplined and
exposed and yet not really exterminated, but instead preserved in
discourse. Only thus—through the dynamics of what Kenneth Burke

23. *The Holy Bible: Revised Standard Version* (New York: New American Library,
1974), Leviticus 20.15–16.
24. Thomas Beard, *The Theatre of Gods Judgements: Or, A Collection of Histories Out of
Sacred, Ecclesiasticall and Prophane Authors* (London, 1597), sig. Aalv.

has called "pure persuasion"[25]—can Beard claim to be performing a necessary social service; his is a moral economy of monsters.

"My mistress with a monster is in love" (III.ii.6): Puck fixes Bottom with Beard's own favorite epithet for sexual deviants. Indeed Beard's sense of the term recalls an early parallel to the animal voyeurism of Oberon in *A Midsummer Night's Dream*. The Borgia Pope Alexander VI could enter popular myth as a libertine "who enjoyed nothing so much as watching with his daughter Lucrezia as horses copulated,"[26] and if this tale seems improbably removed from Shakespeare's England, consider its reappearance in Aubrey's *Brief Lives*, where it attaches not to a pope but rather to Mary Herbert, Countess of Pembroke:

> She was very salacious, and she had a Contrivance that in the Spring of the yeare, when the Stallions were to leape the Mares, they were to be brought before such a part of the house, where she had a *vidette* (a hole to peepe out at) to looke on them and please herselfe with their Sport; and then she would act the like sport herself with *her* stallions.[27]

Aubrey ends this passage by remarking that "one of [Mary Herbert's] great Gallants was Crooke-back't Cecill, Earl of Salisbury,"[28] known affectionately to James I as his spaniel; the anecdote thus transforms its female subject into the figurative lover of literal beasts and the literal lover of figurative beasts, more or less simultaneously. Moreover, the same gesture—a lewd peeping from out of the established moral and/or social center—occurs with greater complexity in a work like Donne's "Satyre IV." There the narrator laments his recent con-

25. Burke's discussion of pure persuasion (*A Rhetoric of Motives* [New York: Prentice-Hall, 1952]) is of considerable theoretical interest for a reading of such Puritan texts as Beard's *Theatre* and Philip Stubbes's *Anatomy of Abuses*. As Burke explains the term, "pure persuasion involves the saying of something, not for an extra-verbal advantage to be got by the saying, but because of a satisfaction intrinsic to the saying" (p. 269)—and yet it is a satisfaction, like that of Beard's tales, "always . . . embodied in the 'impurities' of advantage-seeking" (p. 285). This form of persuasion, Burke continues, betrays itself as a principle of "self-interference" (p. 272) or internal contradiction instituted so as to prolong the process of persuasion itself (p. 271). In effect, Burke posits a model of language that contradicts its own acknowledged material aims, and that does so—like Beard's *Theatre*—as a prior condition of its own existence.

26. David O. Frantz, *Festum Voluptatis: A Study of Renaissance Erotica* (Columbus: Ohio State University Press, 1989), p. 45.

27. John Aubrey, *Aubrey's Brief Lives*, ed. Oliver Lawson Dick (London: Secker and Warburg, 1949), p. 138.

28. Aubrey, *Brief Lives*.

versation with an obnoxious courtier: "A thing more strange, then on
Niles slime, the Sunne / E'r bred; . . . / A thing . . . / Stranger . . . /
Then Africks Monsters."29 Indeed, the source of this fellow's monstrosity is to a large extent the substance of Donne's own text: "Who
wasts in meat, in clothes, in horse, he notes; / Who loves Whores, who
boyes, and who goats" (127–28). The narrator himself stands "more
amas'd" at this discourse "then Circes prisoners" (129), and the poem
therefore fashions a moral diatribe out of its own latent voyeurism. In
effect, it ends up satirizing itself.

The bestial metamorphosis of Donne's narrator parallels the dynamics of Shakespeare's comedy. Donne's speaker in effect becomes
an animal—"more amas'd then Circes prisoners"—by attending to
the represented bestial behavior of others, and he then hands his
amazement on to his audience through yet another level of representation. Aubrey turns himself—and his readers—into a series of dupli-
cate Mary Herberts, peeking through the cracks of his text at the
original Mary Herbert peeking at her rutting horses. Likewise, Shakespeare's Oberon, himself the principal audience at a scene of bestial
transformation and misbehavior, constructs that bestiality as entertainment for another set of viewers entirely. In the process, both
Oberon and Donne's narrator (and, in a less aggressive way, Aubrey as
well) claim to represent the stabilizing influences of domestic order
and moral indignation; they are, as it were, doing the wrong thing for
the right reasons.

For William Franklin's judge, for Thomas Beard, for Aubrey, and
arguably even for Donne, the discourse of traditional morality runs
on despite—even because of—its own slippages, unperturbed by the
fact that it depends for its existence upon the very categories of behavior and of being that it seeks to extirpate. In Book VIII of *Paradise
Lost*, our grand forefather Adam is demonstrably smarter. He recognizes that something is wrong when the Son implicitly offers him
sexual companionship among the newly created animals—"with
mee / I see not who partakes"30—yet he also recognizes that the solution to his problem—Eve—is not really a solution at all. The difficulty

29. John Donne, *The Satires, Epigrams and Verse Letters*, ed. W. Milgate (Oxford:
Clarendon Press, 1967), Satyre IV, 18–22. Further citations are to this edition and
appear parenthetically in the text.

30. John Milton, *Paradise Lost* VIII.363–64, in *John Milton: Complete Poems and Major
Prose*, ed. Merritt Y. Hughes (New York: Odyssey Press, 1957). Further citations are to
this edition and appear parenthetically in the text.

with animals, after all, is that they are animals; they are inferior to Adam, having been constructed with internal deficiencies of mind and spirit that render them unsatisfactory as company or as mates:

> Among unequals what society
> Can sort, what harmony or true delight?
> Which must be mutual, in proportion due
> Giv'n and receiv'd . . . Of fellowship I speak
> Such as I seek, fit to participate
> All rational delight.
>
> (VIII.383–91)

Yet Eve's own composition as Adam's mate pushes her relentlessly into the category of the unequal, away from the rational delight that Adam needs her, by definition, to share:

> For well I understand in the prime end
> Of Nature her th'inferior, in the mind
> And inward Faculties, which most excel,
> In outward also her resembling less
> His image who made both.
>
> (VIII.540–44)

Adam does not make the claim in so many words, but remarks of this sort unfortunately tend to situate Eve in the animal kingdom— precisely where we discover her distant descendants Helena, Hermia, Hippolyta, and Titania. Small wonder that—as James Grantham Turner has recently illustrated—scriptural exegetes like Jakob Boehme sought to bestialize Eve still further by accusing her of sexual intercourse with the serpent.[31] Such efforts comprise the logical end-point of any rigorous attempt to hierarchize conjugal relations.

   How, then, does one mediate between the opposing claims of con-jugal companionship and patriarchal authority? This question in-forms the "irresolvable doubleness" that scholars such as Turner have seen "at the heart of Milton's apprehension of wedded love."[32] Adam, for whom Eve's status is constantly threatening to accelerate out of the order of the inferior and into that of the all-too-equal (while just as constantly threatening to decelerate from equal to animal), sees this

   31. James Grantham Turner, *One Flesh: Paradisal Marriage and Sexual Relations in the Age of Milton* (Oxford: Clarendon Press, 1987), p. 145.
   32. Turner, *One Flesh*, p. 286.

issue as a pressing one, and therefore he gives it pride of place at the
end of his conversation with Raphael. Acknowledging Eve's deficiencies, Adam still cannot help regarding her as "more than enough" of
himself, endowed with "too much of Ornament" (VIII.537–38); it is
as if there were something inherently excessive about her very character as a human being, some equal-but-unequalness that assailed
Adam's own personal integrity.

Raphael's advice on this point is remarkable, for it initiates the
order of language that this essay has been busily surveying. Use your
reason, he effectively counsels Adam; don't forsake it; keep it constantly on guard, elaborating, defining, affirming, and reaffirming
the differences that make you what you are; never stop doing this job,
for it is literally of your essence:

> [Nature] hath done her part;
> Do thou but thine, and be not diffident
> Of Wisdom, she deserts thee not, if thou
> Dismiss not her, when most thou need'st her nigh,
> By attributing overmuch to things
> Less excellent . . .
> 　　　　　　　　Weigh with [Eve] thyself;
> Then value.
>
> 　　　　　　　　　　　　　　　(VIII.561–71)

This exercise of "Wisdom"—as Raphael calls it—evolves within the
compass of a conversation, coextensively with the linguistic distinctions between man and woman and man and beast. Moreover, it involves a vigorous, ongoing projection of Adam's own deficiencies onto
Eve—pulling the man's own beastliness out of himself in order that he
may recognize it in the woman instead. If this process is at all suspended, male privilege evaporates; the man himself becomes the
beast, sunk in passion and ripe for the carnal blandishments of the
local fauna:

> If the sense of touch whereby mankind
> Is propagated seem such dear delight
> Beyond all other, think the same voutsaf't
> To Cattle and each Beast . . .
> 　　　　　　　　　　　　Love refines

The thoughts, and heart enlarges, hath his seat
In Reason, and is judicious, is the scale
By which to heav'nly Love thou may'st ascend,
Not sunk in carnal pleasure, for which cause
Among the Beasts no Mate for thee was found.

(VIII.579–94)

It is Adam's ceaseless responsibility to weed out the bestial pleasures in his human composition, and failure to do so will automatically promote his inferior and wife to the position of "Guide /
and Head" (IV.442–43).[33] In short, being a man—as opposed to a woman
or a beast—requires constant discursive police-work. Milton, concerned as always with preceding his historical predecessors, has here
created the great original of Renaissance morals critics, out-Bearding
Beard and outdoing Donne. In the process, he has paid the same
price the others have paid before him; he has constructed the immor-
al and bestial as intrinsic to the human male subject himself, requiring
continuous surveillance and ongoing exorcism.

Beyond *A Midsummer Night's Dream*, Shakespeare offers a further
perspective on the coupling of people with animals. For Falstaff in *The
Merry Wives of Windsor*, zooerastia supplies a model not just of heroic
but of godlike behavior; wearing a buck's head for his final ren-
dezvous with Mistresses Page and Ford, Falstaff justifies his appearance by invoking classical myth:

Now the hot-blooded gods assist me! Remember, Jove, thou wast a bull
for thy Europa, love set on thy horns. O powerful love, that in some
respects makes a beast a man; in some other, a man a beast. You were
also, Jupiter, a swan for the love of Leda. O omnipotent love, how near

---

33. Such bestial pleasures, of course, later form the basis for Adam and Eve's first
experience of fallenness; after their discovery of "Carnal desire" (IX.1013), the first
couple falls curiously silent—"as struck'n mute" (IX.1064). This muteness—testimony
to their bestial degradation—stands in specific contrast to the deceptive loquacity of the
serpent, which upsets Eve's ability to distinguish between human and animal forms:
"What may this mean? Language of Man pronounc't / By Tongue of Brute, and human
sense exprest?" (IX.553–54). Man and animal have thus traded places, as it were, on the
chain of being; Adam yields his ascendancy over nature (and Eve) by exchanging
Raphaelic "Wisdom" (whose principal index is speech) for "foul concupiscence"
(IX.1078). Then, as the consequences of his behavior emerge, Adam responds to them
in familiar fashion, seeking in turn to hand his bestiality on to Eve through the operations of metaphor: "Out of my sight, thou Serpent, that name best / Befits thee with
him leagu'd, thyself as false / And hateful" (X.867–69).

the god drew to the complexion of a goose! A fault done first in the form of a beast (O Jove, a beastly fault!) and then another fault in the semblance of a fowl—think on't, Jove, a foul fault! (V.v.2–11)

Such transformations, Falstaff reasons, betoken extraordinary passion, and thus—although they may constitute a "fault" to be chuckled over indulgently—they ultimately redound to the lover's credit. Mistress Ford continues the scene in a like vein by coincidentally mocking Falstaff's animal pillow-talk: "Sir John? art thou there, my deer? my male deer?" (V.v.16–17).

A Midsummer Night's Dream thus furnishes us with a king and semideity who acts like a peeping Tom with a taste for animal fornication. *The Merry Wives of Windsor,* by contrast, offers us a sodden, hornbedecked roué who justifies his antics in part by claiming that they are of royal and divine inspiration. In either case, as with Donne, Beard, and others, the audience is left with the fundamental problem of sorting out morality—of determining where a given social police-action ends and where the gratification of forbidden desire begins. And thus, despite their differences, Oberon and Falstaff comprise a rhetorical continuum: a society of those who claim to preserve the order of things by being above that order, and who resort to the most grossly dehumanizing of behavior in the name of human values such as love and domestic harmony. Theirs is, as Falstaff would put it, a beastly fault.

DEERLY DEFLOWER'D

"To bring in (God shield us!) a lion among ladies, is a most dreadful thing; for there is not a more fearful wild-fowl than your lion living; and we ought to look to't" (III.i.30–33): Bottom expresses tender concern for his audience's comfort at the upcoming ducal performance of *Pyramus and Thisbe,* and his concern takes immediate shape as an awareness of sexual difference. The lion threatens not men but "ladies"; and the obvious way to countervail this threat is, in effect, to make the lion act the part of a man:

Your lion . . . must speak through, saying thus, or to the same defect: "Ladies," or "Fair ladies, . . . If you think I come hither as a lion, it were pity of my life. No! I am no such thing; I am a man as other men are";

and there indeed let him name his name, and tell them plainly he is
Snug the joiner. (III.i.32–46)

Thus, while seeking to straighten out the relations between men and
women, Bottom's advice hopelessly confuses the relations between
people and animals. Starting with the assumption that his play *does*, in
fact, threaten to "bring in . . . a lion among ladies," Bottom's language foregrounds its own patent inability to keep species separate;
the lion is a "wild-fowl," and—in the mechanicals' arsy-varsy syntax—
the beast winds up declaring himself "a man *as other men are*" (my
italics). Bottom addresses a fictional audience of "Ladies," and urges
Snug to frame words to "the same defect" as his own; that "defect" is
coterminous with his own inability to conceive of men and women as
comprising a single race.

Snug follows Bottom's advice in a way that once again thoroughly
muddles the distinction between sex and species:

> You, ladies, . . .
> May now, perchance, both quake and tremble here,
> When lion rough in wildest rage doth roar.
> Then know that I as Snug the joiner am
> A lion fell, nor else no lion's dam.
>
> (V.i.219–24)

For the ladies, apparently, Snug threatens to assume the aspect of a
"lion fell"—at least as like as not. Yet Snug's attempt to distinguish
himself from his (other) dramatic character simply confuses matters
further by claiming that Snug, as Snug, *is* a lion; and Snug then ends
his explanation by triumphantly noting that otherwise he is no lion's
dam. Beginning with the earnest concern that an alien sex might
mistake him for an alien species, he ends up getting his own sex
wrong; and that is arguably because, by adopting the character of
another creature, his language has confused itself as to its own gender.

Given such repeated confusion, Bottom's words as Pyramus take on
a decidedly peculiar cast. "O dainty duck!" (V.i.281), he exclaims upon
discovering Thisbe's bloody mantle; and his language quickly assumes
the quality of a mock-heroic lament: "O, wherefore, Nature, didst
thou lions frame? / Since lion vile hath here deflowr'd my deer"
(V.i.291–92). If Nature has framed Snug as a lion, one might reason-

ably wonder, has it then framed Thisbe as a duck or a deer—or both? And given Bottom's persistent tendency to conflate differences of species with differences of gender, his ambivalent use of the verb "deflowr'd" seems fully preconditioned. For defloration in *A Midsummer Night's Dream* is almost by rule a thing done between total aliens: Athenian dukes and Amazon warriors, fairy queens and asses, men and their mares, lions and deer. As Stephen Greenblatt has remarked of another Shakespearean comedy, "Licit sexuality . . . depends upon a movement that deviates from the desired object straight in one's path toward a marginal object, a body one scarcely knows. Nature is an *unbalancing* act."[34]

Of all the mechanicals, Bottom is presented as the one with the greatest taste for acting. Flute, who apparently would like to play "a wand'ring knight" (I.ii.45) shrinks from the part of Thisbe: "Nay, faith; let me not play a woman; I have a beard coming" (I.ii.47–48). But Bottom is agreeable to the task and he promises to do it justice in his tone of voice: "And I may hide my face, let me play Thisbe too. I'll speak in a monstrous little voice, 'Thisne, Thisne!'" (I.ii.51–53). In short, he proposes to impersonate a woman by speaking monstrously; then he further confirms his passion for histrionics by offering to act the other monster in *Pyramus and Thisbe* as well—the lion: "Let me play the lion too. I will roar, that I will do any man's heart good to hear me" (I.ii.70–71). For Bottom, that is, femininity presupposes monstrosity, and thus the lion becomes the one character in the play with whom Thisbe has most in common; both require the hiding of one's face and form, both demand virtuoso modulations of voice and expression, and both provide outstanding opportunities for the display of one's theatrical skill. From an actor's (or at least *this* actor's) standpoint, the beast is the woman's perfect mate. It is an attitude Bottom shares with Oberon.

Hence Shakespeare's burlesque subplot supplies a running commentary on the concerns of the play's central characters, as well as on itself. At the heart of this commentary lies Bottom's animal transformation, which offers him a very real opportunity to speak "in a monstrous little voice" and also, coincidentally, to join with Titania as the star attraction in a fairy freak-show. Unable to distinguish between monsters and women, Bottom himself becomes a monster; and his

34. Stephen Greenblatt, *Shakespearean Negotiations: The Circulation of Social Energy in Renaissance England* (Berkeley: University of California Press, 1988), p. 68.

metatheatrical appearance as Pyramus—"A lover, that kills himself most gallant for love" (I.ii.23–24)—further deepens the irony of his situation by expanding its frame of reference. For while Shakespeare's audience watches Theseus, Hippolyta, and company watching Bottom, it in effect watches itself; the audience of *Pyramus and Thisbe* sees Bottom's folly without recognizing it as a part of *them*selves—that is, as a product of the very discursive practices whereby they maintain social order. Their ox is gored, their deer deflowered.

Separating the Men from the Goats

Peter Stallybrass and Allon White have advanced a powerful explanation for the relationship between low and high characters in *A Midsummer Night's Dream*. For Stallybrass and White, "the 'top' [of any social hierarchy] attempts to reject and eliminate the 'bottom' for reasons of prestige and status, only to discover . . . that the top *includes* that low symbolically, as a primary eroticized constituent of its own fantasy life."[35] Thus Shakespeare's wedding-couples signify their rejection of the Bottom repeatedly through the condescending in-jokes that punctuate the play-within-a-play. Yet Bottom himself emerges as a prerequisite to the very social discriminations that privilege the wedding-couples in the first place; he occupies the necessary place of the other without which Shakespeare's aristocrats could not begin to conceive of themselves as such. No quantity of in-jokes can sever this connection, nor can any quantity of male discipline deny the bestial/female other a controlling share in conventional models of "marital harmony . . . predicated upon the wife's obedience to her husband."[36]

This complex interdependence of high and low tends to wither in the hands of contemporary commentators, who like to replace it with

---

35. Peter Stallybrass and Allon White, *The Politics and Poetics of Transgression* (Ithaca: Cornell University Press, 1986), p. 5.

36. Montrose, "Shaping Fantasies," p. 70. Thus Robert Weimann (*Shakespeare and the Popular Tradition in the Theater: Studies in the Social Dimension of Dramatic Form and Function*, ed. Robert Schwartz [Baltimore: Johns Hopkins University Press, 1978]) also notes the degree to which *A Midsummer Night's Dream*'s aristocratic element is predicated upon "that which was naïve and down-to-earth in the folk mythology" (p. 196). The result, he argues, is a play that transforms both high and low rhetoric and traditions into "something totally new" (p. 196)—and, we might add, totally interconnected.

the now-famous containment-subversion debate. And indeed, the containment-subversion debate—which resolves ambiguities into a binary distinction between conservative Shakespeare and radical Shakespeare—has this to be said for it: it has become an academic social indicator in its own right, much like the in-jokes that Shakespeare's high characters bounce off Bottom. What kind of a Shakespeare critic you are (straight white male fake-radical, black lesbian real-revolutionary, or some awkward admixture of the two) has come very largely to depend upon where you stand on the question of Shakespeare's subversive potential. Leonard Tennenhouse thus argues that "the introduction of disorder into [A Midsummer Night's Dream] ultimately authorizes political authority,"[37] and that the ritual contest between order and disorder—between Oberon and Titania or Theseus and Hippolyta—may thus amount to little more than an affirmation of traditional social arrangements. Certainly the disciplinary character of the play's bestiality may lend itself to such interpretation. Yet, as C. L. Barber long ago observed, Shakespeare's play (and the clown subplot in particular) is pervaded by an acute "consciousness of the creative . . . act itself,"[38] and thus one may view the plot's traditionalisms as self-consciously ironic. From this second, competing standpoint, the element of bestiality in A Midsummer Night's Dream may perform a unique function, deploying biology against institutions (such as marriage and monarchy) that typically advertise themselves as natural and given. By equating social and sexual differences with difference of species, A Midsummer Night's Dream may contest the ultimate morality of class and gender distinctions; to this extent, the play conforms to Catherine Belsey's pro-subversion claim that "Shakespearean comedy can be read as . . . calling in question that set of relations . . . which proposes as inevitable an antithesis between masculine and feminine, men and women."[39]

These opposed positions have very nearly managed to monopolize recent discussion on the political character of Shakespeare's work. I disagree with both. So does Theodore Leinwand, who smartly re-

37. Leonard Tennenhouse, *Power on Display: The Politics of Shakespeare's Genres* (New York: Methuen, 1986), p. 74.

38. C. L. Barber, *Shakespeare's Festive Comedy: A Study of Dramatic Form and its Relation to Social Custom* (Princeton: Princeton University Press, 1959), p. 148.

39. Catherine Belsey, "Disrupting Sexual Difference: Meaning and Gender in the Comedies," in *Alternative Shakespeares*, ed. John Drakakis (New York: Methuen, 1985), p. 167.

marks that "it is a thorough falsification of historical processes to argue that subversion offers the only alternative to the status quo."[40] Where Stallybrass and White, on the one hand, would replace the containment-subversion model with one of conflicted interdependence, Leinwand on the other hand would substitute an ongoing process of negotiation whereby high and low figures accommodate and make use of each other more or less mutually, more or less all of the time, for more or less differing purposes. In both of these cases, one emerges with a considerably more complex (and therefore, perhaps, more disturbing) picture of Shakespeare than any that the containment-subversion dialectic can offer; as Leinwand maintains, "a heteroglot Bottom . . . better captures the Shakespeare function than does any univocal voicing."[41]

Shakespeare's bestiality in *A Midsummer Night's Dream* resolutely resists critical attempts at univocal characterization; the play's weird, hybrid sexiness—or more important, the scariness of its sexiness—has never been effectively foreclosed by efforts at interpretation. To this extent, Shakespeare problematizes the standard Renaissance judicial approach to bestial sexuality, which relies upon clear distinctions between the natural and the perverse, the bidden and the forbidden, and which thus tends to obfuscate the very discursive conditions that make it possible in the first place. As Alan Bray has observed in his book on Renaissance homosexuality (an offense that Renaissance law elided with bestiality under the common name of buggery), individuals did not tend to recognize their own acts as perverse; perversity was always the province of the other, not of the subject in society.[42] Shakespeare's Oberon might have been created especially to illustrate the point. Indeed, by following the discourse of sexual difference to its logically dehumanizing end, *A Midsummer Night's Dream* creates a world in which it is impossible to separate the men from the goats, or the goats from the audience.

The consequent ambiguity is best embodied in the protean figure of Puck, who encompasses all shapes but holds to no proper shape himself, and who thus furthers yet another of Oberon's Borgia-like voyeuristic entertainments:

40. Theodore B. Leinwand, "Negotiation and New Historicism," *Publications of the Modern Language Association of America* 105 (1990): 479.

41. Leinwand, "Negotiation and New Historicism," p. 487.

42. Alan Bray, *Homosexuality in Renaissance England* (London: Gay Men's Press, 1982), pp. 67–70.

> I jest to Oberon and make him smile
> When I a fat and bean-fed horse beguile,
> Neighing in likeness of a filly foal.
>
> (II.i.44–46)

In a passage such as this, distinctions of biological category are buried almost as deeply as the sexual element itself. Puck—who is after all not a man, although he appears to the audience in a human shape— becomes the perfect similitude of a "filly foal," luring its mare (or perhaps its stallion—as assumed by at least one nineteenth-century theater director)[43] forward to a consummation that is specifically Oberon's and that parallels the misrecognition of species. It is a jest that Puck repeats at large for the play's audience, when he both "follow[s]" and "lead[s]" (III.i.106) the mechanicals "through bog, through bush, through brake, through brier" (III.i.107): "Sometime a horse I'll be, sometime a hound, / A hog, a headless bear" (III.i.108–9). These, for him and his master, are apparently the shapes of pleasure.

"O happy horse,"—as another of Shakespeare's characters might put it—"to bear the weight of Oberon!" Puck's multiform services for Oberon depend repeatedly upon his ability to transgress limits—of gender, species, class, and even shape itself. To this extent Oberon's own capacity to maintain order—including husbandly authority in marriage and royal authority in the state—relies upon the violation of those very kinds of order he himself constructs. As Stallybrass and White observe, "the result is a mobile, conflictual fusion of power, fear and desire in the construction of subjectivity: a psychological dependence upon precisely those Others which are being rigorously opposed and excluded at the social level."[44] In a word, the result is Puck.

If, then, the containment-subversion model asks readers of *A Midsummer Night's Dream* to choose between Theseus and Bottom, traditional patriarchalism or carnivalesque misrule, I would decline both options in favor of Puck. Admittedly, a Puckish Shakespeare is an uncomfortable Shakespeare; it deprives readers of social and ideological certainty, just as Puck himself (itself?) deprives the young lovers and bumbling mechanicals of confident knowledge about what is

---

43. Thus Charles Shattuck (*Shakespeare on the American Stage: From Booth to Sothern and Marlowe*, 3 vols. [Washington, D.C.: Folger Books, 1987], 2:71) notes that Augustin Daly's 1888–96 productions of *A Midsummer Night's Dream* "did *not* include a fat and bean-fed horse beguiling a filly foal [*sic*] with sexy neighing"; this passage and others were expurgated in the interest of decency.

44. Stallybrass and White, *Transgression*, p. 5.

going on around them. Such a Shakespeare—and such a Shakespearean character—gains force and complexity from the persistent
refusal to identify with a single binary term (human, male, conservative, traditional, moral) at the expense of its opposite. For this playwright, the inside is always the outside, and vice versa; he toys with the
slippages—between woman and beast, for instance, or man and
monster—that ground the system of meaning of which he is a part.
He does so not for specifically disruptive or subversive purposes, nor
yet against them, but rather because it is only through such toying—
and such slippages—that the system ever emerges (or recedes).

The resulting Shakespeare is neither unambiguously conservative
nor unquestionably radical, but complexly and unremittingly compromised. His work, in this sense, becomes a textual analogue for the
processes of bestial copulation that this essay has been about: a com-
posite figure that blends from conservative into radical and back
again, from human being into goat, in an incessant pattern of statement and self-interference. If *A Midsummer Night's Dream* supplies a
particularly acute instance of this process, it is because this play dwells
so centrally upon the imbricated issues of class and gender difference;
its running metaphorical equations of low class, low gender, and low
species eventually leave its characters with no real avenue for unimpaired commerce with others. In short, the play gives itself and its
audience no place in which to be finally and unambiguously human; it
attests to what Stephen Orgel has called "the radical instability of our
essence."[45] Shakespeare's comedy thus denies us the certitude—
about who we are, and about what it means to be us—that Renaissance disciplinary texts on perversion uniformly, naïvely, and necessarily presuppose.

Appendix
Bestiality and the Law in Renaissance England

The church-court case of William Franklin cited earlier in this essay
certainly is not typical of Elizabethan and Jacobean prosecutions for
bestiality (or "buggery," as it is called in sixteenth- and seventeenth-

---

45. Stephen Orgel, "Nobody's Perfect: Or Why Did the English Stage Take Boys for
Women?" *South Atlantic Quarterly* 88 (1989): 16.

century legal records). On the contrary, during the Tudor period the English legal system expended a great amount of theoretical effort to remove buggery from the church-court purview and into that of the secular magistrate. Thus, as part of its attack on the papacy, Henry VIII's Parliament of 1533 declared "the detestable and abhomynable vice of buggery committed with mankynde or beaste" to be a felony without benefit of clergy and carrying an automatic death penalty.[46] As B. R. Burg has observed, this act was an integral part of Henry's expansion of royal authority,[47] and as such it affords a prime instance of what I have called the rhetorical character of buggery laws. Created more to affirm the royal supremacy than to prosecute sodomites, the Henrician buggery statute's main job was, in effect, to make a political point; hence it was predictably rescinded under Mary and reenacted under Elizabeth. In the process, bestiality came to be formally regarded as "confusion of the natural order,"[48] and thus Coke claims in the third part of his *Institutes* that "Buggery is a detestable and abominable sin, amongst Christians not to be named, . . . against the ordinance of the Creator and order of nature."[49]

Yet this fearsome rhetoric is not accompanied by any demonstrable obsession with buggery in Renaissance legal practice itself; buggery cases under Elizabeth I and James I are numerically insignificant. Bruce Smith rightly observes that prosecutions for homosexuality were far less frequent than for bestiality, and he notes that the assize records for Kent during the reign of Elizabeth list only two indictments for homosexual behavior out of approximately three thousand—"about .07 percent."[50] Against this minute quantity, the ten cases of bestiality listed in the same volume may seem a lot, but they still comprise only 0.3 percent of the overall records. Clearly courts were not much exercised by either offense.

For the reigns of Elizabeth I and James I, I have been able to

46. *Statutes at Large From the First Year of King Edward the Fourth To the End of the Reign of Queen Elizabeth* (London: King's Printer, 1786–1866), 25 Henry VIII, c.6. Also see 28 Henry VIII, c.6; 31 Henry VIII, c.7; 32 Henry VIII, c.3; 2 and 3 Edward VI, c.29; 1 Mary, c.1; and 5 Elizabeth, c.17.

47. B. R. Burg, "Ho Hum, Another Work of the Devil: Buggery and Sodomy in Early Stuart England," *Journal of Homosexuality* 6 (1980–81): 70.

48. Caroline Bingham, "Seventeenth-Century Attitudes toward Deviant Sex," *Journal of Interdisciplinary Study* 1 (1970–71): 447.

49. Edward Coke, *The Third Part of the Institutes of the Laws of England: Concerning High Treason, and Other Pleas of the Crown and Criminal Causes* (London, 1660), sig. I3v.

50. Bruce Smith, *Homosexual Desire in Shakespeare's England: A Cultural Poetics* (University of Chicago Press, 1991), p. 48.

Table 4.1. Indictments for bestial buggery in the reigns of Elizabeth I and James I

	Elizabeth I	James I	Combined
Cases	31	9	40
Convictions	18	2	20
Acquittals	9	7	16[a]

Sources: Calendar of Assize Records (London: Her Majesty's Stationery Office, 1980), Elizabeth I, vols. 1–5, James I, vols. 1–5; *Middlesex County Records*, ed. John Cordy Jeaffreson (Clerkenwell: Middlesex County Records Society, n.d.), vol. 1; *County of Middlesex: Calendar to the Sessions Records*, ed. William Hardy (London: C. W. Radcliffe, 1937), n.s. vol. 3.

[a] In four cases—all Elizabethan—the accused is listed as still at large or as having died before sentencing.

identify forty cases of bestiality handled by the secular authorities (no indictments appear in church court records for the same period). The aggregate character of these cases is illustrated in Table 4.1, and although Alan Bray correctly observes that "any statistical analysis [of this material] is out of the question,"[51] the following points are still perhaps worth noting. First, given that Elizabeth's reign was roughly twice as long as James's, the available records include about 33 percent more indictments for bestiality in the Elizabethan years than in the Jacobean. And second, the proportion of convictions to acquittals is spectacularly higher in Elizabeth's reign than in James's, comprising a ratio of 2 to 1 as opposed to a ratio of 1 to 3.5. Further, Table 4.2 demonstrates that horses (and, to a lesser degree, cattle) were easily the favorite objects of abuse in these cases. (Buggery indictments scrupulously document the species, color, and owner of the maltreated beast.)

Finally, it is perhaps worth returning from these figures, and the generally blasé attitude they inscribe, to the lurid rhetoric that Renaissance authors invariably attached to bestiality—and that regularly associates such misconduct with women. The late Stuart pamphlet *Ravillac Redivivus* (1671), for instance, describes as follows the behavior of Thomas Weir, Mayor of Edinburgh during the Interregnum: having seduced his sister when he was ten and lived with her incestuously thereafter, the violently anti-royalist Weir had also "had sexual intercourse with cows and mares, and especially with one of his mares, upon which he once rode to New Mills."[52] Again, Alan Bray

51. Bray, *Homosexuality*, p. 40.
52. Quoted in Ivan Bloch, *A History of English Sexual Morals*, trans. William H. Forstern (London: Francis Aldor, 1936), p. 461.

Table 4.2. Animals abused in English Renaissance
bestiality indictments

	Number	Percentage
Sows	3	7.5
Sheep	1	2.5
Dogs	1	2.5
Cattle	13	32.5
Mares	20	50
Unspecified	2	5

Sources: same as Table 4.1.

has noted the passage in Marston's *Scourge of Villainy* in which a young voluptuary, deprived of his mistress, replaces her with a "perfumed she-goat."[53] And finally, Coke explains in his *Institutes* that the original Henrician act declaring buggery to be a felony was occasioned because "a great Lady had committed Buggery with a Baboon, and conceived by it, etc."[54] Clearly the main work performed by Renaissance English attacks on buggery was discursive, rather than material, in nature.

53. Quoted in Bray, *Homosexuality*, p. 16.
54. Coke, *Institutes*, sig. I4r.

5

News from the New World

Miscegenous Romance in Aphra Behn's *Oroonoko* and *The Widow Ranter*

MARGARET FERGUSON

Boy.   Our curl'd embraces shall delight
            To checquer limbs with black and
            white.
Nymph.   Thy inke, my paper, make me guesse,
            Our Nuptiall bed will prove a Presse;
            And in our sports, if any come,
            They'l read a wanton Epigram. . . .

                    —JOHN CLEVELAND,
                "A Fair Nimph scorning
          a Black Boy Courting her," 1647

Once Cromwell snatched Jamaica from the Spaniards in 1655 and the end of . . . the Civil War signalled England's wholehearted participation in the slave trade, the purity of the national bloodstream could not be maintained.

                    —FOLARIN SHYLLON,
             Black People in Britain
                1555–1833, 1977

Many students and colleagues have helped with the research for and writing of this essay. I am particularly grateful to Anthony Barthelemy, Catherine Gallagher, John Guillory, Richard Halpern, Ann R. Jones, Joseph Loewenstein, David Lee Miller, Karen Newman, Sharon O'Dair, Mary Poovey, David Simpson, and Harold Weber.

Born sometime in the 1640s, Aphra Behn died in April 1689, shortly after a "Glorious Revolution" she deplored. In the years just before her death, she wrote the two texts I focus on here, texts that seek to dramatize, and profit from, exotic "news" from the new world. The news derives, explicitly in one text, implicitly in the other, from an experience Behn herself claimed to have had in the British colony of Surinam when she was a young woman. The texts in question—a drama titled *The Widow Ranter, or the History of Bacon in Virginia* (probably written in 1687 or 1688, but first performed in November 1689, after Behn's death, and published the following year) and a novella called *Oroonoko, or the Royal Slave* (1688)—transpose elements of Shakespeare's *Othello* to a New World setting.[1] In each text, a male hero kills a beloved and virtuous woman before colluding in his own death. In both texts, Behn at once explores and mystifies the moral ambiguities of England's early imperial venture;[2] she does so in part by dramatizing the romantic death of a non-white heroine with whom she obscurely identifies, while identifying more clearly with the male hero she endows with kingly virtues that are vastly undervalued by the English colonists. By the late 1680s an ardent if by no means uncritical supporter of the Stuarts,[3] Behn weaves a complex strand of domestic royalist ideology into her portrait of these two male heroes, one white and one black, whose tragedies unfold abroad.

In both texts, the hero behaves and is characterized in ways that make him politically labile, indeed overdetermined with reference to

1. I discuss Behn's use of motifs from *Othello, Titus Andronicus*, and Restoration versions of both dramas in "Transmuting Othello: Aphra Behn's *Oroonoko*," in *Cross-Cultural Performances: Differences in Women's Re-Visions of Shakespeare*, ed. Marianne Novy (Urbana: University of Illinois Press, 1993), pp. 15–49. I thank Ann Lowry, editor at the University of Illinois Press, for granting me permission to reuse some materials from this essay.

2. For useful summaries of the early history of English imperialism, see Eric Williams, *From Columbus to Castro: The History of the Caribbean, 1492–1969* (New York: Random House, 1984), chap. 1, and Laura Brown, "The Romance of Empire: *Oroonoko* and the Trade in Slaves," in *The New Eighteenth Century: Theory, Politics, English Literature*, ed. Felicity Nussbaum and Laura Brown (New York: Methuen, 1987), pp. 40–61.

3. Though critics regularly insist on Behn's Tory politics—and note that a number of her plays from the period of the Exclusion Crisis are highly propagandistic—her political views in the 1660s, when she went to Surinam, cannot simply be assumed to have been identical with those she held twenty years later; moreover, even in the 1680s, her obvious sympathies with the Stuart absolutists did not preclude her from criticizing James's incompetence in the period just before he lost his throne; see Sara Heller Mendelson, *The Mental World of Stuart Women* (Brighton: Harvester, 1987), p. 174, for a discussion of Behn's satire, titled "Caesar's Ghost," on James's 1686 Hounslow Heath encampment.

any topical allegory. Though modern critics have almost all read Oroonoko straightforwardly as a royalist hero and, more specifically, as a
figure for the martyred Charles II and for the soon-to-be-deposed
James II, this reading neglects the fact that Oroonoko rebels against a
villainous tyrant figure—William Byam, who was historically a rabid
Royalist. He was opposed, according to the historical record and in
Behn's novella as well, to Behn's family and to one of the characters
she treats admiringly, Colonel George Martin, "brother to the great
Oliverian," as she describes him (p. 50)—that is, to the regicide Henry
Martin.[4] The hero of *The Widow Ranter*, Nathaniel Bacon, is also a
profoundly ambiguous political figure: he oscillates between a position resembling that of a Cromwellian rebel justly resisting tyranny
and the position of a kingly figure whose crass subjects (riffraff of the
Good Old Cause) fail to recognize his superior abilities to rule.[5]

4. I am indebted for this point to Sara Mendelson, *Mental World*, p. 120; alone
among the scholars I've read, she comments on the "unexpected" Republican perspective that pervades (I wouldn't follow her in assuming it governs) the novella—
unexpected because Behn had become a "fanatical royalist" only two years after the
events of *Oroonoko* took place. It seems to me, however, that Mendelson oversimplifies
the question of the novella's political allegory (or rather, I'm arguing, its overlapping
allegories). She explains the Republicanism of the story—written in 1688, long after
Behn had "matured" into Tory views—as a function simply of her youth and the fact
that her lover, a man named William Scot who does not appear (as such) in the narrative, was an exiled Republican and son of a regicide.

5. The historical Bacon, characterized in the *Strange News* pamphlets as an appeal-
ing but finally culpable example of rebellion against true royal authority, has often been
read as a Republican hero, especially by North American scholars who see in Bacon's
Rebellion a prototype of the American Revolution and in Bacon a forerunner of
George Washington, as Wilber Henry Ward remarks ("Mrs. Behn's *The Widow Ranter*:
Historical Sources," *South Atlantic Bulletin* 41 [1976]: 94–98). See also Anne Witmer and
John Freehafer, "Aphra Behn's Strange News from Virginia," *Library Chronicle* 34
(Winter 1968): 7–23, for an argument that Bacon is a figure for Behn's Republican
lover William Scot (esp. pp. 19–20). No one, to my knowledge, has suggested that a
different political valence attaches to Bacon in Behn's play, but the similarities between
Oroonoko and Bacon suggest that both may allude to Stuart kings. In both texts, a
legitimate exerciser of royal authority is absent from the scene, even though Behn had
to alter the historical record to create that absence in *Ranter*. The play substitutes an
incompetent and fictitious interim governor, Wellman, who is aided by a council of
"rifraff" and dunces, for the actual legitimate governor Sir William Berkeley, thus
offering a parallel to the situation in *Oroonoko* where the colony is ruled by the corrupt
Byam in the absence of the (always awaited) true governor (Willoughby, according to
the historical record). Both texts thus figure the Interregnum government in the corrupt colonial government awaiting the "Restoration" of a true king. The political complexities of these texts arise in part from the fact that both were written in the late 1680s
about colonial experiences of the 1660s when battles fought in England during the
1640s and 1650s were being "replayed"—and constantly reinterpreted—in the colonies. As Harold Weber has astutely observed in a letter to me (October 25, 1991), those

As the complexity of the political allegory suggests, both of Behn's "American" texts embellish materials drawn from recent British history to brush sometimes with, sometimes against the grain of common British ideologies, including not only those of the emergent Whig and Tory factions but also those that linked skin colors and moral— especially sexual—proclivities. In so doing, both texts at once exploit and interrogate a strand of distinctly imperialist ideology woven into the complex cultural image of the female author as an "outsider"—a social anomaly at best, a "public" woman or whore (a role often associated with "blackness") at worst. Aspects of Behn's deviant role as female author, I contend, are explored in her treatment of noble heroes misunderstood and undervalued by the English colonial society.

In *The Widow Ranter*, set in Jamestown, the hero's character as a leader of a rebellion in Virginia in 1675–76 is based (loosely) on a pamphlet account of a historical rebellion led by Nathaniel Bacon. Printed in 1667 by William Harris, the pamphlet is titled *Strange News from Virginia, Being a Full and True Account of the Life and Death of Nathaniel Bacon, Esquire, Who was the only Cause and Original of all the late Troubles in that Country. . . .*[6] Behn's Bacon, unlike his pamphlet counterpart, has romantic as well as military adventures. In *Oroonoko*,

---

critics who find in Behn's phrase describing the ultimately tortured Oroonoko as a "mangled King" evidence for a straightforward identification between Oroonoko and Charles II may well be oversimplifying the shocking volatility of such a representation even within royalist ideology. Weber writes: "Charles, as Clark Hulse has suggested [at the Symposium where this paper was first presented], was not the only mangled martyr of the civil war"; Cromwell himself was vilified in terms that clearly anticipate Behn's (and many other contemporary writers') descriptions of "disciplined and punished" bodies: for example, Weber cites the anonymous pamphlet *England's Triumph. A More Exact History of His Majesties Escape After the Battle of Worcester* (London, 1660, pp. 93–94).

6. For a description of this six-page pamphlet and its brief sequel, *More News from Virginia*, published later in the same year again by William Harris, see Bertha Monica Stearns, "The Literary Treatment of Bacon's Rebellion in Virginia," *The Virginia Magazine of History and Biography* 52 (July 1944): 163–79, and also Witmer and Freehafer, "Aphra Behn's Strange News From Virginia," cited above. Both pamphlets are reprinted in *Bacon's Rebellion: The Contemporary News Sheets*, ed. Harry Finestone (Charlottesville: University Press of Virginia, 1956). See also the articles by Charles L. Batten, Jr., "The Source of Aphra Behn's *The Widow Ranter*," *Restoration and 18th Century Theatre Research* 13 (May 1974): 12–18, and by Wilber Henry Ward, "Mrs. Behn's *The Widow Ranter*." Both articles argue that Behn must have read, in addition to the *Strange News* pamphlets, the long report by the King's Commissioners titled "A True Narrative of the Rise, Progresse, and Cessation of the Late Rebellion in Virginia" (submitted to the Crown in 1677 and reprinted in *Narratives of Early American History Narratives of the Insurrections: 1675–1690*, ed. Charles M. Adams [New York: Scribner's Sons, 1915]). Though the evidence is intriguing, these articles would be more persuasive if they dealt

the hero is also based on a historical personage, at least if we accept Behn's statement that she herself met him during her youthful sojourn in the then-British colony of Surinam in 1663–64.[7] This hero, whose name intriguingly recalls the South American river (Orinoco) mentioned by Sir Walter Ralegh in his *Discoverie of the Large, Rich, and Beautiful Empire of Guiana*, is characterized by Behn as an "ebony" prince born in Coramantian, on Africa's Gold Coast;[8] he is ignobly entrapped by a lying British slave captain and transported to Surinam just when Behn says she arrived there with her mother and sister. Her (putative) father, who was to assume the Lieutenant-Governorship of the colony, had died en route.

KEY CONTEXTS

Oroonoko and *The Widow Ranter* intersect in complex ways with narratives that exist at various levels of the social formation, and I shall

with the empirical problem of how Behn might have seen such a source. Ward doesn't cite Batten's article but does note that his conclusion parallels that of Kay B. Dennison, "Sources for Aphra Behn's *The Widow Ranter*" (Master's thesis, North Carolina Central University, 1971).

7. Scholars differ substantially on the dating (and duration) of Behn's Surinam visit. Most now agree that it occurred between early fall, 1663, and February or March, 1664: that is, sometime after Lord Willoughby's receipt on June 16, 1663, of a royal patent granting him the power to appoint various deputies among whom was Behn's (putative) father; and before the deputy governor of Surinam, William Byam (who was promoted to the position of lieutenant general that was to have been held by Behn's father), wrote a letter (dated March 14, 1664) to Robert Harley describing his relief at Behn's departure. See Angeline Goreau, *Reconstructing Aphra: A Social Biography of Aphra Behn* (New York: Dial, 1980), pp. 49–69, and, for a slightly different set of "facts," Sara Mendelson, *Mental World*, p. 118. Mendelson doesn't comment on the fact that her dates make Behn's visit no more than a month long (from January to February 1664)— as implausibly short a time as Elaine Campbell's hypothesis of a six-year sojourn seems implausibly long (Campbell, "Aphra Behn's Surinam Interlude," *Kunapipi* 7 [1985]: 23–35).

8. Oroonoko could well be a Yoruba name, according to my colleague Adéléke Adéèko, but it also evokes the name of the river that Ralegh describes in his *Discoverie*; he spells the name in various ways including "Orenoque." Ralegh's text, first published in 1596 and reissued in three editions that year, was even more widely read after it was reprinted in the second edition of Richard Hakluyt's *Principal Navigations . . .* (1600). This text is available in the modern edition of the *Navigations* by Walter Raleigh, 12 vols. (Glasgow: J. Maclehose, 1903–5, rpt. 1969), 10:338–41. I am indebted for bibliographical information and for my general understanding of Ralegh's *Discoverie* both as "text" and as "event" (the published work includes in its full title the phrase *Performed in the yeere 1595*) to Louis Montrose, "The Work of Gender in the Discourse of Discovery," *Representations* 33 (Winter 1991): 1–41. See also Joyce Lorimer, "Ralegh's First Reconnaissance of Guiana? An English Survey of the Orinoco in 1587," *Terrae Incognitae* 9 (1977): 7–21.

begin by outlining several of these large contextual narratives which
bear on my interpretation of Behn's two New World texts. These
contextual narratives point to sets of (changing) social facts we can
only partially reconstruct. The partiality of our knowledge of such
facts is strikingly evident in biographical contextual narratives. If the
facts about Aphra Behn's life continue to be the subject of speculation
and dispute, that is partly because she herself contributed to the biographical narrative(s) in ways that show her to have been an adroit
self-fashioner. Like Daniel Defoe, she "counterfeited" herself in many
ostensibly autobiographical moments, and she did so by means of a
pen with which she famously said she was "forced" to use to earn her
bread—"and [was] not ashamed to owne it."[9] It was clearly to her
advantage to represent herself as belonging to the gentry, though she
may well have been humbly born or even illegitimate.[10] In *Oroonoko*,
she represents herself as the daughter of a "gentleman" with connections to the powerful Lord Willoughby. The gentleman, surnamed
Johnson, was very probably her adoptive rather than natural father,
and in any case he left her without a dowry when he died in 1663,
during a voyage with his family to Surinam.[11] Whatever the facts of

9. This and all subsequent quotations from Behn's plays are from *The Works of Aphra Behn*, ed. Montague Summers (1915; rpt. New York: Phaeton, 1967), 6 vols; 4:7.

10. According to Behn's anonymous first biographer, she was a "Gentlewoman, by Birth, of a good Family in the City of Canterbury, in Kent" (*On the Life of Mrs. Behn, Written by a Gentlewoman of her Acquaintance*, in *Histories and Novels* [London: printed for S. Briscoe, 1696], sig. A7v, quoted from the British Library Copy, Wing B1711). In the late 19th century, Sir Edmund Gosse argued for lowering Behn's social status on the evidence of a scribbled note, "Mrs. Behn was daughter to a barber," in the margin of a newly discovered manuscript by Anne Finch, the Countess of Winchelsea. Goreau gives an account of Gosse's "discovery" (given authority in his *Dictionary of National Biography* article on her) and subsequent biographical arguments in *Reconstructing Aphra*, pp. 8–10. Acknowledging the scanty and conflicting evidence about Behn's origins, Goreau herself proposes that Behn was the illegitimate daughter of Lady Willoughby, whose husband held the Governorship of Surinam; this theory helps explain why one 17th-century source describes Behn's mother as a "wetnurse" (illegitimate children of upper-class parents were often deposited with wetnurses) and also helps account for the problematic description of Behn as the "adopted" daughter of a man named Johnson, a relative of Lord Willoughby whom the latter appointed his lieutenant governor of Surinam. Behn's other major recent biographer, Maureen Duffy, arrives at very different conclusions about the evidence: in *The Passionate Shepherdess: Aphra Behn, 1640–89* (London: Jonathan Cape, 1977), chap. 1, Duffy argues that Behn's real parents were Bartholomew Johnson, a yeoman, and Elizabeth, née Denham, who was the daughter of a "gentleman." For further discussions of the mystery of Behn's birth and the manifold speculations it has engendered, see Sara Mendelson, *Mental World*, pp. 116–20, and Mary Ann O'Donnell, *Aphra Behn: An Annotated Bibliography of Primary and Secondary Sources* (New York: Garland, 1986), pp. 2–3.

11. For information about the evidence for Behn's trip to Surinam, see O'Donnell,

Behn's birth or of the trip to Surinam, there is no doubt that her education was more determinative of her social status than her blood-lines were.[12] Although she lacked both Latin and Greek—and lamented that women in her society had less access to education than men—her ability to read and write English, as well as several other European languages including French and Dutch, nonetheless allowed her to earn a living, albeit never a stable one.[13] After working for several years as a spy in the Netherlands for Charles II, during which time she perhaps met and married a Dutch merchant whose

---

Aphra Behn: An Annotated Bibliography, p. 3; and see also Campbell, "Aphra Behn's Surinam Interlude," pp. 25–35.

12. For the view that Behn never really went to Surinam but rather plagiarized her descriptions of the colony from Warren's text, see Ernest Bernbaum, "Mrs. Behn's Biography a Fiction," *Publications of the Modern Language Association of America* 28 (1913): 432–53. Goreau and other recent literary historians have convincingly discredited Bernbaum's theory, citing documents by contemporaries, including William Byam, the "villain" of *Oroonoko*, which testify—sometimes testily—to Behn's presence in the colony. See Goreau, pp. 12–13, for a discussion of how Aphra's education constitutes a strong objection to the theory that a lower-class girl might have been simply "adopted" by a gentry family; "a possible exception to this rule of class might have been an illegitimate child passed off as a relative of some sort."

13. See Behn's "*To Mr. Creech (under the name of Daphnis) on his Excellent Translation of Lucretius*," in which she describes herself as "unlearn'd in Schools," a victim of her birth, her education, and "the scanted Customes of the Nation" that don't permit "the Female Sex to tread, / The Mighty Paths of Learned Heroes dead." She then wittily alludes to Milton's (in)famous characterization of Eve falling because of her ambition to equal Adam through the acquisition of forbidden knowledge:

> The God-like *Virgil*, and great *Homers* Verse,
> Like Divine Mysteries are conceal'd from us.
>   We are forbid all grateful Theams,
> No ravishing thoughts approach our Ear . . .
>   [until Creech comes]
>
>   .   .   .
> . . . by this Translation . . . [to] advance
> Our Knowledge from the State of Ignorance,
> And equals us to Man!
>   (*Works*, 6:166–67)

For an interesting discussion of these lines, see Jessica Munns, "'I By a Double Right Thy Bounties Claim': Aphra Behn and Sexual Space," *Curtain Calls: British and American Women and the Theater, 1660–1820*, ed. Mary Anne Schofield and Cecilia Macheski (Athens: Ohio University Press, 1991), pp. 193–210, esp. pp. 203–4. The best account of how she earned her living is by Catherine Gallagher in her book *British Women Writers and the Literary Marketplace from 1680 to 1820* (New York: Oxford University Press, forthcoming). Professor Gallagher has kindly allowed me to read these chapters in draft, and my subsequent page references are to the manuscript; a version of one of the chapters, on Behn's plays, titled "Who Was that Masked Woman? The Prostitute and the Playwright in the Comedies of Aphra Behn," has been published in *Last Laughs: Perspectives on Women and Comedy*, ed. Regina Barreca (New York: Gordon & Breach, 1988), pp. 23–42.

surname she took, she returned to England, only to be arrested and briefly imprisoned for debt; the king had ignored her letters pleading for the remuneration she had been promised. Released from prison through friends (Mr. Behn had evidently died by this point, if he ever really existed), she began to earn her living by writing plays for the London stage. In her later years, barred from the theater and perhaps briefly imprisoned because of an attack on Charles II's disloyal son Monmouth, she also published poems, translations, and some short fiction, including *Oroonoko*.[14] Much of the fiction, however, appeared only after her death, when others were exploiting her fame. Among her posthumous works was *The Widow Ranter*; while less overtly autobiographical than *Oroonoko*, this play nonetheless draws on Behn's youthful colonial experience and advertises itself as her property through numerous authorial self-references.

Interwoven with the biographical contextual story is a set of cultural narratives testifying to lively dispute about the question of female "nature." Feminist scholars have done much in recent years to excavate these narratives, and two areas of research are particularly relevant to an understanding of Behn's—and her society's—construction of her persona of female author. The discourse of "normative" womanhood, which proclaimed that women should be "chaste, silent, and obedient," is a dark ground upon which Behn's figure shines brightly (for modern readers seeking models of rebellion from prescriptive and often misogynist norms of female nature) or luridly (for contemporaries assessing Behn's status as a "licentious" widow who earned her own living).[15] And this discourse of "normative" womanhood had

14. For this very condensed biographical account I have drawn on materials in the books by Goreau, Duffy, and Mendelson cited above, note 11. For more details on the financially consequential attack on Monmouth—in the epilogue she wrote for an anonymous play called *Romulus and Hersillia* (August 1682)—see Goreau, *Reconstructing Aphra*, pp. 251–52. As Goreau observes, it was not only her arrest but a general depression in the London theater that prompted Behn's turn to the (less lucrative) role of poetry and fiction writer. The theatrical depression was the result, in large part, of the amalgamation of the two great companies in 1682, which meant "new plays were for a time hardly required" (Janet Todd, *The Sign of Angellica: Women, Writing and Fiction, 1660–1800* [New York: Columbia University Press, 1989], p. 74). See also O'Donnell, *Aphra Behn*, pp. 5–6; she remarks that between 1682, "when her slur of Monmouth in the epilogue to the anonymous *Romulus and Hersilia* [*sic*] resulted in the warrant for her arrest," and her death, Behn produced and published only two more plays (though she wrote two others); but "all her prose fiction was written (although not all was published) between 1682 and 1689, along with her three poetry miscellanies."

15. For an excellent account and bibliography of the Renaissance ideology of normative femininity, see Ann Rosalind Jones, *The Currency of Eros: Women's Love Lyric in*

an old misogynist obverse that was being newly inflected, during the seventeenth century, in a set of texts about colonial life that depicted Englishwomen seeking their erotic and marital fortunes "licentiously" in the New World.[16] At the same time, however, there was an emergent cultural narrative of proto-feminist protest against the subordinate role prescribed for women which is equally important for understanding Behn's colonialist writings. According to this story, British women, especially wives, resemble slaves. Both groups are demeaned by being the "property" of white men, and members of both groups become, for some writers, objects of sentimental concern.[17] Linked to, possibly even enabling, this emergent cultural narrative protesting women's legal and ideological status as property of men is a strand of a Renaissance skepticism we can call perspectivism. It appears when European writers from Peter Martyr through Montaigne to Thomas Browne and George Herbert interrogate ideologies of ethnocentrism and also those early modes of color prejudice that would, over the

---

Europe, 1540–1620 (Bloomington: Indiana University Press, 1990), chap. 1. For a discussion of the attacks on Behn mounted by some of her contemporaries, see Goreau, *Reconstructing Aphra*, chap. 11 and passim.

16. For examples of this gendered "colonial" cultural discourse see David Brion Davis, *The Problem of Slavery in Western Culture* (Ithaca: Cornell University Press, 1966), p. 277, where he notes that the State of Maryland reversed the old convention of *partus sequitur ventrum* (the child follows the mother) in the late seventeenth century in order to "inhibit the lustful desires of white women." Davis also cites an eighteenth-century colonialist document that displays a fear of female sexuality that is yoked with, or channeled through, an ideology of class: "The lower class of women in *England*," wrote Edward Long, the noted historian of Jamaica, "are remarkably fond of the blacks, for reasons too brutal to mention; they would connect themselves with horses and asses, if the law permitted them" (*Candid Reflections upon the Judgement Lately Awarded by the Court of King's Bench . . . on What is Commonly Called the Negro Cause* [London, 1772], cited in Davis, *Problem of Slavery*, p. 277).

17. See, for instance, Lady Mary Lee Chudleigh's argument in "To The Ladies," that "Wife and servant are the same, / But only differ in the name" (*Poems on Several Occasions* [London, 1703]), quoted from *First Feminists: British Women Writers 1578–1799*, ed. Moira Ferguson (Bloomington and Old Westbury, Conn.: Indiana University Press and Feminist Press, 1985), p. 237. Cf. the statement in a famous pamphlet titled *The Levellers*, also from 1703, that "Matrimony is indeed become a meer Trade[.] They carry their Daughters to *Smithfield* as they do Horses, and sell to the highest bidder," quoted in Maximillian E. Novak and David Stuart Rodes's edition of Thomas Southerne's *Oroonoko* (Lincoln: University of Nebraska Press, 1976), p. xxiv. And see Jacqueline Pearson, *The Prostituted Muse: Images of Women and Women Dramatists, 1642–1737* (New York: St. Martin's Press, 1988), p. 114, on the way in which Southerne followed Behn in making a "symbolic equivalence between women and slaves." For an example of this analogy from later in the century, see Margaret Cavendish's equation of marriage with slavery in *CCXI Sociable Letters* (1664; facsimile ed., Menston, Eng.: Scolar Press, 1969), p. 427.

course of the next few centuries, develop into what we call racism.[18]
Behind the apparently liberal views of a character like Desdemona or
the first-person female narrator of Behn's *Oroonoko*, both of whom
find great beauty in a black man, lies a strong if by no means culturally
dominant line of philosophical speculation and its accompanying
pleasures—among them, I maintain, the erotic pleasure of experimenting with the unfamiliar. Such erotic pleasure could be legit-
imized, like so much else in early modern culture, by reference to
biblical authority: "Thus we that are of contrary complexions,"
Thomas Browne wrote, "accuse the blackness of the Moors as ugly.
But the Spouse in the *Canticles* excuseth this conceit, in that description of hers, I am black, but comely."[19] The witty poem by Cleveland
cited in my epigraph and several remarkable poems by George Herbert and his brother Edward elaborate on this significant albeit relatively unfamiliar "minority" view of black-skinned people as beautiful.

The third contextual narrative (really a set of narratives) that I
want to adduce pertains to two significant, and complexly linked,
institutions of seventeenth-century England, the theater and book
publishing. Behn's efforts to construct marketable authorial personae
were shaped by, and addressed to, the specific kinds of audience—
and patrons—available to her. Catherine Gallagher, who has brilliantly analyzed Behn's material circumstances as a writer, usefully
cautions us against misunderstanding Behn's claims, lauded by Virginia Woolf in *A Room of One's Own*, to have earned her "bread" by her
pen.[20] Mediating in crucial ways between pen and profits was the
institution of the theater and also the need to appeal to actual or
potential patrons; as Gallagher shows, Behn could not have supported herself just on the income from her published books, numerous though these were.[21] Unable to acquire patrons at all during her

18. For a concise account of the (relatively small) group of early Renaissance texts
that remarked the fact that "ethnocentrism works in two directions," see Elliot H.
Tokson, *The Popular Image of the Black Man in English Drama, 1550–1688* (Boston: G. K.
Hall, 1982), pp. 6–7; see also Tokson's discussion in chapter 2 of a set of English lyric
poems (by George Herbert and his brother Edward, Henry King, Henry Rainolds, and
John Cleveland) that offer more complex depictions of black persons as objects and
subjects of erotic passion than most English Renaissance texts do.

19. *The Works of Sir Thomas Browne*, ed. Charles Sayle (Edinburgh: John Grant,
1912), 2:386; cited in Tokson, p. 6.

20. See Catherine Gallagher, *British Women Writers*, and also Deborah C. Payne,
"'And Poets Shall by Patron-Princes Live': Aphra Behn and Patronage," *Curtain Calls*,
pp. 105–19.

21. Gallagher, MS of *British Women Writers*, p. 12.

early career, as Deborah Payne has argued, Behn was trapped—as were Dryden and other non-aristocratic members of her generation of writers—"between a regressive system of patronage and an emergent marketplace of print."[22] And, as Gallagher has persuasively demonstrated,

> Behn, like most of the age's "professional writers," . . . was a playwright partly because the structure and financing of drama allowed for the support of writers. The theater as an institution changed abruptly when, after a twenty-year hiatus, it was restored along with the monarchy. The changes made playwrighting a much more discrete, potentially independently lucrative and chancy activity than it had been. Earlier playwrights had either been members of the theater companies that produced their scripts and therefore simply shared in the company's profits, . . . or . . . were heavily reliant on aristocratic or royal patronage. In contrast, Restoration playwrights were paid the receipts (above the House Charges) for the third day's performance of their plays. . . . Consequently, if a play was not popular enough to hold the stage for three days, the playwright got nothing; if it lasted until the "author's benefit" performance, the playwright's fee would be roughly proportionate to the play's reputation based on its first and second nights' reception. The London theater-going population was small enough for word-of-mouth reporting to spread rapidly through the potential audience.

Gallagher suggests that Behn's construction of an authorial persona, especially in her prefatory epistles to her readers and in the spoken prologues and epilogues of her plays, needs to be understood in the context of this "quite specialized financial arrangement"; like other Restoration playwrights, she tries "to engender a relationship of mutual obligation that will bring in an audience on the third night." As part of this seduction effort, she must work "to keep herself interesting, to dispel the boredom of familiarity." And it is here that Gallagher locates one of Behn's most striking gender-marked innovations, namely her construction, from common misogynist stereotypes of female sexuality, of an unprecedented persona: "the professional woman playwright as a new-fangled whore." Part of the "new-fangledness" as it is exhibited in her late colonial narratives—in some contrast to the plays Gallagher is mainly concerned with and to the *Oroonoko* she interprets mainly as a royalist allegory about the "black-

22. Payne, "Aphra Behn and Patronage," *Curtain Calls*, p. 111.

ness" of ink and of absolute monarchy—is an implicit erotic rule, developed for the female author, that draws a line between titillation or seduction, on the one hand, and, on the other, any sexual pleasure or behavior connected with procreation.[23]

Behn not only adapts the image of the prostitute for her own purposes; she also seeks to revise and partly to revalue the common cultural association of the color black with female unchastity. She herself had been satirized for her literary ambitions in a poem that bawdily alludes to the female genitals as a "black ace." Written (anonymously) in 1676, the satire depicts "the poetess Aphra" as an aging whore (she was then 36) whose designs on the Laureate's crown come too late. Though she swears "by her poetry and her black ace / The laurel by a double right was her own / For the plays she had writ and the conquests she's won," Apollo denies her plea, suggesting that she's a dozen years too old for sexual conquest.[24] Barely a year later, Behn obliquely counters this type of attack by creating a prostitute heroine in *The Rover* whose name not only wittily inverts the stereotype of "moral color" but also points teasingly to Aphra Behn herself as a maker of signs or masks. This character, named Angelica Bianca, recalls Cassio's mistress in *Othello* as well as many other less than physically or morally pure women named Bianca in English Renaissance drama. This witty character, moreover, bears Aphra Behn's initials, as Janet Todd observes, and also displays an inviting and provocative sign of herself to attract male patrons.[25] Behn underscores her identification with Angelica when she lays paradoxical claim to that sign in a fascinating "post-script" affixed to the first edition of the play, a passage defending it against the charge that it was a piece of rampant plagiarism (from Thomas Killigrew's *Thomaso, or The Wanderer*, first published in 1663–64). Though she has, she confesses, "stol'n some hints," unlike other poets who *conceal* their thefts, she has taken the (by implication superior) tack of calling attention both to her source and to her own witty ways of "appropriating" it: "I, vainly proud of my Judgment hang out the Sign of Angelica (the only Stol'n Object) to give Notice where a great part of the Wit dwelt" (*Works*, 1:107). Angelica the "White's" sign, as Behn erects it to

23. Gallagher, MS of *British Women Writers*, pp. 13–14, 19, 20.
24. "A Session of the Poets," in *Poems on Affairs of State*, ed. George de F. Lord (New Haven: Yale University Press, 1963), 1:355; cited in Goreau, *Reconstructing Aphra*, pp. 232–33.
25. Todd, *The Sign of Angellica*, p. 1.

advertise the products of her own wit, is clearly analogous to the black masks worn by prostitutes in the theater. As Gallagher remarks in her discussion of Behn's prologue to her first play, *The Forc'd Marriage* of 1670, "the poetess like the prostitute is she who 'stands out' . . . by virtue of her mask," the "black velvet case" which, as the Prologue says, "disguises"—but also paradoxically identifies—"every face" of a prostitute in all parts of the theater.[26] In the years between the first King James and the second, England had gone from being a small island nation seeking to whittle away the monopolies that Spain and Portugal held on New World treasure—a whittling that occurred partly through the efforts of state-supported buccaneers such as Sir Francis Drake and Sir Peter Hawkins—to enjoying, in Eric Williams's phrase, an "astounding commercial efflorescence" based on the Negro slave trade and Caribbean sugar production. This trade moved from England to Africa to the Caribbean and then back to England.[27] By 1697, to the great joy of mercantilist theorists intent on promoting the ideal of a favorable balance of trade, the "triangular" cycle had given an enormous stimulus to England's own industry and agriculture, and represented, in the view of an able seventeenth-century economist named Charles Davenant, "a minimum of 36 percent of Britain's commercial profits."[28] By the time Behn wrote her colonialist play and novella, England was well on the way to becoming, in Folarin Shyllon's phrase, "the leading slave mistress, slave trader, and slave carrier of the world."[29] Because Behn had to work with as well as against cultural perceptions of the female playwright as a fallen or "kept" woman (like the actress turned royal mistress Nell Gwyn), and because that role had traditional associations with erotic slavery and indeed with the color black, she was in a peculiarly apt position to articulate a paradoxical perspective on England's colonizing venture, a perspective I would describe as *partially critical*. Behn's professional and economic interests deviated just enough from those we may ascribe to England's dominant male property owners and investors in the colonies to provide a fascinating example of a female author oscillating among multiple subject positions and between complicity with and critique of the emergent institution of New World slavery.

26. Gallagher, MS of *British Women Writers*, pp. 30–31.
27. Williams, *From Columbus to Castro*, p. 144.
28. Cited in ibid., p. 143.
29. Folarin Shyllon, *Black People in Britain, 1555–1883* (London: Oxford University Press, 1977), p. 8.

Aspects of the Texts

In *Oroonoko* and *The Widow Ranter*, the British characters' perceptions
of the New World are mediated through European conventions of
heroic romance and also through a set of ideological inconsistencies
quite typical of colonial discourse, namely those that arise from the
tendency both to conflate and abruptly to distinguish American Indians and Africans as representatives of "otherness" and also as persons
who are, or are not, currently (or "naturally") enslaved.[30] In Behn's
two texts, one narrative, one dramatic, the condition of slavery itself,
as well as the differences of skin color which (partly) determine one's
vulnerability to a literal form of slavery, are products of overlapping
and sometimes competing signifying codes, chief among them the
erotic, the moral, the political, and the economic (broadly construed).
These codes generate many complexities. The "white" male hero Bacon, for instance, looks politically dark to his countrymen—indeed
indistinguishable from the enemy Indians—in part because he prefers an Indian lady to one of his own people: he declares himself the
passionate "slave" or "captive" of an Indian Queen who is, in his eyes,
supremely "fair."[31] Her actual skin color is never mentioned.

   This detail—or rather, the absence of one—might be interpreted
with reference to Karen Kupperman's argument, based on colonial
texts written in the period 1580–1640, that the English initially perceived the Indians as "naturally" white-skinned beings whose "tan" or
"tawny" (not red) color was artificially produced, whether by the sun's

   30. See Karen Kupperman, *Settling with the Indians: The Meeting of English and Indian
Cultures in America, 1580–1640* (Totowa, N.J.: Rowman and Littlefield, 1980), p. 176, on
Edward Waterhouse's "official" account of the 1622 Jamestown massacre of settlers by
Indians; this account, reprinted by Hakluyt and Purchas, stressed the Indians'
"beastliness"—in contrast to earlier emphasis on them as "younger brethren" to the
English—and argued that they could legitimately be enslaved (in contrast to earlier and
some subsequent arguments that as our "kinsmen" they could not be so treated). For a
discussion of the Aristotelian theory of "natural" slavery as applied both to Amerindians and to black Africans, see Anthony Pagden, *The Fall of Natural Man: The American
Indian and the Origins of Comparative Ethnology* (Cambridge: Cambridge University Press,
1982), chap. 3.
   31. The rhetoric of erotic "enslavement" was of course pervasive in Restoration
writing; see, for example, the exchange of love lyrics between the Earl of Rochester and
his wife where she replies to his request that she be "kind" with the lines: "I to cherish
your desire, / Kindness us'd, but 'twas in vaine. / You insulted on your Slave; / Humble
Love you soon refus'd" (quoted from "The Answer," in *The Poems of John Wilmot, Earl of
Rochester*, ed. Keith Walker [Oxford: Basil Blackwell, 1984], p. 21).

action or by practices such as dipping Indian infants in walnut juice.[32] I submit, however, that for Behn and her contemporary audience, the Indian Queen's non-white skin color is both perceptible and perceived to matter, albeit in ways we cannot too securely fix. Thomas Southerne, who adapted Behn's novella for the stage in 1696, was attacked for failing to give a New World heroine "an Indian *Air*, / . . . an *Indian* Hue"—and the question of dramatic "decorum" becomes only more intriguing when we remark that the specific heroine in question is Southerne's version of Behn's dark-skinned heroine who is, in Behn's story, African, not Indian at all.[33] Kupperman herself argues, moreover, that during the second half of the seventeenth century the seeds of racist "separatist" ideologies began to grow—and were critically fostered by the increasing use, by the English, of black African slave-labor: "When English colonists later in the century began to rely massively on African slaves . . . and to categorize servants purely on the basis of race, this could meld with the [developing] idea that Indians were permanently different from Europeans to make them co-victims of racism."[34] As a product of this transitional era in the perception and categorization of various forms of human "otherness," Behn's play invites us to ask how—and how forcefully—we should mark the difference between Bacon and his beloved Indian Queen.

32. See Kupperman, *Settling*, pp. 35–37. Her argument that Indians were perceived by Englishmen not as red but rather as "tawny" (understood as browned by the sun or by "artificial" means) until the end of the seventeenth century, which echoes the conclusion of Wesley Frank Craven, *White, Red, and Black: The Seventeenth-Century Virginian* (Charlottesville: University Press of Virginia, 1971), p. 41, seems to me to oversimplify an enormously complex problem in the history of colonial perception of skin color as a sign of otherness. One problem—and it is common among modern historians—is that Kupperman bases her conclusions about English perceptions of Indians, a group she assumes to have been absolutely distinct from that comprised by "black" Africans in colonists' eyes, on evidence drawn solely from North American colonial records. In an era when England's Caribbean holdings were much more economically important than its North American ones, however, it seems questionable to separate one's evidentiary terrain in the way that Kupperman does. I contend that no firm conclusions about colonial perceptions can be drawn without at least considering the problem of the "metropole," that is, of London as a center of printing, economic activity, politics, and fashion.

33. The attack on Southerne is from "The Triall of Skill," *Poems on Affairs of State: Augustan Satirical Verse, 1660–1714*, ed. Frank H. Ellis (New Haven: Yale University Press, 1970), 6:708; I found the citation in the excellent introduction to the Novak and Rodes edition of Southerne's *Oroonoko*, p. xxxvii, n. 73.

34. Kupperman, *Settling*, p. 187.

By reading Behn's seldom-studied *Ranter* in conjunction with the somewhat better known *Oroonoko*,[35] I hope to show that the romance in the former text, like a romance titillatingly implied in the latter, relies for its narrative effects on an unevenly but distinctly emergent sense of *taboo* about what a later age would name "miscegenation."[36] John Rolfe's famous marriage to Pocahontas (1613)—the only formal instance of intermarriage in the earlier colonial period, according to Kupperman—had been tolerated, and even approved, by some English authorities, despite the disapproval of others who adduced God's warning to Abraham not to "marry nor give in marriage to the heathen, that are uncircumcized."[37] By the 1680s, however, such tolerance was much less prevalent. Behind the tragic scenes of Bacon's romance lurk not only general cultural prejudices against (and also fascination with) cross-group intercourse, social and sexual, but also a set of relatively new laws proscribing the latter phenomenon in the colonies and frequently lumping Negroes, Indians, and Mulattos together for purposes of legal punishment.[38]

In *White over Black*, Winthrop Jordan cites a declaration by the

35. Most scholarly commentary on *Ranter* has focused on Behn's sources for the play; see above, note 7. Maureen Duffy devotes two quite interesting pages to the play and implies its connection with *Oroonoko* by remarking that *Ranter* provides the "structure" for Southerne's dramatic version of *Oroonoko* (*The Passionate Shepherdess*, p. 295). There is also a brief, somewhat condescending account of the play in an article by Paul C. Wermuth titled "Bacon's Rebellion in the London Theater," *Virginia Cavalcade* 7 (Summer 1957): 38–39, and several brief mentions in Jacqueline Pearson, *The Prostituted Muse: Images of Women and Women Dramatists, 1642–1737* (New York: St. Martin's Press, 1988). Only recently, with Margo Hendricks's fine essay "Civility, Barbarity and Aphra Behn's *The Widow Ranter*," has the play begun to receive serious critical attention. Hendricks's essay is forthcoming in *Women, "Race," and Writing*, ed. Margo Hendricks and Patricia Parker (New York: Routledge).

36. On the history of miscegenation laws (the word "miscegenation" was not used in its modern sense to denote prohibited behavior until the nineteenth century, according to the *OED*) see Winthrop D. Jordan, *The White Man's Burden: Historical Origins of Racism in the United States* (New York: Oxford University Press, 1974), pp. 70–71.

37. Kupperman, *Settling*, pp. 118–19. For John Rolfe's own rather tortuous attempt to justify his marriage, see the account in Ralphe Hamor, *A True Discourse of the Present Estate of Virginia* (London, 1615). Kupperman notes that fornication between Indians and whites was punishable in the early period of the Virginia colony, but the penalties were the same as for fornication among whites.

38. See, for instance, Winthrop Jordan's discussion of the groups affected by new laws permitting castration as a punishment in the colonies (never in England) in *White over Black: American Attitudes toward the Negro, 1550–1812* (Chapel Hill: University of North Carolina Press, 1968), p. 155. Jordon argues, however, that black men were perceived as a substantially greater sexual threat to white women than Indians were (pp. 161–62).

Virginia Assembly of 1670 barring both Indians and Négroes, even though "baptised" and free, from the "purchase of christians." Indians and Africans were, however, not debarred "from buying any of their owne nation."[39] In the tortuous language of this declaration we can see the term "christian" being reserved, but not yet with the appearance of "natural" logic, for white Englishmen alone. Indians and Africans (including the "brown" Africans Aphra Behn seems to classify as "natural" slaves, in contrast to the noble jet-black Oroonoko) were also yoked together, albeit differentially so, as prohibited mates for English persons of either sex, who, according to Jordan, began to refer to themselves collectively as "white"—as well as "English" and "Christian"—around 1680.[40] Non-white men, moreover, whether Indian or African, were easily interchangeable in the minds of Englishmen either as members of insurrectionary groups (African slave revolts began to be no less terrifying than Indian raids in the Virginia of the 1670s) or as sexual threats to English women, and hence to the purity of English bloodlines. It is worth noting that castration of both Negro and Indian men became a widely deployed method of punishment in the late seventeenth century, and that miscegenation statutes frequently betray the lawmakers' fear that English women, if left to their own devices, would rush to satisfy their lusts with bestial non-white men. If, as Kupperman argues, "status, not race, was the category which counted for English people of the early years of colonization,"[41] by the time Behn published her stories about America, the categories of status, gender, and race were starting to overlap, sometimes in causal narratives and certainly with significant social consequences.

Social status is clearly important to Behn's hero Bacon when he nobly—if perhaps mistakenly—undertakes to defend Jamestown, in the colony Ralegh named after his "Virgin Queen," against angry Indians who claim the land is theirs. In so doing, he reminds us of Othello defending Cyprus against the "general enemy Ottoman" (I.iii.48); but in contrast to Othello, Bacon is not explicitly called to his military role by the powers of the State. On the contrary, communication from England to the colonies being slow and the colonial govern-

---

39. Jordan, *White over Black*, p. 94; cf. Kupperman, *Settling*, pp. 110–11, on linguistic evidence suggesting that the English "did not come to grips with the general problem of how one designates Christian Indians."

40. Jordan, *White over Black*, p. 94.

41. Kupperman, *Settling*, p. 122.

ment, as Behn represents it, extremely petty and inefficient, a legal commission for the hero fails to materialize. This detail, which makes him an outlaw in the eyes of the colonial Council, serves finally to deepen his resemblance to Othello insofar as both heroes, despite their difference of color, are regarded as potentially (and by some, actually) dangerous to the society's health. In the course of his military action, after falling in love with Semernia, an Indian princess, Bacon ambivalently acknowledges her husband's historical claims to America. Bacon rejects, however, the king's *present* claims to the land with breezy pragmatic cynicism. "[We] were Monarchs once of all this spacious World," the Indian King says, "till you, an unknown People, landing here, distress'd and ruin'd by destructive Storms, abusing all our charitable Hospitality, usurp'd our Right, and made your Friends your Slaves." Bacon replies: "I will not justify the Ingratitude of my Forefathers, but finding here my Inheritance, I am resolv'd still to maintain it so, and by my Sword which first cut out my Portion, defend each Inch of Land, with my last drop of Blood" (II.i; *Works*, 4:245).

This exchange allows considerably more room for interrogating the morality of the colonial enterprise than many contemporary texts do: in the Prologue of Dryden's and Howard's *The Indian Queen* (1663–64), for instance, an Indian boy is made to justify as a fated necessity his country's conquest rather than protest its injustice as Behn's King does.[42] The ideological limits of, and fissures in, Behn's sympathy for the Indians' point of view appear, however, quite strikingly when her figure of exotic female nobility softens her husband's protest by expressing an admiration for a member of the conquering people which focuses on his romantic attractions. The Indian Queen's first words in Behn's play suggest already her attraction to Bacon, an adulterous passion that works to cover over, and implicitly justify through the gloss of romance, the British appropriation of the Indians' land. "Even his Threats have Charms that please the Heart," says the Queen (II.i; *Works*, 4:245); thus does a symbolic personification of the New World land implicitly approve the conquest and so transform a rape into a romance of mutual attraction among noble subjects.

Bacon eventually kills the Indian King, removing that obstacle to an

42. "By ancient Prophesies we have been told / Our World shall be subdu'd by one more old," says the Boy in Dryden and Howard's *Indian Queen*, in *Dryden: The Dramatic Works*, ed. Montague Summers (London: Nonesuch, 1931), vol. 1; the quotation is from p. 207.

Englishman's possession of land and lady. Though he soon learns that his love is indeed reciprocated, he is not permitted to enjoy the fruits of passion, partly, it seems, to punish him for appearing to his fellow Englishmen, if not unequivocally to Aphra Behn, as a threat to legal institutions and therefore to property rights. Meeting the now-widowed Indian Queen during a forest battle when she is disguised in breeches, Bacon wounds her fatally with his sword. She thus becomes a tragic foil for the comically lustful and wealthy older white woman of the play's title, a ranting Widow who also changes her skirts for breeches late in the play, and who seems for several reasons—among them her eloquence and bold embrace of unchastity—a self-ironizing figure for Aphra Behn herself.

Despairing at the loss of his love and what appears to be the loss of his battle with the Englishmen, Bacon commits suicide, just before discovering that his men, led by his lieutenant Daring, have in truth achieved a great victory. Like the ancient hero Hannibal, to whom Bacon explicitly compares himself, Bacon takes poison to keep himself from "falling into the hands of his enemies."[43] The classical allusion works to ally the British with the imperial Romans and to mark out an ideological site for at least some sympathy with a character who resists Britain's laws, including the newly emerging colonial statutes against miscegenation.[44] The site for sympathy has distinct limits, however, one of them signalled by a character who remarks, early in

43. The quotation is from Montague Summers's introduction to the play (*Works*, 4:219); for Bacon's own allusion to the famous Carthaginian as his model, see 4:304: "Come, my good Poison, like that of *Hannibal*."

44. Given the historical fact that one of the ringleaders of Bacon's rebellion, a man named Richard Lawrence not mentioned in Behn's play, had scandalously buried his learning and abilities "in the darke imbraces of a Blackamoore, his slave," thereby offending the English women "in or about towne," it seems plausible to see Behn as contributing quite deliberately, if somewhat obliquely, to the discourse of "news"—analytic and scandal-mongering both—about interracial romance. The story about Lawrence does not appear in the *Strange News* pamphlets but rather in a seventeenth-century narrative entitled "The History of Bacon and Ingram's Rebellion" that wasn't published until the nineteenth century (when it was found in a unique MS). Though usually discounted on that ground as a possible source for Behn's play (see, e.g., Batten, "The Source," p. 13), we cannot assume that such a narrative—or parts of its contents—would not have been known to Behn's contemporaries. Positivistic assumptions about transmission seem particularly inadequate to describe the world of overlapping oral and printed routes whereby information circulated in this era. For the mention of Lawrence, see "The History" as reprinted in *Narratives of the Insurrections: 1675–1690*, ed. Charles M. Andrews (New York: Charles Scribner's Sons, 1915), p. 96. See also Wilcomb E. Washburn, "Essay on the Sources," in *The Governor and the Rebel: A History of Bacon's Rebellion in Virginia* (Chapel Hill: University of North Carolina Press, 1957), pp. 171–81.

the play, that "this Country [British America] wants nothing but to be
peopled with a well-born Race, to make it one of the best Colonies
in the World" (I.i; *Works*, 4:229). Bacon's union with the Indian
Queen would have been seen by many as *not* contributing to this
genetic aim.

His likening of himself to the black African Hannibal is one of
many textual details that make this white "Outlaw" a symbolic double
of the eponymous hero of Behn's *Oroonoko*. That African prince, ironically renamed Caesar when he is transported to Surinam and sold as
a slave, also invokes Hannibal as his model at a late moment in his
tragic story; urging his fellow slaves to revolt against the English,
Oroonoko describes Hannibal as "a great Captain" who "cut his way
through Mountains of solid Rocks."[45] Oroonoko doesn't, however, tell
his less well educated followers about Hannibal's ultimate fate in his
battles against Rome. Oroonoko has obviously had a European education (he was tutored by an atheistical Frenchman during his boyhood
in Coramantian); he is moreover described by Behn as having "Roman" not African features (p. 8). Reshaped though he is for European tastes, Oroonoko like Othello clearly does not so transcend his
color as to be an acceptable son-in-law for Englishmen, not even for
those characters in Behn's story who profess to admire him greatly.
Oroonoko indeed occupies an ambiguous outside/inside position with
respect to the ruling culture; he's officially a slave but has been promised his freedom by one of the "middle level managers," Trefry, and
also by the narrator herself, who tells us that she occupies a high social
position and the best house in the colony, and who is, at the time she
meets Oroonoko, a fatherless, unmarried young woman far from
home and without a dowry.[46]

In contrast to Bacon, Oroonoko is apparently allowed to fulfill his

45. All quotations from *Oroonoko* are from the edition by Lore Metzger (New York:
W. W. Norton, 1973); the passage cited here is from p. 40. Subsequent citations appear
in the text.

46. The text is, however, significantly ambiguous about whether Behn could or did
own slaves in her own right, as a fatherless, unmarried woman. In her prefatory letter
to Lord Maitland, she refers to Oroonoko as "my Slave," but she suggests, in the course
of the story, that she lacked the key power to dispose of her chattel property: she relates
that she "assured" him, falsely, as it turns out, that he would be freed when the Governor arrived. Her assertion that she occupies the "best house" in the colony is on p. 45 of
the Norton edition; in her prefatory epistle to Lord Maitland—not printed in the
Norton edition—she states that "I had none above me in that Country, yet I wanted
power to preserve this Great Man [Oroonoko]"; quoted from *Oroonoko, or The Royal
Slave: A Critical Edition*, ed. Adelaide P. Amore (Lanham, Md.: University Press of
America, 1987), p. 3.

sexual desires according to a hoary romance formula: two young lovers are separated by a *senex* figure, Oroonoko's erotically greedy but, as it turns out, physically impotent grandfather, who takes the prince's beloved Imoinda into his own harem in the novella's opening section. In the second part of the story, set in the American colonies, the lovers are miraculously reunited, in a scene that the narrator calls a pleasing "novel" (p. 44). The lovers' bliss, however, is shadowed by their condition of chattel slavery and filtered, for the reader, through the "eye-witness" consciousness of the narrator herself, the young white woman who plays the role of Oroonoko's "*Great Mistress*" (p. 46). Soon after learning that Imoinda is pregnant, Oroonoko kills his beloved. Sexual jealousy reinforced by a principle of patriarchal property rights in women and children looms large among Oroonoko's motives. Specifically, he fears that Imoinda may be "*ravished* by every Brute," thus becoming a "Slave to the enraged Multitude" (p. 71) after his own death comes—and he's sure it will—as the result of his scheme to avenge himself on the cruel Deputy Governor of the colony, Colonel Byam. With Imoinda's prompt approval of his plan of revenge, Oroonoko gives her the "fatal Stroke, first cutting her Throat, and then severing her yet smiling Face from that delicate Body, pregnant as it was with the Fruits of tenderest Love" (p. 72).

The reasons for Imoinda's death are complex and multiple, but chief among them, let me reiterate, are two centered on property. Oroonoko is unable to bear the thought that his child will be born a slave, the property of others; and he's equally outraged by the idea that Imoinda will perhaps also be alienated from his patriarchal ownership—she may become, after his death (or indeed at any time), the sexual slave of a white man. Interestingly, when Oroonoko first hears, from Trefry, of Imoinda's presence in Surinam, but before he learns her name and recognizes her as his own long-lost wife, he expresses considerable surprise that her owner should be pining fruitlessly for her favors: he asks Trefry "why, being your Slave, you do not oblige her to yield?" (p. 42). Here is a moment in the text where a gender ideology of masculine dominance clearly overshadows differences *among* men arising from skin color or social class. Nonetheless, in the end Oroonoko's black skin color and, even more, his status as a rebellious slave outweigh the solidarity effects associated with male gender and shared "noble" class origins. Like the white-skinned Bacon, Oroonoko is ultimately destroyed because of the threat which his "outsider" status poses to the dominant social group and, specifically, to the male property owners of that group.

The text's response to that threat is to ratify, albeit ambivalently, even guiltily, the "necessity" of the outsider's punishment and his ultimate death. Oroonoko suffers a narratively dispersed and lengthy process of death in which others' hands as well as his own carry out a gruesome dismemberment of his body—a punishment he has knowingly incurred by pursuing his schemes of revolt and subsequently vengeance. The first stage in the hideous process involves Oroonoko being whipped and tortured after the aborted rebellion, with "Indian pepper" being rubbed in his wounds. Imoinda is "spared" the sight of this torture, not because of any kindness on the part of the Governor but rather, the narrator says, "for Fear she should die with the Sight, or miscarry, and then they should lose a young Slave" (p. 67). After killing his wife and explaining to her the "Necessity" of his deed, he lies drained of power by her side for two days, until he is found by a party of Englishmen. At this point, he takes up his knife, declaring histrionically that he is unafraid of dying, "and at that word, cut a piece of Flesh from his own Throat" (p. 75). He subsequently "rip'd up his own Belly, and took his Bowels and pull'd 'em out," in a gesture that Charlotte Sussman has brilliantly discussed as an uncanny repetition, on his own body, of his murder of the pregnant Imoinda.[47] Several long paragraphs later, others complete Oroonoko's work of self-mutilation: "The Executioner came, and first cut off his Members, and threw them into the Fire . . ." (p. 77).

Unlike Oroonoko's black body, Bacon's white one is not tortured before his death, but he too serves as a "necessary" sacrifice in—and to—the plot. To understand the ideological economy of that plot and its resemblances to *Oroonoko*'s, we need to look briefly at the comic story that Behn interweaves with the tragedy of Bacon's miscegenous romance, a story that ends in multiple marriages for Englishmen and women of varying social ranks and moral complexions. In that comic plot, the Widow Ranter herself, like the two virtuous young Englishwomen Madam Surelove and Mrs. Chrisante, acquires a suitable mate; if, as I have suggested, the Widow Ranter is a figure for the aging Aphra Behn herself, and a comic foil to the Indian Queen, it is particularly significant that she chooses Bacon's best lieutenant, a man named Daring, for the role of husband. Daring and the Widow are each subversive characters, Daring because he fights with and for

47. See C. Sussman, "The Other Problem with Women: Reproduction and Slave Culture in Aphra Behn's *Oroonoko*," in *Rereading Aphra Behn: History, Theory and Criticism*, ed. Heidi Hutner (Charlottesville: University Press of Virginia, 1993), pp. 212–33, esp. p. 220.

Bacon, the Widow because she is openly unchaste, has money of her own to spend as she sees fit, and uses it to achieve respectability and also to gain sexual satisfaction with a younger man who enters into the institution of matrimony with jovial cynicism. But these two characters are less subversive, Behn's plot suggests, than Bacon and the Indian Queen, who singly and together break too many social laws to be allowed to live. One might indeed argue that the Widow and Daring acquire their license to live at the price of their doubles' deaths. If this interpretation of one aspect of the play's complex ideological economy is right, then it seems fair to suggest that Aphra Behn seeks to please her English audience, and profit from a clever revision of the *Othello* plot, by representing with titillating sympathy "forbidden" modes of behavior and finally legitimating that representation by punishing her most transgressive characters with deaths presented as "inevitable," fated. If Bacon is like Hannibal, we know he can't win in the end, and the contemporary colonial project is rendered safe for British audiences by being thus assimilated to an old imperial plot in which the black Carthaginian hero loses the battle. The author thus manipulates the audience's sympathy for the tragic hero and heroine in a way that does not finally disrupt the reassuring ideological economy whereby the threat to England's slaveholding trade economy is— as it were inevitably—contained. In *Oroonoko*, Behn represents an analogous containment but with significant differences, chief among them the first-person female narrator's explicit economic and moral implication in the tragic deaths of Oroonoko and Imoinda.

"We trade for Feathers," Behn writes in *Oroonoko*, and the "we," a complex shifter throughout the novella, clearly refers here to English persons of both sexes who are trading with the native Indians, a group designated in this passage as Other, as "them." The Indians, Behn goes on to explain, order the feathers "into all Shapes, make themselves little short Habits of 'em, and glorious Wreaths for their Heads, Necks, Arms and Legs, whose Tinctures are unconceivable. I had a Set of these presented to me, and I gave 'em to the King's Theatre; it was the Dress of the *Indian Queen*, infinitely admir'd by Persons of Quality" (p. 2). Though she gives rather than sells the "inimitable" feathers to the "King's Theatre" (actually, the Theatre Royal where the King's Company played), it is clear that the gift is made in the hope of future authorial benefit; Behn's own plays were produced by the King's Company and though she was unable to get a play performed in 1688, she clearly hoped to do so again in the future. She may even have meant this passage to advertise her own as yet unseen "Indian Queen," a character clearly inspired by Dryden's heroine who might well have inherited her feather headdress if ever *The Widow Ranter* reached the stage and made its bid for the Third Night favors of "Persons of Quality." When the play was performed after Behn's death, the actress Anne Bracegirdle evidently wore such a feather headdress and was attended by putti-like black boys (Figure 5.1).

Unlike some English visitors to the colonies who brought Native American persons home with them as "curiosities," Aphra Behn brought instead theatrical feathers, "some rare Flies, of amazing Forms and Colors" (*Oroonoko*, p. 2), and of course material for the verbal representations of exotic bodies contained in the book she wrote many years later. Imoinda's body is described, in *Oroonoko*, in a way that highlights its status—and value—as an exotic artifact: as Catherine Gallagher has shrewdly observed, it is a body described as if its "natural" state were artificial.[48] Behn tells us that all nobly born Coramantians "are so delicately cut and raised all over the Fore-part of the Trunk of their Bodies, that it looks as if it were japan'd, the Works being raised like high Point around the edges of the Flowers" (p. 45). Some, she goes on to explain, are only carved "with a little Flower, or Bird"; this is the case with Caesar-Oroonoko. Others, however, and the example suggests yet another significant asymmetry of gender, are carved all over. Imoinda, the narrator remarks, as if it were an afterthought ("I had forgot to tell you"), has "fine Flowers and Birds all over her Body."[49]

Behn remarks that carvings such as those on Imoinda's body are "more delicate" than those on "our antient *Picts* that are figur'd in the Chronicles"; this observation alludes, almost certainly, to the famous set of engravings Theodor de Bry made (with significant alterations) from John White's paintings of Indians and published in 1590 with Thomas Harriot's *The Briefe and True Report of the New Found Lande* (1588).[50] White had followed his paintings of Indians "with drawings

48. Gallagher, MS of *British Women Writers*, p. 104.

49. Gallagher remarks, with reference to Behn's parenthetical gesture of "I had forgot to tell you," the "clumsy yet strong scoring" of Imoinda's body; MS of *British Women Writers*, pp. 103–4.

50. I am indebted to Richard Halpern for the reference to de Bry. For a discussion of the ways in which he "softened and Europeanized" White's paintings of Native Americans (White's own watercolors weren't published until the twentieth century), see Kupperman, *Settling*, p. 33; both the watercolors and the engravings are reproduced in *The American Drawings of John White, 1577–1590*, ed. Paul Hulton and D. B. Quinn (London: Trustees of the British Museum, 1964).

Figure 5.1. Engraving by W. Vincent said to represent Anne Bracegirdle playing Semernia in Behn's *The Widow Ranter*. Courtesy Harvard Theatre Collection

of ancient Picts and Britons who looked very much like his Indians, particularly in dress and body decorations."[51] Behn's passage, then, with its allusion to a famous work of travel literature, dramatizes her effort to establish a scale of comparative value for an emergent market in which books and bodies and bodily adornments all jostled as commodities. I argue, indeed, that in *Oroonoko* Behn constructs an ambiguous reflection on the role of intellectual producers and consumers in this international market. The novella's opening pages announce that this is a "true" "eye-witness" account of things that happened in the "new Colonies," most notably the encounter between the young female narrator and Oroonoko and Imoinda. Though these noble slaves are clearly the object of the author's interest and sympathy, they are also "curiosities" she offers her readers back in England; as she is well aware, she must offer "novelty" to pique her metropolitan reader's interest (for "where there is no Novelty, there can be no Curiosity" [p. 3]). The author herself, as I have already suggested, is both a producer and a consumer of novelty or "news" whether oral or written. Indeed in a fascinating passage about her own role in one of the novella's climactic episodes—the slave rebellion Oroonoko leads after he discovers Imoinda is pregnant and despairs of the promises the narrator herself as well as Trefry have made to free him—Behn represents her identity as well as her agency as an ambiguous function of the *circulation* of information.

In the passage in question, Behn draws, as Shakespeare does in *Othello*, on a stereotypical scenario of English Renaissance drama, a scenario in which sexually vulnerable (and valuable) English women are pitted against a black man imagined as a villainous rapist. After describing how Oroonoko leads other male slaves in a rebellion, is deserted by all but one of his fellows, and is then recaptured and brutally punished by white male property owners, the author-narrator interrupts the plot's temporal progression to return to a point in the just-recounted story when the outcome of Oroonoko's rebellion was still uncertain. That uncertainty is oddly preserved for Behn's readers by her shift from the simple past tense to a subjunctive formulation that mixes past, present, and the possibility of a different future:

> You must know, that when the News was brought . . . that *Caesar* had betaken himself to the Woods, and carry'd with him all the Negroes, we

51. Kupperman, *Settling*, p. 113.

were possess'd with extreme Fear, which no Persuasions could dissipate, that he would secure himself till night, and then, that he would come down and cut all our Throats. This Apprehension made all the Females of us fly down the River, to be secured; and while we were away, they acted this Cruelty; for I suppose I had Authority and Interest enough there, had I suspected any such thing, to have prevented it: but we had not gone many Leagues, but the News overtook us, that *Caesar* was taken and whipped like a common Slave. (pp. 67–68)

In this passage, the authorial "I" seems at once extraordinarily lucid and disturbingly blind about her own complicity in her hero's capture and humiliating punishment. Had she been present, she "supposes" she could have prevented the cruelty that "they"—white men—wrought upon the black male slave.[52] Her claim to possess some singular social authority, however, is belied by her representation of herself as part of a group of weak females, a passive group prone to illness: as Martine Brownley has noted, Behn later rather guiltily claims sickness as an excuse for her absence from Oroonoko's final torture.[53] In the earlier scene of female flight, the women are possessed not by men, black or white, but rather by an agent named Fear and quickly renamed Apprehension. That oddly abstract agent turns out, if we look closely, to be a product of something the passage twice calls *News*—a mode of verbal production that in this text is often defined as unreliable, and that belongs, as we have seen, to a semantic complex that names crucial features of Behn's own discourse in *Oroonoko*.

Here, as in many other parts of the book, the narrative oscillates between criticizing and profiting from a "system" of circulation which includes both bodies and words, among them the lies Oroonoko discovers to be characteristic of Englishmen and even, the text obliquely suggests, of the narrator herself.[54] This disturbing oscillation has

52. Note that the most logical syntactic antecedent of "they" would be a group of *black* men composed of Oroonoko and his band, perpetrating the rape that one might easily construe as the referent for "this cruelty." The grammatical ambiguity points, it seems, to the struggle between the narrator's original perception of danger and her "corrected" but guiltily impotent retroactive perception that the white men not the black ones were her true enemies.

53. See Martine Watson Brownley, "The Narrator in *Oroonoko*," *Essays in Literature* 4 (1977): 174–81.

54. See, for instance, the passage discussed below where the narrator explicitly invites her reader to reflect on her manipulative narrative powers when she tells Oroonoko stories to "divert" him from thoughts of mutiny. Her promise that he will eventu-

been shrewdly analyzed by Laura Brown and Michael McKeon but
has prompted other critics less comfortable with ideological contradictions to (mis)represent Behn's text either as an "anti-slavery" document or as a royalist allegory which is opposed not to the institution of
slavery but only to the enslavement of kings.[55] Building especially on
Brown's work, I contend that in Behn's shifting and sometimes contradictory perspectives on the slave trade, we can see the lineaments
of a more complex model of European colonization than Tzvetan
Todorov posits in *The Conquest of America*.[56] In contrast to Todorov's
book and most instances of Renaissance travel literature I've read,
Behn's novella construes the relation between Old World and New not
only in terms of a binary opposition between self and other but also in
terms of a highly unstable triangular model which, in its simplest
version, draws relations of sameness and difference among a black
African slave, a white Englishwoman, and a group of native Americans who are described, in the book's opening pages, as innocents "so

---

ally be freed is also an example of the ways in which her first-person narrative participates in the Cretan liar paradox that encompasses all English-born speakers in this
novella. I credit her with considerably more authorial self-consciousness, especially with
regard to her complicity in Oroonoko's fate and in his "education" about the little
"credit" that should be accorded to white men's (and women's) words (p. 66), than
Michael McKeon does in his generally illuminating remarks on the epistemological
"instability" of the novella (*The Origins of the English Novel, 1600–1740* [Baltimore: Johns
Hopkins University Press, 1987], p. 113): "she never is moved, like Congreve, to disclose the manipulative power of the author 'to impose any notions or fictions upon' the
reader."

55. See Brown, "The Romance of Empire," and McKeon, *Origins*, esp. pp. 111–13
and 249–50. For examples of critical accounts that don't allow for symptomatic contradictions and ambivalences in Behn's novella, see George Guffey and Angeline Goreau
on the issue of Behn's representation of black slaves: for Guffey, who reads confidently
"through" the sign of Oroonoko's blackness to an English political subtext, the novella's
ideological argument is not anti-slavery but against the enslavement of *kings*, specifically, the Stuart king tenuously on England's throne in 1688: "through a series of
parallels between James and the mistreated royal slave Oroonoko, [Behn] attempts to
gain the sympathy of her reader for James, who . . . was in great danger of imminent
deposition or worse," writes Guffey ("Aphra Behn's *Oroonoko*: Occasion and Accom-
plishment," in *Two English Novelists: Aphra Behn and Anthony Trollope*, coauthored with
Andrew White [Los Angeles: William Andrews Clark Memorial Library, UCLA, 1975],
pp. 16–17). Goreau, in contrast (and equally confidently), sees Behn's "impassioned
attack on the condition of slavery and defense of human rights" as "perhaps the first
important abolitionist statement in the history of English literature" (*Reconstructing
Aphra*, p. 289).

56. See Tzvetan Todorov, *The Conquest of America: The Question of the Other*, trans.
Richard Howard (1982; New York: Harper, 1984), and, for a cogent critique, Deborah
Root, "The Imperial Signifier: Todorov and the Conquest of America," in *Cultural
Critique* 9 (Spring 1988): 197–219.

unadorn'd" and beautiful that they resemble "our first Parents before
the Fall" (p. 3). Neither the white Englishwoman nor the black African
man shares the Indians' (imputed) quality of primeval innocence, but
Behn's stress on the Indian culture's concern with artifice (body painting, ornamentation, and even self-mutilation, p. 2; cf. p. 57) suggests
that her representation of the Indians offers no stable "base" for the
triangle in question. On the contrary, the Indians will turn out to be as
ethically volatile as the black African man and the white Englishwoman: later in the story Behn describes a time when the English in
Surinam occupied precisely that position of fear toward hostile Indians which she dramatizes for the English colonists in *The Widow Ranter*. "In many mortal Fears" about disputes "the *English* had with the
Indians," the narrator and her cohorts were unable to venture into
Indian territory except in "great Numbers"; she goes on to project
into the future a terror based on past experience, or rather, on an
experience that was past when Behn wrote her novel but still to come
according to the chronology of her narrative: the Indians, she explains, had attacked the colonizers—now mainly Dutch rather than
English—"immediately after my coming away": "they cut in pieces all
they could take . . . and hanging up the Mother, and all her Children
about her; and cut a Footman, I left behind me, all in Joints, and
nail'd him to Trees" (p. 54). If dismemberment—the fate of both the
footman and Oroonoko—seems ominously likely for male servants of
this particular English lady (as well as for her procreative female
servants), that is perhaps symptomatic of the multiple divisions, the
repeated doublings, which characterize Behn's cultural subject matter
and her own subject positions.

One cause of the psychological and ethical doubleness of the narrator and (male) hero is evidently their educations; both received training in European history and literature, albeit less good training, we
may suppose, than that accorded to privileged white men. One consequence of their shared quality of "civilized" doubleness is that both
are at once victims and beneficiaries of socio-economic systems that
discriminate kings from commoners and support the privileges of the
nobility with the profits of the slave trade. Oroonoko is described as
having captured and sold black slaves in African wars before he was
himself enslaved, and the narrator not only belongs to a slave-owning
class but clearly supports the nationalistic colonizing enterprise which
fueled and depended on the African slave trade. She laments the loss
of Surinam to the Dutch a few years after the events of the novella

take place (interestingly, the English traded the colony for New Amsterdam, in "our" America, in 1667) and even uses a lush description of a gold-prospecting river trip to suggest the desirability—in 1688, on the eve of the Dutch William of Orange's accession to the British throne—of retaking the lost colony and its lost profits: "And 'tis to be bemoan'd what his Majesty lost by losing part of *America*," she remarks (p. 59).[57] By thus presenting a narrator and a hero who are both victims and beneficiaries of the international system of the slave trade, and by contrasting and comparing both characters, at different moments, to the exotic, sometimes innocent, sometimes dangerous Indians, Behn provides a perspective on "the Conquest of America" that complicates among other binary oppositions the ethical one, infinitely labile in the literature of the imperial venture, between "we" as good and "them" as "evil"—or vice versa. The "triangulation effects" of Behn's text have as one of their several hermeneutic horizons, I argue, the "triangular trade" analyzed by Eric Williams and mentioned early in this essay.

What even this account of the complexity of Behn's novella leaves out, however—as does Laura Brown's otherwise rich critique—is the specific ideological modality of the "other" black slave in the story, the character who is a major if relatively silent player in the book's shadowy plot about an erotic *triangle*. Imoinda is doubly enslaved—to the whites, male and female, who have bought her and also, as the narrative insists, to her black husband. In striking contrast to the unmarried narrator, who plays the role of the Petrarchan mistress and ladylord toward Oroonoko as vassal, Imoinda is an uncanny amalgam of European ideals of wifely subservience and European fantasies about wives of Oriental despots. She is thus the perfect embodiment, with the exception of her dark hue, of an image of the ideal English wife as the property, body and soul, of her husband. Wives like Imoinda—that is, *African* wives, as refracted in the mirror a white female English author holds up to this example of the Other—"have a respect for their Husbands equal to what any other People pay a Deity; and when a Man finds any occasion to quit his Wife, if he love her, she dies by his hand; if not he sells her, or suffers some other to kill her" (p. 72).

57. Cf. p. 48, where the narrator laments that "certainly had his late Majesty [Charles II], of sacred Memory, but seen and known what a vast and charming World he had been Master of in that Continent, he would never have parted so easily with it to the *Dutch*"; the passage goes on to advertise the natural riches of the (once and future) colony. On the British loss of Surinam (later Guiana) in exchange for New York, see Williams, *From Columbus to Castro*, p. 81.

In this passage, which rationalizes and immediately precedes the gruesome scene where Oroonoko severs Imoinda's head from her pregnant body, the narrator's relation to her black heroine is revealed to be anything but straightforwardly sympathetic. On the contrary, Behn as author uses Imoinda's death scene to inscribe the authority and agency of the *white woman writer*, figured in the narrator, as a function of a set of finely calibrated *differences* from the female "other" embodied in Imoinda. That Other against which Behn constructs her authorial agency is a creature of extremes. On the one hand, Imoinda is presented as utterly passive and obedient; on the other, she is presented as violent and powerful, a creature who threatens the white civilization in ways that are arguably analogous, as we shall see, to those dramatized when Oroonoko kills not one but two mother tigers. Imoinda is, significantly, the only non-white character in the story who's allowed actually to wound with an arrow the supreme figure of white patriarchal authority, Colonel Byam.[58] Her deed of Amazonian aggression is, however, described by the narrator as being quite literally undone—and by another woman of color. Byam's life is saved, though the narrator clearly regrets this, by his Indian mistress, who sucks the poison from his wound (pp. 65, 68). The narrator's own ambivalent relation to male English authority is figured here—but also symbolically divested of its power to harm—by the device of splitting "other" women into the extreme roles of dangerous rebel and erotically complicitous slave.

By implicitly associating both these extremes with Imoinda, through the symbol of a mother tiger I discuss below and through the anagrammatic link between the unnamed Indian woman who nurses Byam and the black woman whose name suggests "I'm Indian" or even more punningly, "I-me [moi] am Indian," Behn effectively presents her own agency as safe—or safe enough—by contrast to Imoinda's figure. The text thus both stages and preordains the outcome of a competition between the white female author and the non-white female slave/potential rebel. The competition is focused on possession of Oroonoko's body and its richly symbolic power to engender something that will outlive it. That power remains latent, in the sense of impotent, without a female counterpart, and for this Behn offers two

58. See *Oroonoko*, pp. 64–65, where Imoinda's exploit is first described as incontrovertible "fact"; and p. 68, where it is oddly described again, this time through the epistemological filter of "news": "the first News we heard, was, That the Governour was dead of a Wound Imoinda had given him; but it was not so well."

distinct images: Imoinda's pregnant body, holding a potential slave-laborer ("for," as the text reminds us, "all the Breed is theirs to whom the Parents belong" [p. 45]); and, alternatively, the author's own "Female Pen" (p. 40), which she deploys to describe, with an unnerving blend of relish and horror, the novella's concluding scenes of Oroonoko's bodily dismemberment, including his castration. She uses that pen also, as she tells the reader in the final paragraph, in hopes of making Oroonoko's "glorious Name to survive all Ages" (p. 78).

The narrator seems to win the competition hands down, though the production of the text, years after the events it describes, testifies to a certain intractible residue or, we might say, psychic fallout from the narrator's comportment toward her slaves. If, however, she signals guilt and some chagrin at her impotence to save Oroonoko (she deserts him in the middle of his torture, for instance, because his smell is too much for her suddenly acquired and typically "feminine" delicacy [p. 76]), she also demonstrates the powers of her pen and implies some degree of choice in how she deployed her verbal skills, oral and written both. Through her "Female Pen" flow at least some of the prerogatives of the English empire and its language, a language she shows herself using, in one remarkable scene, as a potent instrument of sexual and political domination. In this scene, which explicitly pits an image of politically "dangerous" biological reproduction against an image of "safe" verbal production, the author presents herself most paradoxically as both servant and a beneficiary of the eroticized socioeconomic system of domination she describes. When some unnamed English authority figures perceive that Oroonoko is growing sullen because of the "Thought" that his child will belong not to him but to his owners, the narrator is "obliged," she tells us, to use her fiction-making powers to "divert" Oroonoko (and Imoinda too) from thoughts of mutiny. Mutiny is specifically tied to a problem in population management, a problem about which Behn's text—like much colonialist discourse, including chilling debates on whether it is better to "buy or breed" one's slaves—is fundamentally and necessarily ambivalent.[59] Mutiny, the narrator observes, "is very fatal sometimes in those Colonies that abound so with Slaves, that they exceed the Whites in vast numbers" (p. 46). It is to abort the potential mutiny that the narrator is "obliged" to "discourse with Caesar, and to give him all the

59. On the "buy or breed" debates, see Daniel P. Mannix in collaboration with Malcolm Cowley, *Black Cargoes: A History of the Atlantic Slave Trade 1518–1865* (New York: Viking, 1962), p. 52.

Satisfaction I possibly could"—which she does, entertaining him with stories about "the Loves of the Romans, and great Men, which charmed him to my Company." In an interestingly gendered division of narrative goods, she tells Imoinda stories about nuns.[60]

Dramatizing a complex mode of authorial "ownership" of characters who are cast in the role of enthralled—and feminized—audience, Behn represents herself creating a paradoxical *facsimile* of freedom for herself, her immediate audience, and by implication, her readers back home as well. In this facsimile, servitude, which Oroonoko during his revolt describes scornfully as a condition of being "sport of Women" (p. 61), is rendered (perhaps only temporarily) tolerable by being eroticized, fantasized, "diverted" from activities, either sexual or military, that might work to dislodge the English from their precarious lordship of this new world land. Just how precarious was their lordship the narrative acknowledges by repeatedly lamenting their loss of the land to the Dutch. The deeper problems of the logic of colonialism are also signaled, albeit confusedly, by the contrast between the description of slave mutiny quoted above and the explanation offered early in the story for why the British do *not* enslave the native Indians, a group that, like the Africans, is essential to the colonialists' welfare: "they being on all occasions very useful to us," the narrator says, "we find it absolutely necessary to caress 'em as Friends, and not to treat 'em as Slaves, nor dare we do other, their numbers so far surpassing ours in that Continent" (p. 5).[61] This passage sheds an

60. See Amore, introduction to *Oroonoko*, for the hypothesis of Behn's Catholicism, a hypothesis I think is well founded though it does not adequately gloss the sexual division of narrative labor whereby Imoinda is given stories of nuns. For Behn's own nuns' stories (and the late tale *Oroonoko* seems to be full of authorial self-citations), see *The History of the Nun, or, The Fair Vow Breaker* and *The Nun; or The Perjur'd Beauty*, both in *Works*, vol. 5.

61. Since the blacks also greatly outnumbered the whites in the colony, Behn's explanation for the distinction in the English treatment of the two non-white groups is clearly problematic. The matter continues to be a site of debate in modern histories of slavery in the New World, for even though Indians were frequently enslaved, all of the colonial powers came, eventually, to prefer African to Amerindian slaves for reasons that confusingly blended economic, theological, and cultural explanations. Some modern historians, for instance Winthrop Jordan in *White over Black*, invoke color difference as an explanation for why Africans came (eventually) to be seen as better (more "natural") slaves than Indians, but this view seems anachronistic and reductive. More satisfactory discussions are in Davis, *Problem of Slavery*, which describes the distinction as an "outgrowth of the practical demands of trade and diplomacy" (p. 178) bolstered by ideological fictions about blackness (the biblical color of evil) and "noble savages"; and in William D. Phillips, Jr., *Slavery from Roman Times to the Early Transatlantic Trade* (Minneapolis: University of Minnesota Press, 1985). In discussing the commonly cited

ironic light on the later moment when the narrator uses stories to divert Oroonoko from thoughts of mutiny, for we see that one logical solution to the mutiny problem, a solution that her stories to Oroonoko suppress but that her larger narrative only partially represses, is the possibility of *not* enslaving a group of "others" who outnumber you. Such a solution, with respect both to Africans and to Indians, had been recommended by a few early critics of the colonial enterprise; but Behn is far from joining the tiny group who voiced criticisms of the whole system of international trade based on forced labor by persons of many skin colors, including freckled Irish white.[62]

In its characteristically disturbing way, Behn's novel shows us just enough about the author's competition with Imoinda, and about the way that competition is enmeshed in a larger socio-sexual-economic system, to make us uneasy when we hold the book *Oroonoko* in our hands. The text invites us to see that book as a safe sex substitute for the potentially mutinous, economically valuable black slave child Oroonoko might have had with Imoinda—or indeed with Aphra Behn had she given physical rather than verbal "satisfaction," playing Tamora, as it were, to Oroonoko's Aaron and thereby activating longstanding English anxieties about the "genetic" strength of blackness, since babies born of mixed unions were thought inevitably to follow the darker and "lower" hue.[63]

---

adage that "one Negro is worth four Indians" in terms of labor power, Phillips suggests that the difference between the Africans' experience in agricultural societies and the Amerindians in mainly hunting-gathering cultures helps account for this sobering ideological distinction (p. 184)—a distinction that makes a person's economic value stand in antithetical relation to his or her moral value (in European eyes which equated freedom with "natural" nobility).

62. For discussions of early critics of slavery such as Las Casas (who came only late in life to decry the enslavement of blacks as well as Indians) and Albornoz, see Davis, *Problem of Slavery*, p. 189 and passim; Eric Williams, *From Columbus to Castro*, pp. 43–44; and Goreau, *Reconstructing Aphra*, p. 289, on the Quaker George Fox's opposition to the system of slavery. On the legal and ideological distinctions very unevenly and gradually introduced between white and black slaves, see Phillips, *Slavery from Roman Times*, p. 183.

63. See, for instance, the passage from George Best's *Discourse* (1578; rpt. Hakluyt, 1600) where he insists that "I my selfe have seene an Ethiopian as blacke as a cole brought into England, who taking a faire English women to wife, begat a sonne in all respects as blacke as the father was, although England were his native countrey, and an English woman his mother" (quoted from Hakluyt, *Principal Navigations*, ed. Raleigh [cited above, note 9], 7:262). I am indebted to Karen Newman's discussion of this passage in "'And Wash the Ethiop White': Femininity and the Monstrous in *Othello*," in *Shakespeare Reproduced: The Text in History and Ideology*, ed. Jean E. Howard and Marion F. O'Connor (New York: Methuen, 1987), p. 146. Folarin Shyllon also discusses this

In an apparently conservative and reassuring twist of the old trope of book as child, however, Behn offers her contemporary English readers a representation of a white woman who is apparently attracted to a strong black hero but who in the end refrains—as Shakespeare's Tamora and Desdemona did not—from transferring her sexual "treasure" from its rightful owner and disposer, her father or his proxies, to an alien. That contemporary readers would have remarked the text's coy dramatization of an erotic "road not taken" by the narrator is suggested by Thomas Southerne's revisionary dramatization of Behn's tale, a play in which Oroonoko loves a *white* Imoinda.[64] The frontispiece from a 1735 production of Southerne's highly popular play is reproduced, intriguingly, on the cover of the Norton edition of Behn's story (Figure 5.2), and this representation—like Southerne's play itself—arguably capitalizes on the cultural prestige of *Othello*'s drama of tragic miscegenous romance. Southerne's play and its frontispiece also exploit the posthumous notoriety of Behn herself, a notoriety she may well have helped fashion. In 1696, the same year that Southerne's play was first produced, a biography of Behn appeared as a preface and advertisement to a posthumous collection of her novels. The biography, which has been ascribed to Charles Gildon and also (in part) to Behn herself, elaborately and titillatingly *denies* a rumor that the author of *Oroonoko* had a romance with her hero: "I knew her intimately well," the author affirms, "and I believe she wou'd not have conceal'd any Love-affair from me . . . which makes me assure the World, there was no Affair between that Prince and Astrea. . . ."[65] Whatever the status of this rumor

passage by Best; its formulation of a theory of racial domination is clearly significant for understanding the first racially discriminatory law in England, namely the one passed in 1596, under Queen Elizabeth: "Her Majesty, understanding that there are late divers blackmoores brought into this realme, of which kind there are already too manie, considering how God hath blessed this land with great increase of people of our owne nation . . . those kinds of people should be sent forth the lande" (*Acts of the Privy Council of England [New Series], 1596–97*, ed. John Roche Dasent, 26:16–17; cited in Shyllon, *Black People in England*, p. 93).

64. For a discussion of this "recoloring" of Behn's heroine and other significant changes Southerne makes, see Novak and Rodes's introduction to their edition of Southerne's *Oroonoko*; see also Maureen Duffy, who rightly suggests that Behn's *Widow Ranter* provides much of the structure for Southerne's play, particularly for its subplot of young Englishwomen seeking husbands in the colonies but also, I maintain, for its representation of Oroonoko and Imoinda's love (*The Passionate Shepherdess*, p. 295).

65. *The Life of Mrs. Behn* (cited above, n. 11), sig. b1r. Montague Summers identifies the author of this biography (which was retitled and considerably expanded in the 1698 edition of *The Histories and Novels*) with Charles Gildon but suggests that Gildon couldn't

Figure 5.2. Frontispiece from Thomas Southerne's *Oroonoko,*
London, 1735. Courtesy Rare Books and Manuscripts Division, The
New York Public Library, Astor, Lenox and Tilden Foundations

(which is reproduced, again only to be denied "credit," in the introduction to the modern Norton edition of Behn's text [p. x]), it forms part of the larger discursive field in which Behn's text was and continues to be read. At least a part of this field is evidently governed by an ideological economy in which the white woman's book is born, quite starkly, from a self-willed (albeit partial) censoring of her own sexuality and from the death and silencing of black persons, one of them pregnant. Behind the scene of Oroonoko's final torture is the murder-sacrifice of the black woman and her unborn child. And the threat represented by the black woman, I suggest, is obscurely acknowleged to be even greater than the threat represented by the black man, so that the text finally has to enlist him, through enticements of European codes of masculine honor and Petrarchan romance, to suppress the one character who uses physical force rather than words to attack the highest legal representative of the colonial system, namely the male Lieutenant Governor. According to the old Renaissance commonplace, deeds are masculine, words are feminine; but Imoinda, like the Amazon maidens Sir Walter Ralegh sought in Guiana, has performed the kind of deed that Desdemona, Othello's "fair warrior," was never allowed.[66]

Imoinda's rebellious power—and the need to destroy or at least disguise it—are figured most strikingly, I think, in the two juxtaposed episodes where Oroonoko first kills a mother tiger and lays her whelp at the author's feet (p. 51) and then kills a property-destroying tiger— again female—and extracts her bullet-ridden heart to give to the English audience. At this moment Oroonoko is most transparently shown as a figure for the author of *Oroonoko*, a repository of novel curiosities which Behn offers to her readers as he offers the tiger's cub, and then heart, to his owner-admirers: "This Heart the Conqueror brought up to us, and 'twas a very great Curiousity, which all the Country came to see; and which gave *Caesar* occasion of many fine Discourses, of Accidents in War, and strange Escapes" (p. 53). Oroonoko woos his "Great Mistress" and other British ladies as Othello

---

possibly have composed the text "unaided"; rather, he was (purportedly) using material Behn intended to have "worked up into a novel" (see *Works*, 1:xxi–xxii); Robert Adams Day argues for Behn's authorship of much of *The Life* in "Aphra Behn's First Biography," *Studies in Bibliography* 22 (1969): 227–40.

66. On Ralegh's quest for Amazons as described in his *Discoverie* ("[I] was very desirous to understand the truth of those warlike women, because of some it is beleeved, of others not"), see Montrose, "The Work of Gender," pp. 25–29, and esp. p. 26.

wooed Desdemona with his eloquent story of his "most disastrous chances . . . moving accidents . . . hairbreadth scapes i' th' imminent deadly breach" (I.iii.133–35). With respect to the power relation between a narrator and an audience, this scene offers a mirror reversal of that in which the narrator entertains her sullen, potentially mutinous hero with her culture's stories of "great [Roman] men." We can now see even more clearly that the "ground" of both scenes, the "material," as it were, from which the production and reception of exotic stories derives, is the silent figure of the black woman—silent but by no means safe, as is suggested by the image of the female tiger and the narrative device of duplicating it.

In *Oroonoko* as in *The Widow Ranter*, then, Aphra Behn uses her "female pen" to ward off the overdetermined set of dangers she associates with or projects onto the non-white heroine; among these dangers, I have suggested, lurks pregnancy, the consequence and all too visible sign, for women, of one form of sexual pleasure.[67] In both texts, moreover, Behn not only kills the Indian or African woman in the end but performs an ideologically significant gesture of cultural appropriation and justification by making the heroine voice, as if it were her own, a desire for death at the hands of a lover, a desire founded, moreover, on precisely the European ideal of female "honor" as chastity which Behn mocked and interrogated in so many of her works. In thus making her non-white heroines participate verbally in the mystification of the complex causes of their deaths, Behn at once exposes some of the dire contradictions of her society's ideologies of gender and at the same time takes advantage, we might fairly say, of the particular historical condition of silence which affected the vast majority of non-white women who lived in England's early imperial territories. That historical condition of course affected non-white men too, but differently, especially, I maintain, because of the differ-

---

67. The narrator's lavish descriptions of Imoinda's "carved" body suggest, of course, the possibility of female homoerotic pleasure as yet another alternative to procreative sexuality. I am grateful to Michèle Barale for this suggestion, which is supported by Behn's publication, in the same year as *Oroonoko*, of a poem "To the Fair Clarinda, who made love to me, imagined more than woman." This poem praises Clarinda for combining virtues of males and females in one body—the same vein of praise that one of Behn's admirers accorded her in a poem printed in the same volume—and thanks the nymph for bringing to "our sex" a way "That we might love, and yet be innocent" (quoted from "Poems Appended to *Lycidus*," *Works*, 6:363; cited and discussed in Goreau, *Reconstructing Aphra*, pp. 205–6). For the poem by Daniel Kendrick praising Behn as the sole exemplar of a super "Third Sex," see *Works*, 6:296–98.

ent *sexual* myths which attached (again differently) to the European image of both the African and the American Indian male. Such silence derives from lack of access to what we might call "literacy," if we define that term, paraphrasing John Guillory, as "a complex of social facts containing answers to the following questions": who reads English? who writes English? for whom? and who has access to education and publication apparatuses?[68] The historical women of color "represented" by figures such as the Indian Queen and Imoinda mostly did not possess the skills of literacy Behn enjoyed.[69] That point may seem obvious, but for that very reason it merits attention from those of us who continue to enjoy the privileges conferred by literacy in English. We should in any event not forget that literate metropolitan women sometimes promoted and rationalized, as well as interrogated, the colonizing process figured, not infrequently, as a rape of a female or feminized "other." "Guiana," as Ralegh famously wrote in 1596, "is a countrey that hath yet her maydenhead" (*Discoverie of Guiana*, in Hakluyt, *Principal Navigations*, 10:428). Aphra Behn arguably contributed to the English effort to deflower that colony. But the author who was praised in her own time as belonging to a "third" androgynous sex ("Ah, more than Woman! more than man she is")[70] not only contributed to this still-ongoing project of once and future rape in ways that perpetuated a tradition of misrepresenting non-white characters on English stages and in the pages of English books; she also invited us to see and ponder the fact that we are *not* seeing the "whole truth" about her white or non-white characters, including herself. In thus producing some quantity of skepticism about the believability or "credit" of her depiction of Oroonoko and Imoinda, or their shadowy doubles the outlaw Bacon and his Indian Queen, Behn was, at the least, a better interpreter and maker of news from the New World than many who have followed her.

68. John Guillory, "Canonical and Non-Canonical: A Critique of the Current Debate," *English Literary History* 54 (1987): 483–527; my paraphrase is from a sentence on p. 485.

69. For a modern attempt to counter the "invisibility" of black women in Caribbean history, see Barbara Bush, *Slave Women in Caribbean Society, 1650–1838* (Bloomington: Indiana University Press, 1990).

70. Quoted from a poem by Daniel Kendrick published with Behn's own *Lycidus* in 1688; cited above, note 70, and in Goreau, p. 268.

6

Dead Man's Treasure

The Cult of Thomas More

CLARK HULSE

The grave, said Andrew Marvell, is a fine and private place, and for most of us it will be. Yet for a few, it is not so: for Stalin, moved from his place next to Lenin to a modest grave by the Kremlin Wall; for Elvis in his mausoleum at Graceland, the lure for armies of tourists; or for the nameless souls dragged from mass graves in Bosnia or Central America, the flickering images of their torn corpses playing across our television screens in endless repetition. No, for some, the grave is not private, not quiet at all.

Death makes the body into a thing, stripping it of all the appearances of spirit and of life. When Hans Holbein painted the famous Erasmus (Figure 6.1), he sought to capture the qualities known to the man's friends and, through his writing, to the world: inwardness, humor, more than a little vanity, brilliance of mind in the feeble body of a hypochondriac. When Hans Baldung Gruen sketched the corpse (Figure 6.2), he saw instead the leaden flesh, the fixed eyes, and the missing teeth.[1] The body in death is an object of pity or of revulsion; its loss of humanity threatens our own.

In death the body no longer can talk back or look back. It is indeed a thing, and suffers the fate of all things at our hands, which is to be

---

1. Christian Müller, "A Drawing of Erasmus on His Deathbed Attributed to Hans Baldung Grien," *Burlington Magazine* 132 (1990): 187–94.

Figure 6.1. Hans Holbein. *Desiderius Erasmus,* 1523. Oil on panel. Private Collection.
Photo: Courtauld Institute of Art

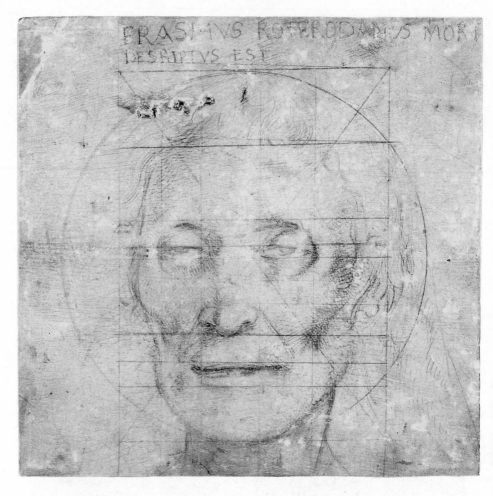

Figure 6.2. Hans Baldung Grien. *Erasmus of Rotterdam on His Deathbed,* 1536. Silverpoint on yellow prepared paper. Öffentliche Kunstsammlung Basel, Kupferstichkabinett

put to use, whether by enshrinement or by mutilation. It is used in ceremonies of lamentation that arouse and cast out grief, in ceremonies of remembrance that define and solidify communities, in ceremonies of embalming that cast out pollution, and in ceremonies of desecration that ward off the demons that affright us. The body is caught up in social economies and monetary exchanges: the embalmer, the gravedigger, the taxman all demand their pieces. Or rather, through the ceremonies of death, the body offers a new promise, to reveal at last all the hidden social and economic roles of the living person. It is like a chest opened to show the wealth or poverty inside.

If the body in death is a thing, it is therefore like a work of art, for art likewise is a thing that we use to exorcise demons, to ward off pollution, to arouse and cast out emotions, and to define and solidify social groups. And art, for all its aloofness, is like other things in being a part of economies, partaking in the exchange of cash as well as of symbolic capital. The buying, the selling, the using and consuming of art are essential to its original production and its continued reproduction. Only by tracing this consumption and reproduction of the work of art can we see how it is like the human body, or, for that matter, how it is unlike, how it is art.

In linking art to death and to use, I am intentionally reversing several of the great commonplaces on which the art of the Renaissance and our understanding of that art are based: that art is a substitute for the living body; that it competes with divine creation in setting forth the very image of life; that the Renaissance is the time of the rebirth of the individual, whose image, in all its variety and nuance, is contained in the portrait of life, which partakes of freedom.

Take Holbein's famous portrait of Sir Thomas More—or Saint Thomas More, if you will. Sir or Saint—humanist author of the *Utopia*, friend of Erasmus, utopian communist philosopher, City lawyer, Lord Chancellor, defender of the faith, martyr—all these roles are projected, or can be projected, through the portrait. In the preparatory drawing (Figure 6.3), the precision of the facial features contrasts with the quickly sketched clothing, suggesting the momentary arresting of an animated figure. Indeed, the very stiffness of the neck and the posed quality of his gaze suggest how very hard it was for him to hold still for the artist. And yet, the features seem so precisely drawn in part because their outlines are pierced with tiny pinholes (Figure 6.4) which are used to transfer the design to a panel for a painting. The very element that produces the image of life is also a sign of use,

Figure 6.3. Hans Holbein. *Sir Thomas More*, 1526–28.
Black and colored chalk on paper.
The Royal Collection
©1993 Her Majesty Queen Elizabeth II
Figure 6.4. *Opposite*. Detail

a sign that this wondrous drawing is a device for production, a sort of machine tool in the artistic industry. The finished painting, now in the Frick (Figure 6.5), replicates the design of the drawing, but now a golden chain of royal office rests about More's neck, symbolizing the position of favor with, and subservience to, the king, that More had just attained. The chain rests there uneasily, like a garment donned in order to be put off. His inwardness is, if anything, even more intensely rendered in the sharper outline of the nose and the drawn mouth (Figure 6.6). Yet if much about him attempts to escape or transcend the body, the world, and the king, simple details draw him back to the realm of decay and death: the unmowed stubble of his chin, the slight pouching particularly evident under the left eye, and above all, the vanity of his red sleeve (Figure 6.7).

If More, like Erasmus, like any of us, is a bit of flesh caught between living and dying, then the portraits of More and of Erasmus are all the more inanimate things suspended between life and death. They are dead things that are of interest only as false images of a life that itself wends toward thingness and toward death. More proclaims himself a character in the Renaissance theater of individuality, and yet makes himself into a symbol first of humanist reform, then of ecclesiastical resistance, and finally of endurance in the face of annihilation. Alive, he can wrestle with his own thingness—his body, his desires, his roles and obligations. Dead, he is altogether a thing for others to use, a bodily metaphor in the struggle between the Church and the king, or, in our own era, a floating sign in the struggles to define the utopian element in humanism. His portraits, whether in paint or in writing, are signs of signs that are produced, circulated, and consumed in furtherance of this transformation of the body into metaphor and the incorporation of metaphors in the body.

I want to look at this process of the transformation of the body of Thomas More into a thing, and the transformation of that thing into art and the economy, as an example of the production of culture.[2] I call this dead man's treasure because it is filled with riches left behind

---

2. In posing the question this way, I must acknowledge the conceptual influence of the emerging subject of body criticism, including Francis Barker, *The Tremulous Private Body: Essays on Subjection* (London: Methuen, 1984); *The Making of the Modern Body: Sexuality and Society in the Nineteenth Century*, ed. Catherine Gallagher and Thomas Lacquer (Berkeley: University of California Press, 1987); *Fragments for a History of the Body: Zone 3–5*, ed. Michael Feher, 3 vols. (New York: Zone Books, 1989); Carolyn Walker Bynum, *Fragmentation and Redemption: Essays on Gender and the Human Body in Medieval Religion* (New York: Zone Books, 1991); Lucy Gent and Nigel Llewelyn, *Renaissance Bodies: The Human Figure in English Culture c. 1540–1660* (London: Reaktion

by others—financial, political, social, aesthetic abundances—riches that rise from the buried chest in the earth. But before turning to Thomas More in some detail, I want briefly to connect his story with that of another Thomas, Thomas Becket, who likewise became a dead man's treasure.

In 1534, Henry VIII began to solidify the changes in the fabric of English culture that he had precipitated by his divorce from Catherine of Aragon. He began to gather to himself the wealth and revenues of the Church, declared himself its Supreme Head, and settled the Succession to the Crown, at least for the moment, on his new-born daughter Elizabeth. Thomas More, who had resigned the Chancellorship in 1532, now refused the oath to uphold the Succession Act, which would have involved acknowledging the legality of the divorce and repudiating papal authority, and so he was committed to the Tower. More died on the block in 1535, and the following year the northern counties rose in the great rebellion known as the Pilgrimage of Grace, but the work begun by Henry and his new chief minister Thomas Cromwell continued unabated.[3] In the summer and fall of 1538, Thomas Cromwell set about the dissolution of the greater monastic houses and the eradication of saintly cults, along with the shrines and relics that were associated with them and that brought revenues to the monks. In September, 1538, the Royal Commissioners reached the Cathedral of Canterbury, the same to which Chaucer's pilgrims had traveled, and dismantled the shrine of Thomas Becket, archbishop and martyr.

This elaborate shrine housing the dead body of Becket is known only from written descriptions and from three depictions, two in the windows of the Cathedral (Figure 6.8),[4] and the other a drawing on a charred fragment of paper now preserved in the British Library (Figure 6.9).[5] The shrine was, by all reports, a thing of staggering rich-

---

Books, 1990); Barbara Stafford, *Body Criticism: Imaging the Unseen in Enlightenment Art and Medicine* (Cambridge: MIT Press, 1991); and Marcia Pointon, *Hanging the Head* (New Haven: Yale University Press, 1993).

3. The finest summary of events and analysis of how they evolved in Cromwell's mind from makeshift measures into a conscious plan is G. R. Elton, *Policy and Police: The Enforcement of the Reformation in the Age of Thomas Cromwell* (Cambridge: Cambridge University Press, 1972).

4. Trinity Chapel aisle, window 5, medallion 1, and window 12, medallion 22, described in Bernard Rackham, *The Ancient Glass of Canterbury Cathedral* (London: Lund Humphries, 1949), pp. 91, 111.

5. British Library MS Cotton Tiberius E. viii, fol. 269; damaged by the fire of 1731. The manuscript is largely similar to John Stow's description of the shrine in his *Annales*, and may be Stow's source.

Figure 6.5. Hans Holbein. *Sir Thomas More,* 1527. Oil on panel.
©The Frick Collection, New York

Figure 6.6 and 6.7. *Opposite.* Details

ness. The lower section, about five feet in height, was made of stone, with arches either open, as they appear in the window, or in a blind arcade, as in the drawing. The arches carried a pediment, which in turn carried the upper portion. Its outer layer was a plain wooden canopy, visible in the drawing. It could be lifted away by ropes to reveal the shrine itself, also made of wood, but plated with gold and damasked with gold wire, into which were worked the pearls, rubies, and other precious stones that had been donated by wealthy pilgrims. Finally, within the golden chest was an iron one—depicted separately in the drawing (Figure 6.9)—which actually held the bones of Thomas Becket.

The wealth of the shrine demonstrates that the monks of the Cathedral priory, like others throughout Christendom who possessed the relics of the saints, had found a very good use for the dead body. The income of the shrine was substantial, with a high of £1,142 in 1220, the year the relics were translated to the shrine. It fell off to about £500 per annum in Chaucer's time and dwindled to a mere £13 13s 3d in 1532.[6] In return for their money, the pilgrims received hospitality from the monks, intercession from the saint, and indulgence from a merciful god. This indulgence was particularly visible in the marks it left on the bodies of pilgrims, or, one might more accurately say, in the marks of affliction that were removed from their bodies through the saint's miraculous cures of the lame, the halt, and the blind.

But at root this transaction involved a category violation, the exchange of material goods for spiritual goods. The violation was felt within medieval culture as a contrast between small shrines and the great, ostentatious pilgrimage sites, and as a contrast between the sincere devotion of the ordinary worshipper and the avarice of a priesthood suspected of corruption. This violation could be endured, the tensions mitigated, and the economy of the shrine maintained, only if its elements underwent a change akin to transubstantiation, asserting a spiritual identity for matter. Most important was a transformation within the site of exchange, that is, within the body of Thomas Becket. For the rest of us, the soul departs from the body at death. For the saint, this is not quite so. The soul is both with God and lingering at the site of the body, so that it may continue to act in the

6. Francis Woodman, *The Architectural History of Canterbury Cathedral* (London: Routledge & Kegan Paul, 1981), p. 221; based on E. Woodruff, "The Financial Aspect of the Cult of St. Thomas of Canterbury," *Archaeologia Canterburiana* 44 (1932): 13–32.

Figure 6.8. *St. Thomas Becket Issuing from His Shrine,* ca. 1220. Stained glass.
Canterbury Cathedral, Trinity Chapel aisle, window 5, medallion 1.
Photo: RCHME Crown Copyright

Figure 6.9. *The Shrine of St. Thomas Becket,* sixteenth century. Ink on paper.
British Library MS Cotton Tiberius E. viii, fol. 269.
By permission of the British Library

material world. Hence the devout speak of the bodies of saints as remaining fresh and uncorrupted, even though to skeptical eyes they appear putrid and rotten. And hence the Becket window (Figure 6.8) shows the saint emerging from the shrine, as if the soul still inhabited its body, in order to work a miraculous cure.

The transaction at the shrine, then, is a triple one: an exchange of money for grace; an exchange between the spiritual and the material realms; and an exchange between the living and the dead. The nature of this transaction is written in the peculiar architecture of the shrine, whereby a nondescript exterior reveals a rich interior which in turn conceals a core of corruption. The middle layer of gold stands as a transitive term between the merely inert on the outside and the once animate but now dead on the inside. It stands as a transitive term between the mortal life of the pilgrim and the presumedly immortal life of the saint; for the saint's death is now hidden away, replaced by a vision of gold. Because it is both true gold and metaphoric gold, it also stands as the transitive term between material and spiritual goods.

Through this transaction, Becket was himself transformed, as his putrid corpse was supplanted by the golden body of the shrine. Becket had been an intensely worldly man who as Lord Chancellor was renowned for the splendor of his appearance. The gold of the realm had flowed in for the bedecking of his body. After becoming Archbishop of Canterbury, he reversed this, or at least so legend claims. Luxury gave way to asceticism, and the gold now flowed outward as alms for the poor. Yet Becket remained as avaricious and ruthless in pursuit of the property rights of the Church as he had been for the crown. No matter whose version one accepts, the dispute in which he died was, at root, over Church lands and revenues which he believed were being alienated to the benefit of the crown or its adherents. The shrine of Becket, with its middle stage of gold, is itself a sign for the alternating flows of revenues away from or toward different sectors of the population.

These complex movements between the material and the spiritual are also theatrical ones. The revelation of the shrine, like the parting of a curtain, or the sudden appearance of a ghost out of the trap, or the apprehension of a vision, moves the witness from one zone of reality to another. The effect of the shrine, as Erasmus describes it, was stupefying: "within the wooden chest is a golden chest; when this is drawn up by ropes, it reveals inestimable treasure. . . . The cheapest part was gold. Everything shone and dazzled with rare and surpassingly large jewels, some bigger than a goose egg. Some monks stood about reverently. When the cover was removed, we all adored. The prior pointed out each jewel by touching it with a white rod, adding its French name, its worth, and the name of the donor. The principal ones were gifts from kings."[7] Like the prologue or epilogue of a Shakespearean history, like the character who stands at the margin of a painting pointing to the main action, like a modern tour guide or some literary critic, the prior with his white rod draws the pilgrim into the action. He keeps his audience fixed within the mimetic world, and guides their response toward catharsis, a momentary state of oblivion to their own physical being that purges off sickness, so that when they leave the interior space of the vision they feel as if they have reentered the world afresh.

But audiences are unruly, and some did not care for the performance, and read the signs otherwise. Erasmus is again the most clever observer, as he describes, in his quasi-fictional way, the reactions of John Colet to the relics. "An arm was brought forth, with the blood-stained flesh still on it. [Colet] shrank from kissing this, looking rather disgusted." Likewise revolting were "some linen rags, many of them still showing traces of [Becket's] snivel. With these, they say, the holy man wiped the sweat from his face or neck, the dirt from his nose, or whatever other kinds of filth human bodies have. . . . [Colet] touched the piece with his fingers, not without a sign of disgust, and put it back scornfully." Confronted with the golden splendor of the shrine, Colet reminded the monks of Becket's generosity to the poor in his lifetime: "Don't you think he'd gladly consent, now that he's so rich and needs nothing, if some poor wretched woman with hungry children at home, or daughters in danger of losing their virtue because they have no money for dowries, or a husband sick in bed and penniless—if, after begging the saint's forgiveness, she carried off a bit of all this wealth to rescue her family, as though taking from one who wanted her to have it, either as a gift or a loan."[8] Colet's uncathartic reaction is nothing less than a denial of the validity of the transaction of material goods for spiritual wealth, a denial that the shrine can bring a purga-

    7. Desiderius Erasmus, "A Pilgrimage for Religion's Sake," in *Ten Colloquies*, ed. Craig R. Thompson (Indianapolis: Bobbs-Merrill, 1957), p. 86.
    8. Erasmus, "Pilgrimage," p. 84. In a few places I have followed the more vivid wording of the anonymous Tudor translation, *The Pilgrimage of Pure Devotion* (1536), reprinted in *Tudor Translations of the Colloquies of Erasmus, 1536–1584*, ed. Dickie A. Spurgeon (Delmar, N.Y.: Scholars' Facsimiles, 1972), pp. 76–77.

tive effect solely through emotion, without social action. He imagines another economy, in which spiritual wealth arises from the redistribution of gold from the dead to the living, with a consequent purgation of the sickness of the body politic. His reshaping of the saintly economy is evidence that the metaphors of the shrine were themselves decaying, wearing out. Like gold coins rubbed by too many hands, they were ready for new imprints.

The wearing out was a long and complex process, involving overlapping critiques of icons and relics by Lollards and Lutherans as well as by skeptical humanists.[9] The new imprint, in contrast, came suddenly, in the form of a royal authority which interceded between the economy of the shrine and the economy imagined by Colet in order to pose as the defender of the people against the predations of the monastic orders. And so, when the shrine was destroyed in September of 1538, its wealth was conveyed not to the poor but to the king's treasury. As John Stow described it, "the spoile of which shrine, in golde and precious stone, filled two great chestes, such as 6. or 8. stronge men could do no more than conuey one of them at once out of the Church."[10] The entire Cathedral treasure amounted to 5020 ounces of gold (worth over two million dollars at today's price), 4425 ounces of gold plate, 9376 ounces of silver or silver-gilt, plus unset jewels, jeweled mitres and croziers, and gold cloth.[11]

The king's chief minister, Thomas Cromwell, understood acutely that the destruction of saintly shrines and relics was essential if the king were to seize the political and financial power held by the Church. He must have glimpsed, at least dimly, the enormity of what he was doing. Contesting the Church meant contesting the Church's power over the body in death. It meant not only the eradication of saintly intercession, but also the eradication of the doctrine of purgatory, the alteration of funeral services and memorial practices, and the redefinition of the nature of the images and records of the dead. The actual seizure of the treasure at Canterbury was a mere skirmish in a long propaganda campaign to rewrite the entire history and significance of Becket's death. A proclamation issued in November of

9. Amid the increasingly rich literature on iconoclasm, see especially Margaret Aston, *England's Iconoclasts*, vol. 1: *Laws against Images* (Oxford: Clarendon Press, 1988), chaps. 4–6.

10. John Stow, *The Annales of England* (London, 1592), p. 972.

11. C. Everleigh Woodruff and William Danks, *Memorials of the Cathedral and Priory of Christ in Canterbury* (London: Chapman and Hall, 1912), p. 218.

1538 gives some indication of its ferocity. Becket, it maintained, was not a martyr but a rebel and traitor, had died in a violent squabble incited by his own bad temper, and had been canonized by the pope merely as a political maneuver against the king. Therefore, the proclamation concluded that:

> from henceforth the said Thomas Becket shall not be esteemed, named, reputed, nor called a saint, but Bishop Becket, and that his images and pictures through the whole realm shall be put down and avoided out of all churches, chapels, and other places, and that from henceforth the days used to be festival in his name shall not be observed, nor the service, office, antiphons, collects, and prayers in his name read, but erased and put out of all the books; and that all other festival days, already abrogate, shall be in no way solemnized, but his grace's ordinance and injunctions thereupon observed, to the intent his grace's subjects shall be no longer blindly led and abused to commit idolatry as they have done in the past, upon pain of his majesty's indignation and imprisonment at his grace's pleasure.[12]

What became of the bones of Becket is not certain, although John Stow and Nicholas Harpsfield, writing from opposite camps, agree that they were burned.[13] The papal bull issued to denounce the destruction of the shrine claims that Becket was subjected to a posthumous treason trial, condemned, and only then burned.[14] In one sense, it is a matter of no importance which of these accounts, if any, is true, since Becket was in any case very dead. But for a culture where the metaphorization of the dead was a matter of profound significance, a culture which at times seemed to care more about the mutilation of dead bodies than about living ones, the issue was very important indeed. For even in its final disposal, the body of Becket was still a site for a cataclysmic struggle over the re- and de-metaphorization of the dead.

12. "Proclamation Prohibiting Unlicensed Printing of Scripture, Exiling Anabaptists, Depriving Married Clergy, Removing St. Thomas a Becket from Calendar," Westminster 16 November 1538, 30 Henry VIII. *Tudor Royal Proclamations*, ed. Paul L. Hughes and James F. Larkin, 3 vols. (New Haven: Yale University Press, 1964), 1:276.

13. Stow, p. 972; Nicholas Harpsfield, *The Life and Death of Sr Thomas Moore, Knight, Sometimes Lord High Chancellor of England*, ed. Elsie Vaughan Hitchcock and R. W. Chambers, Early English Text Society, original series no. 186 (London: Oxford University Press, 1932), p. 215.

14. Elton, *Policy and Police*, p. 257 n.1; Arthur Penrhyn Stanley, *Historical Memorials of Canterbury* (London: Murray, 1887), p. 254; Howard Loxton, *Pilgrimage to Canterbury* (London: David & Charles, 1978), p. 179.

The history of the Becket shrine shows a hagiographic process working both forward and in reverse. A living man meets death. The putrid body is transformed into a splendid body, a saintly richness, surrounded by sacred images and writings. What seems more horrible becomes treasured. As Peter Brown observes in his study of saintly cults in Mediterranean society, the ancient taboos about contact with a corpse were violated, as the Christian cult of saints "rapidly came to involve the digging up, the moving, the dismemberment—quite apart from much avid touching and kissing—of the bones of the dead, and, frequently, the placing of these in areas from which the dead had once been excluded."[15] Indeed, those spaces, far from being polluted by the presence of death, became all the more holy for its presence. The writings and images surrounding the saint became centered upon the miracle of death. The destruction of the shrines in the Reformation is an attempt to reverse this process, not just for an individual but a whole culture. The treasure is pillaged, the writings debunked, the images defaced. The body is rematerialized, stripped of its metaphors and its aura. The bones are burned, buried, or scattered.

Which brings us, at last, to Thomas More, in whose life and in whose death this process is repeated, though with a difference. It is repeated because More was, like Becket, a Londoner who became a chancellor, and a worldly man who became a champion of the Church and eventually a saint. It is repeated because More thought of himself as being like Becket, made that similarity part of his public image, and even managed to die on the eve of the feast of St. Thomas of Canterbury. It is repeated because his death instantly provoked a conflict between the iconoclastic and iconodulic forces within his culture. And it is different because the culture had irretrievably changed even before he died or before Cromwell had ordered the destruction of the shrine of Becket. The steady decline of revenues at Canterbury and the withering irony of More's own friends Erasmus and Colet were evidence enough that, in England at least, the cult of the saint could never again hold the same public place. The economy of sainthood had been altered, and the metaphorics of the relic were transformed.

The killers employed by Henry VIII were not so foolish as to leave Thomas More's body lying in the church, as Becket's was. More was beheaded on Tower Hill and his body, along with that of Bishop John

15. Peter Brown, *The Cult of the Saints: Its Rise and Function in Latin Christianity* (Chicago: University of Chicago Press, 1981), p. 4.

Fisher, was buried in the Chapel of St. Peter within the precincts of the Tower. More's daughter Margaret Roper and foster-daughter Margaret Giggs Clement were allowed to dress the body, and they bore away his bloodstained shirt. More was not canonized until 400 years later, in 1935, but quickly he was spoken of as a martyr for the faith. In 1556 Nicholas Harpsfield compared him to St. Thomas of Dover and St. Thomas Becket. In 1585 Pope Gregory allowed the relics of English martyrs to consecrate altars, and in 1588 Thomas Stapleton claimed that Margaret Clement had given him a piece of the bloody shirt as a relic.

But with no tomb or shrine, there could be no pilgrimages, no public ceremonies. The cult of Thomas More developed instead in the interior and exile spaces of Tudor culture. It flourished in the secret underground of a now-illegal English Roman Catholicism, and above all in the privacy of the recusant family. Deprived of a body, a public site, a shrine, and driven into hiding, the cult of Thomas More centered instead around substitute bodies, namely the portraits and written accounts of More that already existed or were soon produced. Hence it was a cult centered not on the metaphorized body but on metaphors for the body, or even on metaphor itself.

This change points to a certain convertibility between body and portrait and between relic and image. I can do no more than hint here at the relationship of this change to the general ideology of the Renaissance portrait. The making of a portrait was thought of as the fashioning of a substitute life and the mass copying of a portrait image was likened to biological reproduction. Through this visual fecundity or copiousness, the portrait artist manifested in the features of his subject the inner treasures of the soul. The spiritual resonance of even the most secular of portraits was maintained by the common derivation of their artistic composition from the compositional schemes employed for images of saints.[16] The living physical body

16. Johannes Wilde outlines the relationship of portraiture to monumental painting in his chapter "Titian as a Portrait-Painter," in *Venetian Art from Bellini to Titian*, ed. Anthony Blunt (Oxford: Clarendon Press, 1974), pp. 212–65. Larry Silver traces the transformation of saintly types into individual portrayals in his paper "Face as Figure: Portraits as Exempla in Northern Europe," delivered at the session "Transformations of the Northern European Portrait," Renaissance Society of America Annual Meeting, Harvard University, March 31, 1989. Following David Piper, Stanley Morison describes Holbein's composition of the More family as "an example of the kind of adaptation of a religious formula to a secular purpose, which was no doubt thrust on Holbein from his earliest years by the changing sense of values in the city in which he grew up. In the

was transformed and perfected through the creation of an inert replica. Portraits were consumed through a series of ceremonies in everyday life, in which friends, families, dependents, and admirers acted as if the portrait were the living person and might do everything except converse with them. Thus the use of a portrait as a substitute for the lost but perfected body of a saint—that is, the use of a portrait image as an icon—is in a sense only a spectacular variation on the normal economy of portrait representation.

The problems posed by this conjunction were explicitly recognized by Henry VIII's government in its directives to the Church. The Injunctions of 1536 focused on the spiritual and financial economy of the shrines, providing that,

> to the intent that all superstition and hypocrisy, crept into divers men's hearts, may vanish away, they shall not set forth or extol any images, relics, or miracles for any superstition or lucre, . . . seeing [that] all goodness, health, and grace ought to be both asked and looked for only of God, as of the very Author of the same, and of none other, for without Him that cannot be given; but [the clergy] shall exhort as well their parishioners as other pilgrims, that . . . it shall profit more their soul's health, if they do bestow that on the poor and needy, which they would have bestowed upon the said images or relics.[17]

Quickly, however, the authorities realized that the removal of relics was not enough. The images of saints and martyrs had long supplemented or substituted for the actual bodies, and short of a complete eradication of images along the lines of Islam, they would continue to do so. What was needed was a reformation of the metaphorics of images. Hence the Injunctions of 1538 addressed what we have called the theatrical problem, or rather, the problem of iconicity itself, when it proclaimed:

'Darmstadt Madonna', which he painted in 1526, the Meyer family are grouped round, and radiate from, the Madonna and Child in the top centre: if there were a similar nucleus in the empty foreground of the More family group, it would become an Adoration" (*The Likeness of Thomas More: An Iconographical Survey of Three Centuries* [New York: Fordham University Press, 1963], p. 21). The connection between the Darmstadt painting for the Meyer family and the painting of the More family is ratified by John Rowlands, *Holbein: The Paintings of Hans Holbein the Younger* (Oxford: Phaidon, 1985), p. 71.

17. "The First Royal Injunctions of Henry VIII, A.D. 1536," in *Documents Illustrative of English Church History*, ed. Henry Gee and William John Hardy (London: Macmillan, 1914), p. 271.

that such feigned images as you know in any of your cures to be so
abused with pilgrimages or offerings of anything made thereunto, you
shall for avoiding that most detestable offence of idolatry forthwith take
down and delay, and shall suffer from henceforth no candles, tapers, or
images of wax to be set afore any image or picture, but only the light
that commonly goeth across the church by the rood loft, the light before
the Sacrament of the altar, and the light above the sepulchre, which for
the adorning of the church and divine service you shall suffer to remain; still admonishing your parishioners that images serve for none
other purpose but as to be books of unlearned men that cannot know
letters, whereby they might be otherwise admonished of the lives and
conversation of them that the said images do represent; which images,
if they abuse for any other intent than for such remembrances, they
commit idolatry in the same to the great danger of their souls.[18]

Even after the destruction of the physical relics, the regime could
keep the sacred dead in their places only through such subtle stage
managing, down to the details of the lights and candles, in order to
erect a distinction between idolatry and remembrance. The regime's
policy gestured back to the ancient claims, dating to the sixth century,
that images were for the unlearned, that they served only for remembrance, and that they were venerated but not worshipped. At the
same time, the policy superimposed upon the religious icon the practices of remembrance that surrounded the secular portrait. The image now showed a person like us, not a divine figure, and so the
viewer was to see it as a cue to life and to conversation. In the same
transformation, a crime of deed—the pilgrimage or offering—was
replaced by a crime of thought, idolatry. The new site of this subtle
distinction between the true presence and the feigned image was the
inward consciousness of the worshipper, the precinct that the regime
would find the most difficult to police.

It was across these fault lines of image and presence, of remembrance and adoration, that the posthumous portraits of Thomas
More were constructed. There were, of course, multiple portraits of
More already in existence when he died. More's death, however,
seems to have unleashed an explosion of images whose first wave
alone lasted for a century. I want to focus here on two instances of the
More icon, both of which are reworkings of images originally created
for purely secular purposes by Holbein, who was himself something

18. "The Second Royal Injunctions of Henry VIII, A.D. 1538," in Gee and Hardy,
Documents, pp. 277–78.

of a Lutheran. But the meanings of an artifact lie only in a small way in original intention, and in a very large way in subsequent use. The killing of More transformed the paintings from representations of life into posthumous assertions of sanctity and so into vehicles of religious and political resistance.

Holbein's images of More in life consist of the Windsor drawings (Figure 6.3) and the related painting, now at the Frick (Figure 6.5). There are dozens of copies from the late sixteenth and early seventeenth century, some related more closely to the drawings, others to the painting. In a society where the display of portraits was a political action, an assertion of admiration, fealty, and loyalty, the large number of copies is striking. Of course it is wrong to assume that all of them express admiration for More's last actions and disapproval of the king's judicial murder. Any copy based on the Frick portrait, displaying the chain of office around More's neck, could simply be an acknowledgment of his fame and eminence as Chancellor of England. But a late sixteenth-century copy now at Knole (Figure 6.10) is quite blatant.[19] The Tudor rose is replaced with a cross. More's hands, touching in the Frick portrait, are separated so that the thumb and index finger of the right may touch the pearl at the end of the cross. The left, no longer bejeweled, points to an unidentified text, but the letters, if not the exact meaning, of a key phrase are decipherable: "sed causa": "but the cause," perhaps, or "but for the cause." In a more pointed irony, the chain of office remains about his neck, rebuking those who put political opportunism ahead of religious obligation.

This apparently simple reinscription of the Holbein portrait conceals interesting metaphorics. By substituting the cross for the rose and by indicating a cause that cannot be openly named, the maker of the painting has portrayed More in death. Yet the image that he has used is not the severed head, much less the headless body, but the body and head in life. The fact of death, which is the cause of the painting, is annihilated even as it is named. The pearl, depending from the cross, may through traditional associations suggest the soul, pure in its dependence on Christ. More's fingers gently squeeze the tip of the pearl even as his eyes look beyond the frame, as if he were showing it to someone else, or as if the point of contact between flesh and spirit were so sensitive that it is enough to feel the touch, without seeing it. In the image of the death of More, that death itself becomes

19. Morison, *The Likeness of Thomas More*, p. 74, calls it "a good, probably sixteenth-century copy." Roy Strong with more certainty calls it sixteenth-century in *Tudor and Jacobean Portraits*, 2 vols. (London: Her Majesty's Stationery Office, 1969), 1:231.

Figure 6.10. After Hans Holbein. *Sir Thomas More*, late sixteenth century.
Oil on panel. Private Collection

the bridge between matter and spirit, like the shrine of Becket, the bridge to its audience, the community of the faithful. But this is no public and ostentatious shrine or relic. Indeed, it masks its identity as a relic, enveloping it in all but the smallest details with the mantle of secular portraiture, even as it masquerades its audience of the faithful in the guise of consumers of the images of famous men.

The second portrait I want to look at enacts the same metaphorics of life and death, but in a more complex way, since it explicitly constitutes the community of the faithful as the More family. This picture derives not from the single figures by Holbein but from his group drawing (Figure 6.11), executed in preparation for a painting done in 1527 of the More household. The figures in the drawing are, from left to right, More's daughter Elizabeth Dauncey; his foster daughter Margaret Giggs, later Margaret Clement; his father Sir John More; Anne Cresacre, his son's wife; Thomas More himself; his son John More; his fool Henry Patenson; his youngest daughter Cecily Heron; his eldest daughter Margaret Roper; and finally Alice More, his wife. This is the quintessential Renaissance portrait of life, depicting the family circle as humanist circle. The drawing was carried to Erasmus by Holbein himself, and when Erasmus wrote to More to thank him, he claimed that the drawing made him remember his own days among the family.

The finished painting that Holbein made from the drawing does not survive, but late sixteenth century copies of it do. In the Nostell Priory version (Figure 6.12), which is probably very close to Holbein's original, the two figures on the left, Elizabeth Dauncey and Margaret Clement, are reversed from their positions in the drawing, and a new figure, More's secretary John Harris, is introduced at the doorway at the right rear. The history of Holbein's original is extremely vague, but assuming that it was originally painted for the More family itself, it may have been sequestered with the rest of More's estate at his death, and then passed back into family hands briefly in 1590 or into friendly hands who allowed it to be copied, before it passed to the Earl of Arundel's collection in the seventeenth century, and then to the Continent, where it perished.[20]

20. See Morison, *The Likeness of Thomas More*, pp. 22–25, on the process of transmission and copying. Strong, *Tudor and Jacobean Portraits*, 1:348–51 suggests plausibly that Holbein's original was purchased in 1590 by John, Lord Lumley, who was both a Catholic and an avid collector of Holbein's work, and that he allowed the More family to have a copy made. Lumley's collection passed on his death to his son-in-law, the Earl of Arundel.

Figure 6.11. Hans Holbein. *The Family of Sir Thomas More,* 1527–28. Ink on paper.
Öffentliche Kunstsammlung Basel, Kupferstichkabinett

Figure 6.12. Rowland Lockey after Hans Holbein. *The Family of Sir Thomas More*, ca. 1593. Oil on canvas. Nostell Priory, by permission of the Winn Family and the National Trust. Photo: National Trust Photographic Library

The surviving copies painted in the 1590s almost certainly derive from within the More family. The Nostell Priory copy, dating to 1592, was painted either for Thomas Roper, the son of William and Margaret Roper, or for Thomas More II, the son of young John More and Anne Cresacre. Another version of the picture (Figure 6.13) was painted almost simultaneously for Thomas More II. In it, the Holbein composition is radically altered. Margaret Clement is removed from the left edge and Alice More from the right edge, while Elizabeth Dauncey is moved to Henry Patenson's position between Cecily Heron and Margaret Roper. Hence the entire composition is shifted to the left, creating room on the right for a new set of figures, the family of Thomas More II (Figure 6.14). Facing him is his wife, Mary Scrope, and behind them are two of their sons, John More and Cresacre More. Above Cresacre's head hangs a portrait of his maternal grandmother Anne Cresacre.

The painting very carefully preserves the body of Thomas More by renewing it within the family. The painting shows five generations of patrilineal descent, from John I to Thomas I to John II to Thomas II to John III and Cresacre. By the absorption of the physical body into genealogical repetition, the effects of time and death are both annihilated and affirmed. Anne Cresacre appears twice, once as a young woman of fifteen and once as a woman in her fifties. Thomas More II appears as old as his great-grandfather, old enough, that is, to be grandfather to his own father.

The portrait reworks the Holbein composition in order to perpetuate ancestral life through family memory. But it does more than that, for this is not just any family. The perpetuation of the More family is the perpetuation of a central element of the Roman Catholic Church in England. John More the younger was imprisoned. Cecily Heron's husband was executed. Thomas More II was himself a reluctant recusant who after years of quietism reasserted his Catholicism, suffered in prison from 1582 to 1586, and remained under surveillance when the painting was executed. His son Cresacre would write a biography of Sir Thomas More, the third to be written by a family member. For the More family, the reworkings of the tangible artifact are themselves acts of both family memory and religious devotion. Nor do the reworkings stop in 1593 with this composition. A series of subsequent retouchings, removed in a recent cleaning but visible in an older photograph (Figure 6.15), added six additional coats of arms, two surmounted with banners reading "Christiano Catholico More." In an age of iconoclasm, this artifact intensified its iconicity with each generation.

Nor does the inclusion of the family of Thomas More II, or the appearance and disappearance of crests and mottoes, end the reworking of the image. For there is another version of the family group, also probably executed for Thomas More II around 1593 (Figure 6.16). The generations again appear all together, although the portrait of Anne Cresacre on the right has been replaced by a window with a garden view, and Sir Thomas More's fool Henry Patenson has reappeared at the center rear peeking through a curtain. But unlike the other picture, which is enormous in size (over 10' × 7'), this is a so-called "cabinet miniature" less than 10" × 12". The miniature is the most private, the most secret, the most inward and personal of the Tudor forms of painting. This miniature was later mounted in a curious way: in a walnut frame, with double-leaf doors. (The hinges of the left door are just visible in Figure 6.16.) With this mounting, the picture takes on the form of a tiny, portable altarpiece, enclosing for private devotion the image of a martyr and the community of blood that he founded.

The pattern etched out in these portraits is reiterated in the hagiography of More in the sixteenth century. There are distinct campaigns of biography writing for More, corresponding to stages in the struggle between the Catholic and Protestant communities. The first campaign, producing the biographies by More's son-in-law William Roper, by his grand-nephew Ellis Heywood, and by Nicholas Harpsfield, takes place during the reign of Mary Tudor. The second, comprising Thomas Stapleton's *Tres Thomae*, parallel lives of the Apostle Thomas, Thomas Becket, and Thomas More, comes from the center of exile resistance at Douai in the Armada year of 1588. And the last campaign, including biographies by one Ro. Ba. and by More's great-grandson Cresacre More, was the work of a community which knew that its exile or suppression was permanent. Of all these works, only two, those of Heywood and Stapleton, were printed: one, in Italian, at Florence and the other, in Latin, at Douai. These are works addressed to the international European community of the Counter-reformation. The others, written in English and circulated in manuscript, were essentially clandestine works, a Tudor analogue to the *samizdat* literature that circulated in the former socialist states of Eastern Europe.

Like the painted portraits, the biographies act as substitute relics.

Figure 6.13. Rowland Lockey after Hans Holbein. *The Family and Descendants of Sir Thomas More,* 1593. Oil on canvas. National Portrait Gallery, London

Figure 6.14. *Opposite.* Detail

Figure 6.15. Rowland Lockey after Hans Holbein. *The Family and Descendants of Sir Thomas More* (detail of background before cleaning). National Portrait Gallery, London

They are passed from hand to hand, treasured for their power to counter the official history of More's life and death promulgated by the government. They strengthen conviction, exorcise fear, and confirm the underground or exile communities. And like the painted portraits, they are subject to a process of revision and iconoclasm. This is most strikingly visible in the case of the Emmanuel College manuscript of Harpsfield's *Life of More*. It belonged to Thomas More II, and was in his possession when he was arrested on 13 April, 1582. It was seized along with his papers, apparently forming evidence in the case against him. It later passed into the hands of a Protestant reader who was not content merely to dislike its subject or its prior owner.[21] This unknown iconoclast defaced the margins with quarrelsome scribblings emphasizing More's reputation for irreverence and accusing him of a phony religiosity. When Harpsfield describes how the young More, in the household of Cardinal Morton, would "vpon the [Sunday] stepp in among the Christmas players, and forthwith, without any other forethinking or premeditation, playe a part with them himselfe," the Protestant annotator scoffs, "A fit exercise for Sunday!"[22] When Harpsfield claims that More "vsed . . . another rare and singuler kinde of almes of his owne body, as to punish the same with whippes, the cordes knotted," the iconoclast gleefully scribbles, "Whipp on, and smart enough!"

These few examples must serve to indicate the entire posthumous career of Thomas More, his conversion into an uncanonized saint, and his place in the histories and counterhistories of the Reformation. Beyond that—and perhaps of more interest now that the internecine wars of Christianity are no longer the primary struggle of our culture—they may serve to indicate something about the formation of the early modern metaphorics of death. In More's images we see the human longing to reassemble the mangled body, to perpetuate it beyond the grave, to transform it into its opposite, a sublime and beatific object, and through it to perpetuate the well-being of the living. In them too we see the skepticism and doubt over sainthood, the inevitable suspicion that death is the end, that worms shall feast on

21. Nicholas Harpsfield, *The Life and Death of Sir Thomas Moore*, ed. Elsie Vaughan Hitchcock, Early English Text Society no. 186 (Oxford: Oxford University Press, 1932), pp. xiii–xv, 294–96.

22. Harpsfield, *The Life and Death*, pp. xv, 11. MSS Emmanuel 76 and Yelverton 72 are alone among the eight early Harpsfield MSS in reading "upon the Sunday." The others read "upon the sudden," or some variant thereof, and this is the reading accepted by the modern editor.

Figure 6.16. Rowland Lockey after Hans Holbein. *The Family and Descendants of Sir Thomas More,* 1593–94.
Watercolor on vellum, in a walnut cabinet with double locking doors.
Victoria and Albert Museum, London

us, and that all claims to the contrary are fraud or treason. We see both the longing and the doubt being transformed from elements in the financial economy of the shrines into elements in the political economy of the Reformation and monarchy. We see the site of the metaphorized body, the place of its spiritual or financial or political transactions, moved from the public space of the cathedral to the interior spaces of the political underground, of the family, and of the individual mind. With that interiorization, we may see the strains of longing and doubt locked permanently within the early modern subject, locked permanently within us.

Perhaps I can best summarize the Tudor struggle over the body in death by recounting a final incident. I said earlier that Thomas More's body had been buried in the Tower, safely out of reach of the devout. But this is not entirely so. His head, severed from the body, was placed on a stake on London Bridge, where, according to Stapleton, "it remained for nearly a month, until it had to be taken down to make room for other heads. . . . The head would have been thrown into the river, had not Margaret Roper, who had been watching carefully and waiting for the opportunity, bribed the executioner whose office it was to remove the heads and obtained possession of the sacred relic."[23]

"There was no possibility of a mistake," said Stapleton, although there was of course every possibility of a mistake. After a month of exposure in July, little could have been left to recognize. The features of the living face would be grossly disfigured and replaced by the markings of sun or weather or insects. But Margaret Roper, with the help of others, had kept track of its position on the bridge, and knew when it was taken down. Besides, there were, Stapleton claimed, unmistakable signs of identity. "A tooth was missing, which he had lost in life." Now that seems persuasive, but Stapleton goes on: "his countenance was almost as beautiful as before. One remarkable fact that his friends noted was that his beard, which before his death was almost white, now appeared to be of a reddish brown colour."[24] We can see at work here the progress by which the beatific body has begun to replace the corruptible one.

23. Thomas Stapleton, *The Life and Illustrious Martyrdom of Sir Thomas More*, ed. E. E. Reynolds, trans. Philip E. Hallett (New York: Fordham University Press, 1966), p. 191. Subsequent references are to this edition.
  24. Ibid., p. 191.

The significance of Margaret Roper's action was not lost on the authorities. She was summoned before the Privy Council and charged with keeping a sacred relic, as well as forbidden books. Through its prohibition, the Council in effect recognized the lingering infectious power of More's death, as contained in his body and in his texts. Their prohibition was an attempt to block the old metaphoric process by which the physical became spiritual and horror became beauty. Instead, they pointed to the danger that those who pursued a fallacious metaphorics of sainthood would simply spread their untransfigured physical infection to the social body.

In her reply to the Council, Margaret Roper maintained that "she had saved her father's head from being devoured by the fishes, with the intention of burying it," and that "she had hardly any [of his] books and papers but what had been already published, except a few personal letters, which she humbly begged to be allowed to keep for her own consolation."[25] Her defense is both equivocal and unanswerable. It appeals first to the ancient fears of the dismemberment of the corpse which have haunted Western culture for millennia, the very fears which the relics of the saints had always violated and transcended. Like Antigone, Margaret Roper claims to have done no more than give to the dead those last offices that the gods have commanded and that secular authority cannot prohibit. Her response appeals secondly to the secular cult of memory and consolation, the very cult with which the authorities had proposed to replace the cult of the saints. If these responses were blatant subterfuges, they were ones that the Privy Council had no way of challenging, so long as she established no shrine and did no public ceremony of devotion.

In this standoff between prohibition and subterfuge, the economy of sacred death is nonetheless transformed. The ostentatious and public exchange of money for spiritual goods at the shrine of the saint is now replaced with the clandestine bribery of an officer of the Crown. The public declaration of faith is supplanted by its public denial and its reaffirmation in private. The realm of icon worship is driven into the interior of private devotion, and enveloped by a new public world of iconoclasm. This is a world where it is well known that bribery and dissent lie just out of sight, but they are ignored so long as they do not insist on proclaiming their presence. It is, in short, a world

25. Ibid., p. 193.

of open secrets,[26] where hypocrisy is a fundamental constituent of being.[27]

What took place between Margaret Roper and the Privy Council, then, was that most characteristic of Tudor exchanges. She denies her sincere beliefs, tucking them away within the secrecy of her own mind and within the privacy of the Roper-More family, and in return, they let her live. They do not attempt to police the thought-crimes they have created, and she does not attempt to display the defaced head of the traitor as the golden image of a martyr. Instead she preserved the head with spices, Stapleton tells us, and after her death it was placed in the Roper family vault in St. Dunstan's, Canterbury, near the former site of Becket's shrine. It is there today, safe and private, in the silence of the tomb.

26. I am indebted here to Jonathan Goldberg's analysis of Renaissance homosexuality as an "open secret" in "Colin to Hobbinol: Spenser's *Familiar Letters,*" *South Atlantic Quarterly* 88 (1989): 107–26. See also D. A. Miller's concluding chapter "Secret Subjects, Open Secrets," in *The Novel and the Police* (Berkeley: University of California Press, 1988), pp. 192–220.

27. Ronald J. Corthell, "'The secrecy of man': Recusant Discourse and the Elizabethan Subject," *English Literary Renaissance* 19 (1989): 272–90, argues that this position of hypocrisy was a specifically Protestant characteristic of later Tudor society. Not liking to "make windows into men's hearts," the government maintained a distinction between people's inner selves and outward actions and claimed to limit its policing to the latter. But this distinction, argues Corthell, placed the Tudor recusants in an impossible position, because the central tenets of their religious belief denied such a distinction and demanded a full correspondence between private belief and public devotion. Thus the very device of hypocrisy that the government held out to the recusant community as its means of survival was a clever test of belief and a form of oppression.

7

Treasures of Culture

Titus Andronicus and Death by Hanging

FRANCIS BARKER

To articulate the past historically does not mean to
recognize it "the way it really was" (Ranke). It means
to seize hold of a memory as it flashes up at a moment
of danger. Historical materialism wishes to retain that
image of the past which unexpectedly appears to man
singled out by history at a moment of danger. The
danger affects both the content of the tradition and
its receivers. The same threat hangs over both: that of
becoming a tool of the ruling classes. In every era the
attempt must be made anew to wrest tradition away
from the conformism that is about to overpower it.
The Messiah comes not only as the redeemer, he
comes as the subduer of Antichrist. Only that historian will have the gift of fanning the spark of hope in
the past who is firmly convinced that *even the dead* will
not be safe from the enemy if he wins. And this enemy has not ceased to be victorious.

—WALTER BENJAMIN, "Theses on the Philosophy of
History"

This essay is based on editorial excerpts from a developed version of the lecture I
gave at the "wisemens threasure" symposium under the title "'A Wilderness of Tigers':
Titus Andronicus, Anthropology, and the Occlusion of Violence." The full version appears in my volume *The Culture of Violence* (Chicago: Chicago University Press, 1993). In
particular, an extended discussion of the appropriation of cultural anthropology by the
New Historicism and a critique of the resulting culturalism have been omitted. In the
sustained version, that material triangulates, in the manner of a Benjaminian constella-

Materialist possibilities are suggested by the phrase "wisemens threasure," with its mapping—perhaps it is a remembering—of the thesaurus onto treasure. Words and money articulated and fused in this way beckon a materialist, if not fully Marxist, definition of what the title of this volume directs our attention toward, "the production of English Renaissance culture." Adjacent to that task of positive theoretical elaboration, I have chosen to focus my argument on "culture," a word and a concept that, given much recent Renaissance criticism, I hear in the specific register of a certain anthropology, if one that I find deeply problematical.

I

Judging, for example, from the early incidence of human sacrifice or from the prominence that it gives to an act of cannibalism, one could argue that *Titus Andronicus* represents Rome as a primitive society. This impression persists in the host of related, accessory ways in which the text not only displays the beliefs and practices of the ancient culture, from such large-scale practices as the habit of enslaving captives taken in war (and the attending spectacles of triumph and tribute with which the play begins), to details like the fetishization of bodily emissions, especially tears, blood, and breath, but displays them as "marked behaviour" in a manner that signifies its primitive

tion, the present, reduced, address to the anthropology of the Shakespearean text and its occlusion of the systematic state violence of early modern England. Traces of a critical polemic, especially via my juxtaposition of the evidence of routinized mass execution to such key new historicist motifs as "cultural performance," the "display" of power, or the remarkable claim that Elizabethan power "is constituted in theatrical celebrations of royal glory and theatrical violence visited upon the enemies of that glory" (Stephen Greenblatt, "Invisible Bullets: Renaissance Authority and its Subversions, *Henry IV* and *Henry V*," in *Political Shakespeare: New Essays in Cultural Materialism*, ed. Jonathan Dollimore and Alan Sinfield [Manchester University Press, 1985], p. 44), remain in the present rescension and have been noticed in the footnotes.

I am indebted for their criticisms and support to my fellow members of the Essex Early Modern Research Group who sat variously through one, two, and in some cases, three versions of this paper: Jerry Brotton, Maurizio Calbi, Al Constantine, Tracey Hill, John Joughin, Angelica Michelis, and Steve Speed contributed immeasurably. Both his published writing and several long conversations with Peter Hulme helped generate and clarify some important ideas. I am grateful to Elizabeth Weall for her help with the production of the text. Jonathan White gave generous intellectual and moral support, particularly in the closing stages of the work. And above all I owe a debt of gratitude to my beloved wife, Marijn.

character. Equally, the formal production of the representation of
Roman society is also "marked." One of the play's editors notes the
way in which "ceremonies provide an almost uninterrupted series of
spectacles"; the sense of the depicted society being shot through by
ceremonial and rite is itself conveyed in the ceremonial character of
the depiction.[1] Thus, although the Rome of *Titus Andronicus* is not a
preliterate society, as most cultures designated "primitive" are held to
be, and not in that sense prehistoric, the play foregrounds ritual
practices, ceremonial spectacle, and the charging of the sacred by
fetishism and taboo in a way fully reminiscent of the representation of
that undeveloped, native, ancient, indigenous condition which the
various discourses of anthropology have insistently called primitive.
The Rome of *Titus Andronicus* is a society organized by the signs of the
primitive.

This is perhaps most clear if we consider its representation of the
treatment of the dead. Early in Act I comes Titus's entry into Rome
after his victory over the Goths. Captured Goths, including their
queen Tamora, her three sons, and her lover Aaron, a Moor in her
entourage, are led in formal triumph into the city. But this triumph is
also a funeral procession to the ancestral tomb of the Andronici,
where the remains of an unspecified number of Titus's sons killed in
the war are buried, and where later in the act another son, Mutius,
slain by Titus himself, is also interred. The disposal of the sons' remains is considered "burial amongst their ancestors,"[2] a rite that unless properly observed will leave them "unburied yet, / To hover on
the dreadful shore of Styx" (I.i.87–88). To ensure that "the shadows
be not unappeas'd" (I.i.100) a human sacrifice is needed and their
living brothers demand Tamora's eldest son, Alarbus, for the pur-

1. Eugene M. Waith, Introduction to *Titus Andronicus* in The Oxford Shakespeare
(Oxford: Clarendon Press, 1984), p. 58. The quotation continues by enumerating the
"spectacles"; I cite it more fully here as further evidence of the "ceremonial" representation of Rome: "the confrontation of Saturninus and Bassianus, the entrance of Titus
drawn in a chariot in a procession which is both triumph and funeral, the sacrifice of
Alarbus following the unsuccessful intercession of Tamora, the burial of Titus's sons,
the election of an emperor, preparations for a wedding, the burial of Mutius. . . .
Another procession and another unsuccessful intercession . . . the shooting of arrows
with messages to the gods; the masque-like visitation of Tamora and her sons disguised
as Revenge, Rape, Murder; the final banquet; and the election of Lucius as emperor to
restore order in Rome. We know that for at least one viewer at the private performance
in 1596 the '*monstre*,' or spectacle, was worth more than the '*sujet*' . . ." (pp. 58–59).
2. *Titus Andronicus*, ed. J. C. Maxwell, The Arden Shakespeare (London: Methuen,
1968), I.i.84. Subsequent references are to this edition.

pose, "That we may hew his limbs, and on a pile / *Ad manes fratrum* sacrifice his flesh" (I.i.97–98). The sacrifice—"Our Roman rites"—is "perform'd" and "Alarbus's limbs are lopp'd," his "entrails feed the sacrificing fire, / Whose smoke like incense doth perfume the sky" (I.i.143–45). One would hardly need look further for evidence of a typically primitive account of the sacred incarnate in a material, indeed corporeal, ritual of sacrificial propitiation of the unseen spirits of the dead. With the further addition only of their sister Lavinia's "tributary tears" (I.i.159), the dead brothers are then interred in "peace and honour" (I.i.156).

The significance of these rites and practices, what I term their "marking," is then underlined by the burial of Mutius. At first Titus denies him interral in the ancestral tomb: "Traitors, away! he rests not in this tomb: / This monument five hundred years hath stood, / Which I have sumptuously re-edified: / Here none but soldiers and Rome's servitors / Repose in fame" (I.i.349–53). These terms—the allegation of treachery, the invocation of half a millennium of ancestral tradition and military service, the protection of the elaborately maintained monument from pollution or abuse—are, of course, heavily charged. But so are those of the intercession of Mutius's paternal uncle and his brothers for proper funeral, an intercession that depends upon naming the transgression of the self-same senses of honor, virtue, and nobility which would be offered if the rite were denied. The rhetorical *summa* of their counter-invocation of the constitutive pieties consists in citing what turn out to be the most charged categories of all: "Thou art a Roman; be not barbarous" (I.i.388). Titus concedes and, the "impiety" (I.i.355) avoided, Mutius's "bones" are laid in the tomb until the ritual can be in proper course completed by the decoration of the monument with "trophies" (I.i.388).

The play gives considerable detail of Rome's mortuary practices, from its custom of tomb burial to the monumentalism of its funerary architecture, and from the importance of propitiatory sacrifice (and the role of olfactory sensation in its appeasement rituals) to the habit of decorating male graves with war goods. But beyond mortuary practice itself we also learn much of the significance of its funeral rites as instances of the wider ideological formations and social structures of the culture. Its funerals not only disclose ideational patterns such as the belief in postmortem survival which are apparently central to Roman society but also articulate in important ways its kinship structure, especially the bonding of male siblings, living and dead, and the importance of male ancestral lineation. In other words, if we cast the eye of a certain anthropology over the Rome of *Titus Andronicus* we would learn a great deal that would be convenient to the expectations we would thus arouse: it would be quite possible to derive from the text insights into what Rome means by peace, and how it uses familiar names; we could describe the significance of consecration or expiation, and that of the act of kneeling or of raising the voice; we could establish the lexicon of its warriors' honor code, or write the grammar of the metonyms and synecdoches it uses to speak of corpses; and so on. Read thus, the text discloses much of what would be necessary to what we might indeed call a positive anthropology, or at least a descriptive ethnography, of this primitive Rome, from the inner structure of its metaphysics to the cultural texture of its daily life.

Something crucial, however, is disclosed in that invocation of the notion of "the barbarous" as an antithetical or exclusive category when compared with what it is to be "a Roman." Its importance lies in the sense that beyond—or perhaps within—the cultural positivity I have been describing there are underlying forms of categorial and representational organization in *Titus Andronicus* which disclose an anthropology that is properly speaking structural. It is valuable in this context to compare the elaborate and elaborated senses of the "culture" of Rome, especially as it is embedded in the funeral rites of Act I, with the mortuary treatment of Aaron, and more especially of Tamora, with which the play ends. Where the proper burial of the slain Andronici at the beginning provides the signs of culture, and its neglect risks barbarism, the killing of Aaron and the disposal of the remains of Tamora are very differently coded. The last scene of the play leaves Titus, Lavinia, the emperor Saturninus, and Tamora dead, with Aaron captive to Titus's son Lucius, who, now in command of the victorious Gothic army, accedes to power in Rome. It is Lucius who pronounces the final "settlement." First Aaron is sentenced: "Set him breast-deep in earth and famish him; / There let him stand and rave and cry for food. / If any one relieves or pities him, / For the offence he dies" (V.iii.179–82). The contrast between this and the treatment of the Roman dead is marked: "Some loving friends convey the emperor hence, / And give him burial in his father's grave. / My father and Lavinia shall forthwith / Be closed in our household monument" (V.iii.191–94). But the contrast is greater still when this is compared in turn with Lucius's orders for the disposal of the remains of Tamora which provide the last lines of the play: "As for that ravenous tiger,

Tamora, / No funeral rite, nor man in mourning weed, / No mournful bell shall ring her burial; / But throw her forth to beasts and birds to prey" (V.iii.195–98). While the Roman corpses will be assumed or re-assumed, with proper ritual, into the order of culture, Aaron is planted in the earth in a kind of vivid parody of pious burial, by which he will be made to "rave and cry" like an animal for food. He will not grow; there will be no further culture for him. And the body of Tamora, a "ravenous tiger" (l. 195) whose "life was beastly" (l. 199), is merely thrown away. Her waste corpse is symbolically jettisoned "forth" from the order of culture into that of nature, from the human world into that of the beasts, from society into the wilderness, or into whatever it is that is outside, and constituted in opposition to, Rome.[3]

The text is thus bracketed by elaborate funeral ritual on the one hand, and its marked lack for those who are not of Rome on the other: rites are counterposed to waste. This contrast represents the formation of an "anthropological" structure that is rehearsed over and over again in the play. As distinct from the "positive" description of the custom and belief of the world of the play, this structure establishes, rather, a boundary between behavior and belief that is marked as being within the community, and that which is not. To one side of the boundary lies culture, and to the other lies either unmarked behavior, or behavior which is marked as the determinate "other" of culture.

This boundary is constituted in and by *Titus Andronicus* in two principal ways: by mutually exclusive, mutually defining categorial antitheses, and by a bi-polar topographical distinction. In the former case the contrastive construction of the civilized is achieved in the counterdistinction with behavior which is, for example, not human, or simply by the deployment of the explicit language of barbarism (itself bringing with it of course a ready-formed and very ancient "anthropology"). A language of monstrousness and bestiality, of the inhuman and the less than human, reinforces and reciprocally constitutes the civil, which is itself thus mapped to the human as such. Examples among others are V.ii.177, where Chiron and Demetrius,

3. It is worth remarking the frequency with which imputations of bestiality occur in the language of the demonization of Tamora; in particular she is several times called a tiger, here and at II.iii.142. (Aaron is a "ravenous tiger" at V.iii.5.) Associated with this is Tamora twice being referred to as Semiramis, at II.i.22 and at II.iii.118 where she is "Semiramis, nay, barbarous Tamora." The beautiful and the lustful alien conjured by the invocation of the mythical Assyrian queen articulate with the bestial and barbarous in the Goth Tamora.

the sons of Tamora who rape and mutilate Lavinia, are called "Inhuman traitors," and V.iii.14, where Aaron is called "inhuman dog"; at II.iii.78 and V.iii.4 Aaron is called a "barbarous Moor," at II.iii.118, as we have noted, Tamora is "barbarous Tamora," and at V.i.97 Lucius speaking to Aaron refers to Chiron and Demetrius as "barbarous beastly villains like thyself." Except in the minatory case of Titus noted above, these words are not used of Romans. In the latter case the text has a highly-charged topography by which the city is marked—tautologically—as the place of civilization, while that which lies outside it is the place of the barbarous or of the barbarian. Rome is, of course, archetypically "the City," a notion powerfully sedimented in the tradition of the West, and one that contributes to the politico-anthropological structure of *Titus Andronicus*, which designates the place beyond the boundaries of the city as the place of the Goths, the vandals and barbarians who are not Roman. One of the main acts of the play's extravagant violence, the rape and mutilation of Lavina by Tamora's sons, takes place in the woods beyond the gates. The place of Roman civility is by definition Rome, the place of Gothic barbarism is by mutual constitution not-Rome, the wilderness outside.[4]

If Rome is *the* place of civility as such—by which, for example, the idea of banishment as a punishment, like that of Lucius in III.i, depends for its sanction on the degradation and danger offered by expulsion beyond the limits of the city—it is thus also important to remark the way in which the crossing (if not the transgression) of the boundary—or its confusion, about which I shall say more below—serves to reinforce it. The miscegenation between Tamora and Aaron, for example, serves such a purpose inasmuch as, by being demonized by the text, it is marked as a practice whose negativity resides in the mixing of what should properly be separate. It thus the more strongly delineates—rather than subverts—the original and constitutive structure of separation. And it is with this in mind that I have emphasized the parodic "burial" of Aaron, and the treatment of

4. I am of course simplifying the way in which such "anthropological" structures actually work. For an illuminating discussion of the way in which "boundaries of community are often created by accusing those outside the boundary of the very practice on which the integrity of that community is founded," see Peter Hulme, *Colonial Encounters: Europe and the Native Carribean 1492–1979* (London: Methuen, 1986), p. 85 and passim, who is in turn drawing on Walter Arens, *The Man-Eating Myth: Anthropology and Anthropophagy* (Oxford: Oxford University Press, 1979). A cognate idea is developed later in this essay.

Tamora's body as detritus. Not least do they figure and connote that marking of the boundaries of the culture that is elucidated—in an exemplary way—by the work of Mary Douglas on pollution and taboo, and in particular on the significance of dirt, filth, or refuse in the constitution of the community by delineating of its limits and warding off the "formlessness," as she puts it, that lies beyond the frontiers of the community. If dirt, as Douglas famously defines it, is "matter out of place," then Aaron the Moor and Tamora the queen of the Goths are, *in Rome*, examples of the matter of such ritual pollution: a defilement cleansed by their final removal from the city to the true place and condition of dirt without.[5]

According then to the reading which, with some detachment, I have been outlining, two connected but slightly differently weighted anthropological perspectives have been at work. One involves the observation of the cultural marking in *Titus Andronicus* of the ritual customs, religious pieties, metaphysical convictions, and ideological norms, as well as the societal and familial structures of Roman society as it is represented by the play. This is a marking which makes Rome appear a "primitive" society inasmuch as the text's representations are made of the stuff that anthropology or its practical support, ethnographic fieldwork, investigates when it interrogates primitive societies, in particular the belief-structures of traditional societies as they are revealed embedded in ritual and in senses of pollution or taboo, and the structures of kinship and authority. But this positive anthropology of the forms of meaningful organization that define, order, and sustain the physical and the metaphysical worlds, plays an important part in the text not least as it is articulated with the second and more important anthropology: the circumscription of culture. At the first level the emphases on "marked behavior" are signs of culture, signs that Rome has, in the way that "primitive" societies do, a culture. I have emphasized the funerary, which is doubtless highly charged, highly marked in terms of the positivity of the processes of a culture. But it is not, therefore, an entirely arbitrary instance, for the pieties and tabooings with which these cultural practices are charged then act, at a second level, as markers of civility vis-à-vis a countervailing barbarism or savagery. This then engages signs not of cultural primi-

5. For Douglas's work on pollution and taboo, see especially her *Purity and Danger: An Analysis of the Concepts of Pollution and Taboo* (London: ARK, 1984); chaps. 6, 7, and 8, "Powers and Dangers," "External Boundaries," and "Internal Lines," are particularly relevant here.

tivism but a-cultural or anti-cultural savagery, so that at the second
level, the other sense in which the play can be seen to engage an
anthropological perspective involving the way in which the marked
practices of the depicted world are themselves representations structured in such a way as to *constitute* an "anthropology." In forming the
boundary between civility and humanity on the one hand and that
which is not civil and human on the other, the play enacts an anthropology rather than simply providing a depiction of Roman society as
one which is of anthropological interest, or defining its own interest in
Rome as principally an anthropological one.

Thus if I began with the sense that Rome is represented as a primitive society, it is now important to see how in another sense it isn't
primitive at all. I have indicated how what I called above a descriptive
ethnography or a positive anthropology is possible, and I have tried to
illustrate some of its possible resources by noting the charging of
materials and phenomena to which such anthropology characteristically attends. But the world of *Titus Andronicus*, and especially its Rome,
is certainly not constituted by the "positivity" of these materials alone.
Rather, or in addition, it is the "structure" of oppositions established
between these marked terms and what they are not that is culturally
constitutive. Thus, despite my opening formulation, the world of
Titus Andronicus is in fact only "primitive" in the special and ambiguous sense to which the anthropological perspective has so frequently,
if not systematically, committed itself: the primitive resides at once in
those societies which have—studiable—culture and in those which
have none, those which in being savage or *sauvage* are beyond and
outside culture.

If the primitive is both the site of "culture" and the absence of
culture, then the marking of the primitive in the representation of
Rome in *Titus Andronicus* is doubly formed, although there is a coor-
dination between the two anthropological perspectives at work in it. A
society that has the stuff of anthropological inspection looks "primitive" because it has "anthropologically" marked ritual, belief and behavior; but the perspective which marks the marking as markable is
itself originatively committed to constituting and reinforcing the
boundary, and the structure of the boundary, between what is civil
and what is barbarous, what is human and what is savage. If the world
of the play looks at first glance primitive, this disposition is subsumed
by the way in which that marking is then coordinated categorially and
topographically within the second, structural anthropology of bi-

polar civility and barbarism. Primitivism in the sense of the savage is expelled beyond the signs of the civil, and where once precisely these signs had seemed "primitive" in the cultural sense, now they appear as the very presence of culture.

For the moment then, one can speak, in these coordinated senses, of *Titus Andronicus* as an "anthropology," or at least of the "anthropologism" of the way in which it gives us a primitive world, but in a manner committed to describing the boundary of its culture. This delineation, constructed by constituting the categories of the civilized and the barbarous, is itself constitutive of the anthropological perspective as such, both in the broad sense that this marking goes back, it seems, to the beginning of the West and *its* "anthropologism," and also in the sense that anthropology—in more restricted, recent and even technical, academic, and professional senses—is, arguably, constituted by the very concept of "culture," and one arguably so constructed.

II

But if we attempt to read *Titus Andronicus* thoroughly in the light of this culturalist perspective, in IV.iv. something strange happens. There is a violence unseen. Amid the spectacular brutalities and exotic theatrical barbarisms with which the play is otherwise laden, there is, by contrast, an instance of the representation of the exercise of power so undemonstrative and marginal that it has consistently escaped notice.

It begins in IV.iii., a scene organized by Titus's conviction that the goddess of Justice has left earth and must be sought elsewhere, first below in "Pluto's region" (IV.iii.13) and, when she is reported not to be in hell either, among the empyreal gods above. It is one of the scenes of Titus's real or assumed derangement, in the unhinged energy of which his associates are caught up. Significantly, it is also one of the play's scenes of foregrounded theatrical spectacle: Titus, Marcus his brother, "other Gentlemen," and the boy Lucius, grandson to Titus, prepare and shoot arrows with petitionary letters addressed to the gods attached to them. To Titus's mind they shoot the arrows into

the heavens; according to Marcus they are launched into the court
where "We will afflict the emperor in his pride" (IV.iii.62). At this
point there enters, as it were unannounced and unprepared for, a
"Clown" who is himself on his way to petition the emperor Saturninus
in a lawsuit. Having, it seems, a less elevated sense than Titus of what
justice entails and how judicial process works, he carries a basket of
pigeons which he intends to offer the emperor as a bribe in the case, a
matter of a brawl between his uncle and one of the emperor's men.
Titus, affecting to regard the Clown as a messenger from heaven,
demands an answer to his airborne petitions: " . . . Sirrah, what tid-
ings . . . / Shall I have justice? what says Jupiter?" (IV.iii.77–78). The
Clown's reply depends upon the representation of a linguistic and
cultural miscommunication or equivocation. Lacking in any case a
classical education—he is drawn not in the aesthetic register of Shakespeare's Roman vocabulary but in that of his English-rustic idiom—
the Clown hears "Jupiter" (or, in his non-elite diction, "Jubiter") as
the dialect-word "gibbeter" and answers accordingly: "Ho, the gibbet-
maker? He says that he hath taken them down again, for the man
must not be hang'd till the next week" (IV.iii.79–81). Or at least, not
until the next scene. It is, of course, what we must be constrained to
think of as a comic moment. There is at least a discrepancy, measured
by a certain "humor," between Titus's overblown, distract railing and
madcap scheming on the one hand, and what is represented as the
only half-intended wit of the Clown's simplicities and misunderstand-
ings on the other: "Why, didst thou not come from heaven?" Titus
asks incredulously; "From heaven? alas, sir, I never came there. God
forbid I should be so bold to press to heaven in my young days" is the
Clown's ingenuous and, as it turns out, unwittingly ironic reply. In a
sequence which in this same vein both mocks and utilizes the Clown's
lack of sophistication, Titus enlists him to carry a message on his
behalf to the emperor in the form of an "oration" or "supplication."
Titus gives the Clown money for his "charges" and promises him that,
presenting the quickly-written message to the emperor along with his
pigeons, he will "have justice at his hands" (IV.iii.96–97, 100–105). In
an opaque passage Titus then asks the Clown for his knife and has
Marcus wrap it in the petition.[6] The Clown is dispatched.[7]

6. See Maxwell's note to IV.iii.115, p. 95.

7. The representation of the Clown is contained within that comic-grotesque
stupidity—sometimes flecked with low cunning—in the light of which plebian figures
almost invariably appear in the high-cultural tradition, when not dangerous, or

But whatever laughter may have been produced in this scene will seem perhaps less appropriate when in the next the Clown delivers his pigeons and Titus's oration to Saturninus. I reproduce the moment here in all its brevity:

> *Tam.*   . . .
>
>   How now, good fellow! would'st thou speak
>   with us?
>
> *Clo.*   Yea, forsooth, and your mistress-ship be emperial.
>
> *Tam.*   Empress I am, but yonder sits the emperor.
>
> *Clo.*   'Tis he. God and Saint Stephen give you godden. I
>   have brought you a letter and a couple of pigeons
>   here.
>
>   [*He reads the letter.*
>
> *Sat.*   Go take him away, and hang him presently.
>
> *Clo.*   How much money must I have?
>
> *Tam.*   Come, sirrah, you must be hanged.
>
> *Clo.*   Hang'd by'lady! then I have brought up a neck to
>   a fair end.
>
>   [*Exit.*
>   (IV.iv.39–49)

This moment is stunning. The Clown is simply taken away to execution. Without cause given. We can speculate that the written "oration" the Clown delivers contains threats or curses, or that Saturninus interprets the knife wrapped in it as a symbolic offer of violence. But the point is that *our* interpretations would remain speculative. The emperor's action in ordering the Clown's death is inexplicable. Unexplained in the literal sense that no overt reason for it is given (and this

---

simply—normally—invisible. He is part of that Shakespearean vernacular by which non-elite, and especially peasant, figures are comic as are, by definition of this mode of representation, rustics and other "lower class" figures are figures of fun. Compare it with the "comic closure" (Francis Barker and Peter Hulme, "Nymphs and Reapers Heavily Vanish: The Discursive Con-texts of *The Tempest*," in *Alternative Shakespeares*, ed. John Drakakis [New York: Methuen, 1985], p. 203) of Caliban's subplot in *The Tempest*. The Clown is not of course grotesque in exactly the same way as we have argued that Caliban is. At least he is not, as far as can be told from the text, physically demonized. He is nonetheless always-already "safely" comic, like Caliban; and this is of course grotesque. There is also, doubtless, comedy in the wit of the Clown's responses to the extravagantly mad or feigned-mad Titus, although again it is a condescending humor. If there is some mockery of Titus, the Clown is not much more than an instrument of its expression, cloaked no doubt in the mode of Shakespeare's notedly "affectionate" portrayal of his menials.

is important because it contributes to the uncanniness of the incident),
it is also unjustified in other senses. Not only does it lack credence
according to the positive norms of behavior the play assumes, but
equally it fails to conform to the protocols of the deviations from
those norms which the play more prominently foregrounds as the
reality of Roman life. Characters in *Titus Andronicus* may act "barba-
rously," but their behavior is rarely random or arbitrary; on the contrary it is invariably ad hominem and selfishly purposeful. Here the
rueful lack of protest in the Clown's last line, his last words—"Hang'd
by'lady? then I have brought up a neck to a fair end" (IV.iv.49)—
bespeaks an apparently cheerful acceptance, and equally cheerful in-
comprehension, of what is to be done to him. The poor are happy to
be hanged by their betters. It is a well-known fact. Without his killing
even represented as an articulation of a Rome in general given over to
the tyranny or savagery that maims the Andronici, the Clown, so
evidently a dupe of Titus's rather than a conspirator or accomplice,
the Clown who heard, eerily perhaps, "Jupiter" as "gibbeter," thus
dies on the gallows, "dazed" (we might imagine after the Wyatt poem)
and "with dreadful face."[8]

And this brief episode remains as a whole entirely enigmatic and
arbitrary. It is as if, running your hand along a surface, something
snags here. It is formally unmotivated in the sense of being aesthet-
ically discrepant from the primitivism and the classicism of the rest of
the play, and of lacking convincing preparation or legitimation in the
thematic, narrative, or hermeneutic codes of the text. It is inexplicable, as I have said, and never mentioned again. It is simply *there*:
strange, *unheimlich*, and, I have found, haunting.

III

Unlike the Clown in *Titus Andronicus* the majority of people who died
on the gallows in early modern England were killed after convictions
for felony sustained in the course of what is frequently called "the
administration of justice." For this purpose lay magistrates, Justices of

8. The image seems compelling if one imagines, as I do, the contrast between the
bizarre levity of the discourse of this moment and the reality of the death by strangula-
tion with which it is but barely articulated. In Wyatt's poem *Stond whoso list upon the
slipper top*, of course, death "grip'th right hard" him who is "much known of other": this
is clearly not the Clown's case.

the Peace, sat in Quarter Sessions in each county hearing petty offenses, while the superior provincial courts, presided over by a judge,
were the Courts of Assize which heard the capital offenses. England
was divided into six assize "circuits," the South-Eastern or "Home"
circuit, the Midland, Norfolk, Oxford, Northern, and Western Circuits. Wales was divided into a further four. (London and the so-called
"metropolitan" county of Middlesex were not included in the circuit
system, having separate but equivalent courts.) Twice each year, usually in the Lent and Trinity vacations, two royal justices empowered by
commissions of Oyer and Terminer and of Gaol Delivery would "ride"
each of the circuits. They convened assize courts in appropriate towns
in each county, hearing pleas and delivering the gaols of those who
had been committed by the Justices of the Peace to await trial on more
serious offenses than could be dealt with by magistrates, and of those
who had been arrested since the last quarter or assize sessions.

It happens that relatively full records survive for the Home circuit,
which consisted of the counties of Essex, Hertfordshire, Kent, Surrey,
and Sussex, as they do for the Middlesex Sessions, and it is these
which provide the basis for what I feel compelled to say—in a decidedly unanthropological way—about hanging in Elizabethan and
Stuart England and Wales. Initially, setting aside considerations of the
quality of justice, and other evaluative issues concerning the relation
between Elizabethan and Stuart power and the mass of the people,
this involves simply attempting to enumerate the instances of death by
hanging (and other related causes) as a result of judgments in the
assizes. In order to count the dead I have drawn very fully in the first
instance on Professor J. S. Cockburn's painstaking work on the bundles of what have come to be called "indictment" files (although their
actual content is more varied) which comprise the main records of the
Home Circuit Assizes in our period.[9]

9. From 1975 to 1982 Professor Cockburn published the records of the Home
Circuit in ten volumes, one for each of the circuit's constituent counties for each of the
reigns of Elizabeth and James. His introductory volume to the *Calendar of Assize Records:
Home Circuit Indictments, Elizabeth I and James I: Introduction* (London: H.M.S.O., 1985)
discusses the organization and procedures of the assizes, and tabulates in summary
form data distilled from the county volumes. I have reproduced many of those data
here, sometimes without further acknowledgement; in most instances I have submitted
them to further arithmetical or statistical processing, and occasionally I have interpo-
lated information from other sources. Interpretation of the significance of the figures
and of their likely reliability is either mine, or it is the work of either Cockburn or of
other commentators, in which case my indebtedness is noted accordingly. The same
general principles govern my use below of John Cordy Jeaffreson's work on the records

According to these files it appears that in Essex, in the period 1559–1624,[10] of the 3,449 people indicted for felonies, 801 were sentenced to death. In Hertfordshire the figures are 1,291 and 320, respectively; in Kent, 2,684 and 732; in Surrey, 2,872 and 623; and in Sussex, 1,435 and 352. Of a total of 11,731 people (10,107 men and 1,624 women) indicted in the five counties of the Home Circuit, 2,828—2,571 men and 257 women—were sentenced to be hanged. This figure must be adjusted however to take account of the known pardons issued in the relevant period. The figures for the Home Circuit in the reign of Elizabeth are as follows: Essex, 105; Hertfordshire, 66; Kent, 148; Surrey, 120; and Sussex, 55. These numbers, which total 494, must then be adjusted to encompass the reign of James as well.[11] The resulting total is 729. When this figure is subtracted from the total of felons sentenced to death in the period it yields the number hanged as 2,099.

To this number must be added, however, the numbers sentenced by Justices of the Peace. Although in theory the more serious offenses should have been dealt with by the royal justices at the twice-yearly assizes, and in practice this was probably increasingly the pattern during the period, there is nevertheless sufficient evidence that the lay magistrates were also hanging felons at a considerable rate. Although the surviving records for quarter sessions are not, so far as I am aware, anything like as full as for the Home Circuit Assizes and for

---

of the Middlesex Sessions and F. G. Emmison's work on the Essex county records: *Middlesex County Records, Vol. 1: Indictments, Coroners' Inquests-Post-Mortem and Recognizances from 3 Edward VI. to the End of the Reign of Queen Elizabeth* (London: Greater London Council, 1972) and *Middlesex County Records, Vol. 2: Indictments, Recognizances, Coroners' Inquests-Post-Mortem, Orders and Memoranda, temp. James I [With Summaries from 1549]* (London: Greater London Council, 1974); *Elizabethan Life: Disorder, Mainly from the Essex Sessions and Assize Records* (Chelmsford: Essex County Council, 1970). For information about the general operation of the assizes I have relied on Cockburn's *A History of English Assizes 1558–1714* (Cambridge: Cambridge University Press, 1972). Subsequent references to all of these texts are to these editions.

10. Following Cockburn's tables, these 65 whole years have been taken, for arithmetical and statistical purposes, as the numerical representation of the extent of the period under consideration, i.e., the reigns of Elizabeth I and James I. (Neither of these monarchs had the forethought to be born or to die at the exact beginning or the exact end of what we think of as the calendar year.)

11. This figure is derived from Cockburn's. On the basis of his own data, Professor Cockburn appears to err when he gives the number pardoned as 495 in the body of his text (*Calendar*, p. 128). The number of pardons for both reigns has been derived by averaging the Elizabethan figure for the years of that reign and multiplying it up for the 65 years of the two reigns.

Middlesex, there are some telling exceptions. Fairly detailed records exist, for example, of the disposition of felons for both the Quarter Sessions and the Assizes held in Devon between 1598 and 1639 (see Cockburn, *A History*, pp. 94–96). Where in this period the judges of assize are recorded as having had 511 people hanged, the Justices of the Peace were responsible for the execution of a further 109, or about another 20 percent of the figure for the assizes. This excludes the 15 people recorded in the same documents as dead before judgment (not to mention the 1,600 who are recorded as having other forms of corporal punishment inflicted on them in the same Sessions in the same period). If it is at all statistically responsible to generalize from the Devon figures and from other instances where records of executions ordered by quarter sessions exist side by side with the figures from the equivalent assizes—and it should be remembered that Devon was not a populous part of the country compared with the Home Circuit, so any resulting distortion is likely to be in the direction of underestimation—it appears that figures given above for executions in the Home Circuit should be increased by a fifth to account for the Justices of the Peace acting in lieu of assize judges. This would mean that the total of people hanged within the jurisdiction of the Home Circuit assizes during the years under consideration is not 2,099 but 2,518.

When we turn to the records for London and Middlesex, it is necessary no doubt to note the slightly different forms of organization and legal basis of the courts which were nonetheless the equivalents of the quarter sessions and assizes in the provincial counties.[12] But although the sessions of the peace held in London and in Middlesex were not, strictly speaking, quarter sessions, and nor were the superior courts strictly assizes, the general pattern, by which inferior courts and courts of first instance were presided over by lay justices while judges empowered by commissions of gaol delivery and oyer and terminer heard felony cases in superior courts, also held good in the metropolis and the metropolitan county. Middlesex justices sat at Westminster and elsewhere in the county, while London justices sat at Guildhall. Sessions of gaol delivery, however, were held for both Middlesex and London at the Old Bailey which stood adjacent to Newgate, the principal prison for both the capital and the county.

In the records for Middlesex the most extensive material is the

12. See Cockburn, *A History*, pp. 29–31; Jeaffreson, *Middlesex 1*, pp. xx–xxvi.

bundles of files known collectively as "sessional rolls."[13] But the Middlesex archives also contain a number of volumes of folio record books, among which is a Gaol Delivery Register begun in the fifth year of James's reign. This was a record of the actual disposition of the cases of felons, rather than the more or less reliably annotated indictments and recognizances of the Sessional Rolls proper. The Register records, among other things, actual executions, while the latter documents may contain such information if they have been annotated to that effect, or may only provide information from which such data can be, at best, inferred. Thus for my purposes the Gaol Delivery Register is in principle a far more accurate document than the sessional rolls themselves. Jeaffreson's original analysis of this material suggests that in practice as well it was kept with great accuracy, at least for certain periods in the early seventeenth century. While during the last seven years of James's reign the Register was kept "with a remissness that in certain passages wanted nothing of scandalous negligence," from the sixth to the fifteenth years of the reign it seems to have been "kept with sufficient care and exactitude; and from the entries made in the folios during these years, one learns even to a unit how largely the criminal code of our ancestors was destructive of human life in one of the smallest of the English counties," as Jeaffreson puts it (*Middlesex* 2, p. xvii).

According to the Middlesex Gaol Delivery Register in the ten years from 6 James to 15 James, the numbers of people hanged were 55, 55, 52, 77, 46, 98, 84, 91, 71, and 75 respectively, a total of 704. On this evidence, then, at least 70.4 people on average were executed by hanging each year in the metropolitan county.[14] In the case of Lon-

13. At the instigation of the Middlesex County Records Society, the Middlesex records were investigated and described in the nineteenth century by John Cordy Jeaffreson, who published his two volumes at Clerkenwell in 1886 and 1887 (*Middlesex 1* and 2). They were republished by the Greater London Council before its demise at the hands of a Conservative government. Jeaffreson's volumes, as well as analyzing—in the strict sense—the material, print numerous documentary examples of indictments, coroners' inquests, recognizances, sessional orders, minutes, memoranda and other "entries of record"; a systematic tabulation of the results of his search of the Middlesex records, giving numbers of indictments for various classes of crime, of convictions, grants of benefit of clergy, sentences, reprieves and numbers of felons at large, etc., for each of the reigns, is printed at the end of the second volume.

14. In giving this as the average annual figure (the equivalent total for the whole period is 4,576), and in adducing and aggregating later not only numbers of executions by hanging but also of "related" deaths in Middlesex (execution by the *peine forte et dure* and "prison deaths" discussed below), I have thus decided to base my calculations and extrapolations on the qualitatively best evidence available, i.e., on that of the ten accu-

don, as distinct from Middlesex, the figures I present are calculated, or, to be precise, are only evidential in as much as they are estimations based on the Middlesex records. I have followed Jeaffreson in cautiously estimating the incidence of penal demise as at least no less in the city and the liberties than in Middlesex, whose population was probably significantly lower than that of London (see *Middlesex 2*, pp. xx–xxi). Therefore to the Middlesex figure of 70.4 executions a year on average may be added a further 70.4 for the metropolis itself.[15]

In enumerating the extent of the taking of life which the records of the assizes and of the equivalent metropolitan courts represent, however, it is important not to forget two other causes of death besides executions by hanging: mortality resulting from the *peine forte et dure*, and deaths in prison while captives were awaiting trial, sentence, further investigation, or other judicial procedure (gaol sentences as such were of course rare in the period).

A prisoner who refused to plead, or who entered a "perverse" plea, was subjected to the *peine*, which consisted of being pressed with heavy weights until the prisoner either pleaded or died (Cockburn, *Calendar*, p. 72). A first taste of the penalty was applied in the courtroom itself, and if the prisoner still refused to plead he or she was incarcerated and the weights applied permanently, or at least until one or other of the desired results was achieved.[16] It is incredible that

---

rate years of the Stuart Gaol Delivery Register. In applying them to the whole period I have accepted Jeaffreson's reasons for thinking that the generalization of these figures (and of those given below for executions by the *peine* in Middlesex) to the rest of James's reign and to that of Elizabeth is not only statistically convenient but historically probable. See Jeaffreson, *Middlesex 2*, pp. xxi–xxii. In view of the principles of methodological and numerical caution outlined below, however, I think it important to indicate that the figures yielded by this apparently high-grade but chronologically limited record differ from those which can be derived from the sessional rolls as such, which embrace the entire period but are very imperfect both in their original comprehensiveness as records of actual executions and also in their state of preservation. The latter figure is somewhat lower than the former.

15. As in the case of the Home Circuit, it is probable that lay justices in Middlesex and London were also ordering executions despite the fact that felonies were supposed to have been referred to the higher courts. Estimates for likely levels of such executions in London and Middlesex, based on the adjustment already noted of the Home Circuit figures in light of the records of the Devon Sessions, are given below along with the aggregated figures, national estimates and projected modern equivalents.

16. See Cockburn, *Calendar*, p. 72; for a discussion of the distinction between the *peine* as a form of torture designed to extract a plea and a sentence imposed on conviction for refusing to plead, see Jeaffreson, *Middlesex 2*, p. xix. Cf. note 18 below.

anyone chose to endure this torment unto death rather than to plead, but some did: it is conceivable that they held out in order to protect their family from destitution, for to be executed in this way meant that the prisoner had not died a convicted felon whose real property would have been forfeit to the Crown (the prisoner's "moveables" were forfeit even under the *peine*) (Cockburn, *Calendar*, p. 72). According to the Home Circuit records at least 23 prisoners were killed in this manner during the two reigns, although this is a questionably low figure when compared with the 48 who, according to Cockburn, were ordered pressed to death at the Old Bailey in the same period (*Calendar*, p. 72, n. 135).[17]

According to the Gaol Delivery Register the figures for Middlesex were as follows. In the ten years from 6 James to 15 James, 6, 3, 6, 2, 1, 3, 5, 2, 1 and 3 people were pressed to death, a total of 32 and an annual average of 3.2. On the basis established above these figures should be doubled to include the London jurisdictions, resulting in a total of 64 and an average of 6.4. The aggregate for deaths by the *peine* in Middlesex and London over the full period 1559–1624 would be 416.

The *peine forte et dure* should properly be considered both a form of judicial torture and a method of execution.[18] But clearly it would not be wholly accurate to count those who otherwise died in prison—of natural causes—among the number executed. However, it is arguable that no death is the result of "natural causes," or at least it cannot be known that a death is natural except in the context of a society which has achieved every possible condition for the prolongation of life. And even if to call a death "premature" might be to engage the unfathomable metaphysics of a pre-destined span believed to have been allotted either to a given individual in particular or to humanity in general, it is nonetheless quite possible to establish under the conditions prevailing in given societies at given moments normal, or at least

17. In fact, Jeaffreson's figures for the Old Bailey are higher than Cockburn suggests, but I have resisted the temptation to adjust the Home Circuit figures to take account of the likely real level of executions by the *peine* suggested by comparison with the more reliable evidence of Jeaffreson's Middlesex hanging book, which I summarize immediately below.

18. Cf. note 16 above. According to Jeaffreson, *Middlesex* 2, p. xix, the *peine* was certainly used in the later part of the seventeenth century as a form of torture designed to extract a plea as well as a sentence for "standing mute" or failing to plead. The figures which I have given here for our period, based on Jeaffreson, are for convictions.

average, life expectancies. It is reasonable to assume that had they been at liberty the deaths of those who succumbed in gaol to disease or starvation might not have occurred when they did, and in this sense are consequential upon the "administration of justice" rather than on nature or destiny. As Cockburn puts it, "Gaols in the early modern period were uniformly overcrowded and insanitary, and lengthy incarceration frequently proved the equivalent of death sentence" (*Calendar*, p. 36). The so-called "prison deaths" resulted mainly from what was known as "gaol fever," which we call typhus; but deaths in gaol "increased dramatically during periods of dearth," suggesting that malnutrition or starvation was also an important cause of penal fatality (*Calendar*, p. 36). In the scaled-up aggregate figures below I have, of course, recorded "prison deaths" separately from the totals for execution, but I have thought it appropriate to represent them nonetheless as numbers of people killed by the authorities.

Figures are available which indicate the number of those who died in prison on the Home Circuit in this way, as an indirect result of judicial process (Cockburn, *Calendar*, pp. 145–71). They are as follows: Essex, 315 (including two suicides); Hertfordshire, 91; Kent, 243 (three suicides); Surrey, 543 (one suicide); and Sussex 123 (one suicide). In total, then, the records which survive count 1,315 men and women who died in prison on the Home Circuit between 1559 and 1625, of which at least seven took their own lives.[19]

I am not aware of data equivalent to that of the Home Circuit for prison deaths in Middlesex or London. I have had therefore to derive estimated figures for these jurisdictions from likely equivalence with the Home Circuit, for which data have survived. The ratio between the number of executions and the number of prison deaths on the Home Circuit is 1:0.52. I assume a similar ratio for Middlesex and for London. If this assumption is well-founded, then this would indicate

19. With the exception of three who are unidentified we know all of the names of all those who died in prison on the Home Circuit in the period. Indeed we know the names of a great many of the men and women the enumeration of whose deaths are the basis of the figures I am presenting. I cannot help comparing this with the fact of our knowledge of "162 real persons known to have attended playhouse performances" in "Shakespeare's London" (see Andrew Gurr, *Playgoing in Shakespeare's London* [Cambridge: Cambridge University Press, 1987], pp. xv and 191–204), and wondering about the different degrees of critical attention the two vastly disproportionate groups of "real persons" has received. In two cases the Home Circuit records are annotated in ways that might indicate the social standing of the victims of prison death: one is marked "gent.," another "clerk." We may assume that the rank of the other 1,313 who died was beneath notice.

that in addition to those who were executed by hanging or by the *peine*, a further 5,710.8 from Middlesex and London would have died in Newgate and the other metropolitan gaols during the period.[20]

I turn now to the estimation of national totals of deaths by hanging which resulted from sentencing in sessions, and, along with these figures, analogous estimates for executions by the *peine forte et dure* and for prison deaths. Although they are based on the detailed records which are available for the Home Circuit and for London and Middlesex and which I have discussed above, these must necessarily be calculated and estimated figures: equivalent data do not exist for the other English and Welsh circuits. The method adopted is that of calculating a figure for the remaining English and Welsh circuits based on the data for the Home Circuit, and then adding to this the figures for London and Middlesex.

In order to estimate a total figure for the provincial jurisdictions it would seem appropriate, in view of the fact that there were six English assize circuits and a further four in Wales, to multiply the Home Circuit figures by a factor of ten. Even without the aid of anything like realistic demographic modeling or a scientific sociology of early modern penal victimization, however, it is clear that such a multiplication would seriously inflate the figures. The Home Circuit was the most populous and the wealthiest of the English circuits; the population of Wales was disproportionately tiny in comparison with that of England. In line therefore with the mathematical caution which I discuss below, I have in fact first derived a figure for England and then added to this a total figure for Wales based on the comparative sizes of their respective populations. To obtain a figure for England it would seem reasonable to multiply the Home Circuit figures by a factor of six as there were six English circuits in all. I have in fact multiplied by a factor of four: this is an arbitrary figure (although demographically reasonable) but certainly a cautious one, well below that suggested by the administrative form of the organization of the assizes. The result of this calculation is as follows: if, as I have shown above, there were in the period 2,518 hangings on the Home Circuit (or an average of 38.7 each year), in the whole of provincial England there would have been

20. The calculation is as follows: 2,518 executions on the Home Circuit (including those ordered by J.P.s) stand in a ratio of 1:0.52 to 1,315 prison deaths. If the number of hangings in Middlesex and London (including the equivalent adjustment) is 10,982.4 (see below for the derivation of this figure), then the number of prison deaths—assuming a similar ratio—is 5,710.85.

10,072 (or 154.95 each year). However, if the estimates given above for executions ordered by justices sitting in quarter sessions are to be trusted, this figure must be adjusted accordingly and becomes 12,086 for the period or 185.94 annually. A similar multiplication of the Home Circuit figures for executions by the *peine forte et dure* and for prison deaths gives an estimated total of these kinds of fatalities for the English provincial circuits as a whole of 92 (or 1.41 each year) for the *peine* and 5,260 (80.92 annually) for deaths in prison.

The figures for Wales which should be added to these totals are based on D. C. Coleman's estimation of the populations of England and Wales in 1545 as 2.8 million and 0.25 million respectively.[21] In other words, the population of the principality is 8.93 percent of that of England. Assuming a similar statistical relation between population size and number of executions suggests a figure for executions in Wales during the period equivalent to that percentage of the English figure, i.e. 1,079.28 (or 16.60 on average each year).[22] The Welsh figures for deaths by the *peine* and for prison deaths have been derived from the estimated English figures in the same way. They are 8.21 deaths by pressing (or 0.13 on average each year), and 469.72 deaths in prison (7.23 each year).

The aggregate figures for the provincial circuits of England and Wales together which result from these calculations are as follows. During the whole period at least 13,165 people were put to death by hanging, 100.21 by the *peine*, and at least 5,729.72 died in prison. The average annual figures for each of these classes of fatality is 202.54, 1.54, and 88.15.

To these must be added the figures for Middlesex and for London. I have discussed the methods by which these were derived above; here it suffices to give them in summary form. It is estimated that in Middlesex at least 4,576 people were executed by hanging during the period, or 70.4 on average each year. If, however, these figures are adjusted, on the basis noted earlier, to include likely numbers of executions ordered by lay justices, the resulting totals for the jurisdiction are 5,491.2 hanged over the entire period, or 84.48 on average every year. I have estimated that a further 208 men and women were exe-

21. D. C. Coleman, *The Economy of England: 1450–1750* (Oxford: Oxford University Press, 1977), p. 12.
22. These are the *adjusted* figures, taking account, according to the previously stated principle, of likely numbers of executions ordered by Justices of the Peace: the estimates for the Assizes alone are one-fifth lower, or 899.43 and 13.83 respectively.

cuted by the *peine* in Middlesex (or 3.2 each year), while 2,855.4 (or 45.93 annually) died in gaol. Following Jeaffreson's suggestion, noted above, that numbers of executions in London may be conservatively estimated as equal to those of the metropolitan county, the figures I have just given may be doubled in order to obtain aggregates for London and Middlesex together, that is, at least 10,982.4 hangings during the whole period (or 168.96) each year, 416 executions by the *peine* (or 6.4 each year), and a further 5,710.8 (or 87.86 people annually) dying in prison.

Finally, addition of these aggregates gives estimated national totals for England and Wales including London and Middlesex. The resulting figures are as follows: 24,147.4 men and women hanged; 516.21 pressed to death, and 11,440.52 dead in gaol; on average at least 371.5 were put to death by hanging, 7.94 were killed by the *peine forte et dure*, and a further 176 probably died in gaol in each and every one of the 65 years of the reigns of Elizabeth and James.

To give a sense of the extent of the slaughter[23] it is perhaps worth scaling these figures up to modern-day equivalents. One way in which this can be done is by a comparative analysis of population.[24] The early modern population of England and Wales, as estimated by Coleman (*The Economy*, p. 12) to be 4.085 million at the arbitrary but more or less mean date of 1603, is related to the modern population of England and Wales, which on 30 June 1989 stood at 50,562,000, in a ratio of 1:12.38.[25] Multiplying the early modern figures for execution and related deaths accordingly would mean that if a similar proportion of the present-day population were put to death, at least 4,599.17 people on average would be executed as convicted felons each year, a further 98.29 would be pressed to death without plea, and 2,178.88

23. I have tried in this section of this essay not to allow the language to become too heightened. But the process of gleaning, extrapolating, adjusting, and aggregating these figures—before even beginning to assess interpretatively their likely underestimation of the real scale of executions (and still less to account for *that*)—was extremely unpleasant, and one that I found, moreover, morally and politically uneasy, especially in view of the ghastly irony that the higher the eventual figure proved, the stronger the overall case argued by this essay became. The counting often seemed more part of the problem than part of the answer, and it was only possible to do this work for short periods of time before the revulsion became too much. It was not possible to forget—which is what numbers often help us to do—that it is the untimely extinction of real lives which is enumerated in these figures.

24. Although see note 27 below.

25. Coleman, *The Economy of England*, p. 12; H.M.S.O., *Population Trends: Journal of the Office of Censuses and Surveys* 61 (1990): 49.

would die in gaol. A similar "calculation" can be made for the modern United States.[26] The resulting figures are these: 22,383.88 executions by hanging each year, 478.39 executions by the *peine*, and 10,604 prison deaths.[27]

These figures, whether evidential or projected, are horrendous. But there are several kinds of reason for believing that they are radical underestimations of the numbers of people actually put to death, and that the aggregate figures should be very much higher than those given here (and might have been even higher again). In the first place there are technical reasons to do with the nature of the records drawn on, and with their original quality as records, which give every ground for believing them to be a very incomplete account of what must actually have taken place, and one yielding figures which are much below the real values. They have also been subject to varying degrees

26. The population of the United States is estimated at 246,113,000 on June 30, 1988 (see *Population Trends* 61 [1990]: 49). The estimated early modern population stands in relation to this figure at a ratio of 1:60.25. The figures for executions by hanging and by the *peine*, and those for prison deaths have therefore been multiplied by a factor of 60.25 to yield the figures given.

27. I am no more a statistical demographer than I am an anthropologist. These modern equivalent figures are in no sense meant to represent a scientifically accurate extrapolation based on reasonable demographical or sociological equivalences between early modern England and Wales and the demographical and sociological structures of the contemporary populations with which the comparison is made. They are meant as an indicator of the scale rather than the number of the deaths. If the scaling up of the Home Circuit, Middlesex, and London figures to aggregates for England and Wales in the sixteenth and seventeenth centuries is already speculative (given that where statistics survive from the period there are no reliable ones, and that there were in any case no national totals recorded in the period, whether trustworthy or otherwise), still less can mere multiplication provide a reliable value for the modern number of executions equivalent to those carried out in Elizabethan and Stuart England and Wales. Strictly speaking, the results are no more than what they appear to be: the values achieved when the calculated period aggregates are multiplied in the same ratio as that which relates the modern population(s) to the population then. But *as an indicator*, as a suggestion of how many of the modern population would have to be killed in order to correspond to the equivalent proportion of the period population who *were* being killed each year, they are chilling, radical underestimates as they are.

Perhaps more appropriate figures would be produced not by a comparative analysis of population, but by one of crime and punishment. I leave it to the reader to estimate how many people would have to be killed in modern Britain (or in the United States, which has an annual murder rate of about 25,000) if we sought to execute everyone convicted of an offence more serious than the theft of goods worth the equivalent of 12 pence.

of material damage—in some instances quite extensive—both in the
period and subsequently. And there are methodological factors connected with the way in which I have selected and treated the extant
figures, which suggest that the real values were significantly greater
than those recorded: as a general principle I have been careful at
every stage in my choice of data and subsequent arithmetical or statistical treatment of the figures to underestimate rather than risk exaggerating the numerical values involved. Precisely because it is part of
my wider argument to show how great the extent of coercive violence
was, I have thought it appropriate at every point to be as conservative
as possible in my empirical procedures and in my methods of inference both from the data and from the palpable inadequacy of the
data. In selecting values where variant figures are available I have
chosen the lower or lowest quanta; when calculating arithmetically, or
projecting statistically from the empirical calculations, I have
rounded results down rather than up and chosen methods of calculation which tend to err in the direction of low rather than high sums.
Inasmuch as mathematical procedures and methodological infer-
ences from the nature and quality of the records have been concerned, I have been careful throughout to give "the Age of Shakespeare," that high point of English culture, the maximum benefit of
the doubt.

Second, consideration of the county assizes and the Middlesex sessions (with their equivalents in the city of London) by no means ex-
hausts the judicial, para-judicial, summary, and other means by which
the state could and did dispose of its subjects. Not only were there
other jurisdictions—conciliar, municipal, episcopal—which over-
lapped those of the Assizes, but even beyond the purview of the assize
courts and of these competing jurisdictions in the provincial counties,
and that of the equivalent courts in London and Middlesex, a number
of other judicial and quasi-judicial authorities were also busily hanging people. No account has been taken of the myriad special commissions of oyer and terminer which were empowered to deal with particular instances of disorder outside the regular Sessions, and which put
to death anyone from participants in gatherings deemed to be unlaw-
ful protests or riots through to the likes of the less prominent participants in Essex's rebellion. Nor has account been taken of the frequent
occasions on which martial law was declared with the consequent—
undeniably summary—execution of yet further numbers of the pop-

ulation.[28] I have given no place in these calculations to the criminal trials in the higher courts at Westminster such as King's Bench. And I have in particular excluded from consideration the religious and political trials, mainly conducted at the center, whether the big State trials of notorious rebels and traitors, or the more routine but nonetheless political trials of less prominent opponents or alleged opponents of the regime, which were conducted in the Westminster courts and elsewhere.[29]

And third, if one wishes to assess not only the figures but the violence they articulate, it is important to remember that the documents only record—with whatever degree of accuracy or error—those whom the state was *successful* in killing, as distinct from those it failed to apprehend, try, convict, and execute or otherwise destroy. Even if it were possible to obtain perfect information about the actual incidence of all executions, such a total would itself markedly under-

28. For a discussion of martial law in the Tudor period, see John Bellamy, *The Tudor Law of Treason: An Introduction* (London: Routledge and Kegan Paul, 1979), pp. 228–35.

29. In contrasting the "routine" character of the hangings ordered by assize courts with the more spectacular trials and executions at the center, it is important nonetheless to avoid two erroneous implications. It is no part of my argument to suggest that these deaths were less central: on the contrary. Nor is it to allow that the "administration of justice" is somehow neutral, where a show trial or a martial law execution is clearly "political": again, on the contrary. The claim that the ordinary work of the judicial apparatus is not political is a mystification that has served successive regimes well. At a fundamental level, routine administration of justice daily promulgates and reinforces dominant ideologies, protects the existing social structure (its property relations especially), and either subordinates or eliminates those who fail or refuse to serve or satisfy its values and norms of behavior. And as for the Elizabethan and Stuart assize courts in particular, there is no doubt not only that they were an integral part of the transmission and enforcement in the provincial counties of state policy (and not only in judicial matters but across the board of governmental policy) but that they were also sites—I say this at the risk of appearing to concede something of the argument I am opposing—of the spectacular display and practice of the power of the state, and in particular the monarch, whose agents the judges were and whose supremacy they represented. The assize judges gathered in Star Chamber before they left for the circuits and were "charged" with the task not only of carrying out their judicial commissions but also of conveying and reinforcing current policy at large. On arrival in the counties they convened—with, indeed, some display of authority—the great and the good of the locality and in turn charged them with the responsibility of the government of the place according to how the state was currently defining this task. And then set about hanging the less great and the less good. For an account of the political and governmental function of the assize judges see Cockburn, *A History*, pp. 1–11; and for another account, particularly of the coercive spectacle of the convocation of a session of assize, see the Introduction to *Order and Disorder in Early Modern England*, ed. Anthony Fletcher and John Stevenson (Cambridge: Cambridge University Press, 1985), p. 21.

estimate the scale and intensity of what would be involved in trying to assess the general violence of the "culture." My subject is not, after all, merely punishment. In any case there is evidence suggesting that even what we have seen so far is but a fraction of the whole when compared with what the scale of killing would have been if what we might call—borrowing or altering a phrase from Foucault—"the will to punish" had operated or had been able to operate absolutely unimpeded. There is evidence of inefficiency, corruption, and sometimes leniency in the processes of arrest, prosecution, and the determination of verdicts and sentences. There was also overt resistance to arrest and incarceration involving active efforts on the part of the system's victims to contest and to evade the power of the judicial and "police" machinery. And there was also more subtle, but probably more widespread, resistance in forms of indirect recalcitrance—particularly among members of local communities—designed to impede or mitigate the process. Thus a number of factors indicate willed or accidental limitations on the effectivity of a power which would have been even more devastating in its effects. Behind the arithmetic is a dialectic of conflict: the figures given are the result not of *unitary* historical process, but of what can only be imperfectly labeled a "will to punish" as it has been modified by coming up against not just its own inefficiencies and dysfunctions but also, and most importantly, whatever and whoever resisted the ideological authority and the physical capacity of the state to do violence to its subjects.

IV

> The tradition of the oppressed teaches us that the
> "state of emergency" in which we live is not the excep-
> tion but the rule. We must attain to a conception of
> history that is in keeping with this insight.
> —WALTER BENJAMIN,
> "Theses on the Philosophy of History"

In defense of property and the established social order the Elizabethan and Jacobean crown killed huge numbers of the people of England. Their names not wholly unknown, the circumstances of their demise often recorded, the sheer number of them only estimable, men, women, and children in "Shakespeare's England" were strung up on permanent or makeshift gallows by a hempen noose. Sometimes the spinal cord was snapped at once; if not they hung by their necks until they suffocated or drowned, until their brains died of hypoxeia, or until the shock killed them. Pissing and shitting themselves. Bleeding from their eyes. Thinking.

Or they were crushed under slabs of stone and iron. Or they "took their own lives," as the exculpatory phrase has it. Or they became just "prison deaths."

But nothing of this is dramatized in *Titus Andronicus*. The relationship between the text and the "quiet," steady slaughter of the people by hanging is not one of ostentation but occlusion. The play does make violence, extravagant violence, the center of its and our attention, but the graphic violence of the drama serves to direct attention away from, rather than toward, the elimination of huge numbers of the population. For the barbarisms so spectacularly performed by the play are nothing like the common violence of the times. I make no comment on the real incident of cannibalism in early modern England, only on the diversionary effect of such a practice being foregrounded in *Titus Andronicus* at the expense of the representation of a systematic violence which is recoverable but which is thus occluded. Indeed, one might be forgiven for thinking that *Titus Andronicus* is organized around this very occlusion. So extravagant and so insistent is the violence of the play, for which of course it has been dismissed by criticism, that even without attempting to bring to light the material it occludes, an analysis based on the idea that it "has something to hide" would seem almost to suggest itself.

It is the anthropology of *Titus Andronicus* that plays the main part in organizing this occlusion: the "othering" structure of its categorial and topographical anthropology of civility and barbarism locates significant violence in another time, in another place, among other people. I noted above the way in which the Shakespearean anthropology simplified the structuration of otherness (see note 4). It is important to see now how the oversimplification serves the occlusion I am discussing: the clear and simple expulsion of the savage beyond the limits of the civil seeks to locate safely "out there" the violence which it codes as barbarism but which may in fact belong dangerously "in here." But in making violence into the spectacle of the exotic, it serves in a curious way also to domesticate that violence, or at least to render violence *merely* theatrical. No one alive in early modern England could

fully have *believed* that the location of violence was elsewhere, but we
know that ideology—perhaps especially when deployed in the form
of "cultural performance"—works in mysterious but effective ways.

The sense of occlusion at work in *Titus Andronicus*—to return to the
strange episode of the Clown which precipitated these reflections on
violence and its occlusion—is, however, both subtle and complex. For
example, I myself was led to investigate systematic execution by an
uncanny moment in the play itself, by the odd flatness of the incident's intrusion into the otherwise extravagant decorum of the text. It
is an incident that lies at the unnoticed margins of that text: the play
has its guilty secret, *which it keeps.* Certainly it keeps very quiet compared with what an analysis which prioritizes spectacular display
would expect.[30] But it is, of course, "there": just as no repression
disappears *"without trace,"* so the occlusion of violence marks the text
from which it is excluded. One form of the trace is perhaps to be
glimpsed in the artistic incongruity of the episode, which while it is
absolutely uninflected in one sense, in another is not as flattened as all
that. For one thing it is, as I have already said, in several senses comic;
perhaps, in response to the very unmotivated, seemingly "arbitrary"
character of the episode itself and in particular of the summary disposal of the Clown, a nervous and uncomfortable laughter—like that
which *Titus Andronicus* as a whole has engendered and received—may
be appropriate. I have also indicated the discrepancy among the class
idioms involved. The episode is a marginalized "representation"
which but barely represents, an articulation which disarticulates, leaving everything unsaid when viewed in the light of what I have demonstrated above as the actual incidence, both in extent and intensity, of
death by hanging among the ludic rustics and non-elite clowns of
early modern England and Wales—the real dead. It suggests in this
way that the achievement of occlusion depends on an inherently complex form of representation which does not entail simple suppression
of the occluded material, and which is certainly not either socially or
representationally monovalent. It could be argued, for example, that

30. The spectacular display of power—see in particular Leonard Tennenhouse,
Power on Display: The Politics of Shakespeare's Genres (London: Methuen, 1986)—has been,
of course, one of the recurrent themes of New Historicist accounts of the Shakespearean text. Here, and in the following pages, are traces of the critique of culturalism
(to which I have referred above; p. 226) by juxtaposition of my reading of violence and
occlusion to New Historicist accounts of the theatrical display of power. For more
explicit discussion of this issue, see the full version of this essay in my *Culture of Violence.*
See also below, note 35.

Shakespeare does not so much obscure as frequently acknowledge— in examples like the hanging of Cordelia in *Lear*—the killing of the people.[31] But this only seems to me to be clear from a certain, rather specific, class perspective. The death, by hanging, of aristocrats like Cordelia—sentimentalized as "my poor fool"—is represented as tragic, and with appropriate affect. The deaths of some plebian figures are poignant on condition that they form part of the aristocratic story: the hanging of Bardolph, at which the king nods, is part of Henry's "tragedy" and only barely part of Bardolph's—"comic"— narrative. But the lack of affect associated with the demise of the Clown in *Titus Andronicus* makes it casual, more like the reference to the "gallows-maker" whose "frame outlives a thousand tenants" in the gravedigger's scene in *Hamlet* (V.i.43–44), part of the routine, "natural" landscape and lifescape of the poor. If hanging is "addressed," it is nonetheless impossible to claim that because *Titus* glancingly dispatches a minor character in this way—uncanny as the episode itself is—it therefore does not occlude the massive social, historical, and political phenomenon of the execution by hanging of huge numbers of the common people, even although the play is otherwise so massively "centered" in the extravagant, "exotic" violences that it actually does foreground. And still less does the "culture" in which this play, and "Shakespeare" as a whole, has been subsequently embedded address this and similar material. On the contrary, this glancing attention—which is in turn quite distinct from theatrical display—is the very form of the occlusion. To be sure, occlusion does not entail a complete erasure of death by hanging; rather it puts death by hanging "under erasure." Not exactly hidden, it is more naturalized and exscribed at the same time.

This sense of the intricacy of occlusion is particularly important if we consider that there are ways, for example, in which what I have called the "structural anthropology" of *Titus Andronicus* is in the practice of the drama unable to function. Indeed, in a fuller reading of the play—if that were an objective—it would be important to take seriously the complexity of the way in which the categorial structure of barbarism and civility and the boundaries established by their symbolic and topographical distribution are unable to be sustained. Consider these three examples. It is Rome—not the barbarian, Gothic exterior—which Titus describes, in a language redolent of the play's

31. I am particularly indebted to Jonathan White for his interrogation of this point.

anthropology, as "a wilderness of tigers" (III.i.54). When the purging
resolution comes, or at least when something like order is restored at
the end, it comes only partly out of the Roman tradition but more
mainly from a source and a place which, according to the structure of
anthropology, is entirely inappropriate: from Gothic barbarity. Lucius, Titus's son, flees the city, allies himself with the enemy and enters
Rome triumphant but at the head of a *Gothic* army.[32] And, in the
central act of the eating of human flesh, what is to be made of the fact
that Titus cooks Tamora's sons but does not eat; while Tamora eats
but does not *know* what she eats? Who, in such circumstances, is the
cannibal, and where, in such circumstances, is the line between civilization and barbarism? In each case—and there are many others—
there seems to be a transgression of the line which demarcates the
boundary between the civil and the savage. It is a line that throughout
the play can be drawn but not, it seems, held.

This raises important questions about the politics of representation
in the given play *Titus Andronicus*, in Shakespeare's *oeuvre* more widely,
and in the Elizabethan and Jacobean theater as a whole, questions in
particular of the extent to which the theater either underwrites the
signifying practices of the dominant culture (and by way of that the
political and social power of the dominant, as well as its cultural authority), or alternatively unsettles such structures and institutions by
transgressing, erasing, confusing, contesting, or making "dysfunc-
tional" the categories and representations they support and which in
turn support them.[33] But more immediately it is worth remembering

32. I am grateful to Maurizio Calbi, my colleague in the Essex Early Modern Research Group, for alerting me to this aspect of the text.

33. I have written elsewhere recently of the relationship between what I see as the
master-discourse of the Shakespearean tragic text and the failure or the inability in
what I call the event of the drama of that project to be sustained in its full form. See my
Culture of Violence, esp. pp. 3–92. Connected with this, I am grateful to Peter Hulme in
discussion for raising the question of whether the intrusion, in the language of the
representation of the Clown, of Englishness isn't also the intrusion of "England" in the
sense that by virtue of that episode *Titus Andronicus* could be read not so much as an
occlusion but a critique, albeit one which is inevitably coded and displaced. I have to say
that I doubt it. The question of Shakespeare's historicism and his sense of cultural
otherness is very difficult of course, but in *Titus Andronicus* there does seem to be an
attempt to imagine another society, suggested not least by the explicit and somewhat
self-conscious classical borrowing, especially of Ovid, which could be seen as functioning very much like tribal lore in ethnographic description; and above all by way of the
structuration of otherness I have discussed above. In any case, I have looked without
success for historically particular instances of death by hanging—some especially noted
intensification of the norm, or an exceptional atrocity—which would explain contex-
tually this suggestion of "intrusion." By the same token I am skeptical about the "radical tragedy" reading, most famously and persuasively represented in the book of that

the insistence of Mary Douglas—whose work provides so much of our sense of the importance of anthropological limits—that boundaries have to be symbolically crossed *in order* to act effectively as cultural demarcations. Indeed, according to Douglas, order and even the limits of culture "as such" may be not only confirmed by their being transgressed, as a fashionable word has it, but even *produced* in the passage. Dirt is necessary to a clean place, and to the idea of cleanliness. Certainly in *Titus Andronicus* if the civil and the savage seem to be at times in the wrong places, and the line between those places is confused, the sense of the wrongness involved in the confusion is not itself confused. This is so even if these signs of the limits of the civilized and the human are all transgressed or negated, as, in fact, they are. The prohibition against eating human flesh is contravened, and in general—apart perhaps from the transgression of the incest taboo—there seems little that is prohibited which does not in fact occur at the other, barbarous, extreme.[34] But this is, again, how the occlusion works: the exoticization of significant violence depends upon the affirmation, in remarkably complex forms, of the difference between the indigent and the strange.

I am suggesting that even when violence is shown it is occluded, and that occlusion is more than a mere lack of ostentation.[35] Power is not made visible by Titus Andronicus; it is hidden, as we have seen, by other visualities. At best it leaves complex, oblique, easily overlooked

---

name by Jonathan Dollimore, which may risk a recuperation of "Shakespeare," this time as a great, if coded, critic of his society. Eventually this problem will have to be solved: it is the central question of Shakespeare criticism today.

34. Hulme comments in these terms on the marginal character of the eating of human flesh: "Human beings who eat other human beings have always been placed on the very borders of humanity. They are not regarded as *in*human because if they were animals their behaviour would be natural and could not cause the outrage and fear that 'cannibalism' has always provoked" (Hulme, *Colonial Encounters*, p. 14). On the matter of incest cf. Levi-Strauss's claim that the prohibition on incest is the one universal taboo: in *Titus Andronicus* there is certainly no overtly incestuous sexuality in the form of a sexual act committed, although Elizabethan and Jacobean tragedy was quite capable of addressing the issue. But there may be an element of displacement in the fact that Tamora eats her sons.

35. But if the relationship between *Titus Andronicus* and the reality of hanging is as I suggest, then important questions are raised about the political orientation and purposes of any interpretative approach that—most prevalent recently in the form of New Historicism—depends on the culturalist view that the encratic effectivity of the Shakespearean text lies in its explicit display of power. In fact, if the main interpretative assumptions of the New Historicism are brought to bear both on the anthropology of *Titus Andronicus*, and on the evidence of hanging in early modern England which I have presented, a major discrepancy in its vaunted ability to interpret becomes apparent, as I argue in *The Culture of Violence*. See also above, note 30.

traces as the signs of its occlusion. To be sure, there is theatrical display, and it is largely violence that is theatrically displayed; indeed, from the earliest moment of Shakespearean criticism, many have commented on the way in which the play seems to be composed of almost nothing but such extravagant theatricality. But it is not, as I have suggested, the common violence of the times which is made thus so spectacular.

I have not commented interpretatively on the precise nature of the general relationship between the occluded material as such and the text of *Titus Andronicus*—apart of course from positing both the occlusion itself and the complexity of the way in which it works, seeking what the culturalist reading and the cultural performance hide as well as what they disclose, and excavating what has been occluded but which ought, according to the predispositions I have been discussing, to be very fully "on display." And in particular I have not attempted to specify precisely the ratio of significance between coercive violence and cultural legitimation. This is a matter which would need considerable further theoretical elaboration, for surely there was a "moral economy" organized around the assizes, surely hangings were in this way "cultural" events, and of course there is meaning in what cannot otherwise be thought of as acts of purely physical violence. At least it is not impossible to presume, on the basis of the evidence I have offered above, that if there was such widespread state violence there was also an estimable dissemination of fear. The process of arrest, imprisonment, trial, and execution cannot be taken in isolation from some sense of the effects that awareness of this process must have had on those members of the population who were not presently caught up by or involved in it, not least, presumably, because the minatory effect of the process kept them "within the law." In either case a very different account will be needed of the relationship between the theater and power, between culture and violence, than that which is currently available.[36]

36. In using the term "moral economy," and in my deployment of archival material on the assize courts, I might be seen to be privileging a certain kind of social history. Indeed at "wisemens threasure" I thought it important to point out that the balance between symbolic authority and coercive violence in the exercise of Elizabethan and Stuart power had been debated by social historians years ago. In this connection (and I

V

If one asks with whom the adherents of historicism
actually empathize the answer is inevitable: with the
victor. And all rulers are the heirs of those who con-
quered before them. Hence, empathy with the victor
invariably benefits the rulers. Historical materialists
know what that means. Whoever has emerged victorious participates to this day in the triumphal procession in which the present rulers step over those who
are lying prostrate. According to traditional practice,
the spoils are carried along in the procession. They
are called cultural treasures, and a historical materialist views them with cautious detachment. For without
exception the cultural treasures he surveys have an
origin which he cannot contemplate without horror.
They owe their existence not only to the efforts of the
great minds and talents who have created them, but
also the anonymous toil of their contemporaries.
There is no document of civilization which is not at
the same time a document of barbarism. . . . A historical materialist therefore dissociates himself from it as
far as possible. He regards it as his task to brush history against the grain.

—WALTER BENJAMIN,
"Theses on the Philosophy of History"

There is nothing that I or anyone else can do for the dead of early
modern England, other than to remember in the practical, active,
historically redemptive sense that Benjamin recommended. That part
of the past which has passed is truly gone.

But that part of the present which we call the past, that part which
flashes up at a moment of danger, is another matter. . . .

I began with cultural treasures borne along in the triumphal pro-

----

am particularly grateful to Margaret Ferguson for pressing this point) I was taken to
task in the discussion that followed my lecture for allegedly valorizing the Real. It is
difficult to be believed when I point out that despite the national academic stereotypes I
no more accept the unconditional reality of the empirical than I give credence to the
hypostatization of the symbolic. At the risk, to be sure, of raising some—doubtless
unwelcome—epistemological problems, I would insist that even at the theoretical level
the evidence of mass execution I have reported above stands opposed to culturalism,
even if no allowance is made for the extent to which I have deliberately flattened it into
the numerical.

cession of ruling tradition and I shall end with them. From the beginning of the formation of western modernity in the moment of first
contact with "America," anthropological thought, in the constitution
of which Shakespeare participates, has shadowed the idea of culture.
But the anthropology of *Titus Andronicus*, and of the Shakespearean
text at large, in effect legitimates an entire historical culture of violence which it domesticates, in its own society and for us, by the
strategies of occlusion and exoticization I have addressed. Cultural
criticism becomes complicit with this violence if it does not free itself
from the same strategies, remaining equally content to remember in
order to forget.[37] To a terrifying extent, what now counts as culture *is*
the occlusion of that historical violence, then and now. Thus Benjamin's *dictum* that "there is no document of civilization which is not at
the same time a document of barbarism" is resonant.

Clearly the Shakespearean text and its culturalist readings actual
and potential belong among the documents of our civilization; indeed
there are ways in which for the literary culture of the English-
speaking world Shakespeare has come to serve as the very epitome of
civilization. But Benjamin's thesis holds good even when the document in question is not so apparently "about" the antithetical
couple—civilization and barbarism—as *Titus Andronicus*. Texts which
are by their own definition the most civilized must most occult the
barbarism of which he speaks. It is thus that they are documents of
violence, as they occlude the violence which is culture. Or, in the case
of *Titus* it is as if the process works first, by means of an inversion, the
other way round. This dreadful play, so often estimated as itself a
kind of barbarism and thereby not authentically Shakespearean,
serves to confirm by exception the normally civilized protocols of
what we can recuperate as Shakespeare's art, as our tradition, as a
secure past and a cultured present.[38] Even the barbaric text under-

37. For more on the idea of remembering in order to forget, rather than *simple*
forgetting, see my "Which Dead? *Hamlet* and the Ends of History," in *Uses of History:
Marxism, Postmodernism and the Renaissance*, ed. Francis Barker, Peter Hulme, and Margaret Iversen (Manchester: Manchester University Press, 1991), pp. 47–75.

38. *Titus Andronicus* is a play I have come not to regard, in the course of working in
detail on it, as all that inferior either by the—in fact somewhat ramshackle—structural
standards of Shakespeare's dramaturgy, or by the claims made for the cogency of his
skills of characterization and versification. In II.iii.10–29, for example, it has some of
Shakespeare's best early verse. But the play has been scorned or ignored from a very
early moment in a way which suggests to me that more is at stake than bad artistic work.
There is something insistent in the warding off of *Titus*, as if the rejection of material
which is unacceptable for other reasons has been disguised as aesthetic criticism. Ed-

writes the civilization, which is itself in turn barbaric. It is a barbarism which is concealed not least in the occlusion of violence achieved in the very spectacles of the text's own strange savagery. In the evidence of mass execution I have adduced, I have tried to show that that tradition of "civilization" has been abstracted from the history of early modern England and Wales, an occlusion of the violence—by its own terms, "barbarism"—which is its inner structure.

I, for one, will not be party to that violence, nor to its occlusion. Nor to its "anthropology."

---

ward Ravenscroft, one of its earliest recorded commentators, remarked in 1678 that it was "rather a heap of rubbish than a structure" (quoted in Waith, Introduction, p. 1); a recent critic, Gustav Cross, begins his introduction to the play thus: "*Titus Andronicus* is a ridiculous play" (Shakespeare, *The Tragedies*, ed. Alfred Harbage, Complete Pelican Shakespeare [Harmondsworth: Penguin, 1969], p. 11). Its Shakespearean authenticity has been from the beginning repeatedly questioned, and generally the work has been dismissed as early, immature, crude, sensationalist. The common view is, under the circumstances, a happy one: that *Titus Andronicus* is a "primitive" play, in the sense that it is what the language of literary taste used to call a "barbarism." It seems that Shakespeare agreed.

8

"The picture of Nobody"

White Cannibalism in *The Tempest*

RICHARD HALPERN

Tupi or not Tupi, that is the question.
—OSWALD DE ANDRADE, *Manifesto Antropófago*

In his 1971 essay "Caliban," the Cuban critic Roberto Fernández Retamar writes: "A European journalist, and moreover a leftist, asked me a few days ago, 'Does a Latin-American culture exist?' . . . The question . . . could also be expressed another way: 'Do you exist?' For to question our culture is to question our very existence, our human reality itself, and thus to be willing to take a stand in favor of our irremediable colonial condition, since it suggest that we would be but a distorted echo of what occurs elsewhere. This elsewhere is of course the metropolis, the colonizing centers."[1] For a critic writing in a revo-

This essay has benefited enormously from discussion, critique, and editorial queries following its presentation at the Seventeenth Alabama Symposium on English and American Literature. I especially thank Francis Barker, Margaret Ferguson, Christopher Kendrick, and the editors of this volume.

1. Roberto Fernández Retamar, *Caliban and Other Essays*, trans. Edward Baker (Minneapolis: University of Minnesota Press, 1990), p. 3. Subsequent references are to this edition. Retamar's essay originally appeared in *Casa de las Américas* 68 (1971): 124–51.

My epigraph, from Oswald de Andrade's *Manifesto Antropófago*, is taken from Emir Rodríguez Monegal, "The Metamorphoses of Caliban," *Diacritics* 7 (1977): 82. In the Brazil of the 1920s, de Andrade's *Movimento Antropófago* or Cannibal Movement "advo-

lutionary country just ninety miles from a hostile superpower, questions of cultural and human non-existence are more than merely theoretical. Yet for Retamar, they cannot be reduced to the crude but real possibility of actual annihilation, either. To destroy Latin American culture one need only reduce it to the status of an imitation, simulation, or—as he puts it—"distorted echo" (*eco desfigurado*) of the metropolitan culture. Retamar's phrase is both resonant and precise. In Ovid, the mythological Echo is indeed disfigured by her unrequited love for Narcissus: she wrinkles, ages, wastes away to skin and bone before decorporealizing entirely into pure, disembodied voice.[2] Latin America as "disfigured echo" is not only condemned by the dominating metropolis to mere repetition, it is also drained of strength and vitality by a vampire-like extraction of cultural and material wealth. The metropolis itself, according to the logic of this figure, plays the role of Narcissus, caught in a self-enclosed, specular enjoyment of its own cultural productions, and unable to read in the post-colonial world anything more than another, inferior image of itself.[3]

Retamar's response to this paralyzing double bind is the figure of the mestizo, of what José Marti called "our *mestizo* America" (p. 4). The racially mixed figure of the mestizo, compounded of Native American, African, and European blood, represents a culture that chooses miscegenation over imitation; instead of simply repeating *or* rejecting the metropolitan culture, it assimilates, depurifies, and transforms it by mixing it with non-European strains. As employed by Retamar, the notion of a mestizo culture has clear affinities with certain themes of post-structuralist thought: it denies unique or delimited points of origin, it replaces a monological conception of cul-

---

cated the creation of a genuine national culture through the consumption and critical reelaboration of both national and foreign influences. Imported cultural influences were to be devoured, digested, and reworked in terms of local conditions." The Brazilian modernists dated their Cannibal Manifesto "the year the Bishop Sardinha was swallowed," thus commemorating the date on which Brazilian Indians had devoured a Portuguese bishop (*Brazilian Cinema*, ed. Randal Johnson and Robert Stam [London: Associated University Presses, 1982], pp. 81–83).

   2. Ovid, *Metamorphoses*, trans. Frank Justus Miller (Cambridge: Harvard University Press, 1936), 3:393–401.

   3. In Raul Ruiz's film *On Top of the Whale*, a Dutch anthropologist studies two Patagonian Indians kept on the estate of a man appropriately named "Narcisso." In the house of Don Narcisso, the dichotomy between Western subject and indigenous object of knowledge breaks down into a complex array of doublings and self-deceptions.

tural discourse with a dialogical or indeed disseminative one, and it problematizes boundaries and deconstructs binary oppositions, including that of center and periphery.[4] For having once applied the notion of *mestizaje* ("mixedness" or "mestizoization") to Latin American culture, Retamar then insists that "the thesis that every man [*sic*] and even every culture is *mestizo* could easily be defended" (p. 4).[5] Mestizoization is thus not a derivative or peripheralized or parasitic state but the inescapable condition of culture as such, including metropolitan culture.

But unlike some of its post-structuralist cousins, *mestizaje* is not an abstractly textual or discursive concept. It is founded, rather, on the image of the racially mixed body, and insists on this materiality. To borrow Retamar's distinction, it represents human as well as cultural existence. Unlike the emaciated and ultimately disembodied figure of Echo, the mestizo is a corporeal as well as a cultural presence.[6] At the same time, *mestizaje* also invokes a history. For if the figure of the mestizo celebrates cultural mixedness in the present, it also recalls that this mixedness arose from a colonial situation, and that it was originally the product of violence, domination, and desire. *Mestizaje* is, in a sense, a Nietzschean revaluation of the past, a transformation of defeat through the cultural will to power of the colonized.

In taking Shakespeare's Caliban as the literary symbol for American mestizo culture, Retamar joins a tradition of Caribbean, Latin American, and African writers who have adapted or appropriated *The Tempest* in an effort either to represent the colonial situation or devel-

4. When Emir Rodríguez Monegal accuses Retamar of "aping the French intellectuals" ("The Metamorphoses of Caliban," p. 82), he means francophones such as O. Mannoni, Franz Fanon, and Aimé Césaire rather than the French poststructuralists. Nevertheless his expression is a striking one, evoking both imitative Echo and the bestial qualities of Caliban.

5. In "Against the Black Legend" (*Caliban*, pp. 56–73), Retamar develops the theme that Spanish culture is a mestizoized formation of Christian, Moorish, Islamic, and Jewish influences. Under Retamar's gaze, the image of Europe as unified oppressor disintegrates into that of multiple and competing traditions: elite and popular, "central" and "peripheral," and so forth.

6. As employed by Retamar, it also invokes a specifically *male* presence. The implicit opposition of Echo and Caliban clearly genders the resistance to cultural dependency in a troublingly masculinist way. It would be unfair, surely, to place sole blame for this on Retamar; colonialism had already been gendered, both literally and figuratively, for centuries. Yet it is also true that some male contemporaries of Retamar's, such as the filmmaker Tomas Guttiérez Alea, later came to give more serious thought to the sexual politics of postrevolutionary culture in Cuba. See Alea's *Up to a Certain Point* (1984).

op a counter-discourse to it.[7] A colonial reading of the play has long
been available in the Anglo-American critical tradition as well, at least
in the latent form of an awareness of Shakespeare's use of reports
from the New World, his informal affiliations with the Virginia Company, and so forth.[8] However, it is only in the past decade or so that
colonialism has established itself as a dominant, if not *the* dominant
code for interpreting *The Tempest*.[9] Colonialist discourse is typically
buttoned onto the play primarily through allegory: the master-slave
dialectic between Prospero as colonizing subject and Caliban as colonized.[10] Generally it is assumed that Prospero occupies a hegemonic
position not only on his island but also in the play's ideological field;
The Tempest, in other words, somehow endorses or mystifies colonial
domination. It is also frequently noted, however, that Caliban manages at least to question if not undermine the colonizer's assumptions
of superiority, in part through political argument (such as Caliban's
claim that the island was originally and rightfully *his*) and in part
through a poetic side to his nature which remains invisible to Prospero.[11]

7. Rob Nixon, "Caribbean and African Appropriations of *The Tempest*," in *Politics
and Poetic Value*, ed. Robert von Hallberg (Chicago: University of Chicago Press, 1987),
pp. 185–206.

8. On Shakespeare and the Virginia Company, see Charles Mills Gayley, *Shakespeare and the Founders of Liberty in America* (New York: Macmillan, 1917); according to
Frank Kermode, Shakespeare's use of colonial reports and pamphlets was first noted by
Malone in 1808 (Kermode, Introduction to *The Tempest* [London: Methuen, 1954],
p. xxvi).

9. Deborah Willis, "Shakespeare's *Tempest* and the Discourse of Colonialism," *Studies in English Literature* 29 (1989): 277–89. Willis both traces the ubiquity of colonial
readings and devotes considerable polemical energy to arguing that *The Tempest might*
be about something other than (or rather, something in addition to) colonialism.

10. Two important examples are Paul Brown, "'This thing of darkness I acknowl-
edge mine': *The Tempest* and the Discourse of Colonialism," in *Political Shakespeare: New
Essays in Cultural Materialism*, ed. Jonathan Dollimore and Alan Sinfield (Ithaca: Cornell
University Press, 1985), pp. 48–71; and Francis Barker and Peter Hulme, "Nymphs and
Reapers Heavily Vanish: The Discursive Con-texts of *The Tempest*," in *Alternative Shake-
speares*, ed. John Drakakis (London and New York: Methuen, 1985), pp. 191–205.

11. See, for example, Stephen J. Greenblatt, "Learning to Curse: Aspects of Linguistic Colonialism in the Sixteenth Century," in *First Images of America: The Impact of the
New World on the Old*, ed. Fredi Chiappelli, 2 vols. (Berkeley: University of California
Press, 1976), 2:561–80: "Ugly, rude, savage, Caliban nevertheless achieves for an instant an absolute, if intolerably bitter, moral victory" (p. 570). Compare Stephen Orgel,
"Shakespeare and the Cannibals," in *Cannibals, Witches, and Divorce: Estranging the Renaissance*, ed. Marjorie Garber (Baltimore: Johns Hopkins University Press, 1987), p. 54;
and Willis, p. 284.

Such readings have tended to "Americanize" the play, or at least Caliban, by identifying him with the natives described in colonial reports. Leslie Fiedler epitomizes this Americanist reading, arguing that by the end of *The Tempest*, "the whole history of imperialist America has been prophetically revealed to us in brief parable: from the initial act of expropriation through the Indian wars to the setting up of reservations, and from the beginnings of black slavery to the first revolts and evasions."[12] Even if we hesitate in the face of so closely detailed a prophecy, we ought nevertheless to admit that the play manages in some respects to anticipate later developments, and thereby gains much of its cultural force and pertinence. I myself argue that the play's significance is largely American and anticipatory, and to do so I explore paths blazed by both Retamar and Fiedler. More precisely, I want to examine the ways in which the play both advances and erases the mestizoization of Western culture.

I

I begin by shifting attention away from the Prospero-Caliban axis in the play and toward a possibly unexpected focus: the humanist councillor Gonzalo. Gonzalo, that kind and idealistic if somewhat befuddled character, is generally taken to provide a kind of counterpoint both to the machiavellian plotting of Sebastian and Antonio and to the colonialist domination represented by Prospero. Best remembered, perhaps, for the ideal commonwealth he depicts in II.i., Gonzalo seems to embody an ineffectual utopianism which nevertheless offers a moral contrast to the power politics of the play. In fact, however, Gonzalo's real function is to shift the play's colonialist politics into another mode.

This he does most strikingly when he imagines (or tries to imagine) his ideal commonwealth, accompanied by Antonio's and Sebastian's cynical commentary:

> *Gonzalo.* Had I plantation of this isle, my lord—
> *Antonio.* He'd sow't with nettle seed.

12. Leslie A. Fiedler, *The Stranger in Shakespeare* (New York: Stein and Day, 1972), p. 238. See also Alden T. Vaughan, "Shakespeare's Indian: The Americanization of Caliban," *Shakespeare Quarterly* 39 (1988): 137–53.

Sebastian. Or docks, or mallows.

Gonzalo. And were the king on't, what would I do?

Sebastian. 'Scape being drunk for want of wine.

Gonzalo. I' th' commonwealth I would by contraries
Execute all things. For no kind of traffic
Would I admit; no name of magistrate;
Letters should not be known; riches, poverty,
And use of service, none; contract, succession,
Bourn, bound of land, tilth, vineyard, none;
No use of metal, corn, or wine, or oil;
No occupation; all men idle, all;
And women too, but innocent and pure;
No sovereignty.

Sebastian. Yet he would be king on't.

Antonio. The latter end of his commonwealth forgets the
beginning.

Gonzalo. All things in common nature should produce
Without sweat or endeavor. Treason, felony,
Sword, pike, knife, gun, or need of any engine
Would I not have; but nature should bring forth,
Of it own kind, all foison, all abundance,
To feed my innocent people.

Sebastian. No marrying 'mong his subjects?

Antonio. None, man, all idle—whores and knaves.

Gonzalo. I would with such perfection govern, sir,
T'excel the Golden Age.[13]

When he speculates on getting "plantation" of the isle, Gonzalo expresses the only positive *desire* for colonial dominion in the play. Even Prospero is a colonialist *malgré lui*, and he and the other Italians desert their island at the first opportunity. (Unlike the English or Spanish, Italians in general would not be coded for Shakespeare's audience as fanatical colonizers of the New World.) Only Gonzalo exhibits anything like a colonialist imagination in the play, though an apparently benign and utopian one.

Gonzalo's ideal commonwealth, as has long been recognized, paraphrases a passage in John Florio's English translation of Montaigne's essay *On Cannibals*; indeed, it borrows with such fidelity that little atten-

13. William Shakespeare, *The Tempest*, ed. Robert Langbaum (New York: New American Library, 1964), II.i.148–73. Subsequent references are to this edition.

tion has been paid to the small but significant changes that Gonzalo rings on his source. The passage from Montaigne offers an idyllic or Golden Age description of the life of the Tupi Indians of Brazil as reported in various colonial accounts. Shakespeare's audience might not have recognized the specific borrowing from Montaigne, but such Golden Age descriptions of the New World had become a kind of set-piece in colonial writings from Columbus, Vespucci, and Peter Martyr on, and hence would have been instantly recognizable as a genre.

Gonzalo's first significant alteration comes in the word "planta-tion," which unambiguously signifies an exclusively European colony. Hence the "innocent and pure" subjects of Gonzalo's imagined polity are not Montaigne's Indians but white Europeans, who now somehow occupy an American Indian arcadia. Yet they don't do that either, owing to Gonzalo's second alteration. For while Montaigne's passage at least purported to be a description of a real culture in the New World (and I will take up this issue of accuracy later), Gonzalo's com-monwealth makes no such claim. Though recognizably derived from New World accounts, then, this ideal commonwealth appears to be peopled by Europeans and modeled on Ovidian and Virgilian de-scriptions of the Golden Age. All explicit reference to the New World vanishes, though an implicit and ghostly reference still inheres in the arcadian genre itself.

By substituting Europeans for American Indians in his utopian polity, Gonzalo reproduces a recently current strain of English coloni-alist discourse. Idyllic, Golden Age descriptions of the New World and its native inhabitants were disseminated by propagandists for the Virginia Company in order to lure Englishwomen and men to Ameri-ca by suggesting that they might appropriate and enjoy the arcadian landscape now peopled by friendly Indians.[14] *Eastward Ho* (1605), by Jonson, Marston, and Chapman, parodies such propaganda in ways suggestive for Shakespeare's play:

> *Seagull.* Come, boys, Virginia longs till we share the rest
> of her maidenhead.
> *Spendall.* Why, is she inhabited already with any English?

14. Karen Ordahl Kupperman, *Settling with the Indians: The Meeting of English and Indian Cultures in America, 1580–1640* (Totowa, N.J.: Rowman and Littlefield, 1980), pp. 34, 40–41; William Brandon, *New Worlds for Old: Reports from the New World and Their Effect on the Development of Social Thought in Europe, 1500–1800* (Athens: Ohio University Press, 1986), pp. 66–87.

Sea. A whole country of English is there, man, bred of
those that were left there in '79. They have married with
the Indians, and make 'em bring forth as beautiful faces
as any we have in England; and therefore the Indians are
so in love with 'em, that all the treasure they have, they
lay at their feet.

Scapethrift. But is there such treasure there, captain, as I
have heard?

Sea. I tell thee, gold is more plentiful there than copper
is with us; and for as much red copper as I can bring, I'll
have thrice the weight in gold. Why, man, all their
dripping pans and their chamber pots are pure gold; and
all the chains, with which they chain up their streets, are
massy gold; all the prisoners they take are fettered within
gold; and for rubies and diamonds, they go forth on
holidays and gather 'em by the seashore, to hang on their
children's coats, and stick in their caps, as commonly as
our children wear saffron-gilt brooches, and groats with
holes in 'em.

Scape. And is it a pleasant country withal?

Sea. As ever the sun shined on, temperate and full of all
sorts of excellent viands: wild boar is as common there as
our tamest bacon is here; venison, as mutton. And then
you shall live freely there, without sergeants, or courtiers,
or lawyers, or intelligencers—only a few industrious
Scots, perhaps, who, indeed, are dispersed over the face
of the whole earth.[15]

This exchange has a clarifying effect on Gonzalo's ideal commonwealth, cynically literalizing a number of features that Gonzalo invokes only implicitly and idealistically. In *Eastward Ho* the "Golden
Age" becomes actual gold, and the Indians are described as willing
sexual partners, in an all-too-obvious attempt to lure potential colonists. By merging his white plantation with an Indian arcadia,
Gonzalo also (if only latently) performs or acts out the desires produced by colonialist advertisement. Of course, this dream of expropriation and substitution had already turned sour by the time *The
Tempest* was written. The winter of 1609–10 had caused widespread

15. George Chapman, Ben Jonson, John Marston, *Eastward Ho*, ed. R. W. Van
Fosser, The Revels Plays (Baltimore: Johns Hopkins University Press, 1979), III.iii.15–
46.

starvation in the Jamestown Colony followed by a breakdown in social order and the imposition of strict martial law: the most recent colonial reports would thus have suggested the very opposite of Gonzalo's arcadian vision.[16]

Such topical resonances, which render Gonzalo's commonwealth "utopian" in a bad sense, also point to more fundamental contradictions within the ideology and reality of New World colonization. As is well known, early English settlers found themselves embarrassingly dependent on the technologies of native populations for their own survival—a theme of intermittent interest in *The Tempest*.[17] Appropriation of Native American lands was thus impossible without some *imitation* of their culture, even if this was limited to piecemeal borrowings stripped from any cultural context.[18] Native social, political, and cultural life elicited official reactions ranging from guarded admiration to outright contempt, and even the most openminded colonists never suggested that native culture should serve as a model for Chris-

16. See Stephen Greenblatt, "Martial Law in the Land of Cockaigne," *Shakespearean Negotiations: The Circulation of Social Energy in Renaissance England* (Berkeley: University of California Press, 1988), pp. 129–63. Gonzalo's knowledge of the New World is quite pointedly outmoded; his Golden Age reports, along with his monstrous visions of "mountaineers / Dewlapped like bulls, whose throats had hanging at 'em / Wallets of flesh" and "men / Whose heads stood in their breasts" (III.iii.44–47) derive in the main from medieval and early Renaissance travel literature. Likewise the very figure of the humanist councillor and utopian projector is somewhat archaic. Gonzalo represents a brand of humanism whose time had clearly passed when *The Tempest* was written.

17. Caliban, of course, reminds Prospero that he showed him "all the qualities o' th' isle" (I.ii.337) and later promises to teach Stephano and Trinculo how to fend for themselves (II.ii.155–80). In his song celebrating freedom from Prospero, Caliban exclaims "No more dams I'll make for fish" (II.ii.188), a line Sidney Lee describes as "a vivid and penetrating illustration of a peculiar English experience in Virgina" ("The American Indian in Elizabethan England," in *Elizabethan and Other Essays*, ed. Frederick S. Boas [Oxford: Clarendon Press, 1929], p. 297). Early Virginian settlers were heavily dependent for their food on natives' fish-dams whose construction and operation they could never master themselves. The settlers were thus in a constant state of anxiety lest they alienate the natives and provoke them to destroy the dams. Writes Lee: "The gloomy anticipation of the failure of the dam through native disaffection came true in those early days, and was a chief cause of the disastrous termination of the sixteenth-century efforts to found an English colony in Virginia. The narratives of the later Virginian explorers, Captain John Smith and William Strachey, whose energies were engaged in the foundation of Jamestown, bear similar testimony to the indispensible service rendered by the natives' fish-dams to the English colonists. Caliban's threat to make 'no more dams for fish' consequently exposed Prospero to a very real and a familiar peril" (pp. 298–99).

18. James Axtell, "The Indian Impact on English Colonial Culture," in *The European and the Indian: Essays in the Ethnohistory of Colonial North America* (Oxford: Oxford University Press, 1981), pp. 272–315.

tian Europeans.[19] Nevertheless, this culture and social structure were felt to possess a dangerous appeal. Well into the eighteenth century, colonial officials and others inveighed against so-called "white Indians"—that is, Europeans who either fled to indigenous tribes in order to escape the harsh conditions of life in the colonies, or, having been captured by natives and integrated into their social world, refused to return to their families and friends when released. Cotton Mather denounced the *"Criolian* Degeneracy" which afflicted English youth when they were "permitted to run wild in our Woods."[20] To many colonists, Native American life offered a higher degree of both liberty and social cohesion than did the authoritarian government of the colonies. By inserting European subjects directly into a description of an Indian arcadia, then, Gonzalo's ideal commonwealth might be said to invoke the perilously utopian allure associated with the colonial imitation of native culture, and the subsequent mixing or "Criolian degeneracy" which this could entail. More explicitly, *Eastward Ho* raises the tempting prospect of cultural and physical miscegenation, but then masters it by insisting on the genetic dominance of European blood. ("They have married with the Indians, and make 'em bring forth as beautiful faces as any we have in England.")[21]

I think, however, that the relation of Gonzalo's commonwealth to the colonial project is more mediated than this, and that its primary focus is on the assimilation of New World culture by European, and specifically humanist, thought. While it borrows its descriptive detail from Montaigne, Gonzalo's ideal commonwealth also alludes in a more general way to Thomas More's *Utopia*.[22] More, of course, sets

19. See Axtell, "The Indian Impact," and Kupperman, *Settling with the Indians*, pp. 141–58.

20. Quoted in Axtell, "The Indian Impact," p. 160. See also Axtell, "The White Indians of Colonial America," in *European and Indian*, pp. 168–206.

21. In his dedicatory epistle to King Charles, George Sandys introduces his translation of Ovid by invoking the issue of cultural miscegenation: "It needeth more then a single denization, being a double Stranger: Sprung from the Stocke of the ancient Romanes; but bred in the New-World, of the rudeness whereof it cannot but participate; especially having Warres and Tumults to bring it to light in stead of the Muses." George Sandys, *Ovid's Metamorphosis Englished, Mythologized, and Represented in Figures*, ed. Karl K. Hulley and Stanley T. Vandersall (Lincoln: University of Nebraska Press, 1970), p. 3.

22. As both humanist councillor and philosophical traveler Gonzalo combines the roles played by More and his fictional character Raphael Hythlodaeus; his egalitarian, communist utopia bears a generic though clearly imperfect resemblance to Thomas More's fictive polity. See Arthur J. Slavin, "The American Principle from More to Locke," in Chiappelli, *First Images of America*, 1:147–48.

his utopia in the New World, and colonial reports on native culture inspire the *Utopia* to some degree, though the extent of this influence has been the subject of longstanding debate. In *Eastward Ho*, Seagull borrows More's famous golden chamberpots and chains and relocates these among the Indians of Virginia, suggesting that for early modern audiences, at least, *Utopia* was strongly associated with the indigenous cultures of the New World. Hence Shakespeare's double allusion to Montaigne and More unmistakably draws attention to New World influences on the humanist imagination, and particularly on its utopian, political strain.

It does so, however, only to stage the disappearance or rather the repression of this influence. For in describing his ideal polity, Gonzalo, unlike More or Montaigne, avoids any direct allusion to the New World; his only explicit point of reference is the classical Golden Age, which installs him in a conservative and restrictively humanist genealogy. Gonzalo's utopian project appropriates colonial descriptions of the New World but effaces or occults this influence by reinscribing it within a closed and Eurocentric textual economy. When Antonio cynically remarks that "the latter end of his commonwealth forgets the beginning," he refers to Gonzalo's inconsistency in handling the problem of sovereignty or kingship, yet his words apply as well to the cultural genesis of Gonzalo's vision. This commonwealth actively "forgets" its non-Western beginnings.

Gonzalo's erasure of non-Western influences is completed when he populates his ideal commonwealth with Europeans rather than Native Americans, thereby removing the bodily as well as the cultural presence of those indigenous subjects. Consuming or erasing the racial body covers up all remaining traces of non-Western origin: Gonzalo's commonwealth is now peopled by Europeans and apparently created by the Western philosophical imagination drawing on the classical tradition. This double process of erasure is what I have chosen to call white cannibalism: Gonzalo in effect consumes the body of the racial other in order to appropriate its cultural force. In this respect he becomes a counterpart to Caliban, the anagrammatical cannibal—a connection I pursue later.

Gonzalo and his imaginary commonwealth do not counter colonialist domination in *The Tempest*, then, but rather transpose it to a cultural plane. Gonzalo usurps the Indian utopia in thought, just as Prospero usurps Caliban's isle in fact.[23] Yet it may seem strange to invest

23. Prospero eagerly adopts a specular relation to Gonzalo: "Holy Gonzalo, honor-

Gonzalo with such dire, or even coherent, intentions. Indeed, the erasure of cultural origins I have just outlined might well be ascribed not to imperialist design but to mere forgetfulness, a frequent attribute of the comic *senex* or old man figure. Antonio even mocks Gonzalo by calling him "this lord of weak remembrance" (II.i.236),[24] and there may be an additional irony in the fact that Gonzalo is a forgetful *humanist*, given that humanism is generally associated with the restoration of cultural and historical memory. Yet it is truer to say that Renaissance humanism inaugurated a dialectic of memory and forgetting which is here embodied in Gonzalo. Erasmus's writings on rhetorical copia, for instance, recommended "digesting" classical authors in order to produce new, distinct, and individual styles. As a strategy of appropriation through the consumption or erasure of textual origins,[25] copia converts forgetfulness from a lapse or weakness into a mechanism of stylistic sovereignty and a means of mastering cultural authority. Erasmian stylistics and its cannibalistic metaphors provide a suggestive analogue to Gonzalo's white cannibalism, and they suggest that Gonzalo's gaps in memory can be read not only as a sign of individual weakness but as a characteristic strategy of Renaissance humanism. Gonzalo is indeed a "lord of weak remembrance" in that his forgetfulness is a *source* of sovereignty, guarding the cultural coherence of humanism from the shock of non-Western influence.

A telling, indeed paradigmatic, example of Gonzalo's active forgetfulness occurs in the famous "widow Dido" exchange of II.i., shortly before the utopian reverie:

> *Gonzalo.* Methinks our garments are now as fresh as
> when we put them on first in Afric, at the marriage of
> the King's fair daughter Claribel to the King of Tunis.
>
> *Sebastian.* 'Twas a sweet marriage, and we prosper well in
> our return.
>
> *Adrian.* Tunis was never graced before with such a
> paragon to their queen.

---

able man, / Mine eyes, ev'n sociable to the show of thine, / Fall fellowly drops" (V.i.62–64). The two old men do indeed mirror each other, for better and for worse.

24. Antonio's remark may possibly refer to Francisco, not Gonzalo. The Variorum Edition records differing views (pp. 113–114) but ultimately endorses Gonzalo as the referent of Antonio's remark, as does Stephen Orgel in the Oxford edition. Orgel thinks Antonio refers to Gonzalo's confusion while describing his ideal commonwealth.

25. See Terence Cave, *The Cornucopian Text: Problems of Writing in the French Renaissance* (Oxford: Clarendon Press, 1979), pp. 45, 182.

> *Gonzalo.* Not since widow Dido's time.
>
> *Antonio.* Widow? A pox o' that! How came that "widow" in? Widow Dido!
>
> *Sebastian.* What if he had said "widower Aeneas" too? Good Lord, how ill you take it!
>
> *Adrian.* "Widow Dido," said you? You make me study of that. She was of Carthage, not of Tunis.
>
> *Gonzalo.* This Tunis, sir, was Carthage.
>
> *Adrian.* Carthage?
>
> *Gonzalo.* I assure you, Carthage.
>
> *Antonio.* His word is more than the miraculous harp.
>
> *Sebastian.* He hath raised the wall and houses too.
>
> *Antonio.* What impossible matter will he make easy next?
>
> (II.i.71–93)

The topic of conversation is the marriage of Alonso's daughter Claribel to the King of Tunis: significantly, a mixed or miscegenating marriage of white European and black African. Gonzalo's muddled pedantry, which confuses Tunis with the ancient city of Carthage, leads to the exchange about "widow Dido." Yet Gonzalo's apparently random dithering is hardly unmotivated. By recalling Aeneas's romance with Dido, the non-African queen of African Carthage, Gonzalo both evokes and denies the miscegenous marriage of Claribel.[26] Further, by confusing Tunis with Virgil's fictionalized vision of Carthage, he transforms a real African city into a spot in the literary geography of *The Aeneid*, thus supplanting the material existence of a non-European society with a founding text of the Western tradition and, not incidentally, the great epic of Roman imperialism. Consuming both the cultural presence of Tunis and its material or bodily existence, Gonzalo's forgetfulness performs an act of white cannibalism. *Tunis delenda est* is the ideological maxim here, and Tunis is in fact deleted by being reinscribed within a humanist textual tradition. All of this prepares for a more important and culturally central act: the textual purgation of Gonzalo's utopian commonwealth.

Within Renaissance humanism, the genre of the utopia served as a privileged medium for both the importation and the neutralization of political ideas from the New World. At the level of content, Thomas

26. For a more extended discussion of the importance of Virgil for this scene, see Orgel, "Cannibals," pp. 58–64.

More's *Utopia* is clearly influenced by colonial reports describing communal ownership of property, social equality, and the absence of kingship and marked class differences within some Native American cultures. The New World provides both the content and a hypothetical vantage point for criticizing the dominant social order of late-feudal Europe. Yet this political and geographical exteriority is then abstracted from any specific locale or origin. As a place that is pointedly "nowhere" the utopia posits an inadequacy in all extant cultural systems—Western and non-Western—and is fully at home in none of them. More's Utopia does not, for the most part, legitimate itself by reinscribing New World practices within a humanist genealogy. Instead, it appeals on the one hand to the supposedly self-evident rationality of its social logic and, on the other, to the purely empirical or pragmatic claim that it really exists and works, though not within a known cultural geography.[27] The utopian genre thus aspires to autonomy and self-legitimation. Thomas More's *Utopia* is set in motion when King Utopus separates it from the mainland, a gesture which we may read as the text's desire to cut all lines of cultural influence. But it is precisely because the utopia claims to legitimate itself that it can borrow features from non-European cultures without seriously decentering the West's sense of cultural self-sufficiency. It is not New World culture but utopian culture that indicts the West, and this indictment is so global as to seem to come from nowhere in particular. Precisely because it is autolegitimating, the utopia can be a seemingly innocuous medium for the covert or semi-covert importation of non-Western influences into Western political discourse.

Gonzalo's ideal commonwealth doubly effaces its references to the New World. On the one hand it reinscribes them within a humanist genealogy. Yet insofar as it invokes the generic codes of the utopia, it denies all lines of origin by posing as an autonomous act of philosophical speculation. To the degree that Gonzalo's commonwealth *is* a utopia, it does not suffice to say that its subjects are "Europeans." Rather, they are the abstract subjects of political philosophy, without racial or cultural characteristics: genuinely "white" subjects in the sense that they are blanks inserted in, or rather produced by, a scheme of political reason. Gonzalo's replacement of Native American

27. James Holstun, *A Rational Millennium: Puritan Utopias of Seventeenth-Century England and America* (New York: Oxford University Press, 1987), pp. 63–64, discusses the importance of empirical claims for utopian fiction, as does Slavin, "American Principle," p. 144.

subjects with Europeans is, in this sense, only the first step toward a more complete disembodiment. As utopia, Gonzalo's commonwealth is genuinely "the picture of Nobody."[28]

But Gonzalo's scheme is afflicted by a slippage of genre. It clearly begins as utopia: by dubbing his vision a commonwealth, and by claiming to "execute all things" by himself, Gonzalo seems to invoke the utopian interest in planned, formal institutions. Yet his description passes almost immediately into a neighboring but rather different genre: the pastoral arcadia, which is characterized rather by a lack of formal institutions.[29] Gonzalo's citizens are not the purposefully, even obsessively productive inhabitants of a fully rationalized polity but rather the idle denizens of the Golden Age. The end of Gonzalo's commonwealth forgets its generic beginnings as well. But this slippage of literary genre revives all the questions of cultural origin that the utopia works to suppress. For while the Golden Age was a recognizably classical or Western topos, it had also become inescapably associated with colonial reports from the New World. Whereas Thomas More had incorporated New World arcadia into a humanist utopia, Gonzalo reverses this genetic order, and by so doing he reveals the obscure anatomy of Western utopian discourse.[30]

28. In III.iii., Trinculo, Stephano, and Caliban hear Ariel invisibly playing a tune on a tabor and pipe. Trinculo remarks, "This is the tune of our catch, played by the picture of Nobody" (III.iii.131–32). The phrase refers to an anonymous, early seventeenth-century play titled *No-body and Some-body*, and to the sign of its printer, John Trundle, which depicted a man composed of head and limbs but without a trunk. In the play itself, the characters Nobody and Somebody are employed as satirical devices to depict the displacement or denial of social responsibilities. For instance:

> Come twentie poore men to his gate at once,
> *Nobody* gives them mony, meate and drinke,
> If they be naked, clothes, then come poore souldiers,
> Sick, maymd, and shot, from any forraine warres,
> *Nobody* takes them in, provides them harbor.

(*Nobody and Somebody* [Glasgow: privately reprinted, 1877], sig. B4r). Likewise, when Somebody orders his men to oppress the poor and widows, rack rents, raise prices, and so forth, he tells them to blame it on Nobody. The displacement of social and moral agency carried out by this simple device is relevant to *The Tempest* in general and to Gonzalo's ideal commonwealth in particular.

29. Holstun, *A Rational Millennium*, p. 67.

30. James Holstun's fine discussion of arcadia and utopia in *A Rational Millennium* (pp. 67–77) is crucial to my argument here. Holstun is surely correct in arguing that arcadia and utopia are antithetical in principle, and that "Utopia is the violent civil negation of pastoral arcadia" (p. 74). I nevertheless want to suggest that, in More's case at least, this negation is never fully carried out, that the genre of the *Utopia* remains irreducibly mixed, and that this mixture is both medium and sign of the work's mes-

One of the assumptions of this essay is that European colonialism extracted not only gold, raw materials, and slave labor from the New World, but forms of political, social, and cultural knowledge as well. It might be objected, however, that arcadian descriptions of New World culture reflected only the values, desires, and nostalgias of the colonists themselves. Hence what appears to be cultural expropriation or transfer may in fact be only ideological projection and feedback. Indeed, this latter view has become widely dominant among historians of New World colonization and settlement.[31]

Colonial reports from the New World were, to be sure, marked by factual and ideological distortion, often massive. Yet they were rarely mere hallucinations. Karen Ordahl Kupperman has persuasively argued that the more outlandish and ethnocentric visions of the New World were almost exclusively produced by writers who had never been there, and that settlers who regularly interacted with North American Indians often achieved a fairly sophisticated understanding of their culture.[32] William Brandon, meanwhile, maintains that even the so-called Golden Age reports produced by the earliest explorers were not without *some* factual basis. Brandon points out that other non-Western cultures, in Africa or Asia, did not provoke comparisons to the Golden Age, and that a number of New World cultures did in fact possess certain features that at least roughly corresponded to this western myth, common possession of property being one of the most important. Furthermore, while the myth of the Golden Age was imposed on American cultures from without, and interpreted their structures selectively and ethnocentrically, the process of influence

---

tizoized status. To this extent I disagree with Holstun's insistence that the early modern utopia is *entirely* produced by Western processes of rationalization and technological domination.

31. See Henri Baudet, *Paradise on Earth: Some Thoughts on European Images of Non-European Man*, trans. Elizabeth Wentholt (New Haven: Yale University Press, 1965), pp. 26–27; Robert F. Berkhofer, Jr., *The White Man's Indian: Images of the American Indian from Columbus to the Present* (New York: Knopf, 1978).

32. See Kupperman, *Settling with the Indians*, p. 106 and passim. John Howland Rowe, "The Renaissance Foundations of Anthropology," *American Anthropologist* 67 (1965): 1–20, argues that even Peter Martyr, who did not visit the New World himself, relates "ethnographic information [which] is relatively abundant and is presented in a notably objective fashion" (p. 13). Rowe adds that "no one who makes a general survey of the literature bearing on historical ethnography which has come down to us from 16th century Europe can fail to be struck by the fact that it provides better and more detailed information on New World Cultures than on those of the other parts of the world which the Europeans were exploring at the same time" (p. 14).

was actually more mutual and dialogical than it might seem. For while the classical Golden Age generally depicted an arcadian existence under the rule of a good king, the New World Golden Age generally emphasized political liberty and masterlessness. Thus observation of American Indian culture had a reciprocal influence on the imported model of the Golden Age. Brandon goes on to argue that the conception of political liberty entered Western political discourse largely by means of colonial reports from the Americas.[33] The image of the New World as Golden Age is, clearly, neither a pure European projection nor an accurate description of native societies. It is, rather, a mestizoized formation that enabled a number of cultural and ideological operations, many of them contradictory: operations of advertisement and colonial propaganda, the reinscription of native societies as precultural rather than cultural, and, I would insist, the appropriation of native socio-cultural practices by the West.

Critics of cultural imperialism tend to emphasize the *imposition* of Western cultural norms and practices onto non-Western societies, and to view this as concomitant with political and economic dominion. Yet by depicting non-Western cultures as being too fragile, ineffectual, or inconsequential to exert a counterinfluence on the metropoles, a merely monological or one-way theory of cultural imperialism may actually feed the West's characteristic illusions of cultural self-sufficiency. Moreover, by understanding cultural dominion only as the imposition of Western forms, it may elide very real and equally serious acts of cultural appropriation by the West.[34] In *The Tempest*,

33. Brandon, *New Worlds*, pp. ix, 21, 23, 38, 60, 151. As Karen Kupperman points out in *Settling with the Indians* (pp. 49–50, 143–44), English colonists interpreted the chieftainship of North American tribes as analogous to European monarchy. The imperial structures of the great mesoamerican cultures were also evident to explorers and colonists. Reports of South American, and especially Brazilian, peoples seem more often to have mentioned the absence of kings (see, for example, Brandon, p. 38). The Golden Age theme of masterlessness is, in any case, raised by Caliban, who complains to Prospero that "I am all the subjects that you have, / Which first was mine own king" (I.ii.341–42).

34. By "appropriation" I do not mean the mere fact of cultural borrowing, or even the transformation of foreign cultural practices that inevitably accompanies importation into another socio-cultural system. I mean a mode of appropriation which entails the erasure of origins. At the same time, it is abundantly clear that abstract constructions such as "the West" and "the New World" are only provisionally useful for purposes of analysis. To assume that New World influences were evenly absorbed by some unified entity called "the West" is as naïve as assuming that New World gold was equally distributed among all the citizens of Spain. (Needless to say, the "New World" is an equally artificial construct.) Differences in national and class cultures, theological out-

Gonzalo's ideal commonwealth is the conduit for both appropriating Native American social structures into humanist utopian thought and denying this influence by consuming the body of the racial other. Yet the physical presence, at least, of the repressed other endures in the person of Caliban. If Gonzalo's commonwealth both enacts and erases the mestizoization of Western culture, Caliban is the very embodiment of the mestizo: his mother is an Algerian witch, and he himself exhibits traits of both the American Indian and the European wild man. Again, if Gonzalo's commonwealth is a disembodied social order, Caliban seems at times to be pure body removed from any social order.

One ideological effect of applying the myth of the Golden Age to New World cultures was, as I have said, to reinscribe them as *pre-political*, arcadian existences, and thus to view American Indians themselves as, at best, noble savages. Shakespeare's Caliban, an isolated being lacking any cultural context, is precisely the pre-political, pre-cultural being produced by arcadian myth. An anomic racial body, a bundle of ungovernable drives, Caliban is the ideological precipitate or residue that remains once Gonzalo's commonwealth has abstracted the cultural forms of Native American life.[35]

To speak of Caliban as "pure body" may seem unjust. He is not, after all, some grunting, heaving piece of nature but a complex and articulate character. Though his drunkenness and attempted rape

---

look, and so forth obviously determined both the extent and mode of cultural appropriation. Historically, the New World clearly played a significant role in anti-monarchical and anti-aristocratic thought. It was assimilated more visibly into bourgeois-democratic than into popular-radical discourse, and for fairly obvious reasons it was more apparent in, say, eighteenth-century France than in seventeenth-century England, where it had little visible influence on radical sectarian literature during the revolutionary era. A more materialist version of this essay would insist on specifying the social conditions under which New World reports were, or were not, included in political or literary discourse. My remarks here are limited to humanist and certain post-humanist assimilations of colonial reports.

35. Elsewhere I have argued that More's *Utopia* effects a similar split between a "proto-Hobbesian 'natural man'" and an abstractly rational polity (Richard Halpern, *The Poetics of Primitive Accumulation: English Renaissance Culture and the Genealogy of Capital* [Ithaca: Cornell University Press, 1991], pp. 150–51). In More's case, I maintained, this was entirely a symptom of commodity fetishism: "the reified impulse is the necessary and dialectical mirror image of the reified commodity" (p. 151). The present essay offers another, supplementary explanation of the same phenomenon, this time rooted in the dynamics of colonialism. My earlier reading must be included among the more or less "Eurocentric" readings of the *Utopia*, for which this essay may serve in part as corrective.

signify bodily intemperance, he is not in the end defined by these things. Only to Prospero and Miranda does he appear an ineducable savage whose "vile race" both lacks and positively resists culture. By reducing him to a bearer of firewood, Prospero actually *makes* Caliban into a merely corporeal being, a "natural slave." Gonzalo and Prospero thus cooperate in "processing" the non-European subject. One absconds with his culture, and the other reduces him to bodily labor. Together they create a savagism that they then treat as an antecedent to culture rather than its product. "Pure body," in other words, is not some irreducible substratum but a kind of dramatic role—partly foisted onto Caliban, partly present as an innate disposition, partly adopted as a mode of defense.

When he first spots Trinculo, for example, Caliban deems him a tormenting spirit sent by Prospero, and he pretends to be a corpse in order to avoid further punishment. Trinculo's speculations on the seemingly dead body are instructive:

> What have we here? A man or a fish? Dead or alive? A fish! He smells like a fish; a very ancient and fishlike smell; a kind of not of the newest Poor John. A strange fish! Were I in England now, as once I was, and had but this fish painted, not a holiday fool there but would give a piece of silver. There would this monster make a man; any strange beast there makes a man. When they will not give a doit to relieve a lame beggar, they will lay out ten to see a dead Indian. (II.ii.25–34)

Miming death, Caliban has become pure body. In Trinculo's eyes (and nose) he is not mestizo but amphibian, a mixture of species rather than of race,[36] tending toward brute corporeality. Trinculo's plan to exhibit Caliban in England alludes to the importation and exhibition of American Indians which began during the reign of Henry VII and had become regular policy under King James.[37]

While Trinculo's is a more popular form of spectacle than Shake-

---

36. At III.ii.30–31, Trinculo describes Caliban as "half a fish and half a monster."

37. The natives, it was thought, would learn the virtues of Christian, civilized life and report on the kind treatment they had received when they returned to America. Conversely, it was hoped that they would inspire interest in the New World among the English, thus promoting colonization (Lee, *The American Indian*, pp. 268–69, 282–83). Exhibiting Native Americans as popular curiosities was also profitable in its own right, as Trinculo grasps. While a number of these American "guests" died of disease, cold, or the hardships of travel, this did not much reduce their exhibition-value—if Trinculo is to be believed.

speare's courtly play, it adumbrates Caliban's place within a larger system of colonialist representation which included *The Tempest*. The English beheld American Indians only as isolated specimens, removed from their native lands and cultures and reinserted into a discontinuous, carnivalesque series of curios and wonders.[38] "The Indian," a detached spectacle, is produced by abstracting indigenous subjects from sociocultural collectives and repositioning them within something akin to natural history.[39] As "wonder," Caliban is interchangeable with a great fish; reduced to visual object, to pure body, he is of equal interest alive or dead. When Trinculo speaks of "painting" this fish, he means reproducing it on a sign to be hung outside of a booth at a fair; Gonzalo's picture of Nobody finds its counterpart and completion, then, in Trinculo's picture of mere body, likewise founded both on the erasure of cultural origin and on the death of the represented subject.[40] Disembodied utopia and lifeless body are dialectical products of one system of colonial representation.

"When they will not give a doit to relieve a lame beggar, they will lay out ten to see a dead Indian," remarks Trinculo. Since relieving beggars is a prime motive of More's *Utopia*, Trinculo implicitly designates England both as the negation of Utopia (as More himself had done) and, in the same breath, as the negation of the Indian. The visitors to Trinculo's booth are the descendents of More's idealized petty-producing class, now fully commercialized and hostile to the vagrant population from which, in More's day, they had recently been sundered by the process of primitive accumulation.[41] No longer the potential citizens of a utopian polity, they renounce any imaginary

38. J. H. Elliott, *The Old World and the New 1492–1650* (Cambridge: Cambridge University Press, 1970), pp. 30–32. On *Wunderkämmer*, see also Steven Mullaney, "Strange Things, Gross Terms, Curious Customs: The Rehearsal of Cultures in the Late Renaissance," in *Representing the English Renaissance*, ed. Stephen Greenblatt (Berkeley: University of California Press, 1988), pp. 65–68.

39. John White's watercolor paintings of American Indians, turned into engravings by the Dutchman Theodore De Bry, illustrate the fusion of early American ethnography with natural history. White was sent along with Thomas Harriot to depict unknown and possibly profitable resources in the New World, and his Indian portraits are therefore interspersed with paintings of herbs, plants, and animals. In White's portraits the isolated Indian is at once a natural object and a potential commodity.

40. Lee, *The American Indian*, p. 275, lists more than one instance of American Indians who were imported to England, had their portraits painted by distinguished or fashionable artists, and subsequently died before they could return home.

41. On More's *Utopia* and the petty producing class, see Christopher Kendrick, "More's *Utopia* and Uneven Development," *boundary* 2 13 (1985): 233–66. On primitive accumulation, see Halpern, *The Poetics of Primitive Accumulation*, pp. 61–75.

"fusion" with New World models of a communist society, preferring instead to be regaled with the spectacle of the (dead) Indian body.

Yet if Caliban measures the historical deterioration of More's utopian ideal, he also opens up the space of a counter-utopia. Interestingly, this effort centers on a non-act, or at least an uncompleted one: the reported attempt to rape Miranda. Confronted by Prospero, Caliban is less than remorseful: "Oh ho!, Oh ho! Would't had been done! / Thou didst prevent me; I had peopled else / This isle with Calibans" (I.ii.349–51). His evident pride in this attempted rape is perhaps the play's most difficult moment for those readers, including myself, who elsewhere find Caliban to be an appealing or at least a sympathetic character. Here, for one moment, he seems to correspond exactly with the sickest fantasies of colonialist and racist ideology; as Leslie Fiedler puts it, he is "the first nonwhite rapist in white man's literature."[42] Reduced entirely to a racial being, to the impure, mestizoized body which is extruded by Gonzalo's disembodying utopia, Caliban nevertheless becomes Gonzalo's double as well. For in wishing to "people the isle with Calibans," he, like Gonzalo, produces an imaginary society. Indeed, Caliban here makes the play's first and only allusion, however indirect, to the idea of a non-European collectivity—the very thing that inspired Gonzalo's commonwealth in the first place before disappearing from view.

In glimpsing the "original" of Gonzalo's stolen commonwealth, however, we do not attain to a more genuine or appealing utopia. On the contrary, Caliban's imagined polity is locked into symmetry with Gonzalo's only to be rejected in its turn. By locating utopia precisely in the context of rape, Shakespeare suggests that the way to utopia is always lined with violence—that this path is cut, as it were, in the hide of the other, no matter who does the cutting. Instead of liberating himself, Caliban merely extends the chain of oppression, displacing violence onto new victims as his sole means of revenge.

My reading of Gonzalo's ideal commonwealth may wrongly have been taken to imply that *The Tempest* is a covertly anti-colonial play. It does contain an anti-colonial strain, and this strain does deftly ensnare Gonzalo, but only so that none of the play's characters, no matter how apparently inoffensive or gentle, may escape being implicated in the exercise of power. The critique of Gonzalo's commonwealth does not work on behalf of some more authentic utopian ideal,

42. Fiedler, *The Stranger in Shakespeare*, p. 234.

then, or even on behalf of the colonized as victims, but as part of a rigorously anti-utopian current which swamps both Caliban and Gonzalo. *The Tempest* does not "side" with either colonizer or colonized, but cynically undercuts both in the name of a shared but fallen human nature. The play's political shrewdness, which devastatingly reveals the subtlest folds of power, ultimately serves a game which admits of no solidarities. In *The Tempest*, as in Shakespeare's plays generally, critique is radically disjoined from utopia.

Although apparently evenhanded, Shakespeare's skepticism purveys an ultimately conservative message: yes, the way of the world is a violent one, but utopian projectors only multiply the violence they pretend to oppose. In this particular case, however, such rueful and apparently hard-headed moralizing is rather artfully contrived, for despite their own fantasies it was the colonizers themselves who, in their relations with the colonized, held a virtual monopoly on rape and sexual violence. Readers who find themselves casuistically tallying Caliban's sexual assault against the prior wrongs done to him, or who try to "revalue" this assault in light of the anti-colonial utopia it projects, are caught in a false historical premise, one which builds specious symmetries for conservative ends. Retamar's choice of a rapist as anti-colonial hero not only betrays a striking indifference to matters of gender, but falls into an ideological trap set by *The Tempest*.

Caliban's ideal commonwealth mirrors Gonzalo's not only in its reliance on violence but, ironically, in its apparent attempt to expunge the racial other. Just as Gonzalo requires the New World arcadia to construct his own polity, but then represses this dependency by claiming sole authorship himself, so Caliban's imagined *socius* can be embodied only through the reproductive agency of Miranda, but Caliban then denies his dependency on her by claiming that he would people the isle with Calibans—that is, with racial clones of himself. Yet if this symmetry bars all paths to utopia, it nevertheless admits of some internal difference, because Caliban is *already* a mixed or mestizoized being. The fictive children of Miranda and Caliban would be "Calibans" in the sense that they would further the process of mestizoization which is Caliban's legacy. Unlike Gonzalo, then, Caliban does not try to totalize division by eliminating the racial other; he dismantles division through a disseminative, though violent, practice. (Again, we may contrast Seagull's fantasy in *Eastward Ho!* of mixed couplings producing white children.) As a mestizoized space, Caliban's polity seems to possess a genuinely utopian content—a content which is not neutralized but rather blocked, because its only visible means of access is Miranda's rape.

In mirroring one another, Gonzalo and Caliban are both drawn into the other's field. It is only as read against Gonzalo's ideal commonwealth that Caliban's rape can even hint at a utopian end; conversely, that rape manifests the otherwise latent violence behind Gonzalo's commonwealth. If *The Tempest* does not seem to "prefer" either Gonzalo's or Caliban's brand of violence, it nevertheless allows some distinctions to be drawn between them. For Caliban's violence is at least explicit and thus allows us to take its measure; no reader of the play needs to be reminded of the assault on Miranda. Gonzalo's more symbolic violence, however, conceals itself by annihilating or consuming its victims. While colonial violence is generally quite visible both in the real world and in *The Tempest* (via Prospero), Gonzalo's case suggests that such violence becomes latent, if ever, not when its modalities are gentle but when its effects are total, and no one remains to report it.

Strikingly similar issues of annihilation and cultural memory are raised in an historical context by Bruce E. Johansen's controversial book, *Forgotten Founders: How the American Indian Helped Shape Democracy.* Johansen's thesis is that Iroquoian principles of government, as set down in their constitution, "The Great Law of Peace," had a significant influence on such figures as Benjamin Franklin and Thomas Jefferson when they formulated the principles of American government.[43] According to Johansen, the conceptual armature of both the Declaration of Independence and—more indirectly—the Constitution of the United States were significantly informed by Iroquoian example. No explicit reference to native models survives in these documents, however, and historical memory of any possible contribution tended to disappear with the Iroquois themselves, who were nearly exterminated by their erstwhile allies the English after the successful conclusion of war against the French.

The title of Johansen's book—*Forgotten Founders*—clearly bears on issues central to this essay. In fact, as construed by Johansen, the United States Constitution bears a notable resemblance to Gonzalo's ideal commonwealth in *The Tempest*. Both are utopian documents modeled on (mediated) reports of Native American societies—

43. Bruce E. Johansen, *Forgotten Founders: How the American Indian Helped Shape Democracy* (Boston: Harvard Common Press, 1982). On the Indians' use of wampum as a system of writing, see pp. 29–31.

demonstrably and systematically in Gonzalo's case, possibly and infer-
entially in the case of the Constitution. Yet both utopias are intended
for habitation by Europeans. Both repress their mestizoized origins
by erasing all traces of native influence. And both complete this erasure by consuming or destroying the body of the racial other—
metaphorically in Gonzalo's case, all too literally in the case of America. Johansen's book constructs North American history as a disturbingly real enactment of the white cannibalism implicit in Gonzalo's
ideal commonwealth.

Setting Retamar against Johansen, we may suggest that while Caliban's mestizoized counter-utopia takes historical root in the Latin
American culture of José Marti, Gonzalo's ideal commonwealth af-
fixes itself farther north. More generally, we ought to distinguish
between North and South American "models" when discussing the
topic of colonialism in *The Tempest*. The South American model often
retains the bodies of indigenous occupants in order to employ them as
slave labor. This model is represented historically by Spain's use of
native labor in its American mines, and, in *The Tempest*, by Prospero's
enslavement of Caliban. The North American model, by contrast,
expropriates not the labor power but the socio-cultural forms of indigenous peoples. And having done so it then consumes their bodily
existence in an act of white cannibalism. The result in literature is
Gonzalo's ideal commonwealth; the result in history is the United
States, the picture of nobody.

II

My own reading of *The Tempest*, it should now be clear, involves an
allegorical appropriation of the text—or rather, it elaborates Retamar's. The significance of Gonzalo and his ideal commonwealth
appears when he becomes the symbolic representative of a more general cultural strategy in humanist and neo-humanist discourse, a strategy which is also central to current debates about the canon and
pedagogy. Clearly, conservative arguments for the need to protect a
"core" curriculum from contamination by presumably "peripheral"
or subaltern cultures are complicated by a recognition that the so-
called core is already infected by the periphery, is indeed constituted
by such infection, and that the apparent closure of the Western canon
may obscure a more fundamental state of mestizoization.

To say this, however, raises certain questions about the model of cultural repression that underlies my reading and, indeed, the whole project of alternative histories, which is implicitly filiated with psychoanalysis. The assumption here is that the dominant culture achieves a false, ideological appearance of unity and self-sufficiency by "repressing" its dependence on subaltern strains. Retamar's (merely virtual) image of Echo and Narcissus, which figures the specular self-satisfaction of the West, implies a conception of the dominant culture not entirely unlike the Lacanian ego, whose aggressive unity is both sustained and frustrated by the dialectic of the imaginary. The task of the cultural historian, like that of the psychoanalyst, is thus to liberate repressed histories, thereby restoring a cultural memory whose therapeutic effect may be, paradoxically, traumatic: not so much the resumption of a full and overarching culture that will embrace all social groups (the liberal ideal) but the definitive fracturing of any such illusion. Just as the insistence of the letter reveals the ego and its speech to be, as Lacan puts it, a "privileged symptom," so the restoration of the repressed history serves its function by decentering rather than expanding the discourse of the dominant culture.

In one sense, then, to speak of a "repressed" history means nothing more than to read cultural texts *symptomatically*, through their gaps or contradictions. Pointing to the significant chronological delay experienced by early modern Europe in assimilating New World culture, the historian J. H. Elliott writes: "It is difficult not to be impressed by the strange lacunae and the resounding silences in many places where references to the New World could reasonably be expected."[44] In *The Tempest*, Gonzalo's ideal commonwealth produces just such a "resounding silence" or determinate absence, and his strategic forgetfulness thus seems to locate something like a cultural repression of the New World within European discourse.

In a later essay Elliott continues his implicitly psychoanalytic metaphor when he writes that early modern Europe had a "built-in screening mechanism . . . to limit the range and extent of cultural shock." Elliott argues that the New World did not enter European discourse directly but for the most part had a catalytic and recombinatory effect on already-established traditions: "Rather than pointing Europe in totally new directions, the discovery of America emphasized and strengthened certain elements in European civilization at the expense

44. Elliott, *The Old World*, p. 13.

of others."[45] One of the ideological functions of Renaissance humanism, I would argue, was to close the traumatic gap in cultural discourse produced by the discovery of America. This it did by substituting European elements (largely from the classical tradition) for those
of New World culture, thus creating a new, defensive genealogy which
served as the cultural equivalent of a screen memory.[46] If this is true
the discursive coherence of humanism simply papers over a structure
of trauma, repression, and subsequent resuturing.

The resonant absences in Gonzalo's ideal commonwealth can be
heard in more recent humanist writings on Renaissance utopias.
George M. Logan's 1983 study of More's *Utopia*, for example, insists
that More wrote exclusively for a humanist audience and situated
himself in humanist traditions: "Utopia must be somewhere, so it may
as well be in the extremely topical Americas. . . . But . . . More is not
in any way constrained by the accounts of America. . . . A more interesting class of Utopian features consists of those adopted from Plato
and Aristotle."[47] In one sense, Logan's protocols of reading simply
reproduce Gonzalo's, and those of Renaissance humanism more generally, by writing the utopia into a predominantly Western context.
Yet if Logan is complicit with humanist ideology in denying the mestizoized status of More's work, it is also true that his assumptions are
shared by less conservative critics and that the textual genealogy he
provides for the *Utopia* is more detailed and persuasive than those
offered by proponents of American influence.[48]

45. Elliott, "Renaissance Europe and America: A Blunted Impact?" in Chiappelli,
First Images of America, 1:22, 17.

46. Sigmund Freud, "Screen Memories," in *The Standard Edition of the Complete
Psychological Works of Sigmund Freud*, trans. James Strachey et al., 24 vols. (London:
Hogarth Press, 1953–74), 3:303–22.

47. George M. Logan, *The Meaning of More's Utopia* (Princeton: Princeton University
Press, 1983), p. 195.

48. In her 1982 study, Miriam Eliav-Feldon writes: "It is quite striking, in fact, how
little influence the New World had on the content of utopias during the Renaissance;
one has the impression that they could all have been written even if Columbus had
never set sail" (*Realistic Utopias: The Ideal Imaginary Societies of the Renaissance, 1516–
1630* [Oxford: Clarendon Press, 1982], p. 12). Her view is endorsed by James Holstun,
who, writing from a Foucauldian-Frankfurt School perspective, associates the early
modern utopia with Western processes of rationalization and technological domination
(*A Rational Millennium*). An enthusiastic but flawed effort to demonstrate American
influence on More is Arthur E. Morgan's *Nowhere Was Somewhere: How History Makes
Utopias and How Utopias Make History* (Chapel Hill: University of North Carolina Press,
1946), which tried to prove that the Utopia is systematically patterned after reports of
the Incan empire in Peru.

The proposition that Renaissance utopias were enabled in some fundamental way by the discovery of the New World seems indisputable as a generality. Yet it doesn't bear up as well under close textual scrutiny. Indeed, the "repressive hypothesis" as I have developed it here might be subjected to a Foucauldian inversion: far from denying a deep indebtedness to American culture, works such as More's *Utopia* or Campanella's *City of the Sun* simply parade references to the New World as cultural fashion or empty topicality.[49] Instead of being "repressed," American allusions are multiplied by a discourse whose effect is to implant colonial desire, not to deny cultural dependency. In fact, these functions are not at all mutually exclusive; More's *Utopia* both flaunts a fashionable interest in colonial discovery *and* tends to efface the signs of a more fundamental American influence.[50]

Nevertheless, the repressive hypothesis here seems more successful at grounding a negative than a positive hermeneutic. Able to unsettle Eurocentric self-sufficiency, the notion of a "forgotten" American influence runs into trouble when it aspires to the status of a research project. The generally unfavorable reception accorded by scholars to Johansen's book is symptomatic of a broader trend.[51] While some of the objections leveled against Johansen are either clearly political or easily contestable,[52] others locate genuine weaknesses in his attempt

49. Rosario Romeo admits that reports from the New World influence *City of the Sun* in incidental ways: "But as to the fundamental question of Campanella's communistic conceptions, the presumed derivation from the institutes of Incan Peru is unsustainable." ("The Jesuit Sources and the Italian Political Utopia in the Second Half of the Sixteenth Century," in Chiappelli, *First Images of America*, 1:179.)

50. Here again the Freudian concept of repression is helpful. In his paper on "Fetishism" (*Standard Edition*, 21:153) Freud distinguishes between *Verleugnung* as the denial of an idea or representation (in this case the absence of the maternal phallus) and *Verdrängung* or repression proper, which pertains rather to the affect attached to a representation. Put differently, it is not the object of desire which is subjected to repression but desire itself. In the analytic situation nothing prevents the object of repressed desire from becoming the explicit subject of a speech that is voluble but never quite pertinent.

51. See especially Barbara Graymont's review in *New York History* 64 (1983): 325–27. Scholarly review of Johansen's book has been almost universally unfavorable—e.g., Karen Ordahl Kupperman, *Journal of Interdisciplinary History* 14 (1984): 879–81; and Bernard W. Sheehan, *Indiana Magazine of History* 79 (1983): 368–69.

In reviewing William Brandon's book, *New Worlds for Old*, John H. Elliott likewise found Brandon's arguments for extensive American influence on European political thought largely unconvincing (*Hispanic American Historical Review* 67 [1987]: 504–5). On the other hand, Elliott's views are challenged by Arthur J. Slavin, "American Principle."

52. One reviewer, for example, objects that "Johansen has mistaken Franklin's and Jefferson's rationalist curiosity about natural history, i.e., 'aboriginal government,' for

to demonstrate a direct and relatively unmediated influence of Native American political practices on colonial government. Johansen's detractors will generally allow a more diffuse and mediated form of influence, via the French *philosophes* and Lockean notions of natural right; but as one put it, "The democratic political structure that arose as a result of the American Revolution did not spring from the Iroquois example, admirable though that was, but rather from a century-and-a-half of colonial self-government."[53]

Johansen's argument runs into difficulties similar to those encountered by arguments for New World influence on Renaissance utopias: assertions of cultural influence which seem tenable as generalities founder at the level of concrete political practices, institutions, or genealogies. In both cases the American thesis falls to the historian's version of Occam's razor: it isn't that Native American models are inherently implausible but rather that European or colonial models are always amply available, so that recourse to an alien culture seems both redundant and undemonstrable.[54] While this objection may be based on ideology as much as method, the fact remains that the "repressed" or forgotten history remains irreducibly speculative; it cannot be (or at least has not been) definitively produced.

Gonzalo's ideal commonwealth, with its occulted but easily recoverable subtexts, may thus offer a dangerous interpretive lure. For in the case of Native American influence on Western culture there may be, in the end, no hidden history—that is, no concrete but repressed narrative—to recover. Perhaps the signs of the New World are, like Poe's purloined letter, both fully displayed and invisible in the texts of

visceral commitment and political application" (*Choice* 20 [1983]: 1052). This facile dichotomy is untenable for a period when the concept of natural right occupies a central place in political discourse. Barbara Graymont's review (p. 326) insists that Johansen falls prey to the colonial misperception of the Iroquois kinship state as a political state, while Bernard Sheehan argues more broadly that Johansen confuses ideological images of the "Noble Savage" with the reality of Iroquois society, and that he has "bought in its entirety Benjamin Franklin's 'Deistical Indians'" (Sheehan, p. 368). True, Johansen does not adequately consider the fact that European prejudices may have influenced colonial perceptions of native society. But as I have tried to argue in this essay, misrecognition can be a *mode* of appropriation as well as an impediment to it. To treat colonial perceptions of American cultures as pure illusion, or simply to deny the possibility of cultural influence every time some element of ideological distortion intervenes, is to condemn the study of cultural interaction to the crudest sort of positivism. Johansen's book is guilty of various historical errors. Yet while they certainly vitiate his work, they do not suffice to demolish his central thesis.

53. Graymont, review of Johansen, p. 326.
54. See especially Barbara Graymont's review.

European political thought. It may be that if the traces of American
influence (and hence of mestizoization) tend to disappear from the
products of white culture, this is not because they have been sub-
merged or covered over but because they have been abstracted to the
point of transparency. In the case of Renaissance utopias, the New
World is present as a general social thematics (communal property,
masterlessness, and the like) from which all social specificity, and
hence the signature—the "tint"—of any particular culture has been
drained. (That cultural "tint" is then extruded and registered as the
dark body of the racial other.) Yet while the individual components of
this general social thematics may also be available in the European
and colonial storehouses of culture, they are subjected to a deictic
reorganization by the utopian text, prompted in turn by the image of
America.[55]

By deixis I mean here to denote a complex ideological and referen-
tial process. What the deictic function of America adds to the elements of its social thematics is the fact that one can look and see
them—"point" to them in the world. It thus invests utopian thought
with the empirical force of the real, which fictional or philosophical
polities will necessarily lack. Here visibility is a simple function of
embodiment, contrasted with a textual abstract. At the same time,
however, this looking or pointing *at* is also a looking or pointing *away
from*—specifically, away from the egalitarian social forms which also
existed in Europe, but which were irremediably marked as forms of
class existence. The Diggers and other radical movements of the mid-
seventeenth century were able to draw on longstanding practices of
the English laboring classes in formulating their social programs. Yet
the inescapably popular character of such movements and traditions
tainted them for those political thinkers to whom the American example appealed precisely because it seemed to detach utopian forms
from the practices and values of the laboring classes. Indeed, the
arcadian tradition on which Gonzalo draws for his ideal commonwealth performs an important ideological function by substituting

55. Utopia operates by example and demonstration, deictically. "At the basis of all
utopian debates, in its open or hidden dialogues, is a gesture of pointing, a wide-eyed
glance from here to there, a travelling shot moving from the author's everyday lookout
to the wondrous panorama of a far-off land." Darko Suvin, *Metamorphoses of Science
Fiction: On the Poetics and History of a Literary Genre* (New Haven: Yale University Press,
1979), p. 37. Quoted in Holstun, *A Rational Millennium*, pp. 63–64.

idleness, with its aristocratic associations, for labor as the basis of a communitarian society. Gonzalo's "picture of Nobody" thus purifies itself of the stain, not only of the non-white body, but of the European laboring body as well. More generally, it abstracts the political from the economic, that is, from the realm of real production. The deictic force of America relies, then, on a constitutively *displaced* embodiment whose cultural visibility entails cultural refraction as well.

The deictic status of the American image (no matter how deeply distorted or misrecognized) radically transforms the discursive significance, legitimation, and internal articulation of the elements of its social thematics. Even if America proves to be largely "superfluous" at the level of content, it is nevertheless crucial at the level of form. For the Enlightenment, too, America may or may not add new rights to those imaginable in Europe, but it helps render them "natural"—thus draining them of apparent class-specificity—and, indeed, transfigures the very category of nature. The Noble Savage who incarnates these "natural" rights is doubtless the ideological product of European misrecognition; but this misrecognition is not unmotivated, which is to say, it results from a dialogical though asymmetrical practice.

The New World thus plays the part, in European culture, of the vanishing mediator whose catalytic work is not immediately visible in its products.[56] Yet if this mediator "vanishes," it does not necessarily do so as the result of repression. A better psychoanalytic model might be D. W. Winnicott's transitional object, whose destiny is to be decathected rather than repressed. The disappearance of the transitional object does not, therefore, open a symptomatic gap in the signifying chain, marking the determinate absence of another story or narrative. Rather, the history of the transitional object assumes its afterlife in the form of a distinctive *tone* imparted to the whole field of psychic object-relations. This history cannot be located in individual contents or representations but in the affective "strings" that connect them.[57] So too the mestizoization of European culture tends to

56. I borrow the term "vanishing mediator" from Fredric Jameson's essay "The Vanishing Mediator; or, Max Weber as Storyteller" in Jameson, *The Ideologies of Theory: Essays, 1971–1986. Volume 2: The Syntax of History*, Theory and History of Literature 49 (Minneapolis: University of Minnesota Press, 1988), pp. 3–34.

57. D. W. Winnicott, "Transitional Objects and Transitional Phenomena," in *Playing and Reality* (New York: Basic Books, 1971), pp. 1–25. For the famous case titled "string," see pp. 15–20.

disappear—in part, doubtless, because it is repressed, but also because its effects inhere less in localizable contents than in their discursive articulation.[58] White cannibals are nourished not by what they eat but by how it is digested.

58. Although I have invoked the transitional object rather abstractly, in order to provide a model for a cultural process, I think it also plays a more direct and properly psychoanalytic role in *The Tempest*. Sycorax, Caliban's mother, never appears within the play's system of dramatic representations, but her primitive ur-magic, which precedes Prospero's more masculine and "civilized" thaumaturgy, persists as what Caliban calls the "qualities o' th' isle" (I.ii.337), those strange "noises, / Sounds and sweet airs that give delight and hurt not" (III.ii.140–41), which occasionally transport Caliban to dreams. The dispersal of Sycorax as maternal object, then, leaves its traces in the magical *Stimmung* of the play's landscape. (See Fredric Jameson, *The Political Unconscious: Narrative as a Socially Symbolic Act* [Ithaca: Cornell University Press, 1981], pp. 110–13, on the "*worldness* of *world*" as a constitutive element of romance.) This transformation likewise purges Sycorax's "evil" nature, leaving only a pleasant though impersonal force. Yet its enduring presence unsettles the primacy of Prospero's power, and suggests that the play's "happy" resolution may ultimately depend not on Prospero's dramatic stratagems but on a miraculous matrix that suffuses the isle—not, that is to say, on any given character among others, but on the quality of the dramatic space they all inhabit. For a powerful feminist reading of Shakespeare's plays drawing on Winnicott's work, see Janet Adelman, *Suffocating Mothers: Fantasies of Maternal Origin in Shakespeare's Plays, "Hamlet" to "The Tempest"* (New York: Routledge, 1992).

9

Allegory, Materialism, Violence

GORDON TESKEY

Mens hebes ad verum per materialia surgit.

— Abbot Suger

. . . et ceci pourrait expliquer l'indifférence de cette substance immuable que dévotement nous appelons *Dieu*.

— M. Yourcenar

[The dull mind ascends to the truth by means of material things. . . . and this could explain the indifference of that intractable substance which we devoutly call God.]

When we survey the range of discussions of allegory in the past thirty years we are struck not only by the variety of approaches taken to it but by the persistence with which these approaches turn on the question of how the two parts of the word—*allo, agoreuein*, "other speaking"—are related. The word *allegory* implies a primary narrative pointing to an "other" that is heterogeneous to it and to which that narrative is itself "other." Out of these reciprocal "others" various approaches to the subject can be generated by inclining to either side of the rift at the heart of the word: to the material signifier in its aspect as *writing*, or to the ideal referent in its aspect as *vision*. There can be no radically "true account," no *etymos logos* of allegory that does not look into this rift at the heart of the word, for it runs as deep as any in the philosophical tradition, separating the categories of the material and the ideal.

Of the differences of approach it creates, the most familiar is the question of whether allegory is a *mode* or a *genre*. While the modal approach begins by observing that any literary work whatever is open to an adventitious interpretation, the generic observes how ideological structures, determined more or less in advance, enter into narrative by an adventitious encoding. Even the notion, still crucial in Dante studies, of "figural realism" as a kind of allegory that is superior to psychomachy can be seen as inclining toward the material register of the poet's "earthly world," to use Auerbach's phrase, as opposed to the ideal register of its meaning, where characters represent things like Theology and Reason. Similarly, the question of whether allegory is a kind of writing that entails the translucence of physical signs to the logos, as in the encyclopedic allegories of the medieval cathedrals, or whether allegory is a kind of writing that acknowledges the opacity of the material signifier and the consequent impossibility of what it is trying to do, can be seen as proceeding from the dissonance of the radicals in the word allegory itself.

It would of course be incorrect to suppose that these approaches can be reduced unequivocally to one or the other extreme: all of them make allowances for what they are required to forget. The *modal* approach introduced in Angus Fletcher's ground-breaking study, notwithstanding its tendency to see discourse itself as incipiently allegorical, applies the repetition-compulsion in psychoanalysis to the behavior of personified universals in conventional allegorical texts. The *generic* approach developed by Maureen Quilligan, notwithstanding its intention of setting allegory apart, is founded in a subtle investigation of the polysemous character of language in general as a material background, or landscape, for allegorical persons. The *figural realist* approach to Dante, notwithstanding its Crocean hostility to the poetry of concepts, is deeply concerned with the problem of transcendental reference. The more traditional or "philological" perspectives, typified by Curtius, in which allegory is generated out of the conjunction of a philosophical culture with an ancient literary form, are not unaware of a rift between transcendental thought and its narrative formations, though they may indicate it only by a certain dryness of tone when recounting absurdities.

Even Paul de Man's sustained meditation on questions surrounding his specialized use of the word allegory formulates both sides of the issue in the most practical way: "Why is it," he asks, "that the furthest reaching truths about ourselves and the world have to be stated in such a lopsided, referentially indirect mode?"[1] No one forgets altogether that there are two sides to the problem, as there are two parts to the word. Nor is it at all apparent that a correct approach would try to hold them in balance: they cannot be balanced, which is why extreme approaches have had a way of turning up insights that would not have been turned up by more apparently responsible ones.

Perhaps the most we can ask now of any effort to understand allegorical literature is that it acknowledge the terms within which it inflects itself to either extreme and that it recognize the inevitability of a confrontation with what it denies. For what any "inclined" effort must at least temporarily forget is not just the other side of the question (whatever the "other" in any particular case is) but the rift at its center. This is also the rift that it is the purpose of an allegorical work to conceal.

1. Paul de Man, "Pascal's Allegory of Persuasion," in *Allegory and Representation*, ed. Stephen J. Greenblatt, English Institute (Baltimore: Johns Hopkins University Press, 1981), p. 2.   For allegory as a mode, see Angus Fletcher, *Allegory: The Theory of a Symbolic Mode* (Ithaca: Cornell University Press, 1964); as a genre, see Maureen Quilligan, *The Language of Allegory: Defining the Genre* (Ithaca: Cornell University Press, 1979), and "Allegory, Allegoresis, and the Deallegorization of Language: The *Roman de la Rose*, the *De planctu naturae*, and the *Parlement of Foules*," in *Allegory, Myth, and Symbol*, ed. Morton W. Bloomfield, Harvard Studies in English 9 (Cambridge: Harvard University Press, 1981), pp. 163–86, esp. p. 163. Charles S. Singleton's theory of "figured realism" follows Erich Auerbach in "Figura," *Scenes from the Drama of European Literature* (1959; rpt. Minneapolis: University of Minnesota Press, 1984), pp. 11–76 and in *Dante: Poet of the Secular World*, trans. Ralf Manheim (Chicago: University of Chicago Press, 1961). For references to Singleton's work and to allegory in the Commedia generally, see Robert Hollander, "Bibliography I," in *Allegory in Dante's 'Commedia'* (Princeton: Princeton University Press, 1969), pp. 321–35. The series of *Lectura Dantis Americana* emerging under Hollander's general editorship (vol. 1, ed. Anthony K. Cassell, and vol. 2, ed. Rachel Jacoff and William A. Stephany [Philadelphia: University of Pennsylvania Press, 1989]) provides useful surveys of the scholarship on these cantos. For the philological view of allegory, see Ernst Robert Curtius, *European Literature and the Latin Middle Ages*, Bollingen Series 36 (Princeton: Princeton University Press, 1953), pp. 360–62; Hans Robert Jauss and Uda Ebel, "Entstehung und Strukturwandel der allegorischen Dichtung," in *La littérature didactique, allégorique et satirique*, ed. Jürgen Beyer, ser. Grundriss der Romanischen Literaturen des Mittelalters 6 (Heidelberg: Winter, 1968): 1:146–244. In vol. 2 of *Grundriss* 6 (Heidelberg: Winter, 1970), pp. 203–80, Jauss and Ebel describe medieval allegories under five headings: (1) the development of allegory from Biblical exegesis; (2) the tradition of the *Physiologus*; (3) otherworldly and apocalyptic visions (by Ebel); (4) allegorical epic; (5) erotic allegory. For further references, see my "Allegeory" in *The Spenser Encyclopedia*, ed. A. C. Hamilton et al. (Toronto: University of Toronto Press, 1990).

The last remark indicates that the negativity of the material "other" of an allegory is not solely a methodological problem that can be confined to poetics and redistributed more adequately there. For if the rift we observed in the various approaches to allegory is also at the center of the object of study—is in fact the thing that that object is trying to hide—it runs deeper than both, reaching down into the foundations of an eidetic metaphysics the absurdities of which allegory tries to repair by imaginative means, logical ones being inadequate to the task.

At the heart of what allegory is trying to conceal—that is, at the heart of a more general, metaphysical disorder—is the problem of *methexis* or "participation"—literally, a "having across"—by which abstractions are predicated of individual things only after being predicated of themselves through the trope of personification, as when Justice is said to be just.[2] The absurd supposition that a universal can be predicated of itself, its absurdity concealed behind the tautological appearance of phrases like "justice is just," goes back to Plato; that he was aware of its presence in the theory of the forms, even if he could not identify its character precisely, is indicated by his deployment in the *Parmenides* of an argument against him to which he seems not to have had any answer.[3] This argument, commonly referred to as the "third man," purports to show that the theory of the forms involves an infinite regress: the form of man is connected to any particular man by their sharing (*methexis*) something that is separate (*choriston*) from both; this thing can be nothing other than a third man, which must in turn share something with the first two, and so on.

2. *Parmenides* 132 d. *Metaphysics* 987 b 10–15. See also *Phaedo* 100 d and *Parmenides* 131 a.

3. See Gregory Vlastos, "The Third Man Argument in the *Parmenides*" (1954; with a logical addendum, 1963), in *Studies in Plato's Metaphysics*, ed. R. E. Allen (London: Routledge, 1965), pp. 231–63. If there is a form of Man by which particular men are men, then a particular man and the form Man must share between them the separate quality of being a man; this quality constitutes a "third man" which must share the quality of being a man with both, thus opening an infinite regress. Vlastos argues that the third man argument is rendered invalid by its holding simultaneously the self-predication and non-identity assumptions, but that these are themselves destructive of the copy theory of reality and the hierarchy of being it implies—principles that are also fundamental to allegorical expression. For a defense of the third man argument, see John Malcolm, *Plato on the Self-Predication of Forms: Early and Middle Dialogues* (Oxford: Clarendon, 1991), pp. 47–52.

It should be pointed out that in the *Parmenides* the form of "Largeness" is used, not the form of "Man," and that the phrase "third man" appears in Aristotle's use of the same argument, where it is invoked in what appears to be a technical abbreviation.[4] But the designation "third man" has stuck to the argument up to the present no less adhesively than has the notion that it is the concept of Man that is chiefly at stake in any attack on or defense of the theory of forms. We thus find Aristotle's attack on idealism brilliantly parodied in Milton's "*De Idea Platonica quemadmodum Aristoteles intellexit*," where what is ridiculed is the notion that the form of man must itself be a particular man, though perhaps somewhat larger.

Of course, the strictly logical sense of the argument in the *Parmenides* is unaffected by whether Largeness or Man serves as an example of one of the forms. But the ideological consequences of the difference are obviously great: whereas "Largeness" is a concept sufficiently airless to ensure one's keeping one's attention focused on logical problems, "Man" is an abstraction with more than a few implications that make it hard to see the problems behind it as logical problems at all. These are instead cathected onto the relation of the concept of Man to a feminine "other" it encloses as an internal difference necessary to its self-propagation: as a father stands to his sons, so form stands in relation to its instances, which are begotten in and propagated through an alien subject, matter-as-woman.

Although the most radical formulation of this is in the *Timaeus*, to which I shall turn in a moment, its sexual implications are brought out with particular clarity in Aristotle's *De generatione animalium*, where the female is the material receptacle for masculine form contained in the sperm: "the male provides the 'form' [*eidos*] and the 'principle of movement' [*ten archen tes kineseos*], the female provides the body [*soma*], in other words, the material [*hylen*]." The sexual implications of the Aristotelian identification of form with movement and of matter with passivity are made more explicit in a passage elaborating this assertion: "If the male is the active partner, the one which originates the movement, and the female *qua* female is the passive

---

4. For references to arguments denominated "the third man," see Francis Mac-Donald Cornford, *Plato and Parmenides* (London: Routledge, 1939), pp. 87–90. The extent to which such references include the subtleties of the argument as it stands in the *Parmenides* is of course difficult to say. For Aristotle's use of the third man, and the extent to which he understood its implications, see Gregory Vlastos, "The Third Man Argument," pp. 241 n. 2, 246 n. 5, and 250–51 n. 3.

one, surely what the female contributes to the semen of the male will
not be semen but material [*ou gonen all' hylen*]. And this is in fact what
we find happening; for the natural substance of the menstrual fluid
[*he ton katamenion physis*] is to be classed as 'prime matter' [*prote hyle*]."[5]
The problem of *methexis* as a participatory "having across" is thus
"seated" or "placed" by a *cathexis* in the entirely different context of
gender, where it can appear to be solved under the image of sexual
congress. Consequently, sexual relations in allegory will be invested
with metaphysical significance, and metaphysical problems will appear to be worked out—which is to say concealed—in imaginary,
sexual terms.

To see what is being implied in these terms we need to look closely
at the words used for the intrusion of the economy of gender into the
relations of matter and form, particularly the words used in the *Timaeus*, in which we are introduced to the absolutely featureless "mother" or "receptacle" through which the father propagates his seed in
the world of things.[6] It is through the concept of gender that the
principles of hierarchy (man over woman) and imitation (parent and
offspring) are articulated in the theory of forms. The receptacle is
designated literally as "that which receives from below," the *hyodoche*, a
substantive formed from the verb *hypodechomai*, one of the meanings
of which is simply "to become pregnant": matter becomes pregnant
with form by assuming a subject position with respect to the male.

It is unnecessary here to enter into the relations of this *hypodoche*
with the more common term for matter, the *hypokeimenon* or "subject,"
which in Greek means literally "that which lies underneath" (the Latin
subiectum is more violent), except to note that both words indicate
matter in terms of the proper position for the wife during intercourse. The significance of this is not just that the logical problems
associated with philosophical idealism are hopelessly entangled with
the very different problems of gender: if the case were that simple the
metaphorics of gender would scarcely have adhered so tenaciously to
idealism. The confusion of the two has survived because it is psycho-

5. *De generatione animalium* 729 a 10 and 28–33, Loeb trans. The menstrual fluid is
"prime matter" only relatively, that is, only with respect to the living animal to which it is
prior.

6. *Timaeus* 50 c–51 b. The metaphorics of paternity and generation in Platonic
metaphysics has of course been a major concern of Derrida's writing. One of the more
accessible discussions, centered around *Republic* 506 e, is "Le Père du Logos," in "*La
pharmacie de Platon*," *Dissémination* (Paris: Seuil, 1972), pp. 84–95; English trans. Barbara Johnson, *Dissemination* (Chicago: University of Chicago Press, 1981), pp. 75–84.

logically resonant and politically useful: it is an *ideology*. In Althusserian terms it is also, because it is an ideology, a practice taking the social form of a ritualized reading that will conceal, like a veil, the logical problems inherent in *methexis*.

When engaged by an interpreter who enters more or less uncritically into the conventions of the genre, allegory offers imaginary solutions that universalize hierarchical relations of power in the family so that these can be found in the cosmos and then prescribed in the state. The structure of belief sustained by this ideological practice is especially evident in Neoplatonism, in which the infinite regress opened by self-predication—the third man becoming as it were the first *daemon*—begins to look not like an absurdity but like the unlimited productiveness of the *spermatikoi logoi*, or seminal principles, filling the abyss with transitory forms that emerge from the mother and die. Being independent of matter, the father is untouched by this death.

Through what they imply about the inferior position of matter when receiving the imprint of form, the Greek and Latin words for "matter"—*hypokeimenon, hypodoche, subiectum, substratum*—are metaphorical indications of what is epistemolgically, sexually, and politically at stake in idealism as a cultural force. Idealism in this sense is by no means motivated by the will to discover the truth of the actual world, for such a truth would be entirely different from what we abstractly preconceive it to be—from what, in Platonic terms, we already know and therefore need only remember. Idealism is driven instead by a will-to-power that subjects what it does not understand, epistemologically, sexually, and politically, to an abstract knowledge it imagines it already has. It is therefore committed to reducing to a state of indifferent homogeneity the material basis that it still needs as a place to occur outside itself.

To summarize the discussion so far, we can say that the logical concepts at the basis of Platonic idealism, *methexis* and *chorismos*, "participation" and "separation," enter into a metaphorics of *insemination* and *parturition* by which a form like justice can multiply itself through a featureless, alien, invisible mother—even as it continues, in the empyrean, to father itself. The result of this seating of metaphysical problems within the structure of the family is a totalizing illusion we can call "hierarchical, animated idealism," in which a kind of agency is attributed to the abstractions that predicate themselves before flowing down into things in the world. Allegory is not just the literary mani-

festation of animated idealism but the basis of a social practice, interpretation, by which the integrity of the hierarchy is repeatedly affirmed, weaving a veil of analogies over a heterogeneous, material
substratum. This practice is made possible by the violence of reducing
the other to a featureless substance imprinted by form.

Now the concept of matter, considered apart from the metaphorics
of gender, is a logical instrument for establishing the principle of
individuation beneath the lowest order of abstractions, the *infima species*:[7] it lets us distinguish, under the form of Justice, one just man
from another, and its purpose is the separation of individuals within
an abstract class that unites them. Logically speaking, there can be
nothing material, nothing *alive*, and certainly nothing masculine or
paternal about any abstract class considered apart from its material
contents. Nor can there be anything material, alive, or masculine
about the highest abstraction from which all the others are supposed
to be derived. The father as a conscious, immaterial agent of form
does not exist, which is why he has to be hidden behind subordinate
agents—*daemons* in animated idealism, *personifications* in allegory[8]—
who are abstractions themselves but who seem nevertheless to have
something material about them because they instantiate what they
abstract. Animated idealism needs matter to give the power of agency
to these agents. The grand metaphorics of paternity with its hierarchy
of agents cannot survive as long as matter remains inaccessible to it,
that is, as long as matter remains a purely logical instrument of differ-
entiation beneath the lowest *species*. It is therefore the project of allegory to capture the material and lift it up onto the level of concepts,
making it seem as if the material were not the logical contradiction of
matter but its eschatological destiny.

This capturing and sublation of the material, normally carried out
in secret, is unexpectedly revealed in powerful allegorical texts at
moments that are so shocking in their honesty that they have consistently been misread not as disclosures of what allegory is secretly
doing but as departures from allegorical expression. Such moments
literalize a gender metaphor from Neoplatonism, the moment of *rap-*

7. For the concept of matter in ancient philosophy, see under *hyle* in F. E. Peters,
Greek Philosophical Terms: A Historical Lexicon (New York: New York University Press,
1967), pp. 88–91.
8. For the relation of agency in Neoplatonic *daemons* to the repetitive acts of
personifications (and the relations of both with the repetition compulsion), see Angus
Fletcher, "The Daemonic Agent," in *Allegory*, pp. 25–69.

tio in which matter, because of its perversity—which is to say its resistance to the desire of the male—must be ravished by form before its conversion (*conversio*) and return (*remeatio*) to the father[9]: being ravished is what matter secretly wants. By rapture the material is transformed from a slattern into something *decor* and bears in its substance the imprint of form.

In the moments I am speaking of, however, the real power behind this fantasy of the material is unmasked, so that we see violence being committed on an unwilling woman, and in such a way that there is no fantasy of converting her to the rapist's desire. Nor is there any fantasy of releasing her from it: we are confronted instead with a paralyzed struggle in which the rift between heterogeneous others is forced into view. What we have seen to be the logical impossibility of raising the concept of matter onto the level of abstractions is thus forced into view by the metaphorics of gender, so that what we are shown is the capturing of a feminine principle that continues to resist, in captivity, being converted into an embodiment of the meaning that is violently imprinted in it. Examples from Spenser that come readily to mind are Amoret and Mirabella, the torture of each being an asymptotical progression toward her becoming a personification of wifely consent.

In a literary genre concerned more than any other with the metaphysical implications of gender, such moments, in which the space between matter and form is forced open by violence, are uncommon. It is more broadly characteristic of allegory—though by no means more true of it—for this violence to be concealed so that the feminine figure embodies, with her whole body, the meaning that is imprinted in her without any visible resistance. When this happens we have

9. In the various permutations of the Neoplatonic triad of *emanatio, raptio*, and *remeatio*, the moment of "turning," or *conversio* (Gr. *epistrophe*), can be either independent of the violence of the *raptus* or a part of it—or, oddly, both, in Agrippa of Nettesheim's *De occulta philosophia* (1533), p. 316, where *raptus* is an alienation of the soul from its divine origin and a recovery of the soul to that origin. See Edgar Wind, *Pagan Mysteries in the Renaissance* (New Haven: Yale University Press, 1958), p. 48 n. 1. (See also p. 40 and nn. 4 and 5.) Wind is explicating the passage from Ficino's *De amore* (a commentary on the *Symposium*) on threefold creation, in which God is said to make, seize (*rapit*) and perfect each thing. As Wind points out, *raptus* is a literal translation of *harpazein* in the Chaldean Oracles and in Proclus's commentary on the *Parmenides*, an act of violent seizing by which being is again joined to the one. See *In Parmenidem* V. col. 1033, 27 in Proclus's *Opera*, ed. Victor Cousin (Paris, 1864). That this seizing before union is to be understood in erotic terms is a commonplace of Neoplatonism, *amor* being, as Ficino puts it in *De amore* III.iii, the perpetual knot and copulation of the world ("nodus perpetuus, et copula mundi"). (Cited in Wind, *Pagan Mysteries*, p. 41.)

personification. But the struggle inside personification is exposed when, by a gesture to which I shall give a name in due course, it is turned inside out.

We can describe in more general terms what is at issue in this struggle by saying that at certain moments in allegorical works the negative or "literal" other is disclosed as the thing that remains heterogeneous to the abstract forms that are imprinted on it. The spectacle this disclosure exhibits is of a struggle positioned at the very center of what allegory is trying to do, which is to conceal the fundamental disorder out of which the illusion of absolute order is raised. It is moreover out of this struggle at the rift that the whole process of allegorical figuration is generated, thus creating a veil of analogies behind which we imagine is placed, like the vanishing point in linear perspective, the singularity of absolute truth. The material in allegory is the site of the rift that we have seen to be the purpose of allegorical works to conceal. We can therefore define the *material* in allegory as *that which gives meaning a place to occur while remaining heterogeneous to it.*

The scholastic solution to this heterogeneity is to conceive of the material "other" in terms of the fantasy we have just noted: matter longs for form as a woman longs for a man: *materia appetit formam ut femina virum.* While this strange notion can be traced back to Aristotle's *Physics* (where it is not approved of because it opens the infinite regress we have seen),[10] it appears to have entered medieval culture,

10. *Physics* 192 a 22–23: "what desires the form is matter, as the female desires the male [*thelu arrenos*] and the ugly the beautiful [*aischron kalou*]—only the ugly or the female not *per se* [*kath' auto*] but *per accidens* [*kata sumbebekos*]"; trans. Richard McKeon, *The Basic Works of Aristotle* (New York: Random House, 1941). Aristotle is assessing others' ideas about matter. The final clause shows that he thinks it an error simply to identify matter with the female. This is brought out in the Loeb translation by Philip H. Wicksteed and Francis M. Cornford: "So that if (to borrow their own metaphors) we are to regard matter as the female desiring the male or the foul desiring the fair the desire must be attributed not to the foulness itself as such, but to a subject that is foul or female incidentally." The passage is translated in Calcidius's commentary on the *Timaeus—Platonis Timaeus interprete Calcidio cum eiusdem commentario*, ed. Ioh. Wrobel (Leipzig: Teubner, 1876), p. 317—such that what is earlier described as the desire of matter (*silva*) for form becomes the desire for "purification" ("silva vero adpetit formam et inlustrationem"). The final qualification speaks only of *deformity*, or the ugly, being accidental, leaving us to suppose that the feminine may indeed be essential: "it is only matter therefore that desires purification, as the feminine sex desires the male and deformity beauty, but in such a way that the deformity of matter is not of its nature but

appropriately enough, through Calcidius's commentary on the *Timaeus*, whence it was transmitted to Bernardus Silvestris's philosophical allegory, the *Cosmographia*, in which Matter or Silva is described as follows: "*Silva*, a coagulate mass that is dissonant with herself, chooses in the midst of her crudeness to be united with form, and desiring to leave her ancient tumultuousness demands the embellishment of number and the bonds of musical harmony"; "Silva . . . sibi dissona massa . . . formam rudis / . . . Optat, et a veteri cupiens exire tumultu, / Artifices numeros et musica vincla requirit."[11]

It emerges in what follows that matter is dissonant with herself because her "appetite" (*appetitio*) for the good, that is, for masculine form, is opposed by another impulse in her to "malignity" (*malignitas*), as a consequence of which any form imprinted in her will necessarily be imperfect. It is not hard to see how this notion of matter is a theological modification of the maternal receptacle in the *Timaeus*, introducing noise into the channel through which form is communicated and so establishing the rift in the material. Thus at the outset of the main phase of the allegorical tradition we find the concept of the material explicitly introduced as a place of conflict between "ancient tumultuousness" and a metaphysical desire that is imposed on it from above and then reinterpreted as coming out of matter itself as a more hidden, more ancient desire. It is the fantasy of the repressed smile of the woman who only appears to resist: *materia appetit formam*.

How does this attribution of masculine desire to its object, which we find at the outset of the allegorical tradition, fit into the more general picture of literary history? Curiously enough, it emerges in philosophical allegory at a time when woman, in the imaginative world of romance, was beginning to be understood in precisely the opposite

accidental to it" (p. 317). In his remarks following this passage (p. 318), Chalcidius speaks of matter as female, and as wanting cultivation and ornament, in a manner that indicates he does not think of it as *accidentally* feminine.

11. Bernardus Silvestris, *Cosmographia*, ed. Peter Dronke (Leiden: Brill, 1978), 1:18–22. See Winthrop Wetherbee, trans., *The "Cosmographia" of Bernardus Silvestris* (New York: Columbia University Press, 1973), p. 145 n. 9 and index under "matter." For the influence of the Timaeus at Chartres, see Wetherbee, *Platonism and Poetry in the Twelfth Century: The Literary Influence of the School of Chartres* (Princeton: Princeton University Press, 1972), pp. 28–36. For matter in twelfth-century poetry, see pp. 158–59, 161 n. 12, and 178–79. See also Brian Stock, "*Silva / Hyle*: Bernard's Materialism and Its Sources," in *Myth and Science in the Twelfth Century: A Study of Bernard Silvester* (Princeton: Princeton University Press, 1972), pp. 97–118; see also 228 n. 1 and 232. For an account of ancient materialism and its transmission, see J. C. M. Van Winden, *Calcidius on Matter: His Doctrine and Sources* (Leiden: Brill, 1965).

way: as that which is fleeting, that which resists, that which is desired
by the male. (When consciousness is given to this fleeting, unmaster-
able "other," which actively disrupts by its *malignitas* the structures of
intellectual authority, it speaks through Chaucer's Wife of Bath.) As
they develop independently and interact with one another through
allegory, literary romance and scholastic philosophy have sharply opposed notions of the feminine substance in which meaning and form
are imprinted: the one regards the feminine as that which resists and
evades the desire of the male, the other as that which longs for it. As
the only literary form that has made a sustained effort to do the
impossible—to unite philosophical to imaginative truth—allegory
emerges out of the tension between romantic and scholastic perspectives on the origin and place of desire. In the *Roman de la rose* we find
the notion of woman as that which resists more evident in the first
part, which is closer to the traditions of courtly romance, while the
notion of woman as secretly desiring the male emerges, together with
a vast influx of scholastic philosophy, in the second part of the poem,
where the castle of the lady's resistance is burned down by her unacknowledged desire to be taken.

We noted earlier that this desire is at root a metaphysical desire that
is encoded in erotic terms and translated into a metaphorics in which
the father inscribes form on a willing or unwilling female. For this
reason images of sexual congress, whether they are achieved, de-
ferred, sublated, or transformed into sexual violence have a peculiarly
resonant power in allegories as instances of a broader, structural
problematic of gender. We need only think of the *Commedia*, the *Roman de la rose*, *The Faerie Queene*, and even the second part of *The
Pilgrim's Progress* to see how fundamental this problematic is to the
idealist project of allegory. Sexual relations in allegory, and the violence that is implicit in them, are figurations of the metaphysical
desire to capture the heterogeneity of the material and convert it to
form.

One of the more curious ways in which this desire is served in an
allegory is through the figure of personification. For our purposes
the important thing about personification is not the absurdity of making a quality like justice true of itself but the imaginative problem of

trying to think what could possibly be the *subject*—literally, "that which is cast underneath"—of the predicate, justice, when predicated of itself. Philosophers do not worry about this because they know that it cannot be there. But it is there for the poets, for whom self-predication leaves a residue that is not justice but the thing in which or on which it rests in order to be true of itself. Often the absurdity of this self-predication is foregrounded as a kind of metaphysical wit creating a surface disorder or "noise" that we are to suppose will be recuperated beyond it: "*Disdayne* he called was, and did disdaine / To be so cald."[12] The main effect Spenser wants to achieve here is to make it seem to the reader as if the rift at the heart of Disdain, disdaining to be Disdain, initiates a movement within the sign to a higher level of abstraction where the contradiction at this level would be resolved. Spenserian wit always has this anagogical spin. But the appeal to a higher level of abstraction must be passed through an unacknowledged substance that has disdain as its attribute. This interior substance is a *subject* in both senses of the word: in the sense of "that which is cast underneath" and in the sense of a conscious agent who disdains and therefore *is*.

Whether this substance is something inert, the wax in which disdain is imprinted, or something animate and weird, a consciousness that differs from what it is called by affirming, paradoxically, its identity with its name, it can never be recuperated by the anagogical movement to a higher level of abstraction. Both formulations of the subject in the allegorical figure of Disdain open an infinite regress as soon as we try to appropriate them to the concept of disdain. It is only by *not listening too closely* that the noise of the subject inside personification can be heard as the resonance of a higher truth into which it is absorbed. No one is supposed to listen as closely as we have just now. Personification has been regarded as the *sine qua non* of allegory, at least since the eighteenth century,[13] not because it makes clear what the text is intended to do but because it hides it so well.

How does it do this? One of the more curious things about the operation of this figure is its tendency to give a feminine gender to

12. *The Faerie Queene*, ed. A. C. Hamilton, Longman Annotated English Poets (London: Longman, 1977), II.vii.41. Subsequent references are to this edition.

13. See Bertrand H. Bronson, "Personification Reconsidered," *ELH* 14 (1947): 169, and Richard Blackmore, "Preface to *Prince Arthur*," in *Critical Essays of the Seventeenth Century, 1685–1700*, ed. J. E. Spingarn, 3 vols. (Oxford: Clarendon, 1908–9), 3:238.

personifications that are the agents, not the receptacles, of paternal inscription.[14] These agents are both eminent examples of the qualities they instantiate in themselves and living sources that flow into the material world: "She is the fountaine of your modestee," Spenser's Alma tells Guyon, "You shamefast are, but *Shamefastnesse* it selfe is shee" (II.ix.43). Here a masculine figure, Guyon, is addressed as a lower instance of a higher abstraction that is female. If the project of idealism is normally worked out as a masculine imprinting of a feminine other, why are the genders in the hierarchy reversed? A grammatical explanation—that abstract nouns in Latin are in the feminine gender—is at best a partial one. The feminine gender in personification raises the material from its place below the lowest *species* into the realm of abstractions so that the meaning of the personification will have something to imprint itself in; at the same time the feminine gender prevents us from seeing the material for what it is, which would open an infinite regress. In other words, when the material in allegory is represented as female the metaphor acts as a veil concealing the material from our conscious recognition of it as such while communicating it to us unconsciously. We can say then that the material in an allegorical personification proceeds from the vision of universals as self-predicating subjects, where the subject in which predication occurs is represented as female in order to conceal the absurdity such predication involves. What is the stuff out of which *Shamefastnesse* is made if not matter? She is made of her gender.

This concealing of the material in gender makes the trope of personification untypical of allegory in any deeper sense of what the genre is actually doing. By concealing the material in the feminine gender of an animated abstraction, personification excludes from its structure the more dynamically material substratum of narrative, the engagement of which as a "literal" other is the central problematic of allegorical expression. When Addison remarked that allegorical personification mobilizes "a Scheme of Thoughts traced out upon Matter,"[15] he was following the neoclassical assumption that allegory should have as little to do with narrative as possible: compare Spenser's allegory with Johnson's. It is no accident that the more the narra-

14. Male personifications in *The Faerie Queene*—e.g. Orgoglio, Disdain, Furor, Occasion—tend to be represented in more *significantly* physical terms than are feminine ones, as if to make up for the lack in the male of the substantiality of the female.

15. Joseph Addison, *The Spectator*, ed. Donald F. Bond, 5 vols. (Oxford: Clarendon, 1965), 3:577.

tive counts in an allegory the fewer personifications we see, for personification is an attempt to conceal in a figure the rift that is more or less openly on view throughout an allegorical narrative.

As a material substratum that gives meaning a place to occur while remaining heterogeneous to it, narrative in an allegory at once subverts and complicates the idealist project. We saw that in the *Timaeus* the "receptacle" or "mother" in which the forms are propagated must be absolutely featureless. It is however precisely this condition of homogeneity in the material that allegory cannot fulfill; for in allegory concepts are imprinted in narratological materials that are anything but featureless, materials that persistently introduce noise as they slip out from under the structured antinomies of the idealist project.[16] Allegory encounters this heterogeneity as an independent world, and even as an order of life, that must be subdued for the purpose of making a sign. Its principal means of achieving this end (so far as it is possible to achieve it) is to homogenize the alterity of narrative by calling it "literal," erasing its previous life while preserving its form under erasure. Unlike the indifferent femininity of the material in the *Timaeus*, the narrative captured by an allegory has an order of its own that can only be held up to view and forced to bear the imprint of a meaning to which it is never resigned. To consider allegory at its heart, at the rift where the transcendental and the material "others" are divided, is to consider it in terms of the poetics of capture.

Any logocentric re-encoding of this resistance of the material-as-narrative can never be wholly persuasive because the struggle at the rift can never be wholly concealed. The resulting dissonance is something that the great allegorical poets know and exploit; minor ones do what they can to avoid it. The more powerful the allegory the more openly violent are the moments in which the materials of narrative are shown being actively subdued for the purpose for raising a structure of meaning.

A particularly lucid example of this occurs in a moment of allegorical troping in a work that is not allegorical in its general structure, although the political circumstances in which it appeared could be counted on for it to be seen in that way. I refer to the moment in the fourth act of Verdi's *Rigoletto* when the murderer asks Rigoletto the name of the victim the murderer will be paid to dispatch. Rigoletto

16. I discuss at more length this fundamental incompatibility of narrative and conceptual structure in "From Allegory to Dialectic: Imagining Error in Spenser and Milton," *PMLA* 101 (1986): 12–13.

replies very strangely: "Vuoi saper anche il mio? Egli è Delitto, Pun-
izion son io" ("Would you like to know my name too? He is Crime, and
I am Punishment"). It is as if Rigoletto is unable to rename himself
allegorically without first naming the diacritical complement without
which his new name would have no significance. The peculiarly men-
acing character of the gesture lies in the textualizing violence by which
the underlying, material life of the persons named—the life of the
speaker just as much as his victim—is raised up onto a table of moral
oppositions where nothing exists except in a diacritical relation with
respect to the other: "Would you like to know my name too? He is
Crime." (It is merely a proleptic form of this violence to say that no
violence has occurred because Rigoletto and the Duke are already
parts of a text.) The pleasures we normally associate with allegory—of
recognizing the aptness and wit of an imaginative presentation of
ideas, of building up more complex structures of meaning out of a
narrative unfolding in time, and of seeming to penetrate into the
center of a truth that is hidden within—should not distract us from
what is perhaps the most satisfying, and most deeply concealed, pleasure of all: that of observing the subjection of something we cannot
control to the violence of thought.

We may even see the persistence with which students of Dante
condemn readings that interpret Beatrice as Theology and Virgil as
Reason—readings that, however incomplete, are assuredly elicited by
the text—as a moral reaction to the pleasure we secretly take in such
violence, and thus to some extent an authentic response to what the
poem, and not just its allegorizing critics, is doing behind the work of
the veil. Where such criticisms err is in their assumption that this
violent reduction of life to a text has nothing to do with Dante, who
was more of a Nietzschean interpreter of the world than might be
supposed, and whose strength flows from the violence with which he
reduces persons to substance.[17] The great allegorical poets expose
and even exacerbate the contradiction by revealing the process of
transforming life into meaning as deracinating, violent capture.

This is the difference between a figure like *Philology* in Martianus
Capella and a figure like Dante's Beatrice, or between the various
figures met by the pilgrim in Deguileville's *Pèlerinage de la vie humaine*
and some of the more disturbingly realistic characters in Bunyan,

17. See John Freccero, "Infernal Irony: The Gates of Hell," in *Dante: The Poetics of
Conversion*, ed. Rachel Jacoff (Cambridge: Harvard University Press, 1986), pp. 93–109,
esp. p. 106.

whose actuality we can observe being turned into writing by the hermeneutic project that bends all their actions—and, more to the point, all their destinies—to suit what they are called.

———————

The bending of someone's destiny to suit what she is called is shown with particular force—so much force that we have not yet learned how to read it as allegory—in what is probably the most famous episode in allegorical literature. I refer to that inaugural moment of the semiotic project of Dante's *Inferno* when a woman, Francesca da Rimini, is made, or is almost made, into a sign. Indeed it is the incompleteness of this making-into-a-sign that Dante is setting before us. He does this in the fifth canto of the *Inferno* when the pilgrim descends with Virgil into the second circle, where the real punishments, those that "goad to wailing," begin.[18]

The canto effects a transition from the distribution of souls throughout all Hell to the punishment of the souls in this one circle. The first figure the pilgrim encounters is therefore the infernal judge, Minos, who assigns every soul to its place in Hell by writhing his tail around himself as many times as the soul has to descend levels. Charged with "so great an office"—*cotanto offizio* (l. 18)—Minos must be seen in counterpoint with Francesca, who comes at the end of the canto uttering, among other things, the striking phrase, "so great a lover," *cotanto amante* (l. 134). The significance of the canto is suspended between these terms, the abstract *offizio* and the embodied *amore*; and the punishment meted out by the former never succeeds in subduing what is of independent value in the latter. In other words, Francesca's love is never captured and subdued in such a way as to identify it with her punishment in Hell.[19] In this episode of the *Commedia*, where allegorical punishment is introduced for the first time, the heterogeneity of passionate love and the officiousness of the punishment that tries to absorb that heterogeneity into itself are forced

18. *Inferno* 5.3. I follow the text of Giorgio Petrocchi as reproduced with slight modifications (none of them relevant here) in *The Divine Comedy*, ed. and trans. Charles S. Singleton, *Inferno: Italian Text and Translation*, Bollingen Series 80 (Princeton: Princeton University Press, 1970). Translations are mine.

19. See John Freccero, *Dante*: "If the bodies in hell are really souls, then it follows that their physical attitudes, contortions and punishments are really *spiritual* attitudes and states of mind, sins made manifest in the form of physical punishment. It is therefore correct to say that the punishments *are* the sins" (pp. 106–7).

apart, exposing to our view a struggle between them that can never be resolved.

Once he has passed Minos the pilgrim encounters the storm of winds in which the souls of the carnal sinners are hurled about, blaspheming the divine power as it punishes them for having submitted reason to pleasure. Virgil, as *periegetes* or allegorical guide, points out to Dante (*nominommi a dito*, l. 68) some of the more famous historical examples of lust, such as Semiramis, Cleopatra, and Tristan, not omitting his own Dido, whom he refers to with elliptical frigidity as she who broke faith with the ashes of Sichaeus (l. 62). We then meet Francesca and her lover, Paolo, whose shade weeps quietly in the background while she alludes to the main points of their story—of how she was married by a trick to Paolo's deformed brother,[20] of how she and Paolo were murdered by her husband and finally, at the pilgrim's request, since he knows more about the art of pathos than she does, of how she and Paolo first kissed while reading of Lancelot and Guinevere. She concludes by saying, with striking reticence, "quel giorno più non vi leggemmo avante" ("that day we read in it no farther") (l. 138), whereupon the pilgrim faints for pity and the canto closes.

The first thing to notice about the canto is its balance. It begins with Minos, the grotesque agent of an abstract system of classification. It then proceeds swiftly through the carnal sinners, for whom our sympathy is supposed to be removed by our being told that they blaspheme the divine power. The canto concludes with Francesca, who is beautiful where Minos is grotesque, who is gracious to the pilgrim where Minos has been rough, and whose consciousness is inaccessible to what she represents in the system of Hell whereas Minos's consciousness, which is as absorbed in its operation as is Spenser's Disdain, is obsessively preoccupied with the mechanical distribution of souls.

This is not to compare Francesca and Minos as characters, though they are the only speakers apart from Virgil to address Dante in the canto: the relation between Minos and Francesca is more of the nature of a mechanical operation to its material. But Francesca is never

20. I see no reason to suppose Dante was not thinking of circumstances similar to those recorded by Boccaccio in his commentary, in particular Francesca's having been deceived into thinking she was marrying Paolo instead of his deformed older brother, Gianciotto. For Boccaccio's account of the legend, see Singleton, *Inferno: Commentary*, pp. 84–87.

entirely subjected to that operation or rendered featureless by it. Although like every other soul encountered by the pilgrim in the *Inferno* her consciousness is the material substratum of her being as a sign, it nevertheless largely escapes the imprint of what she means in Hell. Even the mild language Dante uses to describe the souls in this circle—those carnal sinners who have, as he puts it, subjected reason to pleasure "i peccator carnali, / che la ragion sommettono al talento" (ll. 38–39)—is placed at a distance so that no direct judgment is passed on Francesca. It should also be pointed out in this connection, given the frequency with which the word *lust* has been incorrectly applied to Francesca,[21] that the word *lussuria* is used in the canto only to characterize Semiramis (l. 55)—a very special case—while the collective sin of the souls in this circle is that of giving too much importance to "desire" or "inclination," *talento*. The first soul of the damned that we meet is singularly independent of her abstract condition in Hell. This is of course why she has always been hard to read.

Whether we should see Francesca's punishment as a tragic indictment of the justice of God or as a stern corrective to our erring affections is a problem that can never be solved because it is not meant to be solved, even if the best solution we have, John Freccero's, can explain it as arising from "the dialectical relationship of the pilgrim's view to that of the poet." For if the authoritative view that emerges from this dialectic is committed, as Freccero puts it in a phrase that is as revealing as it is magnificent, to "the crushing exigencies of the poet's structure," it remains in our eyes, as we read this canto, closely allied to the function of Minos, the instrument of those crushing exigencies.

Freccero speaks of the poet's global and comprehensive detachment as the perspective to which the movement of the poem is committed, ascending, as he says, from "the problematic and humanistic" to the "certain and transcendent . . . from a synchronic view of the self in a dark wood to a diachronic total view of the entire world as if it were, to use Dante's powerful image, a humble threshing floor upon which a providential history will one day separate the wheat from the

21. Singleton, *Inferno: Commentary*, p. 76, glosses *talento* at verse 39 as "'Desire,' 'appetite'; specifically, 'carnal appetite,' since this is the circle of *lussuria* or lust." He is followed, as we shall see, by critics who are intent on making Francesca worse than Dante did, that is, on making her indistinguishable from Semiramis, to whom the word *lussuria* (l. 55) is exclusively applied. *Talento* is the only word Dante uses in a general sense to characterize this circle, and it means something quite different from *lussuria*.

chaff."[22] What is striking about this description is the way it brings out the thrilling violence of the transcendentalizing project of the *Commedia*, the sheer power with which the crushing exigencies of the poem's intellectual design flatten the complexities of life to the plane of a threshing floor—an image that is terrifying precisely because it is so humble. Freccero's image of crushing, which recalls the Biblical winepress, and his appropriation of Dante's image of the flailing of souls on the threshing floor of judgment, exposes what the agency of signification in the *Commedia* really is: it is wrath, wrath and love being indistinguishable from one another in Christian eschatology—witness the inscription on the gates of Hell[23]—just as hatred and eros are indistinguishable in rape.

What is striking about the canto is the way violence is made into a spectacle that not only discloses what Dante's art is committed to doing but reveals that it can never be done all the way to the end. We thus become detached for a moment not only from our affective response to Francesca's punishment but also from the transcendental violence that corrects our response, observing the two perspectives not as being united in the latter, eschatological plan but as being divided by a rift that can never be closed. No one, even at the conclusion of the *Commedia*, can think of Francesca's torture as a manifestation of the love that moves the sun and the stars. We have to forget her, which at that point is easy to do. But our forgetting the moment when Francesca stops speaking, the moment of rhetorical silence in which her passion escapes being represented and named in the text, does not change what Dante has shown us in that moment about the limits of his art and the limits of the transcendental design it supports. Our mere forgetfulness of Francesca's silence cannot be interpreted as the eschatological recuperation of her love to God's. Although she is captured, she eludes being turned into a featureless substance imprinted by wrath.

This is marked for us in Francesca's final words, which we have already had occasion to note, and in the more general relation of those words to the economy of writing: "quel giorno più non vi leggemmo avante"; "that day we read in it no farther" (l. 138). She is of

22. John Freccero, *Dante*, pp. 25–26. It looks to me as if the places of *synchronic* and *diachronic* should be changed in this passage.

23. *Inferno* 3.5–9: "Fecemi la divina Podestate, / la somma Sapienza e 'l primo Amore . . . Lasciate ogne speranza, voi ch'intrate" ("Divine power made me, the highest wisdom and the originative power of love . . . abandon all hope, you who enter").

course referring to the book she and Paolo stopped reading when they first kissed: "*Galeotto fu 'l libro e chi lo scrisse*"; "a pander was that book, and its writer" (l. 137). But in a larger sense the book represents a realm of textuality that is set over in opposition to life, and it evokes in this way the transcendental comedy through which Francesca is made known to us and into which she is drawn because of her sin.

The significance of reading in this canto has been noted by Robert Hollander and expatiated upon by Giuseppe Mazzotta, who identifies Francesca's sin with reading literally, "according to the flesh," so that she mistakes "the insubstantial shadows of the text for her own self." This mistake is more widely reflected, according to Mazzotta, by a tendency in her character to live out her passion neurotically through the patterns offered her by books, patterns that cause her, as Mazzotta puts it, to "lapse into lust" and that are reflected in her speech, which deploys a "language of love which resembles both Guinizzelli's and Dante's stilnovistic formulas."[24]

I wish to pause here to consider this view of Francesca as what Freccero has called a "medieval Emma Bovary."[25] For a long time I found this a comforting reading. I wanted Francesca to be not only lustful but shallow, and to deserve what she gets more than my affective response told me she does. I was happy to feel less remorse for being, as a reader who must in some part of himself assent to the design of the poem, a voyeuristic party to a torture which, as Hollander describes it so well, "dwells in the memory of almost every literate Western man." I suppose she dwells in the memory of almost every literate western man not because her "power to seduce is so great and so beautiful" as Hollander puts it,[26] but because her suffering is so terrible and so terribly unjust—a *mal perverso* as she calls it[27]—by any standard a literate western man should respect. The

24. Giuseppe Mazzotta, *Dante, Poet of the Desert: History and Allegory in "The Divine Comedy"* (Princeton: Princeton University Press, 1979), pp. 169 and 196.

25. John Freccero, *Dante*, p. 25: "The critical uncertainties about whether Francesca is a heroine of spontaneous human love or merely a deluded medieval Emma Bovary . . . arise from the dialectical relationship of the pilgrim's view to that of the poet."

26. Robert Hollander, *Allegory in Dante's "Commedia"* (Princeton: Princeton University Press, 1969), pp. 107 and 106.

27. *Inferno* 5.93. She is thankful to the pilgrim because he has "pity on our perverse misfortune" ("poi c'hai pietà del nostro mal perverso"). Whether *mal* should be translated here as "ill" (with Singleton) or "misfortune" depends on the extent to which one wishes to make Francesca condemn herself out of her own mouth, or the extent to which one wants to reduce the discomfort one feels at the distance separating her consciousness, and her sense of justice, from the punishment inflicted on her. Sin-

discomfort this causes has therefore prompted some literate western men to try to make the criminal fit the punishment. Thus Charles S. Singleton speaks of Boccaccio's account of the legendary circumstances alluded to in Francesca's narrative as "embroidered nicely to exculpate Francesca as much as possible,"[28] without indicating what more reliable account is being so embroidered. I expect Boccaccio's exculpatory account, if that is what it is, is closer to Dante's intention in the episode, which is to make us uncomfortable, than is the comforting, inculpatory program of modern American critics, from Singleton on, who want the torture of Francesca to make sense in the transcendental project of the *Commedia*.

Calling her what Dante does not, "that lustful lady," Hollander wittily affirms that Francesca is destroyed because she "loved the wrong Paul,"[29] as if a woman should love that misogynist apostle before any man of flesh and blood. Hollander's brilliantly aggressive reading of this canto, which has established the Virgilian, Pauline, and Augustinian substructure of allusion on which it has been read ever since, remains indispensable to a reading that would make a case opposite to his. Such a case would state that while the texts Hollander mobilizes are indisputably at work beneath the surface of the canto, their relation to that surface is much more complex than he allows. They are not just the hidden, orthodox, correct meaning of an episode that is dangerously seductive if read on its surface. For the Augustinian, Pauline, and Virgilian substructure of allusion constitutes the ground of moral and spiritual imperatives—the ground from which a violent imposition of meaning on the "other" is launched—that is undermined by the spectacle of Francesca's punishment. It holds its sadistic shape in the transcendentalizing project of the *Commedia* because Dante had the courage to show us his doubts, just as Plato had the courage to put the third man argument in the *Parmenides* and leave it unanswered.

---

gleton presses too far in trying to eliminate anything discordant with Christian orthodoxy when, commenting on Francesca's statement that love cannot be resisted, he cites the words *mal perverso* as if they are spoken by the poet in reference to such love: "In adducing the ineluctability of love, moreover, Francesca pleads her own excuse: neither she nor Paolo was responsible, for, as she implies, none may withstand Love's power. The perverseness of such love (cf. the "mal perverso" of verse 93) from the point of view of Christian doctrine is evident" (*Inferno: Commentary*, p. 89). Francesca is using the words *mal perverso* to refer to the perverseness not of her love but of her punishment.

28. *Inferno: Commentary*, p. 84.
29. Hollander, *Allegory in Dante's "Commedia,"* pp. 107 and 113.

It is not just the spectacle of Francesca's punishment that does this, however, but our experience of her language. This is why a sensitive critic like Mazzotta, who is committed to Hollander's aggression (which is to say the aggression Dante here exposes as such), focuses on her language and condemns it as an artificial display of stilnovistic formulas. He thus manages to elide—that is, to confuse—the poet's desire to represent Francesca in the best rhetoric he can muster with Francesca's desire for Paolo. Who is the agent behind the literariness of Francesca's speech, Francesca or Dante? She does not strike us at all as someone who speaks affectedly in stilnovistic formulas but as someone who was, and still is, passionately in love, and who can express this in literary language because she is a literary creation:

> Amor, ch'a nullo amato amar perdona,
> mi prese del costui piacer sì forte,
> che, come vedi, ancor non m'abbandona.
>
> (ll. 103–5)

(Love, which never spares the loved one from giving love in return, seized me so strongly with joy in him that, as you see, it still does not leave me.)

This is of course literary language, magnificently poised, but it is designed to strike us as passionate, tragic utterance, not as neurotic affectation. Moreover, the error of which Francesca is accused, of living vicariously through books and confusing what she reads in them with life, is in fact what she should have done, according to the transcendental standard of the comedy, but did not do. If she were to have done what morality required she would truly have mistaken the letter of the text for life, living in a fantasy she can take delight in while innocently reading. This is what she refuses to do when she sins. Her sin is to recognize the difference between what happens in a book and what can happen in life, and to state in her actions that there are some things in life that can never be captured in a book, not even a book like the *Commedia*. She therefore acts on this recognition "according to the flesh" but by no means "literally," since she has just recognized the profound gulf that separates the flesh from the letter, a gulf Pauline and Augustinian violence conceals.

No aporia in the *Commedia*, not even its conclusion, is so clearly marked as this one. The pilgrim simply wakes up somewhere else. What then is the poet trying to show us by means of it? He is trying to show us the violence of an art by which a heterogeneous world of experience—in this case erotic experience—is abstractly classified and then held up for us to inspect as a warning. If the book that shows Francesca what to do is in her eyes a pander, the book that shows what she is, the object of the Father's eroticized hate, is in our eyes, at this moment, a kind of legal rapist, *e chi lo scrisse*. Who is the poet who would make such a terrible confession? She is Crime, and he is Punishment.

Our examination of the material in allegory has elicited two apparently opposed figural moments exemplified by Spenser's Shamefastness and Dante's Francesca. On the one hand we have personification, the trope most typically associated with allegory, which we have seen to be structured around the absurdity of self-predication as a way of covertly absorbing the material into itself: "*Shamefastnesse* it selfe is shee." On the other hand we have the trope without a name, nameless because it reveals what the theory of allegory as well as its practice typically denies: the material substratum that is necessary to the abstract project of meaning but that always escapes being fully subdued by that project, as Francesca da Rimini escapes being coincident with lust. It is, to borrow a phrase, a spectacle of heterogeneity.[30] Indeed if the material this spectacle discloses were subdued entirely to the project of making a sign it would resolve itself into personification and its heterogeneity would vanish, either into the gendered materiality of a figure like Shamefastness or into the conceptualized substantiality of masculine personifications such as Spenser's balloon-like Orgoglio and brittle Disdain.

While personification points to the positive "other" of allegory, the trope with which we are now concerned points to the negative, material "other" that resists, disturbs, and complicates any orderly imposition of meaning. If we must give a name to such a moment we will do best to call it simply the *figure of capture*, *capture* being a word that

30. Peter Stallybrass, "Marx and Heterogeneity: Thinking the Lumpenproletariat," *Representations* 31 (1990): 70, 73, 79, 82, and 91. For the monstrous as the most apt representation of the divine, see René Rocques, "Teratologie et théologie chez Jean Scot Erigène," *Mélanges offerts à M.-D. Chenu*, ed. André Duval, Bibliothèque Thomiste 37 (Paris: Vrin, 1967), p. 429.

implies the appropriation of an other that remains unsubdued in
captivity, like an animal pacing its cage.

The direction in which we are headed may be cause for alarm—at
least on the scale of importance on which such a thing could be cause
for alarm. It might be supposed that what I am trying to show is that
there is a hitherto unrecognized allegorical trope, the figure of capture, that can be set over against the figure of personification for the
purpose of submitting the most rebarbative problem of literary theory to some kind of domestic control. Personification and capture
would thus be seen to stand at opposite poles of a field of rhetorical
possibilities in which allegories work and by which allegories are contained. Within that restricted compass allegories would move without
interruption until encountering the rift at one of the field's limits,
turning away from it and moving in the opposite direction toward
personification, beyond which they cannot pass because personification represents, at this end of the field, the limit of figural intensity,
just as capture, at the other end, represents the limit where figures
disintegrate. Beyond personification waits the absurdity of the third
man, which would force allegory into a confrontation with philosophy. Beyond the figure of capture is the unraveling of the participation of abstractions in particulars, which would force allegory into a
confrontation with history.

This distribution of perils, with the Scylla of philosophy to one side
and the Charybdis of history to the other, is uncomfortably familiar,
reproducing as it does the classic, Aristotelian move of clearing out
the confusion of history and philosophy within literature by expelling
both terms to the periphery. Whether this move is a legitimate one for
literature as a whole, establishing for criticism an independent disciplinary space by expelling its deepest theoretical problems, it is clearly
illegitimate for allegory. For allegory is committed to the impossible
task of bringing history and philosophy together by imprinting abstract form directly in the material of historical life; and its hidden,
productive operation is the violent one we have observed of capturing
the heterogeneity on the other side of the rift and holding it up for
inspection. For allegory, as for its theory, there can be no balance of
extremes or uncontested middle way.

Considered in this light, the trope of personification is a superficial
manifestation of what is happening in an allegorical text, having been
thrown up from below by forces obscurely but dynamically at work in

the struggle at the rift; and the moment of capture is not a trope in any classical sense but a revelation of those productive forces at work. To situate personification and capture at opposite poles of a homogeneous field in which allegory will work without trouble is to banish the trouble that makes allegory work. It is to position the rift outside allegorical expression altogether when in fact it is ineradicably there at its heart, making everything in the allegory seem to correspond with everything else in a play of analogies that is nothing more than an Apollonian veil. The rift is allegory's negative "other." To ignore or forget this is to commit the methodological error we noted at the outset: of reproducing in our analysis the act allegory has already performed in concealing the rift behind a veil of unbroken, analogical correspondences.

When we position the rift where it belongs, in the material substratum that everywhere in an allegory gives meaning a place to occur while remaining heterogeneous to it, we can see that what we have called the figure of capture is not a figure at all but something more fundamental which might be called the *work* of the rift. The work of the rift works behind the work of the veil, in the way that order is built up out of a disorder that it secretly needs and that it therefore interprets as polysemy. Polysemy is the kind of domestic disorder that makes the metaphysical structure supported by allegory seem to come alive, engaging us in the ritual of interpretive play by which the coherence of the system as a whole is affirmed. But despite its centrality to the process of allegorical figuration, the rift cannot openly be shown for what it is except by the poets who have the courage, at brief moments, to do so. I mean the poets (and here, at the end, I want to say that Spenser is second to none in this regard) who draw back the veil of an optimistic, metaphysical illusion to show us the truth that is its undoing.

Notes on Contributors

FRANCIS BARKER is a Reader at the University of Essex, where he teaches contemporary cultural theory. He is the author of *The Tremulous Private Body: Essays on Subjection* (1984) and *The Culture of Violence: Essays on Tragedy and History* (1993); and an editor of *1642: Literature and Power in the Seventeenth Century* (1981), *Uses of History: Marxism, Postmodernism and the Renaissance* (1991), and *Postmodernism and the Re-Reading of Modernity* (1992). He is presently at work on a book about the figure of the artificial man.

BRUCE THOMAS BOEHRER is an associate professor of English at Florida State University. He is the author of *Monarchy and Incest in Renaissance England: Literature, Culture, Kinship, and Kingship* (1992), as well as articles in various journals. At present he is working on a project tentatively entitled "Ben Jonson and the Idea of Revolution?"

MARGARET FERGUSON teaches at the University of Colorado. She is the author of *Trials of Desire: Renaissance Defenses of Poetry* (1983), as well as coeditor of *Rewriting the Renaissance: The Discourses of Sexual Difference in Early Modern Europe* (1986) and, most recently, of *Postmodernism and Feminism*, a special issue of *Boundary 2* (1993). She is currently finishing a book titled "Partial Access: Female Literacy and Literary Production in Early Modern England and France."

RICHARD HALPERN is an associate professor of English at the University of Colorado at Boulder. He is the author of *The Poetics of Primitive Accumulation: English Renaissance Culture and the Genealogy of Capital* (1991). He is currently at work on a project involving Shakespeare and modernism.

CLARK HULSE is the author of *The Rule of Art: Literature and Painting in the Renaissance* (1990) and *Metamorphic Verse: The Elizabethan Minor*

Epic (1981), as well as of essays on Spenser, Sidney, Shakespeare, and Titian. He has held Guggenheim, Newberry Library, and British Academy fellowships. He is professor of English at the University of Illinois at Chicago and has been visiting professor of Art History at Northwestern. The essay in this volume is part of a book he is writing on portraiture in the age of Henry VIII.

CHRISTOPHER KENDRICK is associate professor of English at Loyola Unviersity in Chicago. He is the author of *Milton: A Study in Ideology and Form* (1986) and has been working for some time on a book about the utopian genre in sixteenth- and seventeenth-century Britain.

RICHARD LACHMANN teaches sociology at SUNY Albany. He is the author of *From Manor to Market: Structural Change in England, 1536–1640* (1987) and the forthcoming *Capitalists in Spite of Themselves: Elite Conflict and European Transitions*. He is currently working on a project concerning the professionalization of literary careers in the United States since 1945.

JOSEPH F. LOEWENSTEIN, associate professor of English at Washington University, is the author of *Responsive Readings: Versions of Echo in Epic, Pastoral, and the Jonsonian Masque* (1984) and of a forthcoming book titled *The Authorial Impression: Intellectual Property, Print, and Renaissance Literary Work*.

DAVID LEE MILLER teaches English Renaissance literature at the University of Kentucky. He is the author of *The Poem's Two Bodies: The Poetics of the 1590 "Faerie Queene,"* (1988) as well as essays on psychoanalysis and Renaissance literature.

SHARON O'DAIR is associate professor of English at the University of Alabama. She is the author of essays on Shakespeare, social science and literary theory, and the issue of class in the profession.

GORDON TESKEY teaches at Cornell. The present essay is part of a larger study of allegory and violence.

HAROLD WEBER is an associate professor of English at the University of Alabama. He is the author of *The Restoration Rake-Hero: Transformations in Sexual Understanding in Seventeenth-Century England* (1986). He is currently at work on a project concerning Charles II and the print trade.

Index